State Constitutions for the Twenty-first Century, Volume 3

SUNY series in American Constitutionalism

Robert J. Spitzer, editor

State Constitutions for the Twenty-first Century, Volume 3

The Agenda of State Constitutional Reform

G. Alan Tarr and Robert F. Williams, editors

State University of New York Press

Published by
State University of New York Press, Albany

For information, address State University of New York Press,
194 Washington Avenue, Suite 305, Albany, NY 12210-2384

Production by Michael Haggett
Marketing by Anne M. Valentine

Library of Congress Cataloging-in-Publication Data

State constitutions for the twenty-first century. Volume 3, The agenda of state
constitutional reform / edited by G. Alan Tarr and Robert F. Williams.
    p. cm. — (SUNY series in American constitutionalism)
  Includes bibliographical references and index.
  ISBN 0-7914-6711-2 (hardcover : alk. paper)
  1. Constitutional law—United States—States. 2. Local government—Law and
legislation—United States—States. 3. Finance, Public—Law and legislation—
United States—States. I. Title: Agenda of state constitutional reform.
II. Tarr, G. Alan (George Alan) III. Williams, Robert F. (Robert Forrest), 1945–
IV. Series.

KF4550.Z95S6823 2006
342.7302—dc22

                                           2005014629

ISBN-13: 978-0-7914-6711-4 (hardcover : alk. paper)

10 9 8 7 6 5 4 3 2 1

Contents

Introduction   1
   G. Alan Tarr

Chapter One   Rights   7
                Robert F. Williams

Chapter Two   The Legislative Branch   37
                Michael E. Libonati

Chapter Three   The Executive Branch   67
                Thad Beyle

Chapter Four   The Judicial Branch   85
                G. Alan Tarr

Chapter Five   Local Government   109
                Michael E. Libonati

Chapter Six   Voting and Elections   145
                James A. Gardner

Chapter Seven   Constitutional Amendment and Revision   177
                Gerald Benjamin

Chapter Eight   State and Local Finance   211
                Richard Briffault

Chapter Nine   Education   241
                  Paul L. Tractenberg

Chapter Ten   The Environment and Natural Resources   307
                  Barton H. Thompson Jr.

Bibliography   341

Contributors   355

Index   357

Introduction

G. Alan Tarr

The state constitution is the fundamental law of the state. As such, it should embody the aims and aspirations of the citizens of the state and serve as the foundation for the state's political life. It also should facilitate—rather than retard—political, social, and economic progress in the state.

Despite their diversity, American state constitutions share certain common features. A state constitution establishes the institutions of state government and prescribes how those institutions shall operate. Through its rights guarantees and its prohibitions on governmental action, a state constitution largely determines the scope of state powers, and it distributes those powers among the branches of state government and between state and locality.[1] A state constitution also establishes qualifications for state office and prescribes how state officials are to be chosen. Thus it channels political conflict in the state and provides mechanisms for its resolution. In addition, many state constitutions, not content to structure state government, enshrine fundamental policy choices, sometimes providing broad direction for public policy and sometimes prescribing its content in considerable detail. It is therefore no exaggeration to suggest that the effectiveness and responsiveness of state government, the policies that it pursues and the values that it advances, all depend fundamentally on the state constitution.[2]

As a glance back through history reveals, state constitutions have played a crucial role in the development of American governmental institutions. In part this has occurred through individual states pioneering constitutional reforms that were subsequently adopted by other states throughout the nation. Examples of the operation of this horizontal federalism include the movement to white manhood suffrage that occurred in emulation of the Alabama Constitution of 1819, the adoption of partisan election of state judges that followed the example of the influential Iowa and New York Constitutions of the mid-nineteenth century, and the spread of the initiative that followed its adoption by Oregon in 1902.[3] State constitutions have also had an impact on national politics. In some instances state experiments, such as the enfranchisement of women and the direct election of the upper house of the legislature, have been incorporated into the federal Constitution. Even when state initiatives have not been adopted nationally, they have often furnished the agenda for those seeking to improve the operation of the federal government. Recent examples of this vertical federalism include the campaigns for a presidential item veto and for a balanced-budget requirement.

Finally, state constitutions in a sense "complete" the federal Constitution by including elements not found in that constitution that are essential to American government.[4] For example, the original federal Constitution did not need to define voting qualifications because state constitutions had already done so. Even today, the federal Constitution need not address education and local government, to take but two examples, because state constitutions deal comprehensively with those matters. Thus many matters that are dealt with in the national constitutions of other countries are in the United States addressed in state constitutions.

This is not to say that state constitutions always succeed in achieving the objectives sought by their drafters. Indeed, the history of state constitutions is largely a history of constitutional change, fostered by the conviction that constitutional reforms would improve the performance of state government. Only nineteen states retain their original constitutions, and most states have adopted three or more constitutions. Even when states have not jettisoned their constitutions, they have continued to tinker with them. The states' current constitutions contain more than 6,000 amendments, with most state constitutions averaging more than one amendment for every year they have been in operation.[5] The frequency of state constitutional change through revision and amendment suggests both an acknowledgment of the problems plaguing current state constitutions and an optimism that their defects can be corrected.

The problems that provide the impetus for state constitutional change take various forms. Specific defects in a state constitution may prompt piecemeal reforms designed to address those defects. Many state constitutional amendments serve this purpose. In addition, a state constitution may over time cease to serve the broad social, political, or economic ends for which it was created, in which case fundamental changes may be introduced to achieve those ends more effectively. For instance, the perception at the outset of the twentieth century that state constitutions no longer sufficiently ensured the accountability of government officials prompted constitutional reformers to introduce elements of direct democracy—the initiative, referendum, and recall—into state constitutions. A state constitution may also be changed because the citizenry wishes to make specific substantive choices different from those in the former constitution and wants to devise new institutions or procedures for implementing those choices.[6] Examples include the constitutions adopted in the South after Reconstruction that were meant to reassert white political control, as well as Illinois' "Granger" Constitution of 1870 and Montana's "environmental" Constitution of 1972. Alternatively, a state constitution may be changed to renew original constitutional commitments when political practice departs too much from the original constitutional design. When constitutional reformers do this, they are heeding the admonition of the Virginia Declaration of Rights that "no free government, nor the blessings of liberty, can be preserved to any people but by . . . frequent recurrence to fundamental principles."[7] Finally, a state may adopt a new constitution or substantially alter its old one to respond to new problems or new conditions. In doing so, the states are following the advice of Thomas Jefferson, who claimed that constitution making is a progressive enterprise, that each generation can draw on a broader range of political insight and experience in addressing the changing constitutional challenges confronting it, and that frequent constitutional change is thus desirable.[8] The adoption of the New Jersey Constitution of 1947, the Connecticut Constitution of 1965, and the Florida Constitution of 1968 illustrates this phenomenon.

Although only a few states followed the lead of New Jersey, Connecticut, and Florida in revising their constitutions during the mid-twentieth century, the political, social, and economic changes that promoted constitutional reform were hardly unique to those states. This is true more generally. Many of the problems and concerns that encouraged state constitutional change in the past were common to all the states, rather than idiosyncratic. And this is the case at the beginning of the twenty-first century as well. All the American states are assuming new responsibilities for policy development and implementation as power is devolved from the federal government and as new tasks arise for government at all levels. All the states likewise are seeking to address endemic problems in areas of traditional state responsibility, such as education, economic development, and the environment. All face budget difficulties to a greater or lesser extent. Moreover, all are confronting their responsibilities, new and old, amid rapidly changing political, economic, and social conditions. How effectively individual states respond to the challenges facing them will depend to a significant extent on the quality of their state constitutions, because these constitutions structure and guide the operation of state government.[9]

This, however, is a cause for concern. More than two-thirds of the states now operate under constitutions that are more than a century old, that were designed to meet the problems of another era, and that are riddled with piecemeal amendments that have compromised their coherence as plans of government. In addition, the public disdain for government at all levels, together with the increasing reliance on direct democracy for policy making in the states, suggests a need for constitutional reforms designed to increase the responsiveness of state institutions and to promote popular involvement that does not preclude serious deliberation about policy options. Many state constitutions would benefit from substantial changes designed to make state governments more effective, equitable, and responsive, and to equip them to deal with the challenges of the twenty-first century.

Previous volumes of *State Constitutions for the Twenty-first Century* have focused on overcoming the political obstacles to state constitutional reform and on drafting state constitutional provisions. The present volume, in contrast, is aimed at the substantive direction of constitutional reform. It is designed to assist scholars, public officials, and members of the general public in identifying the constitutional problems confronting their states, in recognizing the range of alternative responses to those problems, and in choosing among those alternatives. To serve these purposes, the book describes the variety of state constitutions, analyzing their strengths and weaknesses, thus providing an overview of the current state of state constitutions. By identifying those strengths and weaknesses, it encourages officials and citizens to examine whether their particular state constitutions will enable their state governments to meet the challenges that will confront them in the early decades of the twenty-first century. Finally, by identifying alternative approaches devised by the states to deal with common constitutional problems and by assessing the advantages and disadvantages of those approaches, this volume provides guidance for those undertaking the task of constitutional reform.

The volume is organized topically, with chapters focusing on each of the major features common to contemporary state constitutions. The chapter "Rights" by Robert F. Williams considers the protection of rights under state constitutions. Four chapters—"The Legislative Branch" by Michael E. Libonati, "The Executive Branch" by Thad Beyle, "The Judicial Branch" by G. Alan Tarr, and "Local Government" by Michael E. Libonati—examine state constitutional provisions dealing with governmental institutions and their operation. Two chapters—"Voting and Elections" by James A. Gardner and "Constitutional Amendment and Revision" by Gerald Benjamin—look at constitutional provisions dealing with the expression of the popular will. Finally, three chapters—"Education" by Paul Tractenberg, "Environment and Natural Resources" by Barton H. Thompson, Jr., and "Taxing, Spending, and Borrowing" by Richard Briffault—consider constitutional provisions pertaining to fundamental areas of state public policy. In dealing with these topics, the chapters share a common approach. They identify the values that should guide constitution makers and constitutional reformers in dealing with these topics, survey the major issues pertaining to each topic, assess how various state constitutions have dealt with each of those issues, and thus clarify potential approaches to constitutional reform.

The use of the plural "approaches" is intentional and important. State constitutions necessarily reflect diverse state constitutional traditions, historical developments within individual states, and the particular political complexion of each state. As a consequence, no single model is appropriate for all states, and this volume eschews the creation of a "model state constitution."[10]

Having said that, one must also emphasize that the constitutional experience of other states is vitally important for state constitutional reformers. State constitutions share a more or less uniform structure, and they deal with a common set of issues (as well as some issues that are distinctive to particular states or groups of states).[11] State constitution makers can therefore learn from the constitutional experience of other states and can draw on their constitutions. In fact, state constitution makers have regularly done so. The history of state constitution making is a history of constitutional borrowing, of drafters looking beyond their borders for how other states have dealt with the problems they share.[12] Judicious consideration of the experience of other states can yield both positive and negative models, as well as helping to identify the range of alternative approaches for addressing common problems. The contributions to this volume have undertaken to facilitate this task of constitutional comparison and borrowing.

The three volumes of *State Constitutions for the Twenty-first Century* represent the culmination of several years of work by a group of scholars and officials dedicated to improving political life in their states. Some of these dedicated individuals have contributed chapters to these volumes. Others too numerous to mention have provided information, encouragement, and critical commentary, and their contributions are likewise reflected in the pages of these volumes. I personally have profited immensely from their efforts and their expertise and want to recognize their importance.

This project would never have gotten off the ground without the generous backing of the Ford Foundation. I would particularly single out the support of Julius Ihonvbere, my grant officer at Ford, whose enthusiasm for the project never flagged. Finally, I would like to thank all those at Rutgers University-Camden who played a crucial role in the completion of the project. Provost Roger Dennis encouraged the formation of the Center for State Constitutional Studies, and he and Dean Margaret Marsh have strongly backed its activities ever since. Robert Williams, my colleague at Rutgers-Camden and Associate Director of the Center for State Constitutional Studies, has made enormous contributions to the project. His breadth of knowledge and his ability to negotiate difficulties have been crucial to the success of the project. Sylvia Somers, the administrative assistant at the Center, has helped keep the project on course with her hard work, her sharp eye for detail, and her eminent good sense.

Notes

1. State governments have historically been understood as possessing plenary legislative powers—that is, all residual powers not ceded to the federal government or prohibited to them by the federal Constitution. This is somewhat oversimplified but largely correct. State constitutions thus operate primarily as documents of limitation

rather than as documents of empowerment. With some notable exceptions, they do not grant powers to the state government but rather impose limits on the exercise of state power, and in the absence of such a constitutional limitation, it is generally assumed that the state government can act. For indications that the situation is somewhat more complicated than the traditional understanding suggests, see Robert F. Williams, *State Constitutional Law Processes,* 24 *Wm. & Mary L. Rev.* 178–79 (1983).

2. For further elaboration of the character of state constitutions and their development, see G. Alan Tarr, *Understanding State Constitutions* (1998).

3. Horizontal federalism refers to interstate relations, the transmission of ideas and policies from one state to another, in contrast with vertical federalism, which involves the relation between the federal government and state governments. See "Editors' Introduction," in *State Supreme Courts in State and Nation* (Mary Cornelia Porter and G. Alan Tarr, eds., 1982), xix–xxii.

4. Donald S. Lutz, "The United States Constitution as an Incomplete Text," 496 *Annals Academy Pol. & Soc. Sciences* 23 (1988).

5. Data on state constitutions and state constitutional amendments are contained in thirty-five *Book of the States* 10, tbl. 1.1 (2003).

6. See Mark E. Brandon, "Constitutionalism and Constitutional Failure," in *Constitutional Politics: Essays on Constitution Making, Maintenance, and Change* (eds. Sotirios A. Barber and Robert P. George, 2001).

7. Virginia Declaration of Rights, sec. 15.

8. Letter to Samuel Kercheval, July 12, 1818, reprinted in *The Portable Thomas Jefferson* (ed. Merrill D. Peterson, 1975).

9. These themes are elaborated in G. Alan Tarr, "The State of State Constitutions," 62 *La. L. Rev.* 3 (2001).

10. The National Municipal League created a "model state constitution" in the early 1920s and periodically revised it over four decades. See *A Model State Constitution,* 6th rev. ed. (1967). For discussion of the political perspective underlying this model and the model's effects on constitutional reform, see Tarr, supra note 2, at pp. 150–57.

11. State constitutions do differ in the level of detail in their treatment of those issues and in the range of other issues they address. Moreover, some problems are so state-specific that no other state's experience is helpful in solving them.

12. For documentation of borrowing during the nineteenth century, see Christian G. Fritz, "The American Constitutional Tradition Revisited: Preliminary Observations on State Constitution Making in the Nineteenth-Century West," 25 *Rutgers L.J.* 945 (1995). More generally, see Tarr, supra note 2, chapters 4–5.

Chapter One

Rights

Robert F. Williams

INTRODUCTION

State constitutions are, by definition, changeable. The possibility of changes in rights guarantees, though, can be both attractive and forbidding. For example, many people would approve (depending on the topic) of the addition of new, more modern, state constitutional rights.[1] On the other hand, one substantial factor in the recent resistance to the calling of state constitutional conventions is the fear of losing existing rights or the specter of acrimonious debates over controversial areas such as abortion, women's rights, public employees' right to strike, and so on. State constitutional rights are neither liberal nor conservative, at least in a conventional political sense. They range from free speech and the rights of those accused of crime to property rights, victims' rights and the right to bear arms. The words of one of the last generation's commentators on state constitutional rights remain true today:

> The present complex social and economic structure of society, with its new concepts of social and economic democracy, the possible improper use of broadening governmental powers, and the bureaucratic character of the modern state have but increased the importance of and necessity for the inclusion of guarantees of individual rights in state constitutions.[2]

Modern state constitutional rights guarantees can be seen as fitting into two categories: (1) those that are worded identically or similarly to federal constitutional guarantees and therefore share a common constitutional history (although state constitutional rights predated the federal Bill of Rights in the original thirteen states); and (2) those that are not identical or similarly worded and therefore do not share a common constitutional history. State constitutions contain many different rights from those in the federal Constitution. They are differently understood and often differ textually. We will return to this distinction later.

A preliminary point about the *judicial interpretation* of state constitutional rights provisions, although not the focus of this volume, is necessary for an understanding of issues relating to state constitutional rights. For most of the twentieth century, litigation relating to the enforcement of constitutional rights primarily invoked the federal Constitution. Originally, of course, the federal Bill of Rights applied only to the actions of the federal government. Most of the federal Bill of Rights has now been applied by the United States Supreme Court to the actions of state and local government through "selective incorporation."

State constitutional rights guarantees, and their enforcement by state courts, provided the primary fuel for the renewed interest in state constitutions during the last quarter of the twentieth century. This increased interest in state constitutional rights, particularly from the standpoint of state judicial enforcement, has been referred to as the "New Judicial Federalism." This phenomenon, always possible but surfacing dramatically in judicial, political, and legal circles after about 1970, involves states courts interpreting state constitutional rights guarantees to provide more protection than the federal Constitution. These developments, in turn, raised a variety of questions about the legitimacy of state courts interpreting their constitutions in this manner. Opinions about the phenomenon ranged from enthusiastic support by civil liberties and criminal defense lawyers, and a number of members of the state judiciary, to strong condemnation, on the ground that state judges were simply "looking for" excuses to reach more liberal decisions than the United States Supreme Court. These legitimacy concerns continue to be raised today.

It is clear, however, that in a legal and political sense state courts are entirely within their authority in reaching decisions that are more protective than those of the United States Supreme Court, even when they are interpreting provisions that are worded identically to their federal counterparts. It is not the *power* or authority of state courts to reach such results, but rather the *wisdom* and propriety of such outcomes that is in contention.

This discussion so far has related to the *judicial interpretation* of state constitutional rights provisions. The primary focus here is the consideration of modifying existing rights clauses, as well as inserting new rights into, and removing old rights from, state constitutions. Understanding the New Judicial Federalism does provide important background for state constitution drafters.

The development of the New Judicial Federalism also has shown that the exercise of popular sovereignty, or voting by the electorate, can not only be used to add new rights, but also to literally overturn or "overrule" judicial interpretations of state constitutional rights guarantees (or, for that matter, other state constitutional provisions). Such overruling can be accomplished either through legislatively proposed amendments, constitutional convention proposals, or in those states that permit it, popularly initiated constitutional amendments.

There are two different approaches. First, state constitutional decisions can be overruled simply by amending the constitution to say that the judicial interpretation no longer applies. For example, several states have overturned state judicial decisions declaring the death penalty unconstitutional by inserting language in the relevant clauses to say that capital punishment will not be deemed to violate the provision.[3] Illustrating a different approach, after some expansive state judicial interpretations, Florida's search and seizure clause was amended in 1982 to require the state courts to interpret the provision the same way as the United States Supreme Court interprets the federal clause.[4] This also happened in California to eliminate a line of state constitutional interpretations that went beyond the federal requirements in the area of school busing.[5] This Florida and California "lockstep" or "forced linkage" amendment approach can be seen as undesirable because it constitutes a blanket adoption, *in futuro,* of all interpretations of the United States Supreme Court, thereby abdicating a part of a state's sovereignty and judicial autonomy.

Some state courts, relying on their state constitution's mechanisms for amendment and revision, have struck down attempts to overrule judicial interpretations of state constitutional rights provisions. For example, the California Supreme Court refused to uphold a blanket "lockstep" amendment for all of the state constitutions criminal procedure clauses, ruling that it was a proposed "revision," and therefore could not be accomplished through the initiative process, which was limited to "amendments."[6] On the other hand, the Florida Supreme Court upheld the search and seizure forced-linkage amendment against a challenge asserting that it was placed on the ballot in a way that misled voters.[7]

GUIDING PRINCIPLES

Several principles should be kept in mind when considering changes to the state declaration of rights, or to rights guarantees in general.

1. *State Constitutional Rights Should Reflect the Fundamental Values and Aspirations of the State:* Although it is primarily the courts that *enforce* state constitutional rights, most other state officials, and even private individuals, *apply* them. State constitutions can reflect ("constitutionalize") the values of the populace.

2. *State Constitutional Rights May Differ from Those Found in the Federal Bill of Rights:* State and federal constitutional rights differ from each other not just quantitatively, but also qualitatively. Federal constitutional rights are intended to apply to the nation as a whole, and some of them, such as the Seventh Amendment right to a jury trial in civil

cases, have not been applied to the states. Further, interpretations by the United States Supreme Court of federal constitutional rights can change over time, or even be judicially overruled or reversed. Thus, how these federal constitutional rights apply within each state can be a matter of some uncertainty.

State constitutional rights, by contrast, are intended to and as a matter of law can only apply within a single state. Therefore, rights debates within a particular state can respond to concerns similar to those reflected in federal constitutional rights, but also to matters of specific local concern. Also, these state constitutional rights can provide either greater or lesser rights than those protected at the federal level, although when there is a lesser level of protection, the federal minimum standards must be enforced. Finally, as will be discussed later, state constitutional rights are much easier to change than federal constitutional rights.

3. *State Constitutional Rights May Include Positive as well as Negative Rights:* Virtually all of federal constitutional rights protect *negative* rights, that is, limits on the power of government to interfere with rights. On the other hand, state constitutions not only provide such negative rights, but also often include *positive* mandates for rights protection or governmental action. These can require very different approaches, particularly from the standpoint of judicial enforcement, to rights protection.

4. *State Constitutional Rights May Be Located Throughout the Constitution, Not Just in the Declaration of Rights:* Most often, state constitutional rights are contained in the first article of a state constitution. This is not always true, however, as some states insert their article on rights within or at the end of the state constitution. In addition, it is important to note that there are a number of enforceable rights guarantees (sometimes through judicial interpretation) included in other parts of state constitutions. For example, a limitation on the Legislature's ability to pass "special laws" (laws creating narrow classifications) is primarily a limitation on legislative power; on the other hand, it provides citizens with equality of rights arguments. The same could be said of state constitutional clauses requiring "uniformity" in taxation and certain other tax limitations. Other examples include provisions requiring a "thorough and efficient," or "uniform" education, and requiring a vote of the public before debt is incurred. These are often seen as providing state citizens with judicially enforceable rights, but they are not contained in the article on rights. Many environmental and natural resource provisions, some of which create rights, also do not appear in the Declarations of Rights.[8]

5. *State Constitutional Rights May Include Restrictions on Private Action as Well as on Government Action:* While virtually all federal constitutional rights guarantees apply only against infringement by *the government* (referred to as the "state action doctrine"), state constitutional guarantees sometimes are applied to private parties, or to quasi-private parties who would not be viewed as government actors for federal constitutional purposes. This is true of state constitutional collective bargaining rights in the private sector such as New Jersey's art. I, par. 19, which expressly provides that "Persons in private employment shall have the right to organize and bargain collectively." On the other hand, California's 1972 state constitutional privacy amendment was applied by the California Supreme Court to the private National Collegiate Athletic Association based on prereferendum information supplied to voters describing invasions of privacy by *business*.[9] There is a tension here, of course, between "constitutionalizing" too many private relationships, on the one hand, and providing significant enforcement of constitutional guarantees against powerful societal actors, on the other hand.[10]

6. *Although State Courts Will Play a Leading Role in Enforcing State Constitutional Rights, These Rights Impose Obligations on All State and Local Officials:* It is well understood in our current time that including rights in a state constitution will virtually always (except where the rights are not "self-executing," because they contain insufficient detail for effective judicial enforcement) result in *judicial* enforcement of such rights. It is often difficult to foresee how the courts will enforce rights in the future. At the state level, courts are often less concerned about rigid standing rules for rights litigants, and may give less deference for "political questions" than the federal courts. Also, state and local government officials other than the courts are also under an obligation to respect, if not to affirmatively enforce, state constitutional rights.

7. *State Electorates Retain the Authority to Change, Add to or Delete State Constitutional Rights by State Constitutional Amendment:* It might initially seem odd that by a mere majority vote of the electorate, a constitutional amendment can be ratified or a new constitution adopted that can change state constitutional rights guarantees. This may well seem to contradict our American notion of constitutional rights guarantees as protecting minorities or the powerless against majority tyranny. Yet this is a fundamental feature of state constitution making.

When, in the 1980s, electorates in a number of states began to "overrule" state constitutional interpretations going beyond national minimum standards, a number of commentators decried this form of "popular supervision" over rights guarantees.[11] One commentator reported that "Since 1970, at least nineteen important amendments to state bills of rights, designed to curtail criminal procedure rights, have been adopted in some fourteen states."[12] In fact, however, most of the amendment activity was limited to the criminal procedure area.[13] It seems that the fear that state constitutional rights would become the "prisoner of majoritarianism"[14] has not materialized. As Janice May has observed:

> The amendment process has not been used excessively, if measured by the number of civil rights amendments during the past fifteen years . . . Furthermore, the amendments represented modifications rather than radical change . . . One might say that there is a bifurcation of roles. Generally speaking, the role is one of contraction in criminal justice, but one of expansion in other areas of law, with few exceptions. Most of the new rights adopted at the polling place, among them the right of privacy, rights of the disabled, ERAs, and environmental rights, are neither expressly protected by the U.S. Constitution nor fully protected by the federal courts. . . .
>
> In a democracy, support for civil rights must ultimately find an anchor in public opinion. For better or worse, the state constitutional tradition tips the scales toward voter participation in preserving or reducing civil rights. The record of civil rights protection during the past fifteen years, while mixed, holds out hope for the state amendment process.[15]

Another commentator, Harry Witte, concluded that popular discussion and debate about rights, as part of the state constitutional process, was a good thing.

> In general terms, our federalism *permits* vigorous popular democracy to operate in the states because the Federal Constitution places checks on majoritarian excesses. At the same time, it *depends* on that popular democracy as the source of its most creative innovations. In matters of rights, the outcomes of the majoritarian processes also help inform the judiciary, state and federal, regarding the status of the living traditions that define our liberty.[16]

Some people have argued, particularly with the state constitutional initiative, that minorities are left in a very vulnerable position with respect to protecting their rights. To remedy this problem, various proposals have been advanced to make the initiative process more difficult, either in terms of the number of signatures required to place an amendment on the ballot or in terms of the number of votes required to adopt an amendment. Lynn A. Baker has argued that these changes should not be made, because, given the federal safety net, minority people have as good a chance of achieving new rights through initiative as they do of losing existing rights.[17]

These principles, or key elements in thinking about state constitutional rights, should be kept in mind by those considering changes in the state constitutions that add, modify, or remove rights. They do not, of course, take the place of the policy arguments concerning the adoption or removal of specific rights guarantees.

THE EVOLUTION OF STATE CONSTITUTIONAL RIGHTS GUARANTEES

State declarations of rights were originally adopted during the revolutionary period separately from the structural provisions of state constitutions. Sometimes these compilations of rights were debated and adopted prior to the adoption of the constitution that structured state government. In fact, though, not all state constitutions originally had declarations of rights, but now all do. When the federal Constitution was proposed, part of the Antifederalist criticism of the document was that it did not contain a list of rights guarantees, as had become standard practice in the states. That defect was, of course, remedied several years later by the adoption of the Federal Bill of Rights, to include the first ten amendments to the federal Constitution. The state constitutional declarations of rights served as important and influential models for the federal Bill of Rights.

For most of the history of our country, of course, the federal Bill of Rights did not apply at all to state or local actions. Slowly, however, beginning early in the twentieth century and accelerating in the 1960s, the United States Supreme Court determined that many of the federal Bill of Rights provisions did apply, based on the Fourteenth Amendment, to limit the actions of states and local governments. This "selective incorporation," together with the aggressive judicial enforcement of federal constitutional rights guarantees by the Unites States Supreme Court from the 1950s through the 1970s, led to the domination of rights discussions by the federal constitution.

The state declarations of rights today still contain, primarily, seventeenth- and eighteenth-century ideas about rights. But, importantly, a number of states acted to add new rights to their constitutions in the second half of the twentieth century. Guarantees of the rights to collective bargaining were added in five states, protection of women's rights was added in more than a dozen states, rights for people with disabilities were added in a few states, as was the right to bear arms, and, most recently, the victims' rights movement has led to the inclusion of victims' rights provisions in state constitutions. State constitutional declarations of rights include both matters that are recognized as of national importance, such as free speech, religious freedom, equality, criminal defendants' rights, and so on, as well as rights guarantees that are more local and regional in nature, such as fishing rights, natural resource protections, water rights, and so forth. Also, as noted earlier, state constitutions include both provisions that are recognizable as analogous to those in the federal Constitution and provisions that are not. A good example of provisions that have no federal counterpart is the "open courts" or "right to remedy" provisions (which can be traced back to the Magna Carta) that are contained in about forty states' constitutions. The history of state constitutional rights guarantees makes it clear that a society's, including a state polity's, ideas about rights can change over time, and can vary according to region of the country.

THE RELATIONSHIP OF STATE AND FEDERAL CONSTITUTIONAL RIGHTS

In our federal system, as in many nations governed by constitutional federalism, federal constitutional rights merely provide the *minimum* of enforceable rights. The states, and their state constitutional rights guarantees, provide an additional source of rights beyond the federal minimum. These rights may take the form of judicial interpretations of state constitutional provisions that are similar or identical to federal constitutional guarantees (and are therefore of less importance for this volume), or they may be reflected in state constitutional rights guarantees that have no analogue, or are dissimilar (and therefore in addition to) federal constitutional rights. It must be remembered that these provisions may or may not appear in the article on rights. It is, of course, technically possible for a state to recognize *less* rights in a particular area under its state constitution, but it must still enforce the minimum federal rights as a matter of national law.

State judicial decisions interpreting any of these kinds of rights provisions, which are clearly based on the state constitutional right at issue, may not be reviewed by the United States Supreme Court because there is no relevant question of federal law involved.

These important relationships and distinctions between state and federal constitutional rights suggest that it is a mistake to view the state constitutional rights guarantees as simply "little" versions of the more familiar federal Bill of Rights.

The Current Picture of
State Constitutional Rights

Civil Liberties: Freedom of Speech, Assembly, and Religion

Freedom of Speech

Many state constitutions protect the freedoms of speech and the press in much more explicit terms than the federal Constitution. Art. I, par. 6 of the New Jersey Constitution provides a good example: "Every person may freely speak, write and publish his sentiments on all subjects, being responsible for the abuse of that right. No law shall be passed to restrain or abridge the liberty of speech or of the press." The New Jersey Supreme Court has distinguished this type of clause from the negative federal constitutional provision in the First Amendment, indicating that the state provision is an *affirmative* right.[18] On this basis, the New Jersey Supreme Court has recognized the right to free speech, including leafletting, in privately owned shopping malls.[19] This ruling has implications for other forms of privately owned property, such as gated communities, condominiums, nursing homes, and so on.[20] Many other state supreme courts, however, have not given such an expansive interpretation to the identical language in their own state constitutions.[21]

Freedom of Assembly

A number of state constitutions contain a separate clause guaranteeing the freedom of assembly, such as New Jersey's art. I, par. 18: "The people have the right freely to assemble together, to consult for the common good, to make known their opinions to their representatives, and to petition for redress of grievances." This clause also gave support to the New Jersey Supreme Court's ruling permitting free speech and leafletting privately owned shopping malls, but similar provisions have not supported the same result in other states. A related provision in some state constitutions guarantees the right of "remonstrance."[22]

Religion

As is the case with the freedoms of speech and assembly, many state constitutions are much more explicit and detailed with respect to religion guarantees than is the federal First Amendment. For example, Ohio's art. I, sec. 7 reads as follows:

> All men have a natural and indefeasible right to worship Almighty God according to the dictates of their own conscience. No person shall be compelled to attend, erect, or support any place of worship, or maintain any place of worship, against his consent; and no preference shall

be given, by law, to any religious society; nor shall any interference with the rights of conscience be permitted. No religious test shall be required, as a qualification for office, nor shall any person be incompetent to be a witness on account of his religious belief; but nothing herein shall be construed to dispense with oaths and affirmations. Religion, morality, and knowledge, however, being essential to good government, it shall be the duty of the general assembly to pass suitable laws to protect every religious denomination in the peaceable enjoyment of it own mode of public worship, and to encourage schools and the means of instruction.

It is important to note that clauses like this also explicitly protect the "rights of conscience." The Ohio Supreme Court has relied explicitly on that provision to protect a prison guard's claimed right to wear long hair based on religious conviction, under circumstances where the federal Constitution would not provide such protection.[23]

The state constitutions contain a wide variety of different, explicit religion guarantees.[24] Many state constitutions contain, in addition, explicit prohibitions on the involvement of religion in public schools, based on the Blaine Amendment.[25] The existence of such clauses has major implications for a variety of the proposals for alternatives to public schools.[26]

Rights of Those Accused of Crime

Criminal procedure rights were among the earliest and most important rights protections in English law. The familiar rights against self incrimination, cruel and unusual punishment, unreasonable search and seizure, double jeopardy, and rights to confrontation of witnesses, jury trial, indictment, speedy trial, and assistance of counsel were all important rights under English law and were carried forward into the first state constitutional declarations of rights. Many of these ancient rights have developed rather standard or accepted meanings, at least at their core. Therefore, proposals to change these rights formulations should be carefully considered, because courts will most likely view a change in language as intending a change in meaning.

Criminal procedure rights may be broken into two categories: (1) those that apply during the investigatory and charging phase of the criminal process, and (2) those that apply during criminal trials. For example, the right against unreasonable search and seizure applies during the investigatory phase (and is most often enforced prior to trial through motions to suppress illegally seized evidence), while the right to confront witnesses applies during the criminal trial phase.

Despite the early origins of these familiar criminal procedure rights, some state constitutions have modified them in the second half of the twentieth century to address modern circumstances more clearly. For example, in Florida the search and seizure clause, art. I, sec. 12, was modified in the 1960s to protect against "the unreasonable interception of private communications by any means . . ."[27] The Michigan search and seizure guarantee, art. I, sec. 2, was also modified in the 1930s and again in the 1950s to state:

> The provisions of this section shall not be construed to bar from evidence in any criminal proceeding any narcotic drug, firearm, bomb, explosive or any other dangerous weapon, seized by a peace officer outside the curtilage of any dwelling house in this state.[28]

Of course an illegal seizure of these items under federal law will lead to their exclusion despite this clause.[29]

As in other areas of the judicial interpretation of state constitutional guarantees that are similar to federal constitutional guarantees, minor differences in wording of criminal procedure guarantees have supported state constitutional interpretations that are independent from federal constitutional interpretation. For example, in the famous 1972 California decision, *People v. Anderson,*[30] the California Supreme Court ruled the death penalty unconstitutional, relying on the California constitution's "cruel *or* unusual" language, in contrast to the federal constitution's "cruel *and* unusual" wording. Another example was the Utah Supreme Court's 1980 decision in *Hansen v. Owens*[31] dealing with self-incrimination. The Utah court interpreted its provision ("no person may be compelled to give evidence against himself") to be more protective than the federal Fifth Amendment provision that no person shall be required "to be a witness" against himself. The Utah court, however, reversed itself five years later based on debates at the Utah Constitutional Convention indicating no intent to adopt meaning different from the federal Constitution.[32] Finally, a number of state courts have relied on the specific "face-to-face" language of their confrontation clauses to interpret such rights guarantees more strictly than required under federal constitutional law.[33]

Despite the overall importance of criminal procedure guarantees under state constitutions, and despite the fact that there is a high volume of litigation under these clauses, there have been surprisingly few serious proposals to add to or change these "rights of the accused." In the criminal procedure area particularly the interpretations of the federal constitution by the United States Supreme Court can have a very strong influence on the court interpretations of identical or similar state constitutional guarantees.

Civil Litigation Rights

There are a number of state constitutional rights provisions that protect litigants' (usually plaintiffs') rights in the civil litigation context. A number of these
have played a central role in the debate over "tort reform."

Tort reform proposals include caps on damages, limitations on punitive
damages, statutes of repose, mandatory alternative dispute resolution, modification of joint liability rules, as well as a number of other approaches. Interestingly, there are virtually no federal constitutional claims that arise for plaintiffs
who feel aggrieved by such state legislative restrictions. It is state constitutions,
rather, that provide a wide variety of avenues of constitutional challenge. General state constitutional provisions on open courts and the right to a remedy,[34]
civil jury trial, due process and equal protection, and separation of powers have
provided fertile grounds for successful constitutional challenges to tort reform
measures. Also, general legislative process restrictions contained in state constitutions, such as the single-subject limit, have supported the invalidation of omnibus tort reform measures.[35] In addition, some states' constitutions contain
specific provisions aimed directly at preserving tort remedies. For example, the
Kentucky Constitution contains the following two provisions:

> The General Assembly shall have no power to limit the amount to
> be recovered for injuries resulting in death, or for injuries to person
> or property.[36]

> Whenever the death of a person shall result from an injury inflicted by
> negligence or wrongful act, then, in every such case, damages may be re-
> covered for such death from the corporation and person so causing the
> same. Until otherwise provided by law, the action to recover such dam-
> ages shall in all cases be prosecuted by the personal representative of the
> deceased person. The General Assembly may provide how the recovery
> shall go and to whom it belongs; and until such provision is made the
> same shall form part of the personal estate of the deceased person.[37]

The Arizona Constitution provides that "[n]o law shall be enacted in this State
limiting the amount of damages to be recovered for causing the death or injury
of any person."[38] The Oklahoma Constitution provides: "The defense of . . . assumption of risk shall, in all cases whatsoever, be questions of fact, and shall, at
all times, be left to the jury."[39]

The issues of state constitutional law and tort reform have become even
more prominent because high-visibility decisions in a number of states have
struck down various tort reform measures on state constitutional grounds. State
high courts in Indiana,[40] Illinois,[41] Oregon,[42] and Ohio[43] struck down a variety
of tort reform laws purporting to restrict plaintiffs' rights. The area of tort

reform and state constitutional law may raise somewhat different legitimacy questions than were raised by the criminal defendants' rights and civil liberties issues that have dominated the New Judicial Federalism. In the area of civil liberties and criminal defendants' rights, there are often federal constitutional provisions that are similar or identical to the state constitutional provisions applied by state courts. This can raise legitimacy questions about state courts resolving constitutional claims under their own state constitutions but in the shadow,[44] or glare,[45] of earlier federal constitutional decisions rejecting similar rights arguments. Whereas the key question in federal constitutional law involves the legitimacy of judicial review itself, the central question in state constitutional law has concerned the legitimacy of state constitutional rulings that diverge from, or "go beyond," federal constitutional standards.[46] In cases involving constitutional challenges to tort reform, in contrast, there are no pertinent federal provisions, and thus the main controversy (as at the federal level) has involved state courts overturning legislative pronouncements.

Rights of Prisoners

Several state constitutions include provisions granting rights to prisoners. The Oregon Constitution is a good example, containing provisions stating that criminal punishments should be "founded on the principles of reformation, and not of vindictive justice,"[47] that convictions may not "work corruption of blood, or forfeiture of estate,"[48] that "all penalties shall be proportioned to the offense,"[49] and that no "person arrested, or confined in jail, shall be treated with unnecessary rigor."[50] The Wyoming Constitution also provides that prisoners shall not be treated with "unnecessary rigor" and that the "erection of safe and comfortable prisons, and inspection of prisons, and the humane treatment of prisoners shall be provided for."[51] The Georgia Constitution provides that "nor shall any person be abused in being arrested, while under arrest, or in prison."[52]

Discussing the Oregon provisions, and their origins, Justice Hans Linde of the Oregon Supreme Court stated:

> Provisions like these have antecedents as early as New Hampshire's 1783 constitution, coming to Oregon by way of Ohio and Indiana. They reflect a widespread interest in penal reform in the states during the post-Revolutionary decades. The clauses are not as universal as more familiar parts of the bills of rights, and ideas of humanitarian "reform" have changed with time and among the states. . . . But while constitutional texts differ the present point is that many states thought a commitment to humanizing penal laws and the treatment of offenders to rank with other principles of constitutional magnitude.[53]

These kinds of provisions, although not widely present in current state constitutions, are prevalent enough, and completely distinct from federal constitutional rights, that they should be taken into consideration.

Victims' Rights

The victims' rights movement that arose beginning in the 1980s and 1990s realized that state constitutional revision was a process that could be used to establish constitutional rights.[54] This demonstrates that state declarations of rights can include rights favored by conservatives as well as liberals. Several state constitutions now include such rights, such as the right to notification of criminal and sentencing proceedings, the right to make statements at such proceedings, and the right to be treated with "fairness, compassion and respect" in the criminal process.[55]

Various issues have arisen with regard to the judicial enforcement of these new victims' rights guarantees. For example, in 1998 the Rhode Island Supreme Court held that the victims' rights amendment was neither self-executing nor did it provide a direct cause of action for money damages when officials violated it.[56] In other states conflicts have materialized between the asserted rights of victims and those accused of crime.

Equality Guarantees

Governmental decisions to treat people differently from others are often challenged as depriving some persons of protected rights. These equality arguments have been made most often under the federal Fourteenth Amendment's equal protection clause.[57] Most state courts have not developed doctrine independent of the federal equal protection clause under their state constitutional equality provisions.[58] Instead, they seem content not to read into such provisions anything other than what the United States Supreme Court has interpreted the equal protection clause of the Fourteenth Amendment to mean.

Most state constitutions do not contain an "equal protection" clause.[59] But they do contain a variety of equality provisions. In some states, broad guarantees of individual rights have been interpreted to require equal protection of the laws generally.[60] Further, most states have generally applicable provisions prohibiting special and local laws, the grant of special privileges, or discrimination against citizens in the exercise of civil rights or on the basis of sex. Finally, many state provisions guarantee equality in specific or limited instances—from requiring "uniform" or "thorough and efficient" public schools to requiring uniformity in taxation. Virtually all of these provisions differ significantly from the federal provision. They were drafted differently, adopted at different times, and aimed at different evils.

A number of state constitutions contain language similar to the classic language of equality in the Declaration of Independence. Sec. 1 of the Virginia Declaration of Rights, adopted a month before the Declaration of Independence, provides:

> That all men are by nature equally free and independent, and have certain inherent rights, of which, when they enter into a state of society, they cannot by any compact deprive or divest their posterity; namely, the enjoyment of life and liberty, with the means of acquiring and possessing property, and pursuing and obtaining happiness and safety.[61]

Other constitutions contain a different type of general equality provision intended to prohibit grants similar to royal privileges. Sec. 4 of the 1776 Virginia Declaration of Rights, for example, provides that "no man, or set of men, is entitled to exclusive or separate emoluments or privileges from the community, but in consideration of public services."[62]

Another type of general equality provision is the Common Benefits Clause of the Vermont Constitution, which states:

> That government is, or ought to be, instituted for the common benefit, protection, and security of the people, nation, or community, and not for the particular emolument or advantage of any single person, family, or set of persons, who are a part only of that community.[63]

Only a few states have such a provision. In 1999 the Vermont Supreme Court interpreted the Common Benefits Clause to require the state to recognize marriage of same-sex couples, or, alternatively, grant such persons domestic partner benefits.[64]

A number of states include in their constitutions a curb on granting "special" or "exclusive" privileges, after a series of abuses by the relatively unfettered state legislatures responding to powerful economic interests. For example, art. I, sec. 20 of the 1859 Oregon Constitution, which was patterned after Indiana's 1851 constitution provides: "No law shall be passed granting to any citizen or class of citizens privileges or immunities which, upon the same terms, shall not equally belong to all citizens." These provisions commonly are found in state bills of rights—not in the legislative articles. They reflect the Jacksonian opposition to favoritism and special treatment for the powerful, as well as the earlier, Revolutionary-era rejection of British hereditary or class-based societal distinctions.

Although these provisions may overlap somewhat with federal equal protection doctrine, closer scrutiny reveals significant differences. As Justice Hans Linde of the Oregon Supreme Court has noted, Oregon's art. I, sec. 20 and the federal equal protection clause "were placed in different constitutions at different times by different men to enact different historic concerns into constitutional policy."[65] A provision like Oregon's, then, does not seek equal protection of the laws at all. Instead, it prohibits legislative discrimination in favor of an economically powerful minority.

Closely related to the provisions prohibiting grants of special or exclusive privileges are prohibitions on "special" and "local" laws. These provisions, found in the legislative articles of state constitutions, contain either general or detailed limitations on the objects of legislation[66]: special laws are those that apply to specified or a limited number of persons; local laws are those that apply to specified or a limited number of localities. In addition, notice requirements are usually included for those subjects that may be dealt with by local laws, giving residents of localities to be affected at least constructive notice of the legislature's intended action. The notice provisions for local laws can also provide a basis for invalidating state laws. The Florida Supreme Court found a statutory referendum requirement for constructing public housing, applicable only in one county, unconstitutional for failure to provide the proper notice before its enactment as a "local law."[67]

Though intended in part to curb legislative abuses, these proscriptions on special and local laws reflect a concern for equal treatment under the law. In 1972 the Illinois Supreme Court held that the state's no-fault automobile insurance act violated art. IV, sec. 13 of the Illinois Constitution, which provides that "[t]he General Assembly shall pass no special or local law when a general law is or can be made applicable."[68] The statute required only owners of "private passenger automobiles" to purchase no fault insurance but imposed substantial limitations on tort recoveries of persons injured by any type of motor vehicle. In distinguishing Illinois' "equal protection" clause,[69] which had been added in 1970, Justice Schaefer observed:

> While these two provisions of the 1970 constitution cover much of the same terrain, they are not duplicates, as the commentary to section 13 of article IV points out: "In many cases, the protection provided by Section 13 is also provided by the equal protection clause of Article I, Section 2."[70]

He concluded that article IV, section 13 imposed a clear constitutional duty on the courts to determine whether a general law "is or can be made applicable," and that "in this case that question must receive an affirmative answer." The constitutionally infirm portions of the statute were therefore invalidated.

Prohibitions on special and local laws have broad application, but they do appear limited to the legislatures, and therefore not to cover executive action. As with other state equality provisions, many state courts interpret special laws provisions by applying federal equal protection analysis.

In the 1960s a number of state constitutions were amended to include provisions prohibiting discrimination in the exercise of civil rights. Pennsylvania, for example, added a provision in 1967 which directs that "[n]either the Commonwealth nor any political subdivisions thereof shall deny to any person the enjoyment of any civil right, nor discriminate against any person in the exercise of any civil right."[71] Similar provisions in other states typically limit the proscription to discrimination on the basis of race, color, or national origin.[72] These antidiscrimination provisions are products of the civil rights movement in the 1950s and 1960s.

Prohibiting this type of discrimination has become increasingly important as state governments have expanded from mere regulation into the provision of services. When state governments merely regulated conduct, prohibiting them from denying persons' civil rights was an effective limit—they did not have the leverage of attaching "unconstitutional conditions" to the provision of services; therefore, it was not as easy to favor one right over another. When the state acts as a service provider, however, as it does in programs such as Medicaid, it has the opportunity, in Professor Lawrence Tribe's words, "to achieve with carrots what [it] is forbidden to achieve with sticks.[73] Thus, these provisions prohibiting discrimination against persons in the exercise of their civil rights are needed to keep states from picking and choosing among citizens' rights they seek to advance or repress.

Several states adopted constitutional provisions banning various forms of sex discrimination at the end of the nineteenth century.[74] Generally speaking, however, the "state ERA" is a phenomenon of the 1970s—the most recent manifestation of equality concerns in state constitutions. More than a third of the states now have amendments prohibiting sex discrimination. As the Maryland Court of Appeals noted:

> [W]e believe that the "broad, sweeping, mandatory language" of the amendment is cogent evidence that the people of Maryland are fully committed to equal rights for men and women. The adoption of the E.R.A. in this state was intended to, and did, drastically alter traditional views of the validity of sex-based classifications.[75]

Despite their powerful mandate, most jurisprudence under these new provisions is dominated by federal equal protection analysis. Indeed, most state courts addressing sex discrimination claims seem preoccupied with federal equal protection constructs, largely undermining the state provisions.

Although many states have interpreted generally applicable rights provisions to guarantee equality under the law, other provisions, not usually found in bills of rights, expressly require equality in specific instances. When applicable, these provisions offer state courts sound textual basis for invalidating state actions. And at the same time they warrant extending equality guarantees beyond those of federal equal protection doctrine, these provisions allow courts to avoid some of the problems of basing decisions on generally applicable equality provisions. For example, the provision in the New Jersey Constitution requiring a "thorough and efficient" education, like provisions in other states, supported a judicial decision requiring equal and adequate educational funding.[76]

State prohibitions on special rights and privileges, special and local laws, discrimination against persons in the exercise of civil rights, and discrimination on the basis of sex may similarly be viewed as specific and limited equality provisions. In addition, most states have uniformity in taxation provisions that provide specific grounds for enforcing equality.[77] Although these provisions may be limited in focus, they can be far reaching in effect.[78]

Property Rights: Eminent Domain, Takings, and Due Process

The general area of property rights has been dominated by the provisions of the federal Constitution. The Supreme Court of the United States has been relatively active in limiting the authority of state governments to regulate the use of property.[79] Recent decisions, however, have provided states with slightly more leeway.[80] Most state constitutions contain provisions similar to the federal Constitution's prohibitions on taking of private property for public use without just compensation (eminent domain),[81] regulatory taking (inverse condemnation)[82] and deprivation of property without due process of law.[83]

Eminent Domain

Many of the state constitutions, from the earliest times, have prohibited the taking of property for public use without just compensation. Over the years the conception of what constitutes a "public use" has been greatly liberalized.[84] Some state constitutions, however, like that of Alaska, prohibit property from being taken *or damaged* without just compensation.[85] Each of the states has developed an elaborate judicial interpretation of the procedures to be followed in eminent domain, the definitions of what constitutes a "public use" and the processes for determining "just compensation."

Regulatory Taking (Inverse Condemnation)

State courts, in similar fashion to the federal courts, have developed the concept of "inverse condemnation" as a response to governmental regulations that unreasonably limit the use of property. In these circumstances, the government has not instituted any formal eminent domain proceedings, yet the property owner sues claiming that his property has been "taken" (or "damaged") without just compensation. This is referred to as *inverse* condemnation because the government has never actually started proceedings to take the property, but the property owner argues that its actions are tantamount to such a taking. The textual basis for such claims is the eminent domain clause. Some state courts interpret their state constitutional provision, in these contexts, to be the same as the similar federal constitutional provisions.[86]

Due Process of Law

Many state constitutions contain prohibitions on deprivation of property without due process of law, in language quite similar to that contained in the federal Constitution. Other states use a slightly different formulation, prohibiting deprivation of property except by "due course of law." These provisions come into play, most often, in judicial challenges to the *procedure* by which the government goes about seizing peoples' property or depriving them of its use.

Positive Rights

The idea of a "positive" right indicates a form of affirmative obligation on the part of the government to provide something to people. By contrast, a "negative" right indicates that the government may not do something to people, or deny them certain freedoms. The federal Constitution is often said to contain only negative rights—for example, the First Amendment merely provides that "Congress shall pass no law" but does not affirmatively guarantee freedom of speech or of the press. On the other hand, state constitutions, in addition to negative rights, also contain a number of positive rights.[87]

In truth, the distinction between positive rights or "mandates"[88] and negative rights is not as great as it seems on the surface. For example, in enforcing the negative right prohibiting government from interfering with free speech, the government may be required to expend substantial resources for police to monitor parade routes, crowds, and so on. Further, vindicating the rights against unreasonable search and seizure or self-incrimination can require substantial outlay for investigatory resources. Despite the difficulties of categorizing rights as negative or positive, however, it is clear that there is a range of issues, such as health care, shelter, and subsistence income, that were already dealt with in some state constitutions and that will likely be issues for further state constitutional development.

The New York Constitution contains a requirement that the legislature "provide for the aid, care and support of the needy";[89] Alabama's constitution requires "adequate maintenance of the poor";[90] Colorado's provision promising an "old age pension to all residents 60 years of age and older";[91] Massachusetts' guarantee of "food and shelter in time of emergency,"[92] together with many other similar provisions form the basis of the conclusion that state constitutions already provide for a number of "positive" rights.[93] Art. XI, sec. 4 of the North Carolina Constitution, provides "Beneficent provision for the poor, the unfortunate, and the orphan is one of the first duties of a civilized and a Christian state. Therefore, the General Assembly shall provide for and define the duties of a board of public welfare."[94]

Professor Helen Hershkoff has provided a strong case for the inclusion of positive rights in state constitutions.[95]

Privacy

Unlike the federal Constitution, where the right of privacy has been inferred from various nonspecific provisions, several state constitutions now contain explicit privacy guarantees. For example, in Florida the voters adopted the following provision in the Florida Constitution in 1980:

> Section 23, Right of Privacy. - Every natural person has the right to be let alone and free from governmental intrusion into his private life except as otherwise provided herein. This section shall not be construed to limit the public's right of access to public records and meetings as provided by law.

Alaska, California, and Montana have similar provisions.[96] The Florida Supreme Court relied on its state constitutional provision to strike down a requirement of parental consent for abortion,[97] and Alaska relied on its provision to strike down a limitation on the private possession of marijuana.[98] The Florida Supreme Court, however, rejected an argument that physician-assisted suicide was protected by Florida's explicit privacy provision.[99] Most privacy provisions are of relatively recent vintage and reflect the evolution of ideas about protecting rights in the states.

Unenumerated Rights

A number of state constitutions contain provisions at the end of their Declarations of Rights responding to the concern that by listing certain rights, others should not necessarily be excluded. For example, art. I, sec. 20 of the Ohio Constitution provides: "This enumeration of rights shall not be construed to impair or deny others retained by the people; and all powers not herein delegated, remain with the people."

Several questions arise immediately from the inclusion of such clauses in state constitutions. First, what are the other rights to which such a clause refers? Second, once the other rights are identified, are they judicially enforceable?[100] An example of a state court that found an unenumerated rights clause to support judicial enforcement was Alaska. In *McCracken v. State*,[101] the Alaska Supreme Court determined that there was a right to counsel, including the right to self-representation, in postconviction proceedings. Such proceedings were *civil* in nature, and therefore the explicit state constitutional right to counsel in *criminal* cases did not apply. The court looked to what it considered to be important or fundamental rights at the time of the framing of the constitution and considered those rights to be included in the unenumerated rights clause. The Mississippi Supreme Court ruled in 1998 that a state constitutional right to privacy and the right to choose abortion arose from its unenumerated rights provision.[102] Other courts, however, find that these clauses, much like the Ninth Amendment to the United States Constitution,[103] do not provide judicially enforceable rights.[104]

From a different perspective, unenumerated rights clauses that proclaim the existence of rights that are not explicitly listed can be seen as conflicting directly with the theory of plenary legislative power. In other words, rights provisions often operate as limits on the legislature (and, sometimes, on the executive and even private parties). When such "unenumerated" rights exist, the legislative power is not quite as plenary, or unrestricted, as it seemed.[105]

Issues for the Future

It is, of course, difficult to predict what rights issues will arise in the future. Also, because it is easier to amend state constitutional rights provisions than their federal counterparts, it is not imperative to try to look too far into the future. The Louisiana Constitution was amended in 1974 to include an equality provision prohibiting arbitrary discrimination on the basis of, among other things, "age," "birth," and "physical condition."[106] The word "birth" was chosen to provide protection for illegitimate children.[107]

Even now we are confronted with a range of new privacy concerns arising from the explosion in electronic data gathering, collection and communication in the cyberspace age,[108] and the increasing use of technology in law enforcement,[109] as well as advances in artificial intelligence. The same could be said for issues arising from biomedical ethics and cloning,[110] as well as from the fast-paced changes in reproductive technology.[111] The accelerating rate of globalization and privatization also may raise a variety of state constitutional rights concerns. Finally, none of us can expertly predict the range of issues that will arise in our post-9/11 world. State constitutions will need to be amended to protect rights in this ever-changing world.

NOTES

1. Views of what constituted "modern," state constitutional rights provisions in the last generation included collective bargaining rights for labor, equal rights for women and civil rights provisions. *See* Robert F. Williams, *The New Jersey State Constitution: A Reference Guide* 16 (rev. ed., 1997); Milton Greenberg, "Civil Liberties," in *Salient Issues of Constitutional Revision* 7, 15–19 (John P. Wheeler, ed., 1961); Robert S. Rankin, "The Bill of Rights," in *Major Problems in State Constitutional Revision* 159, 166–74 (W. Brooke Graves, ed., 1967); Frank P. Grad, "The State Bill of Rights," in *Con-Con: Issues for the Illinois Constitutional Convention* (Victoria Ranney, ed., 1970).

2. Rankin, supra note 1, at 175.

3. On November 2, 1982, the Massachusetts voters approved a constitutional amendment which added a second and third sentence to art. 26: "No provision of the Constitution, however, shall be construed as prohibiting the imposition of the punishment of death. The general court may, for the purpose of protecting the general welfare of the citizens, authorize the imposition of the punishment of death by the courts of law having jurisdiction of crimes subject to the punishment of death," Art. 116 of the Amendments to the Massachusetts Constitution. *See also* Cal. Const., art I, § 27; Ore. Const., art I, § 40.

4. "Searches and seizures. The right of the people to be secure in their persons, houses, papers and effects against unreasonable searches and seizures, and against the unreasonable interception of private communications by any means, shall not be violated. . . . *This right shall be construed in conformity with the 4th Amendment to the United States Constitution, as interpreted by the United States Supreme Court. Articles or information obtained in violation of this right shall not be admissible in evidence if such articles or information would be inadmissible under decisions of the United States Supreme Court construing the 4th Amendment to the United States Constitution.*" Fla. Const., art. I, § 12 (amendment in italics).

5. (a) A person may not be deprived of life, liberty, or property without due process of law or denied equal protection of the laws; provided, that nothing contained herein or elsewhere in this Constitution imposes on the State of California or any public entity, board, or official any obligations or responsibilities *which exceed those imposed by the Equal Protection Clause of the Fourteenth Amendment to the United States Constitution with respect to the use of pupil school assignment or pupil transportation.* In enforcing this subdivision or any other provision of this Constitution, no court of this state may impose on the State of California or any public entity, board, or official any obligation or responsibility with respect to the use of pupil school assignment or pupil transportation, (1) except to remedy a specific violation by such party that *would also constitute a violation of the Equal Protection Clause of the Fourteenth Amendment to the United States Constitution,* and (2) unless a federal court *would be permitted under federal decisional law to impose that obligation or responsibility on such party to remedy the specific violation of the Equal Protection Clause of the Fourteenth Amendment of the United States Constitution.* . . . Cal. Const., art. I, § 7. The amendment was upheld against a federal constitutional challenge in *Crawford v. Board of Educ. of Los Angeles,* 458 U.S. 527 (1982).

6. *Raven v. Deukmejian,* 801 P.2d 1077 (Cal., 1990).

7. *Grose v. Firestone,* 422 So.2d 303 (Fla., 1982).

8. *See* Barton H. Thompson, Jr., "Environmental and Natural Resource Provisions in State Constitutions," in this volume.

9. *Hill v. NCAA,* 865 P.2d 633 (Cal., 1994).

10. *See* John Devlin, "Constructing an Alternative to 'State Action' as a Limit on State Constitutional Rights Guarantees: A Survey, Critique and Proposal," 21 *Rutgers L.J.* 819 (1990).

11. James M. Fischer, "Ballot Propositions: The Challenge of Direct Democracy to State Constitutional Jurisprudence," 11 *Hastings Const. L.Q.* 43, 45 (1983).

12. Donald E. Wilkes, Jr., "First Things Last: Amendomania and State Bills of Rights," 54 *Miss. L.J.* 223, 233 (1984).

13. Ibid. *See also* Fischer, supra note 11, at 79.

14. Fischer supra note 11, at 77.

15. Janice C. May, "Constitutional Amendment and Revision Revisited," 17 *Publius: The Journal of Federalism* 153, 178–79 (1987).

16. Harry L. Witte, "Rights, Revolution, and the Paradox of Constitutionalism: The Processes of Constitutional Change in Pennsylvania," 3 *Widener J. Pub. L.* 383, 475 (1993). *See also* Douglas S. Reed, "Popular Constitutionalism: Toward a Theory of State Constitutional Meanings," 30 *Rutgers L.J.* 871 (1999).

17. Lynn A. Baker, "Constitutional Change and Direct Democracy," 66 *U. Colo. L. Rev.* 143 (1995).

18. *State v. Schmid,* 423 A.2d 615, 626 (N.J., 1980).

19. *New Jersey Coalition Against War in the Middle East v. J. M. B. Realty Corp.,* 658 A.2d 757 (N.J., 1994).

20. Jennifer A. Klear, "Comparison of the Federal Courts' and the New Jersey Supreme Court's Treatment of Free Speech on Private Property: Where Won't We Have the Freedom to Speak Next?" 33 *Rutgers L.J.* 589 (2002).

21. Ibid.

22. *See generally* Robert F. Hall, "Remonstrance—Citizens's Weapon Against Government's Indifference," 68 *Tex. L. Rev.* 1409 (1990).

23. *Humphrey v. Lane,* 728 N.E. 2d 1039 (Ohio, 2000).

24. G. Alan Tarr, "Church and State in the States," 64 *Wash. L. Rev.* 73 (1989); Chester J. Anteau, *Religion Under State Constitutions* (1965).

25. Joseph P. Viteritti, "Blaine's Wake: School Choice, The First Amendment, and State Constitutional Law," 21 *Harv. J.L. & Pub. Policy* 657 (1998); Robert F. Utter and Edward J. Larson, "Church and State on the Frontier: The History of the Establishment Clauses in the Washington State Constitution," 15 *Hastings Const. L.Q.* 451 (1988).

26. *See,* for example, *Chittenden Town School District v. Department of Education,* 738 A.2d 539 (Vt., 1999); James A. Peyser, "Issues in Education, Law and Policy: School Choice: When, Not If," 35 *B.C. L. Rev.* 619 (1994); Note, "The Limits of Choice: School Choice Reform and State Constitutional Guarantees of Educational Quality," 109 *Harv. L. Rev.* 2002 (1996).

27. Talbot D'Alemberte, *The Florida State Constitution: A Reference Guide,* 27–28 (1991).

28. Susan P. Fino, *The Michigan State Constitution: A Reference Guide,* 39–40 (1996).

29. Ibid. at 40.

30. 493 P.2d 880 (Cal., 1972). *See also State v. Bullock,* 485 N.W. 2d 866 (Mich., 1992) (same).

31. 619 P.2d 315 (Utah, 1980).

32. *American Fork City v. Cosgrove,* 701 P.2d 1069 (Utah, 1985).

33. *See Commonwealth v. Ludwig,* 594 A.2d 281 (Pa., 1991). The Pennsylvania voters approved an amendment to overrule this decision, but it was declared unconstitutional by the Pennsylvania Supreme Court because the proposed amendment contained more than one subject. *Bergdoll v. Kane,* 731 A.2d 1261 (Pa., 1999). The amendment was properly proposed and adopted in 2003.

34. David Schuman, "The Right to a Remedy," 65 *Temple L. Rev.* 1197 (1992).

35. *See,* for example, *State* ex rel *Ohio Acad. of Trial Lawyers v. Sheward,* 715 N.E. 2d 1062, 1100 (Ohio, 1999); *Fla. Consumer Action Network v. Bush,* No, 99-6689 (Fla. Leon County Cir. Ct., Feb. 9, 2001).

36. Ky. Const., § 54.

37. Ky. Const., § 241; see *Saylor v. Hall,* 497 S.W. 2d 218 (Ky., 1973).

38. Ariz. Const., art. 2, § 31; *see Hayes v. Cont'l Ins. Co.,* 872 P.2d 668, 676 (Ariz., 1994); *Smith v. Myers,* 887 P.2d 541, 544 (Ariz., 1994); Roger C. Henderson, "Tort Reform, Separation of Powers and the Arizona Constitutional Convention of 1910," 35 *Ariz. L. Rev.* 535 (1993). The Arizona provision is discussed in Stanley Feldman, *Comment,* 31 *Seton Hall L. Rev.* 666, 668–69 (2001).

39. Okla. Const., art. XXIII, § 6; *see Reddell v. Johnson,* 942 P.2d 200 (Okla., 1997); *see also* Mont. Const., art II, § 16; *Connery v. Liberty Northwest Ins. Co.,* 960 P.2d 288, 290 (Mont., 1998); *Trankel v. State Dep't of Military Affairs,* 938 P.2d 614, 621 (Mont., 1997).

40. *Van Dusen v. Stotts,* 712 N.E. 2d 491 (Ind., 1999); *Martin v. Richey,* 711 N.E. 2d 1273 (Ind., 1999).

41. *Best v. Taylor Mach. Works,* 689 N.E. 2d 1057 (Ill., 1997); David Fink, Note, Taylor Machine Works, *The Remittiur Doctrine, and the Implications for Tort Reform,* 94 *N.W.U. L. Rev.* 227 (1999).

42. *Smothers v. Gresham Transfer, Inc.*, 23 P.3d 333 (Ore., 2001); *Lakin v. Senco Prod., Inc.*, 987 P.2d 463 (Ore., 1999).

43. *State* ex rel. *Ohio Acad. of Trial Lawyers v. Sheward*, 715 N.E. 2d 1062 (Ohio, 1999); Christopher M. Winter, Comment, "The Ohio Supreme Court Reaffirms Its Right to Declare Statutes Unconstitutional," 31 *Rutgers L.J.* 1468 (2000).

44. *See* Robert F. Williams, "In the Supreme Court's Shadow: Legitimacy of State Rejection of Supreme Court Reasoning and Result," 35 *S.C. L. Rev.* 353 (1984).

45. Robert F. Williams, "In the Glare of the Supreme Court: Continuing Methodology and Legitimacy Problems in Independent State Constitutional Rights Adjudication," 72 *Notre Dame L. Rev.* 1015 (1997).

46. G. Alan Tarr, *Understanding State Constitutions* 174–75 (1998).

47. Ore. Const., art. I, § 15: "Laws for the punishment of crime shall be founded on the principles of reformation, and not of vindictive justice." *See generally* Stephen Kanter, "Dealing with Death: The Constitutionality of Capital Punishment in Oregon," 16 *Williamette L. Rev.* 1, 30–52 (1979). The Oregon voters amended their constitution specifically to authorize the death penalty. *See State v. Wagner*, 752 P.2d 1136, 1150 (Ore., 1988) and *Clark v. Paulus*, 669 P.2d 794 (Ore., 1983).

The Indiana Supreme Court held that the state constitutional requirement that the "penal code shall be founded on principles of reformation, and not of vindictive justice" did not prohibit the death penalty. *Adams v. State*, 271 N.E. 2d 425 (Ind., 1971). *See also Woods v. State*, 547 N.E. 2d 772, 784–85 (Ind., 1989) (discussing application of the provision).

48. Ore. Const., art. I, § 25: "No conviction shall work corruption of blood, or forfeiture of estate."

49. Ore. Const., art. I, § 16: "Excessive bail shall not be required, nor excessive fines imposed. Cruel and unusual punishments shall not be inflicted, but all penalties shall be proportioned to the offense. . . ."

50. Ore. Const., art. I, § 13: "No person arrested, or confined in jail, shall be treated with unnecessary rigor." *See Stirling v. Cupp*, 625 P.2d 123 (Ore., 1981).

51. Wyo. Const., art. I, § 16.

52. Ga. Const., § 2–114. Georgia's constitutional provision is discussed by Dorothy T. Beasley, "The Georgia Bill of Rights: Dead or Alive?" 34 *Emory L.J.* 341, 380–415 (1985). *See also* Tenn. Const., art. I, § 13; Utah Const., art. I, § 9.

53. *Sterling v. Cupp*, 625 P.2d 123, 128–29 (Ore., 1981).

54. *See* William Van Rogenmorter, "Crime Victims' Rights—A Legislative Perspective," 17 *Pepp. L. Rev.* 59 (1989); Patrick B. Calcutt, Comment, "The Victims Rights Act of 1988, the Florida Constitution, and the New Struggle for Victims' Rights," 16 *Fla. St. U. L. Rev.* 811 (1988); Don Siegelman and Courtney Tarver, "Victims' Rights in State Constitutions," 1 *Emerging Issues in St. Const. L.* 163 (1988); Paul G. Cassell, "Balancing the Scales of Justice: The Case for and the Effects of Utah's Victims' Rights Amendment," 1994 *Utah L. Rev.* 1373 (1994).

55. N.J. Const., art. I, par. 22. *See* Richard E. Weglyn, "New Jersey Constitutional Amendments for Victims' Rights: Symbolic Victory?" 25 *Rutgers L.J.* 183 (1993).

56. *Bandoni v. State* 715 A.2d 580 (R.I., 1998).

57. The federal equal protection clause provides: "No State shall . . . deny to any person within its jurisdiction the equal protection of the laws." U.S. Const., amend. XIV, § 1.

58. *See,* for example, *Love v. Borough of Stroudsburg,* 597 A.2d 1137, 1139 (Pa., 1991); *Commonwealth v. Albert,* 758 A.2d 1149, 1151 (Pa., 2000).

59. *See* Brown, "The Making of the Wisconsin Constitution," 1952 *Wis. L. Rev.* 23, 60 (noting absence of equal protection clause); Hargrave, "The Declaration of Rights of the Louisiana Constitution of 1974," 35 *La. L. Rev.* 1, 6–10 (1974) (discussing Louisiana's equal protection clause); Karasik, "Equal Protection of the Law Under the Federal and Illinois Constitutions," 30 *De Paul L. Rev.* 263, 270, n. 33 (1981) ("Illinois was only the eighth state to include an equal protection clause in its constitution"); Margulies, "A Lawyer's View of the Connecticut Constitution," 15 *Conn. L. Rev.* 107, 108 (1982) (discussing Connecticut's several equality provisions). Georgia added an equal protection clause in 1983. Ga. Const., art. I, § I, par. II.

The Ohio constitution contains an interesting "equal protection and benefit" clause. It provides: "Government is instituted for their equal protection and benefit." Ohio Const., art. I, § 2 (1851).

60. New Jersey's "equal protection" doctrine, for example, is based on a clause that provides: "All persons are by nature free and independent, and have natural and unalienable rights, among which are those of enjoying and defending life and liberty, of acquiring, possessing, and protecting property, and of pursuing and obtaining safety and happiness." N.J. Const., art. I, par. 1 (1947). This provision was revised in 1947, changing "all men" to "all persons," to grant equal property and employment rights to women.

61. Va. Const., Bill of Rights, § 1 (1776). Of course, at that time most states still denied the franchise to blacks, women, and those who did not own property.

62. Va. Const., Bill of Rights, § 4 (1776). For a similar provision, see Mass. Const., pt. 1, art. VI (1780).

63. Vt. Const., ch. I, art. 7.

64. *Baker v. State,* 744 A.2d 864 (Vt., 1999).

65. Hans A. Linde, "Without 'Due Process: Unconstitutional Law in Oregon,'" 49 *Or. L. Rev.* 125, 141 (1970); *see also* Hans A. Linde, "E Pluribus—Constitutional Theory and State Courts," 18 *Ga. L. Rev.* 165, 182–83 (1984) ("Such provisions long antedated the Civil War, and their target, prohibition of special privileges, was quite different from that of the 14th amendment's equal protection clause"). For a listing of similar state provisions, *see* ibid. at 182, n. 43.

66. *See,* for example, Fla. Const., art. III, § 11(a)(1) (1968).

67. *Housing Auth. v. City of St. Petersburg,* 287 So. 2d 307 (Fla. 1973).

68. Ill. Const., art. IV, § 13 (1970). The Illinois "special laws" provision declares further that "whether a general law is or can be made applicable shall be a matter for

judicial determination." Ill. Const., art. IV, § 13 (1970). The Alabama, Alaska, Kansas, Michigan, Minnesota, and Nevada constitutions contain similar provisions.

69. Ill. Const., art. I, § 2 provides: "No person shall . . . be denied the equal protection of the laws."

70. *Grace v. Howlett,* 283 N.E. 2d 474, 479 (Ill., 1974).

71. Pa. Const., art. I, § 26 (1967); *cf.* N.Y. Const., art. I, § 11 (1938) (earlier version of this type of provision). For discussion of similar provisions in other state constitutions, *see* Sturm, "The Development of American State Constitutions," 12 *Publius: J. Federalism* 57, 87–88 (1982); Sturm and Wright, "Civil Liberties in Revised State Constitutions," in *Civil Liberties: Policy and Policy Making* 179, 182–83 (S. Wasby, ed., 1976).

72. *See,* for example, N.J. Const., art. I, par. 5 (1947).

73. L. Tribe, *American Constitutional Law* § 15–10, at 933, n. 77 (1978). For a complete discussion of unconstitutional conditions, see Seth Kreimer, "Allocational Sanctions: The Problem of Negative Rights in a Positive State," 132 *U. Pa. L. Rev.* 1293 (1984).

74. These provisions usually concerned only women's suffrage. *See,* for example, Utah Const., art. IV, § 1 (1894); Wyo. Const., art. 1, § 3 (1889).

75. *Rand v. Rand,* 374 A.2d 900, 904–05 (Md. 1977). *See generally* Paul Benjamin Linton, "State Equal Rights Amendments: Making a Difference or Making a Statement?" 70 *Temple L. Rev.* 907 (1997); Wolfgang P. Hirczy de Miño, "Does an Equal Rights Amendment Make a Difference?" 60 *Alb. L. Rev.* 1581 (1997).

76. See Paul L. Tractenberg, "The Evolution and Implementation of Educational Rights Under the New Jersey Constitution of 1947," 29 *Rutgers L.J.* 827, 890–936 (1998).

77. *See generally* M. Bernard, *Constitutions, Taxation and Land Policy* (1979) (abstracting tax provisions from the federal and all state constitutions); W. Newhouse, *Constitutional Equality and Uniformity in State Taxation* (2d ed., 1984) (analysis of state tax uniformity and equality provisions, organized into nine prototypical clauses).

78. The primary effect of tax uniformity provisions is to mandate equality in property taxation. *See* Note, "Inequality in Property Tax Assessments: New Cures for an Old Ill," 75 *Harv. L. Rev.* 1374, 1377–80 (1962).

79. *See Lucas v. South Carolina Coastal Council,* 505 U.S. 1003 (1992).

80. *See Palazzolo v. Rhode Island,* 533 U.S. 606 (2001); *Tahoe-Sierra Preservation Council, Inc. v. Tahoe Regional Planning Agency,* 535 U.S. 302 (2002).

81. Ga. Const., art. I, § III, par. 1; Ky. Const., § 242.

82. Ibid.

83. U.S. Const., amend. XIV.

84. *See* Wendell E. Pritchett, "'The Public Menace' of Blight: Urban Renewal and the Private Uses of Eminent Domain," 21 *Yale L. & Pol'y Rev.* 1 (2003).

85. Alaska Const., art. I, § 18; Miss. Const., art. III, § 17.

86. *See City of Austin v. Travis County Landfill Company,* 73 S.W. 3d 234, 238 (Tex., 2002).

87. Burt Neuborne, "Foreword: State Constitutions and the Evolution of Positive Rights," 20 *Rutgers L.J.* 881 (1989); Helen Hershkoff, "Positive Rights and State Constitutions: The Limits of Federal Rationality Review," 112 *Harv. L. Rev.* 1131 (1999); Jonathan Feldman, "Separation of Powers and Judicial Review of Positive Rights Claims: The Rule of State Courts in a Era of Positive Government," 24 *Rutgers L.J.* 1057 (1993).

88. *See* Lee Hargrave, "Ruminations: Mandates in the Louisiana Constitution of 1974: How Did They Fare?" 58 *La. L. Rev.* 289 (1998).

89. N.Y. Const., art XVII, § 1.

90. Ala. Const., art IV, § 88.

91. Colo. Const., art. XXIV, § 3.

92. Mass. Const., amend. XLVII.

93. For a fuller listing, *see* Neuborne, supra note 87 at 893–95, Hirshkoff, supra note 87 at 1140, n. 44.

94. This provision, dating from 1868, is discussed in Dennis R. Ayers, "The Obligation of North Carolina Municipalities and Hospital Authorities to Provide Uncompensated Hospital Care to the Medically Indigent," 20 *Wake Forest L. Rev.* 317, 330–34 (1984). *See also* Michael A. Dowell, "State and Local Governmental Legal Responsibility to Provide Medical Care for the Poor," 3 *J.L. & Health* 1, 6–7 (1988–89) ("Fifteen states have constitutional provisions which authorize or mandate the provision of medical care for the poor").

95. *See* Helen Hershkoff, "Positive Rights and the Evolution of State Constitutions," 33 *Rutgers L.J.* 799 (2002). For a differing view, *see* Frank B. Cross, "The Error of Positive Rights," 48 *UCLA L. Rev.* 857 (2001).

96. *See generally* Ken Gormley and Rhonda G. Hartman, "Privacy and the States," 65 *Temple L. Rev.* 1279 (1992); Timothy O. Lenz, "'Rights Talk' About Privacy in State Courts," 60 *Albany L. Rev.* 1613 (1997); 1 Jennifer Friesen, *State Constitutional Law: Litigating Individual Rights, Claims and Defenses,* ch. 2 (3d ed., 2000).

97. *In re T. W.,* 551 So.2d. 1186 (Fla., 1989).

98. *Ravin v. State,* 537 P.2d 494 (Alaska, 1975).

99. *Krisher v. McIver,* 697 So.2d 97 (Fla., 1997).

100. *See generally,* Louis Karl Bonham, Note, "Unenumerated Rights Clauses in State Constitutions," 63 *Tex. L. Rev.* 1321 (1985).

101. 518 P.2d 85 (Alaska, 1974).

102. *Pro-Choice Mississippi v. Fordice,* 716 So.2d 645 (Miss., 1998).

103. Calvin R. Massey, "The Anti-Federalist Ninth Amendment and its Implications for State Constitutional Law," 1990 *Wis. L. Rev.* 1229 (1990).

104. Bonham, supra note 100, at 1327.

105. *See* chapter 3 in this volume.

106. La. Const., art. I, § 3.

107. Lee Hargrave, *The Louisiana State Constitution: A Reference Guide*, 23–24 (1991).

108. *See* Edward J. Eberle, "The Right to Information Self-Determination," 2001 *Utah L. Rev.* 965 (2001).

109. Andrew E. Taslitz, "Enduring and Empowering: The Bill of Rights in the Third Millennium: The Fourth Amendment in the Twenty-First Century: Technology, Privacy, and Human Emotions," 65 *Law & Contemp. Prob.* 125 (2002).

110. Lori Andrews, *The Clone Age: Adventures in the New World of Reproductive Technology* (1999); Mark S. Kende, "Technology's Future Impact on State Constitutional Law: The Montana Example," 64 *Mont. L. Rev.* 273 (2003).

111. John A. Robertson, *Children of Choice: Freedom and the New Reproductive Technologies* (1993); Janet L. Dolgin, *Defining the Family: Law, Technology, and Reproduction in an Uneasy Age* (1997); Marsha Garrison, "Law Making for Baby Making: An Interpretive Approach to the Determination of Legal Parentage," 113 *Harv. L. Rev.* 835 (2000); Marsha Garrison, "The Technological Family, What's New and What's Not," 33 *Fam. L.Q.* 691 (1999); Richard F. Storrow, "Parenthood by Pure Intention: Assisted Reproduction and the Functional Approach to Parentage," 53 *Hastings L.J.* 597 (2002).

Chapter Two

The Legislative Branch

Michael E. Libonati

INTRODUCTION

The state legislative branch is distinctive in comparison with the federal legislative branch in that the Federal Constitution "is an instrument of grant—a document that expressly delegates powers to the federal government," whereas "state constitutions in terms of basic theory, are instruments of limitation."[1] Thus, "the state government, having plenary powers, need not look to the state constitution for any specific grant of powers, but must rather look to it for any limitations it may impose on the state's plenary power."[2] This "basic theory of state constitutional law, namely that state governments has plenary powers, and that, in consequence, any provision included in the constitution will operate as a limitation on its powers"[3] is not uncontroversial. Nevertheless, the plenary power principle has important consequences for the creation, drafting, and interpretation of the article of the state constitution devoted to the legislative branch.

The language of art. I (the Legislative Department) of the United States Constitution is relatively unchanged. But since 1776, when the first state constitutions were adopted, the language of state constitutional provisions concerning the legislative branch reflects change, adaptation, and experiment. As a result, the legislative branch article in most states contains specific provisions embodying such values as: (1) accountability; (2) representativeness; (3) transparency; (4) efficiency; (5) institutional autonomy; and (6) clarity in strengthening or diminishing the policy-making role of the legislature in relation to the judicial and executive branches of government.

POWERS

Distribution of Powers

All state constitutions contain a provision vesting the legislative power in the legislature, and most have a separation of powers provision.[4] The language of the Massachusetts Constitution of 1780 typifies the strict separation of powers approach found in thirty-five states:

> In the government of this Commonwealth, the legislative department shall never exercise the executive and judicial powers, or either of them: The executive shall never exercise the legislative and judicial powers, or either of them: The judicial shall never exercise the legislative and executive powers, or either of them: to the end it may be a government of laws and not of men.[5]

Five state constitutions have a general separation of powers clause that "simply divides the powers of government into three branches, without prohibiting one branch from exercising the powers of another." The other ten states lack an express separation of powers clause. "In these states, separation of powers is inferred from the allocation of powers to each of the branches of government, in a manner similar to its inference from the allocation of power among the branches in the U.S. Constitution."[6]

A realistic appraisal of the distribution of policy-making authority reveals a more complex pattern of shared power. The legislature shares policy making with the Executive (veto; executive orders; implementation; administrative agency rule-making), with the Judiciary (common law; rule-making authority over judicial practice and procedure; judicial review), and, in many states, with the electorate (statutory initiative; referendum).

State framers seeking to address the tension between strict separation of powers and the dynamics of the contemporary policy-making process have a variety of options. First, they might try to create a clear, bright line definition of "legislative powers." But like other aspects of the separation of powers, the concept of legislative powers is deeply contested. And, as James Madison observed about a related issue: "[There are] three sources of vague and incoherent definitions: indistinctness of the object, imperfection of the organ of conception, inadequateness of the vehicle of ideas."[7] An added difficulty stems from the bounded capacity of framers to foresee future interbranch controversies.

Second, framers might leave it to the judicial branch to come up with clear, bright line standards for resolving interbranch conflicts. Yet there is little reason to expect that the judiciary will be successful. Both the state and the federal judiciary have tended to oscillate between strict and permissive approaches, creating a case-by-case indeterminacy that a skeptical observer might view as another example of government by the judiciary.

Third, framers might identify and resolve, on a piecemeal basis, recurrent interbranch conflicts. For example, several state constitutions explicitly grant the governor authority to reorganize executive branch agencies.[8] Again, a provision can precisely delineate the roles of governor and the legislature in the appointment and removal of state officials.[9] So too, a well-drafted provision can clarify the legislature's authority over judicial rules of practice and procedure[10] or executive agency rule-making.[11]

Fourth, framers may rely on the political dynamics created by separation of powers and checks and balances to promote incremental, mutual adjustment between and among the branches of government. Reliance on the push and pull of politics has lead to a considerable strengthening of gubernatorial powers without constitutional tinkering.

The Nondelegation Doctrine

The nondelegation doctrine operates as a significant barrier to the legislature's authority to delegate legislative powers by statute. The constitutional basis for the doctrine is the clause vesting the legislative power in the state legislature. The constitutional assignment of power to the legislature is read to forbid the legislature from delegating legislative power to others. The legislature's authority to delegate is subject to judicial review on separation of powers grounds. However, there is no predictable correlation in the states between strict or lax separation of powers provisions and strict or lax judicial application of the nondelegation doctrine.[12]

The twentieth century saw the emergence, proliferation, and growth of administrative agencies empowered to exercise broad policy-making authority over the private sector. Delegation to administrative agencies is not expressly addressed in most state constitutions. In those states, legislative control over administrative agencies is asserted through appropriations, scrutiny of executive appointments (and removals), and committee oversight. State legislatures have also enacted statutes employing various forms of the legislative veto on administrative rule-making. In the absence of state constitutional language expressly authorizing the legislative veto, it is subject to rejection on a variety of state constitutional grounds: legislative vetoes amount to the enactment of legislation by improper means, they improperly denigrate the governors veto power, they authorize the performance of an executive function by the legislature in violation of the separation of powers doctrine, they constitute an undue delegation of legislative authority, or they amount to a usurpation by the legislature of authority vested exclusively in state courts.[13]

Twenty-first century framers are faced with the challenge of explicitly clarifying the distribution of power to review administrative policy-making among the branches of state government. Three departures from the status quo should be considered: One possibility is strengthening the governor's powers over state administrative agencies. This approach diminishes legislative power in the name of "managerial constitutionalism," which calls for centralization of responsibility and direct accountability for policy making and policy implementation in the executive branch. A second possibility is giving some administrative agencies constitutional status, in order to increase their freedom from legislative interference. For example, in Virginia, the State Corporation Commission has regulatory jurisdiction over corporate charters and public utilities.[14] This autonomy, however, comes at the cost of governmental fragmentation. A final possibility is constitutionalization of some form of the legislative veto, that is providing for various forms of suspension or rejection of administrative rules has been expressly created.[15] In 1982 Connecticut amended its constitution with language that both clearly authorizes delegation of authority and frees the legislature to enact by statute any form of legislative veto:

> The Legislative department may delegate legislative authority to the executive department, except that any administrative regulation of any agency of the executive may be disapproved by the general assembly or a committee thereof in such manner as shall by law be proscribed.[16]

Considerations against the legislative veto include undue delay and politicization of the administrative rule-making process and weakening the governor's veto power. Proponents emphasize that it strengthens the legislative oversight of administrative action.[17]

Fixing the proper boundary between the public and the private sector is a significant issue of state constitutional policy. Vesting legislative power through delegation in the private sector raises the specter of governmental entanglement with and capture by private enterprise. The nondelegation doctrine is used to challenge statutes characterizable as empowering private groups to make law. Perhaps unsurprisingly, judicial determinations as to whether a delegated power is "legislative," whether the entity to which the power is delegated is "private" or "public," and the appropriate standards for appraising the validity of such delegations have produced a body of case law that is unpredictable and inconsistent. There is a tension between legislation authorizing "group self-government democratically organized" and the insistence that "public administration shall be the exclusive mode" of regulation.[18] State constitutions should speak directly to issues surrounding the privatization decision. In the absence of a state constitutional provision expressly authorizing or forbidding contracting out of governmental functions or services to the private sector, state courts will be continually addressing policy issues raised by privatization.

Appropriation and Budgetary Powers

The legislature's appropriations power is entrenched in nearly all state constitutions.[19] Alaska's provision is typical of such clauses:

> No money shall be withdrawn from the treasury except in accordance with appropriations made by law. No obligation for the payment of money shall be incurred except as authorized by law.[20]

The power of the legislative branch over appropriations has not been reined in, as a matter of constitutional policy, at the level of national government. Among the states, Vermont is notable for its minimalist approach toward fiscal and budgetary matters "based upon confidence in the system of representative democracy" and reflecting "these beliefs by leaving to the legislature and the governor, the people's elected leaders, broad responsibility for the conduct of the state's fiscal affairs with ample power to adjust needs to the rapid change characteristic of modern times."[21]

Most state constitutions do not follow the federal or the Vermont model. The reach of the legislature's power over appropriations and budgetary matters is both constrained and contested. One significant countervailing power is provided in the forty-three states that give the governor, in some form, an item veto on appropriations bills.[22] The item, or partial, veto enables the governor, unlike the President, to strike out or reduce items of appropriation. Although state courts have had difficulty in defining the terms "item" and "appropriations bill," there is no question that the line item veto tilts the dynamics of the political process in favor of the executive. The governor's veto power is further strengthened by provisions such as Pennsylvania's that limit the scope of general appropriations bills and define the scope of other appropriations bills:

> The general appropriation bill shall embrace nothing but appropriations for the executive, legislative and judicial departments of the Commonwealth, for the public debt and for public schools. All other appropriations shall be made by separate bills, each embracing but one subject.[23]

Provisions in some states constitutions institutionalize the governor's preeminent role in the budgetary process. For example, in New York, the governor submits a complete plan of itemized expenditures together with an estimate of revenues in a unified executive budget in the form of a budget bill.[24] And in nine states, the constitution fixes a deadline for state legislative action on the governor's budget.[25]

Three late twentieth century issues that implicate the legislature's power of the purse present themselves to twenty-first-century constitution makers: (1) the appropriate role of the governor and the legislature with respect to federal grants; (2) the appropriate role of the judiciary and the legislature in funding expenditures mandated by the constitution; and (3) the imposition of constitutionally mandated spending limits.

Recent figures show that approximately 20 percent of state revenues come from the federal government.[26] State legislatures sought to assert control over these funds by statutes that subject "federal funds to the same legislative appropriations process as state revenue"; that require "legislative screening of grant applications prior to their submission to federal agencies"; that impose "legislative control over the identity and structure of state agencies administering federal grant funds."[27] The legislature contended that the appropriations power justified these measures. Governors responded that these measures violated the separation of powers. Court decisions were split. For example, two leading decisions disagreed on the effect of similarly worded appropriations clauses in their state constitutions.[28] And separation of powers based challenges turned on whether the function performed is characterized as "administrative" or "legislative" in nature.[29] The latter characterization led some courts to sustain significant delegations of power over the administration of federal grant funds to legislative committees or to boards on which legislators served with elected executive officials.

The range of solutions to this constitutional problem includes: (1) an amendment to the appropriations clause expressly affirming the legislature's authority to approve expenditures of available federal funds and to appropriate matching funds; (2) an amendment permitting the legislature to increase the governor's authority over federal funds by statute; or (3) an amendment authorizing the legislature to appoint a joint committee to control federal funds when the legislature is not in session.[30] If twenty-first-century constitution makers fail to address and resolve this question, the ultimate policy decision will be left to the judicial branch.

Interbranch controversies have also arisen over the judiciary's power to compel the legislature to appropriate funds in the context of litigation over school funding, court funding, and public funding of elections. Some state courts have sidestepped the issue by determining that such cases present a nonjusticiable political question. Proponents of strong legislative and executive powers over budgetary and spending priorities are well advised to raise this issue when deliberating over the inclusion of affirmative rights, such as an education clause, in the state constitution.

The appropriations power is also constrained by debt limitation and balanced budget provisions that entrench fiscal values antedating the creation of the welfare state. Elimination of such provisions is unlikely. Indeed, recent amendments in four states have added spending limits. Appropriations caps are imposed with reference to a variety of benchmarks including: an absolute dollar amount ($2.5 billion in Alaska); 7 percent of state personal income (in Arizona); and previous fiscal-year expenditures (California). Growth in appropriations is limited by linkage to such factors as population growth (Alaska, California); inflation (Alaska, California); and economic growth (Texas). Otherwise the spending ceiling can only be exceeded by a two-thirds super majority of the legislature (Arizona, California) or majority vote (Texas). Spending limits entrench antitax, limited-government policies as well as a distrust of majority-rule politics. Opponents stress the loss of policy flexibility and responsiveness. Since these provisions are so new, there is insufficient evidence to show whether the hopes of proponents or the fears of opponents will be realized.

Investigative and Informational Powers

The legislature's power to investigate, including the power to compel the attendance of witnesses and the production of documents, has deep historical roots in British Parliamentary practice. A robust investigative power, coextensive with the scope of the legislative power, flows from the plenary power principle. The Florida constitution contains a detailed provision that may serve as a model for other states:

> Investigations; witnesses. Each house, when in session, may compel attendance of witnesses and production of documents and other evidence upon any matter under investigation before it or any of its committees, and may punish by fine not exceeding one thousand dollars or imprisonment not exceeding ninety days, or both, any person not a member who has been guilty of disorderly or contemptuous conduct in its presence or has refused to obey its lawful summons or to answer lawful questions. Such powers, except the power to punish, may be conferred by law upon committees when the legislature is not in session. Punishment of contempt of an interim legislative committee shall be by judicial proceedings as prescribed by law.[31]

In twenty states, auditing of executive branch expenditures is assigned to an official directly accountable to and elected by the legislature.[32] This strengthens the legislature's hand by insuring that "officials of the Executive branch have made their expenditures in line with priorities established by the legislature."[33]

Two recurrent issues with respect to the legislature's investigative power confront twenty-first-century framers: (1) judicial recognition of an executive privilege implied out of the separation of powers provision in the state constitution;

and (2) limitations on the investigative power stemming from the protections of individual rights in the state and federal constitution.

The United States Supreme Court's decision, *United States v. Nixon*,[34] which recognized a privilege of confidentiality of presidential communications in the exercise of executive powers, spawned a flurry of state litigation in which members of the state executive branch sought recognition of an analogous privilege under state constitutions. Most state courts were receptive to the claimed privilege. These decisions not only quashed requests for information from legislative committees but also limited the effect of state freedom of information (sunshine) laws. And in New Mexico, which like many states, has a plural executive, the privilege extended to the attorney general.

This issue is ripe for resolution by twenty-first-century framers. Proponents of a strong executive will be satisfied with the status quo. Proponents of open government will seek to entrench a broad right of access to public records and meetings in the state constitution that applies to both the legislative and executive branches.[35] And proponents of privileged access for the legislative branch will call for language that, like Florida's, confers a robust investigative power coextensive with the plenary powers principle.

Much of the law dealing with the constitutional rights of witnesses has been federalized and is, therefore, beyond the reach of state framers. The new judicial federalism has, however, played a role in this field as well. For instance, the Pennsylvania Supreme Court reads the search and seizure clause of the state constitution as more protective of the privacy interests of witnesses. Inserting a broad investigative powers provision in the state constitution should have the effect of reining in judicial activism.

Confirmation Powers

In most states, the state senate, like its federal counterpart, has the power to advise and consent to proposed gubernatorial appointments.[36] In a few states, the confirmation power is vested in both houses of the legislature. Since many states elect a wide variety of executive branch officials, for example, attorney general, treasurer, secretary of state,[37] the confirmation power may play a less significant role in interbranch relations than it does at the federal level.

Some state constitutional provisions can strengthen the legislature's powers. For example, the Virginia Constitution bars the governor from granting a recess or interim appointment to a rejected nominee.[38] And the Texas Constitution contains detailed rules limiting the governor's power to fill vacant state offices, make recess appointments, and reappoint rejected nominees.[39] The Texas Constitution also bars a governor who was not reelected from filling vacancies.[40] Some state constitutions, for example, New Jersey's, grant the governor sweeping powers of appointment. But in that state these powers are subject to the custom of senatorial courtesy.[41] Thus, traditions of interbranch comity and state political practice are likely to provide a significant counter-weight to the efficiency and accountability concerns that motivated the framers of the New Jersey Constitution to concentrate appointment powers in the governor's hands.

Impeachment

Forty-nine state constitutions provide for impeachment. Few clearly address the issues that have arisen in state impeachment controversies. These defects can be cured by careful drafting. A well-drafted impeachment clause should: (1) name the officers of government subject to impeachment; (2) specify the offenses for which they may be impeached; (3) determine which branch of government shall impeach and try impeachments; (4) if the legislative branch is involved in the process, determine the number of votes required for impeachment and convic-tion; (5) fix the punishment for conviction; (6) clarify whether a convicted offi-cial can be prosecuted for the conduct in question; and (7) resolve whether session limits apply to impeachment.

The Virginia Constitution provides a useful model in that it addresses each of these issues:

> The Governor, Lieutenant Governor, Attorney General, judges, members of the State Corporation Commission, and all officers appointed by the Governor or elected by the General Assembly, of-fending against the Commonwealth by malfeasance in office, corrup-tion, neglect of duty, or other high crime or misdemeanor may be impeached by the House of Delegates and prosecuted before the Senate, which shall have the sole power to try impeachments. When sitting for that purpose, the Senators shall be on oath or affirmation, and no person shall be convicted without the concurrence of two-thirds of the Senators present. Judgment in case of impeachment shall not extend further than removal from office and disqualification to hold and enjoy any office of honor, trust, or profit under the Com-monwealth; but the person convicted shall nevertheless be subject to indictment, trial, judgment, and punishment according to law. The Senate may sit during the recess of the General Assembly for the trial of impeachments.[42]

But the Virginia model, although superior in its coverage in comparison to impeachment provisions in other state constitutions, raises several questions that state constitution makers ought to consider. First, its detailed language deprives the legislature of the flexibility to add to the class of officials subject to impeachment, or to create statutory procedures for the trial and removal of those officials, or to delegate to the judiciary the authority to try impeachments. Second, the breadth and imprecision of the language defining an impeachable offense gives rise to controversies over whether an official may be removed from office on partisan, political grounds or whether the conduct alleged must amount to criminal offense. Third, the provision does not address whether judicial review of impeachment procedures on the grounds for impeachment is permitted or precluded. In view of the diversity of possible outcomes with respect to judicial review, framers are advised to address and resolve this issue. Finally, framers may consider "depoliticizing" the impeachment process by vesting authority to try these charges in the Supreme Court, as is done in Nebraska.[43] However, the effect of this judicialization has been that impeachment is treated as a criminal process necessitating proof of the charges beyond a reasonable doubt.

Membership

Qualifications and Disqualifications

Nineteenth- and twentieth-century state constitutions show a pattern of eliminating restrictions on eligibility for legislative office holding based on religious affiliation or belief, property ownership, race, and gender. This parallels the trend described by James A. Gardner in chapter 6 with respect to voter eligibility. The remaining qualifications in nearly every state are based on U.S. citizenship, minimum age, and district residency.[44] In many states, a state legislator must be a qualified voter, thus adding such disqualifications as felony conviction or mental incompetence contained in the franchise clause of the state constitution. And most states prohibit individuals from holding federal or state office while serving in the state legislature.

A number of issues confront state framers with respect to the decision to entrench qualifications and disqualifications in the constitution. First, there is the question of which, if any, criteria for legislative office holding are to be put beyond the reach of majority rule politics. There is a clear trend of change with respect to the minimum age requirement. In the last thirty-five years, seventeen states have made eighteen-year-olds eligible for election to either chamber of the state legislature. The district residency requirement may preclude experimentation with statewide or regional at-large representation as well as with forms of proportional representation based on party lists, and the felony disqualification may have a disparate impact on minority groups as well as conflicting with the policy of rehabilitating offenders. It is unlikely that noncitizens will be made eligible for state legislative office, although Germany permits certain noncitizens to vote and hold office at the local government level. Since the qualifications clause only applies to state legislators, local governments are and ought to remain free to experiment.

Second, current state constitutions do not address the issue of whether the relevant provisions are "both a floor and a ceiling in that they can neither be added to nor subtracted from, save as expressly allowed by some other section of the Constitution."[45] A strict interpretation of the qualifications clause prevailed in two seminal United States Supreme Court decisions that are consistent with state court decisions. The plenary powers approach to constitutional interpretation, by contrast, would permit the legislature to add qualifications. Or the clause could be redrafted to read "including, but not limited to, age, citizenship and residency."

Third, combining single-district representation with a district residency requirement for holding office tends to strengthen the link between representative and constituent at the expense of party discipline.

Fourth, the ban on dual or incompatible office holding precludes experiments with cabinet-type government in which executive and legislative functions are mixed.

Term of Office

All states operate on the basis of fixed terms for legislative office. The states differ both from the national legislature and among themselves concerning the length of the term. Thirty-six states fix the term of offices for the senate at four years.[46] In about half of these states, senatorial terms are staggered. In five states, a four-year rather than a two-year term of office is standard for the lower house.

Another issue affecting the term of office will be salient for twenty-first century framers—term limits. From 1990 to 1995 voter initiatives imposed term limits on state legislators in twenty-one states.[47] The policy of term limitations revives a debate familiar to eighteenth-century framers of state and federal constitutions. And it is consistent with the "citizen legislator" concept that is embedded in many state constitutions in the form of restraints on the length and frequency of sessions, low levels of pay, and spending caps on expenditures for the legislature.[48] But it is not in tune with the demand of earlier reform advocates that call for the professionalization of state legislatures. Current research indicates that term limits have neither enhanced the policy responsiveness of state legislatures nor put an end to political careerism.[49] Too little time has passed since the adoption of term limits to determine whether the legislature's capacity to provide a check on the executive branch is unduly weakened by the reform.

Compensation

Twentieth-century reformers targeted constitutional provisions fixing the level of compensation for legislators as a significant barrier to the creation of a full-time, professional legislative body. Their efforts have met with some success. The number of state constitutions specifying compensation levels diminished from twenty-four in 1972 to nine in 2004. In most of states, legislative compensation is set by statute.[50] Many of these states also authorize additional compensation for legislators in leadership positions. In twenty states, the compensation question is first addressed by some type of compensation commission independent of the legislature.[51] The independent-commission device combats public perceptions that compensation increases are motivated by legislators' self-interest. In most states, commission recommendations are subject to ratification or disapproval by the legislature. In Maryland and West Virginia, the recommendations may be reduced or rejected, but not increased. In Arizona and Texas, the commission's recommendations are submitted to the electorate.

These varying arrangements reflect levels of resistance in each state's political culture to the merits of a full-time, professional legislature rather than a part-time, citizen legislature. These opposed views are also evident in constitutional provisions mandating term limits and session limits discussed elsewhere in this chapter.

Leadership

In each state with a bicameral legislature, the house is free to elect and empower a speaker.[52] However, the constitutional rule is different for the senate. In twenty-six states, the lieutenant governor serves, by virtue of office, as president of the Senate.[53] That elected constitutional executive officer is, as is the case in the Federal Constitution, given a deciding vote when the Senate is equally divided. In six states, the lieutenant governor may debate and vote in the committee of the whole. Most likely, issues surrounding the legislative role of the lieutenant governor will be subsumed in consideration of whether to retain that office or to abolish it, as nine states have done. As long as the role exists, much of its impact on the legislative process will turn not on formal constitutional language but on senatorial custom and practice.

Legislative Immunity

Forty-three state constitutions offer legislators some speech or debate immunity.[54] In twenty-three states, the wording of the clause matches the language of the Federal Constitution "and for any speech or debate in either House, they shall not be questioned in any other place." In twelve states, words spoken or uttered in debate are privileged. In five states, legislators get only an immunity from "civil arrest" or "civil process" during legislative sessions and for a brief period prior to and after a session. In two states, legislators have no specified immunity of any sort.

The aims underlying speech or debate immunity are well summarized by the Alaska Supreme Court: protecting disfavored legislators from intimidation by a hostile executive; and protecting legislators from the burdens of forced participation in private litigation.[55]

A variety of outcomes are found in the states as to the scope of immunity. In an early case, the Massachusetts Supreme Judicial Court refused to extend the privilege to a libelous statement made as an aside to another member on the floor of the legislature rather than in formal debate.[56] That limited reading is consonant with the wording of the Texas Constitution, which covers only "words spoken in debate in either House."[57] Another judicial response is to follow federal precedents that focus on whether the legislator's conduct is "within the sphere of legitimate legislative activity."[58] Textual differences between the wording of the Federal speech or debate clause and the language of the state constitution have guided state supreme courts to a broader immunity doctrine than that prevailing in the Federal case law. Accordingly, the Alaska Supreme Court held that "legislative duties" immunity extends to a senator's conversation with the governor in preparation for the performance of the senator's duties at a contemplated joint session of the legislature. And the "legislative function" immunity, granted by the Hawaii Constitution and supported by clear legislative history, privileged off-floor statements made by a legislator to a reporter seeking clarification of the legislator's speech.[59]

"Legislative function" immunity more nearly captures the contemporary roles of legislators. Today's legislators deal with citizen grievances, shape public opinion by taking positions, and oversee the administration of the laws outside the legislative chamber and the committee room. Twenty-first framers should weigh whether legislators' activities in the public sphere, in particular their efforts at informing and representing constituent interests, ought to fall unambiguously within the scope of the privilege. If so, they may adopt "legislative function" language that fulfills that aim.

Legislative Ethics

Individuals who seek and hold public office in the twenty-first century are subject to extensive regulation designed to safeguard the integrity of the deliberative process surrounding the consideration of legislation. Most states now require disclosure of campaign contributions, personal financial disclosure for legislators and their families, and disclosure of lobbying expenditures.[60] Most of these reforms came via statute rather than constitutional change. In view of the demonstrated capacity of most legislatures to respond to the public's demand for higher ethical standards twenty-first-century constitution makers must appraise the merits of entrenching ethical norms in the state constitution.

Nineteenth-century constitutions favor constitutionalizing some ethical norms. Most of these provisions focus on reining in pecuniary conflicts of interest. Some form of ban on dual office holding is nearly universal. Several states prohibit legislatures from giving themselves a pay raise that will take effect during the session in which it was voted.[61] Mississippi bars legislators from eligibility, during their term of office, to any nonelective office of profit created or whose emoluments were increased during that term.[62] Pennsylvania requires "any member who has a personal or private interest in any measure or bill proposed or pending before the General Assembly" to "disclose the fact to the House of which he is a member" and to refrain from voting on that matter.[63]

The Rhode Island Constitution mandates a more sweeping and detailed definition of the content of a code of legislative ethics. The provision covers conflicts of interest, confidential information, use of position, contracts with government agencies, and financial disclosure.[64] Florida goes further by mandating full public disclosure of financial interests by candidates for legislative office and full public disclosure of campaign finances.[65] Florida also bans legislators from personally representing clients for compensation before any nonjudicial state agency. Both states create an independent State Ethics Commission to implement the policies spelled out in the constitution. Neither state empowers the Ethics Commission to remove the offending legislator from offices. However, the Florida Commission can conduct investigations and make public reports concerning any breach of public trust by a legislator. Both provisions view lawmaking as an essentially moral activity and are aimed not only at the fact but also the appearance of impropriety in the conduct of public affairs. Both provisions also manifest the same distrust of the legislature's capacity for self-regulation that led to the creation of independent commissions to determine legislative salaries and legislative apportionment.

Expulsion, Exclusion, and Recall

Expulsion, exclusion, and recall are constitutional devices that may affect the legislator's term of office. The legislature's power to exclude is based on a common provision in state constitutions: "Each house shall be the sole judge of the elections, returns, and qualification of its members."[66] This provision is uncontroversial when applied to election contests. But it is unclear whether the legislature can add to expressly enumerated qualifications. State framers are advised to address the issue of whether the legislature should have unreviewable discretion as to member's qualifications, since such discretion could permit the legislature to exclude a member chosen by the people by majority vote.

Forty-five state constitutions expressly authorize each chamber to expel a member.[67] The expulsion power is often curtly phrased: "Each house . . . may with the concurrence of two-thirds of all members elected thereto and serving therein expel a member."[68] In most states, the power to expel is standardless. Michigan adds a procedural requirement that the reasons for the expulsion be entered in the journal with the votes and names of the members voting on the question.[69] Montana and Idaho provide a "for good cause" standard.[70] Vermont bars expulsion "for causes known to constituents antecedent to the election."[71] And Michigan prohibits a second expulsion for the same cause.[72]

On the one hand, state framers should be aware that each phrase added to the bare-bones grant of the power to expel opens possibilities for judicial review. On the other hand, Michigan's procedural constraint promotes deliberation about and accountability for the expulsion decision. And a good-cause requirement deters arbitrary and capricious use of the power. The Vermont provision emphasizes that the judgment of constituents, not colleagues, should determine who represents them. Michigan's policy prohibiting a second sanction for the same offense articulates a deeply rooted legal principle.

Recall is a device embodying the values of direct democracy.[73] Recall authorizes a constituent of members, rather than their colleagues as in the case of exclusion and expulsion, to remove them from office by referendum. Recall is controversial because it is viewed as violating a fundamental principle of representative government—that legislators can act autonomously during their term of office. Nevertheless, recall is a matter of constitutional policy in eighteen states.[74]

Great variety is found in the expression of that policy in state constitutions. Idaho simply authorizes recall and leaves procedural details to be filled in by the legislature.[75] By contrast, Colorado exhibits distrust of legislative discretion by devoting an entire article of the state constitution to a comprehensive exposition of recall procedures, including the form and sufficiency of recall petitions.[76] States also differ as to the grounds for recall. In Wisconsin, no reasons need be stated.[77] In California, the recall petition must disclose the reasons for recall, but the sufficiency of these reasons is not reviewable.[78] In Minnesota, the constitution limits grounds for recall to "serious malfeasance or nonfeasance" in the performance of the duties of office or "conviction during the term of office of a serious crime."[79]

Framers of a recall provision are thus confronted with two fundamental issues. The first is whether the legislature can be trusted to implement the policy or whether statute-like detail should be enshrined in the constitution. The second is whether standards for the exercise of the electorate's decision should be included, as in Minnesota, thus inviting judicial review, or whether the merits of the cause for recall is for the electorate to determine.

In any case, both state legislatures and the electorate are limited in their power to exclude, expel, or recall a legislator by the rights guarantees of the Federal Constitution.

STRUCTURE

Bicameral/Unicameral

The initial question for constitution makers is whether to opt for a single-chamber (unicameral) or two-chamber (bicameral) legislature. The early constitutions of Pennsylvania (1776), Georgia (1777), and Vermont (1777) provided for unicameral legislatures. Since then, state constitutions makers have extensively debated the wisdom and purpose of maintaining a second chamber,[80] although only Nebraska currently has a one-house legislature. Proponents of a one-house legislature argue that it eliminates problems of interhouse coordination, controlling or regulating conference committees or management of joint committees and also furthers the principle of accountability.[81] Too, a single-chamber legislative body is well accepted at the local government level. Opponents worry that unicameralism lowers the consensus threshold for legislative action, increasing the possibility of drastic policy reversals with each change of government.[82]

Single Member/Multimember Districts

As James Gardner observes in his contribution to this volume: "Today, the great majority of state constitutions provide either expressly or implicitly for the election of state representatives and senators exclusively from single member districts."[83] The Citizens Conference on State Legislatures advanced the following rationale for its endorsement of single-member districts:

> the very idea of democratic government in which a citizen delegates power to a representative and holds him responsible for the exercise of it implies a one-to-one relationship, a single clear connection between representative and constituent. As soon as a constituent must contend with more than one relationship, that connection is weakened, the relationship is blurred.[84]

Countervailing considerations include a tradition of multimember districting in a few states. In addition, single member-district elections determined by a simple plurality of votes have the effect of enhancing the seat shares of majority parties and diminishing the shares of minority parties. Further, considerations of ethnic and racial fairness may be raised if single-member, simple plurality systems have the effect of excluding sizable minority groups from representation.[85]

As James Gardner indicates, current state constitutions have little to offer as a model for the multimember option. In 1970, Illinois abandoned an experiment with cumulative voting aimed at maximizing opportunities for the minority party in multimember house districts. And, in jurisdictions covered by the federal Voting Rights Act, state constitution makers seeking to remedy the perceived evils of single-member districts may confront a claim that multimember districts dilute the voting strength of African-Americans and Hispanics.[86] Although there are some proponents of multimember districts,[87] most reform proposals focus on changes in voting and election practices, such as various forms of proportional representation.[88]

Size

Many state constitutions fix the exact size and ratio of state legislative chambers.[89] The Citizens Conference on State Legislatures raised two difficulties with such provisions.[90] First, some chambers are too big, resulting either in chaotic decision-making or in undue concentration of power in a few dominant leaders. The suggested remedy is downsizing the legislature, particularly the lower house. Second, a constitutionally prescribed number is too inflexible. Virginia permits the legislature to change the size of each chamber within a minimum and maximum.[91] North Dakota authorizes the legislature to fix the number of senators and representatives by statute.[92] However, there is no discernible trend toward downsizing state legislatures either by constitutional amendment or statutory change.

Sessions

"No man's life, liberty or property are safe while the legislature is in session."[93] This popular adage sums up the attitude of distrust and the philosophy of limited government that resulted in the inclusion of constitutional rules designed to rein in the legislature's lawmaking capacity.[94] Such rules include: restricting the legislature to biennial rather than annual sessions; limiting the length of legislative sessions; limiting the compensation of legislators; forbidding the carryover of bills from one session to the next within the same term; granting the governor exclusive power to call special sessions; and restricting the legislature's jurisdiction in special sessions to matters within the scope of the governor's call.[95]

In 1972, the Citizens Conference on State Legislatures made the case for significant change in each of these rules.[96] The costs associated with constitutionalizing constraints on legislative sessions are well documented and include hasty, ill-considered legislation adopted at end-of-session logjams, frequent ad hoc special sessions, vesting significant agenda control in the governor, and fostering strategic use of delay and obstruction to block legislation. Some changes are in place. For example, in 1940, only four state legislatures held annual sessions but, by 1980, forty-three state constitutions authorized annual sessions.[97] Also, thirty-three states now authorize the legislature to call special sessions.[98] But, some are not. For example, thirty-six states retain constitutional limits on the length of regular sessions.[99]

The strongest argument for removing session constraints is that they have not preserved limited government. The regulatory welfare state is a fact of life at the outset of the twenty-first century, and session constraints may diminish the legislature's capacity to deregulate and privatize, as well as to engage in effective oversight of the bureaucracy.

Adjournment and Dissolution

Adjournment of legislative bodies means "the temporary cessation of business, which is to be resumed on the next legislative day or at a time certain . . ."; dissolution signifies the permanent cessation of the legislature's authority.[100] The inclusion in early state constitutions of constitutional provisions governing adjournment and dissolution, expressly vesting the legislative branch with the power to adjourn and dissolve itself, reflects bitter experience with the power of the king and colonial governors to prorogue and dissolve colonial assemblies. In fact, the king's power to dissolve is one of the grievances preferred in Jefferson's indictment of royal abuses in the Declaration of Independence.[101]

Early state framers anticipated strategic use of these powers by each chamber. And so they began to insert provisions, now found in forty-seven states and in the U.S. Constitution,[102] that permit one chamber to adjourn itself only for a limited number of days. When Vermont created a bicameral legislature in 1836, it gave the governor a default power to adjourn the legislature in case the chambers could not agree to adjourn, and this innovation has been adopted in about half of the states.[103]

The next wave of change occurred during the nineteenth century. Framers evidenced their distrust of legislatures by prescribing dissolution rules that limited legislative sessions to a stated number of days. These provisions have led to legislative strategems to evade the letter of the text including expansive notions of "legislative days," when that is the term used in the constitution, as well as the practice of stopping the clock. They have also created end of session logjams and encouraged midnight and twenty-four-hour legislation. Twenty-first-century constitution makers would be well advised to eliminate restrictions on the length of legislative sessions.

PROCESSES

Legislative Procedure

Among the most striking features of the evolution of state legislatures is the entrenchment in state constitutions of rules of legislative practice and procedure.[104] Twenty-first-century constitution makers must decide whether to retain, pare, or eliminate these constraints. The purpose of these regulatory provisions is more easily understood in light of their history. In early state constitutions, the legislature is typically afforded broad autonomy: "The Senate shall . . . determine its own rules of proceedings"; "The House of Representatives shall . . . settle the rules and orders of proceeding in their own house."[105] Despite the promise of autonomy suggested by such language, the incorporation of rules of parliamentary law into the constitution began early on.[106] This tendency is illustrated by the constitutional history of Pennsylvania. The earliest Pennsylvania Constitution, the "radical" constitution of 1776, contains several provisions designed to assure openness, deliberation, and accountability in governance by the unicameral legislature: a two-thirds quorum requirement for doing business, a provision calling for open sessions, weekly printing of votes and proceedings during session including recording "the yeas and nays on any question, vote or resolution where any two members require it"; and a provision requiring a formal enacting clause for all laws.[107]

The distrust of the legislature, seen by Jacksonian democrats as an engine for churning out special privileges for interest groups, produced a wave of constitution making in half of the states between 1845 and 1855. These reformers created "a blueprint for the due process of deliberative, democratically accountable government."[108]

These process reforms continued through the period 1864–1879, during which thirty-seven states wrote and ratified new constitutions. As G. Alan Tarr summarized these developments:

> In 1835 Alexis de Tocqueville observed that "the legislature of each state is faced by no power capable of resisting it." But beginning in the 1830s, state constitution makers sought to impose limits on these supreme legislatures. Initially, their restrictions focused on the process of legislation. Some state constitutions required extraordinary majorities to adopt certain types of legislation, under the assumption that it

would be more difficult to marshal such majorities for dubious endeavors. Others imposed procedural restrictions designed to prevent duplicity and promote greater openness and deliberation, assuming that greater transparency in the legislative process would deter legislative abuses or at least increase accountability for them. Thus, state constitutions mandated that all bills be referred to the committee, that they be read three times prior to enactment, that their titles accurately describe their contents, that they embrace a single subject, that they not be altered during their passage so as to change their original purpose, and so on. Other provisions required that the amendment or revision of laws not proceed by mere reference to their titles, that statutes be phrased in plain language, that taxing and spending measures be enacted only by recorded vote, and, most importantly, that no special laws be enacted where general law was possible. By the end of the nineteenth century, most state constitutions included several of these procedural requirements.[109]

The 1873 Pennsylvania Constitutional Convention, whose primary focus was legislative reform, illustrates Tarr's observations. That convention created an interrelated set of provisions implementing a broad vision of deliberative democracy applicable to each phase if the lawmaking process from drafting legislation to final passage.

Most state constitutions do not follow the Federal model, which has little to say about lawmaking procedures.[110] Instead, like Pennsylvania, they incorporate most of the procedural norms that emerged during the nineteenth century. At the drafting phase, each bill must contain a title that "clearly expresses" the subject matter of the body of the proposed law.[111] In addition to the notice function of the title, each bill, except appropriations, is restricted to "one subject" in order to forestall logrolling and to focus the legislature's attention on discrete policy issues.[112] Values of notice and clarity are furthered by the rule that bills that amend or cross-reference existing laws must include the amended or referenced legislation in their text.[113] Particular rules apply to drafting appropriations measures to ensure notice and bar logrolling.[114] An additional safeguard of clarity stems from the void-for-vagueness doctrine rooted in the due process clause of state and federal constitutions.[115]

Constitutional rules were designed to fix accountability and to enhance participation and deliberation. The state house is directly accountable for originating revenue bills.[116] The committee system is recognized and strengthened by the requirement that all bills be referred to a committee and printed.[117] To prevent surprise and foster public notice, no bill could be altered or amended on its passage through either chamber so as to change its original purpose,[118] and every bill must be read at length and printed before the final vote.[119] Principles of accountability and majority rule are embedded in the requirement that a majority of each chamber cast a recorded vote on every bill, and that the presiding officer of each chamber authenticate by signature the fact that the measure was approved, and the fact of signing must be entered in the journal.[120]

On the one hand, procedural constraints on the state legislature modify both the plenary-power principle and the specific constitutional text granting the legislature the power to determine its rules and proceedings. Procedural constraints seem to embody a historical and retrospective approach to state constitution making by entrenching the results of yesteryear's controversies. On the other hand, one can view procedural constraints as a collective effort by the people of the several states over a period of two centuries to entrench principles of notice, deliberation, and accountability into the legislative process by stipulating rules of due process for legislative bodies.

If twenty-first-century framers choose to include procedural rules, they must confront whether those rules ought to be enforced by the state judiciary exercising its power of judicial review. In many states, judges have refused to enforce all but a few of these procedural constraints. That is because "a substantial number" of state courts adhere to the "enrolled bill" rule,[121] which prevents any evidence outside the text of the enrolled bill itself from being introduced as evidence showing constitutional violations of rules governing the process of enactment.[122] Thus, rules concerning drafting such as the single subject and clear title rules are reviewable, because a violation can be determined from the text of the enactment. But violations of majority vote, referral to committee, printing and reading, limited session, and similar procedural rules are unchallengeable in a jurisdiction adhering to the enrolled bill rule. The pros and cons of the enrolled bill rule as well as various modifications and exceptions to that rule all share the same policy vice—state courts, not constitution makers, are making fundamental decisions about the enforceability of constitutional norms. Even without the enrolled bill rule, a state court can refuse to enforce procedural rules by holding that judicial intervention violates separation of powers doctrine.[123] Therefore, twenty-first-century constitution makers are well advised to clarify in the text of the state constitution as to whether or not judicial enforcement is contemplated.

Local, Special, or Private Laws

Constitutional rules about local, special, or private legislation are vigorous survivors from the nineteenth century. The language and scope of such constitutional provisions varies.[124] Thirty-one states prohibit the enactment of a local or special law when a general law can be made applicable. Six states bar special or local laws when there is an existing general law on the subject. Thirty-seven states forbid local or special legislation on certain enumerated subjects. In some states, the legislature may enact special or local laws if published notice of the intention to do so is given[125] or if the affected locality assents.[126]

The policies favoring inclusion of some constitutional barrier to local, special or private laws are concisely expressed in a leading case:

> The inherent vice of special laws is that they create preferences and establish irregularities. As an inevitable consequence their enactment leads to improvident and ill-considered legislation. The members whose particular constituents are not affected by a proposed special law became indifferent to its passage. It is customary, on the plea of legislative courtesy, not to interfere with the local bill of another member, and members are elected and re-elected on account of their proficiency in procuring for their respective districts special privileges in the way of local or special laws. The time which the legislature would otherwise devote to the consideration of measures of public importance is frittered away in the granting of special favors to private or corporate interests or to local communities. Meanwhile, in place of a symmetrical body of statutory law on subjects of general and common interest to the whole people, we have a wilderness of special provisions whose operation extends no further than the boundaries of the particular school district or township or county to which they were made to apply.[127]

Putting these goals into controlling effect is no easy matter. Few state constitutions contain a definition of what is referenced by the term "local," "general," "special," or "private" legislation. Working definitions are found in the Alabama Constitution:

> "A general law is a law which in its terms and effects applies either to the whole state, or to one or more municipalities in the state less than the whole in a class. A general law applicable to such a class of municipalities shall define the class on the laws of criteria reasonably related to the purpose of the law...."
>
> "A special or private law is one which applies to an individual, association, or corporation. A local law is a law which is not a general law or a special or private law."[128]

The Alabama provisions restate rather than resolve the essential problem, however. That problem is the goodness of fit between the classification scheme adopted by the legislature and the purpose of the law. As is the case with regard to enforcement of constitutional rules governing legislative procedures, much turns on the issue of judicial review.

On the one hand, these provisions reflect "an effort to avoid favoritism, discrimination, and inequalities" that arise out of the pulling and hauling of interest groups in the legislative process.[129] Some commentators have recognized that these provisions bear a close resemblance to the Equal Protection Clause of the U.S. Constitution and, as such, offer significant equality guarantees for individuals.[130] On the other hand, leading cases have shown a strong tendency to defer to the legislature's selection of a classification principle.[131] As a result, the legislature can avoid the rule with ease in most jurisdictions. A few constitutions expressly provide that whether a general act is or can be made applicable shall be a matter for judicial determination.[132] It is not clear, however, that even an express provision produces more judicial enforcement of the ban.

CONCLUSION

The legislative branch is a key institution in a functioning democracy. Representative government is an institutional response to the complex problems and conflicts that emerge in a free society. The legislature's role involves: identifying problems, clarifying goals, and devising means compatible with those goals to solve problems.

Legislative problem-solving involves debate, deliberation, negotiation, and compromise. Those characteristics differentiate legislative policy-making from the alternatives of executive branch dominance and direct democracy.[133] The legislature takes into account diverse values and interests that check and balance the bureaucratic and centralizing tendencies of a dominant executive branch. The legislature's superior information-gathering capacity, greater understanding of the trade-offs among competing policy alternatives, and ability to cut deals are lacking when single-issue propositions are submitted directly to the voters.

The competition for policy-making dominance between and among the electorate as well as the executive, the legislative, and the judicial branches of government is built into the system of checks and balances entrenched in all fifty state constitutions. By careful reflection on the natural history of the evolution of the state legislative branch, twenty-first-century framers can face the challenges of making constitutional choices that channel competing claims over policy making without unduly affecting the dynamic vigor of the competitive process.

NOTES

1. National Municipal League, *Model State Constitution* 42 (6th ed., 1963) [Hereafter cited as MODEL].

2. Frank P. Grad and Robert F. Williams, *State Constitutions for the Twenty-first Century*, vol. II (ed. G. Alan Tarr).

3. Ibid.

4. MODEL, supra n. 1, 42.

5. Mass. Const., pt. I, art. 30.

6. Jim Rossi, "Institutional Design and the Lingering Legacy of Antifederalist Separation of Powers Ideals in the States," 52 *Vand. L. Rev.* 1167, 1191 (1999).

7. Federalist No. 37, 227 (Robert Scigliano, ed., 2000).

8. Alaska Const., art. III, § 22, 23; Haw. Const., art. IV, § 6; N.J. Const., art. V, § IV, par. 1.

9. *See,* for example, N.J. Const., art I, § IV, par. 2–5.

10. *See,* for example, Fla. Const., art. V, § 2 (a).

11. *See,* for example, Conn. Const., art. II.

12. Rossi, supra n. 6, 1198–2000.

13. Arthur Earl Bonfield, *State Administrative Rule Making,* 506 (1986).

14. Va. Const., art. IX, § 2.

15. Two states provide for the appointment of a joint committee between sessions with power to suspend administrative regulations until the legislature reconvenes. Mich. Const., art. IV, § 37; S. Dak. Const., art. III, § 30. Iowa and New Jersey require a concurrent resolution to overturn or modify a regulation. Iowa Const., art. III, § 40; N.J. Const., art. 5, § 4 par. 6.

16. Conn. Const., art. 2.

17. For a thoughtful presentation pro and con, *see* Bonfield supra, n. 13, 457–60, 507–11.

18. Louis L. Jaffe, "Law Making by Private Groups," 51 *Harv. L. Rev.* 201, 212 (1937).

19. MODEL supra n. 1, 93.

20. Alaska Const., art. IX, § 13.

21. MODEL, supra n. 1, 91.

22. Council of State Governments, 35 *Book of the States,* 145–46 (2003).

23. Pa. Const., art. III, § 11.

24. N.Y. Const., art. VII, § 2.

25. Council of State Governments, supra n. 22, 148.

26. U.S. Census Bureau, 1997 Census of Governments, vol. 4, Government Finances 4 (December 2000) (compiled from table 4, column 2).

27. George D. Brown, "Federal Funds and National Supremacy: The Role of State Legislatures in Federal Grant Programs," 28 *Am U.L. Rev.* 279, 280 (1979).

28. Compare *MacManus v. Love*, 179 Colo. 281, 499 P.2d 609 (1972) ("No moneys in the state treasury shall be disbursed by the state treasurer except upon appropriation made by law . . ." Colo. Const., art. V, § 33) (federal payments directly to the state are not subject to the appropriation power) with *Shapp v. Sloan*, 480 Pa. 449, 391 A.2d 595 (1978) ("No money shall be paid out of the public treasury except on appropriations made by law." Pa. Const., art. III, § 24) (federal payments to the state are subject to the appropriations power).

29. Bret Smentkowski, "Legal Reasoning and the Separation of Powers: A State Level Analysis of Disputes Involving Federal Funds Appropriations," 16 *Law and Policy* 395, 403–08 (1994).

30. *See*, Role of State Legislators in Appropriating Federal Funds, Hearing Before the Subcommittee on Intergovernmental Relations of the Senate Committee on Governmental Affairs, 95th Cong., 1st Sess. (1977).

31. Fla. Const., art. III, § 5.

32. Council of State Governments, 34 *Book of the States* 166 (2002).

33. MODEL, supra n. 1, 62.

34. 418 U.S. 633 (1974).

35. *See*, for example, Fla. Const., art. I, § 24.

36. Council of State Governments, supra n. 32, 163–68.

37. Ibid., 161–62.

38. Va. Const., art. V, § 11.

39. Tex. Const., art. IV, § 12 (c), (d), (f).

40. Tex. Const., art. IV, § 12 (h).

41. Robert F. Williams, *The New Jersey State Constitution*, 85–86 (1990).

42. Va. Const., art. IV, § 17.

43. Neb. Const., art. III, § 17.

44. Council of State Governments, supra n. 32, 76–77.

45. A. E. Dick Howard, 1 *Commentaries on the Constitution of Virginia* 366 (1974).

46. Council of State Governments, supra n. 32, 73–74. Twelve states provide for a two-year term. New Jersey, the first senatorial term at the beginning of each decade is two years. In Illinois, all senate seats are at stake every ten years. During that decade, each senate seat is subject to a four-four-two-year term in rotation.

47. John M. Carey, Richard G. Niemi, and Lynda W. Powell, Term Limits in the State Legislature 4–5 (2000). Term limits were implemented in seventeen of the jurisdictions. Ibid., 1.

48. Otto J. Hetzel, Michael E. Libonati, and Robert F. Williams, Legislative Law and Statutory Interpretation 170 (3d. 2001); *see*, for example, Cal. Const., art. IV, § 7.5 (spending caps); Tex. Const., art. III, § 24(a) ($600 per month); Ga. Const., art. III, § IV par. I(a) (forty-day limit on length of legislative session).

49. *See* Jennifer Drage Bowser, *The Effect of Legislative Term Limits,* Council of State Governments, supra n. 22, 87–91.

50. Ibid., 125–35.

51. Ibid., 125.

52. Ibid., 122–23.

53. Ibid., 120–21.

54. Steven F. Huefner, "The Neglected Value of the Legislative Privilege in State Legislatures," 45 *W. & M. L. Rev.* 221 (2003).

55. *Kertulla v. Abood,* 686 P.d 1197, 1202 (Alaska, 1984).

56. *Coffin v. Coffin,* 4 Mass. 1 (1808) (interpreting Mass. Const., Pt. I, art. 21).

57. Tex. Const., art. III, § 21.

58. *United States v. Brewster,* 408 U.S. 501 (1972).

59. *Abercrombie v. McClung,* 55 Haw. 595, 525 P.2d 594 (1974).

60. *See generally* Council on Governmenal Ethics Laws, Campaign Finance, Ethics and Lobby Law Blue Book (8th ed., 1990).

61. N.Y. Const., art. III, § 6.

62. Miss. Const., art. IV, § 45.

63. Pa. Const., art. III, § 13.

64. R.I. Const., art. III, § 8.

65. Fla. Const., art. II, § 8.

66. For example, Mich. Const., art. IV, § 16.

67. *See generally* Jack H. Maskell, Recall and Expulsion of Legislators, 1 *Encyclopedia of the American Legislative System* 547–61 (Joel H. Silbey, ed., 1994).

68. For example, Cal. Const., art. 4, § 5(a).

69. Mich. Const., art. IV, § 16.

70. Idaho Const., art. III, § 11; Mont. Const., art. V, § 10.

71. Vt. Const., art. II, IV, § 16.

72. Mich. Const., art. IV, § 16.

73. *See* Thomas E. Cronin, *Direct Democracy* 125–56 (1989).

74. Cronin, Ibid., 126–27.

75. Idaho Const., art. VI, § 6.

76. Colorado Const., art. XXI.

77. Wis. Const., art. III, § 12.

78. Cal. Const., art. II, § 14(a).

79. Minn. Const., art. VII, § 6.

80. John Dinan, "Bicameralism and the American State Constitutional Tradition," 4 (unpublished paper in files of the author).

81. Citizens Conference on State Legislatures, *The Sometime Governments: A Critical Study of the Fifty American State Legislatures* 251 (1971).

82. Bruce E. Cain, *Epilogue* in George C. Lubernow and Bruce E. Cain, eds., *Governing California* 331 at 333 (1997). For a presentation of arguments for and against unicameral legislatures, see, Maryland Constitutional Convention Commission Report 125–26 (1967).

83. James A. Gardner, *Voting and Elections* (p. 45).

84. Supra. n. 82, 82.

85. Bruce Edward Cain, *Legislative Redistricting*, supra n. 67, 392–93.

86. *See generally* Samuel Issacharoff, Pamela S. Karlan, and Richard H. Pildes, *The Law of Democracy* 673–713 (2d. rev. ed., 2002).

87. For a brief discussion of the variety of multimember district options, *see* Anthony Girzynski, *Elections to the State Legislature*, supra n. 67, 439–41.

88. *See* Lani Guinier, *The Tyranny of the Majority* (1994).

89. Council of State Governments, supra. n. 32, 73–74.

90. Citizens Conference on State Legislatures, supra n. 81, 66–69, 155–56.

91. Va. Const., art. IV, § 2, § 3.

92. N. Dak. Const., art. IV, § 2.

93. Suzy Platt, ed., Respectfully quoted 198 (1963).

94. Jon C. Teaford, *The Rise of the States,* 13–14 (2002).

95. Citizens Conference on State Legislatures, supra n. 81, 156.

96. Ibid. 41, 56, 57–62, 103–04.

97. Teaford, supra n. 94, 200.

98. In eleven of these states the legislature may not determine the subjects considered at the special session. Council of State Governments, supra. n. 32, 69–73.

99. In twelve of these states, a supermajority may vote to extend the length of the regular session. Ibid.

100. Robert Luce, *Legislative Assemblies* 181 (1924).

101. Ibid., 181–87.

102. Citizens Conference on State Legislatures, *State Constitutional Provisions Affecting Legislatures* 26 (1967).

103. Ibid.

104. Robert F. Williams, "State Constitutional Limits on Legislative Procedure: Legislative Compliance and Judicial Enforcement," 48 *U. Pitt. L. Rev.* 797 (1987).

105. Mass. Const., pt. II, ch. I, § II, art. VII; § III, art. X.

106. *See* Robert Luce, *Legislative Procedure* 1–22 (1922); Gordon S. Wood, *The Creation of the American Republic* 226–37 (1969).

107. Pa. Const., I, § 10, § 13, § 14, § 16.

108. Hans J. Linde, "Due Process of Law Making," 55 *Neb. L. Rev.* 197, 253 (1976).

109. Alan Tarr, *Understanding State Constitutions* 118–19 (1998).

110. Abner J. Mikva and Eric Lane, *Legislative Process* 177 (2d. ed, 2002). *See* U.S. Const., art. I, § 5 (majority for quorum, journal, recorded vote on demand of one-fifth of those present); art. I, § 7, cl. 1 (revenue bills must originate in House).

111. Pa. Const., art. III, § 3.

112. Millard H. Ruud, "No Law Shall Embrace More Than One Subject," 42 *Minn. L. Rev.* 389 (1958).

113. Pa. Const., art. III, § 6. *See* Horace Reid, "Is Referential Legislation Worthwhile?" 25 *Minn. L. Rev.* 261 (1941).

114. Pa. Const., art. III, § 11.

115. *See* Anthony G. Amsterdam, Note, "The Void for Vagueness Doctrine in the Supreme Court," 109 *U. Pa. L. Rev.* 67 (1960).

116. Pa. Const., art. III, § 10.

117. Pa. Const., art. III, § 2.

118. Pa. Const., art. III, § 1; *see* Martha J. Dragich, "State Constitutional Restrictions on Legislative Procedure: Rethinking the Analysis of Original Purpose, Single Subject and Clear Title Requirement," 38 *Harv. J. on Legis.* 103, 111–13 (2001).

119. Pa. Const., art. III, § 4.

120. Pa. Const., art. III, § 4, § 5, § 8.

121. C. Dallas Sands, 1 *Sutherland on Statutory Construction* 611 (4th ed., 1985).

122. Williams supra n. 104.

123. For example, *Tuck v. Blackmon,* 798 So. 2d 402 (Miss., 2001) (refusing to enforce art. IV, § 59, Miss Const. requiring that any law or statute be read in full before final passage).

124. 1 C. Dallas Sands et al., *Local Government Law,* § 3.21 nn. 3–5 (1982).

125. Ala. Const., art. IV, § 106; Fla. Const., art. III, § 10; Pa. Const., art. III, § 7.

126. N.Y. Const., art. IX, § 2(b).

127. *Anderson v. Board of County Commissioners of Cloud County,* 77 Kan. 721, 95 P. 587 (1908).

128. Ala. Const., § 110.

129. Howard, supra n. 45, 549.

130. *See* Donald Marritz, "Making Equality Matter (again): The Prohibition Against Special Laws in the Pennsylvania Constitution," 3 *Widener J. Pub. L.* 161 (1993); Robert F. Williams, "Equality Guarantees in State Constitutional Law," 63 *Tex. L. Rev.* 1195 (1985).

131. Sands, supra n. 123, § 3.21.

132. For example, Kan. Const., art. II, § 17.

133. Ian Rosenthal, Burdett A. Loomis, John R. Hibbing, and Karl T. Kurtz, *Republic on Trial* 198–214 (2003).

Chapter Three

The Executive Branch

Thad Beyle

The principle to guide the design of a state's executive branch was clearly stated by former North Carolina Governor, Terry Sanford, "Make the chief executive of the state the chief executive in fact."[1] He continued by arguing "the governor is responsible for leadership within each state. To be able to lead, the governor needs to be freed from the barbed wire of antiquated constitutional barriers. . . . (The governor) must have the tools he needs to lead effectively."[2]

SOME HISTORICAL BACKGROUND

In September 1775, John Adams stood at his writing desk as a committee of one drafting the proposed new Constitution for the Commonwealth of Massachusetts. For resources, he fell back on his own earlier work, *Thoughts on Government,* and on the work of those in other states to develop "A Constitution or Form of Government for the Commonwealth of Massachusetts."[3] He proposed a separation of powers between the three separate departments of government—legislature, executive, and judicial. His work was accepted by the full convention with but a few notable changes and has been called "the oldest functioning written constitution in the world."[4]

But as in all the constitutions adopted in the original thirteen states there were three important trends in the powers provided to those separate departments. One was establishing a separate and independent judiciary. However, it is the second two trends that are of importance to this specific topic—the strength that was lodged in the new state legislatures and the lack of strength that was lodged in the governorships. The greater legislative strength was an obvious reaction to the lack of effective representation of the citizens under the imposed colonial governors, and the lesser gubernatorial strength was in reaction to the strength of those imposed colonial governors. Although the governor would "have veto power over the acts of the legislature," the new Constitution called for an annual election of the governor.[5] There were various restrictions on the governorship placed in other new state constitutions. In

North Carolina, one of the delegates to the 1776 North Carolina convention was asked how much power they had proposed to give the governor, to which he replied: "just enough to sign the receipt for his salary."[6]

So the history of the American state governorship is one of rather weak beginnings, followed over the next two centuries by a gradual and incremental movement to provide the governors with more powers. But with some of these incremental steps came other problems. For example, as more states transferred the selection of the governor from the legislature to the people, they often called for the direct election of other state administrative officials. This meant that governors found that they had to share the executive branch powers with other elected officials even though many felt that their vote for governor was a vote for the person who would run the state's executive branch.

The reforms toward the end of the nineteenth century and early twentieth century brought the concept of "neutral competence" into state and local governments. Responding to the excesses of patronage by some elected officials and corruption in several states and cities, a drive to raise the competence of those serving in state and local governments began. The key to these reforms was to install some form of merit system or civil service personnel procedures in these governments so that "what you know" would replace "who you know" as the key factor in securing and keeping jobs, and for promotions. The goal was to separate politics from government insofar as possible.

Similarly, as new responsibilities faced the states, the answer was often to establish agencies, boards, and commissions, often outside the reach of any elected executive branch official. Governors may have had the authority to appoint members of these boards and commissions, but they often shared that responsibility with the legislature either in appointing them or in having the legislature confirm their appointments. Again, the aim was to separate the politics of the past from the policy making and administration of the present and future. The effect of these reforms was to place restrictions on how much power the governor actually had over the various parts of the executive branch of government.

During the twentieth century, there were at least four waves of reform in the states that have had an impact on state executive branches. The first began in 1917 and focused on creating comprehensive plans of administrative organization. In Illinois the movement was led by Governor Frank O. Lowden and in New York by Governor Alfred E. Smith. This movement culminated in the publication of "A Model State Constitution" by the National Municipal League in 1921, which called for "a centralized plan of State organization, headed by the governor, a single-house legislature, and unified court structure."[7]

The second wave of reform came in the mid-1930s, as the appointment of a federal commission by President Franklin Roosevelt to reform the federal executive branch stimulated consideration of executive branch reorganization in the states. In the twenty-five years that these two waves of reform encompassed, it was estimated that "every state in the Union has at one time or an-other . . . considered the matter of administrative reorganization."[8] Eleven of the states sought "to make the governor in fact, as well as in theory, the respon-sible chief executive of the state."[9]

The third wave of state reform was again stimulated by presidential ac-tions, as Presidents Harry Truman and Dwight Eisenhower established the "Hoover Commissions" to look at the possibilities of executive branch reorga-nization at the national level. These in turn stimulated states and even cities to establish "Little Hoover Commissions" to seek the same goals in their govern-ments.[10] "'Concentration of authority and responsibility,' 'functional integra-tion,' 'direct lines of responsibility,' 'grouping of related services,' 'elimination of overlapping and duplication,' and 'need for coordination' echoed through state capitols."[11]

The fourth wave began in the mid-1960s as a number of developments il-luminated the need to reform state governments. The U.S. Supreme Court's decisions on equal education and the need for redistricting state legislatures brought ferment throughout the states. The "Great Society Programs" of the Lyndon Johnson presidency made clear to the states the need to get their houses in order so the programs could be carried out. And a series of state lead-ers such as former North Carolina Governor Terry Sanford and former Cali-fornia Speaker of the House Jess Unruh were given foundation grants to help the fifty states develop their roadmaps for reform.[12] By 1983, Larry Sabato ar-gued, "Within the last twenty years, there has been a virtual explosion of reform in state government. In most of the states, as a result, the governor is now truly the master of his own house, not just the father figure."[13]

In a sense, this fourth wave of reform continues to this day as states con-tinue to make changes as new leadership is faced with problems that need to be alleviated. By 1992, major state executive branch reorganization efforts had taken place in twenty-seven states since the 1960s.[14] While there is a sense that the states are between waves now, it would not be too surprising to see some states begin undertaking major executive branch reorganization due to the fis-cal problems they are facing at the beginning of the twenty-first century. The goals articulated in these reorganization efforts were "modernization and streamlining of the executive branch machinery, efficiency, economy, respon-siveness, and gubernatorial control."[15] Other reforms and changes affecting the state executive branches were also occurring.

WHERE STATE EXECUTIVE BRANCHES STAND NOW

The first way to view what has been happening since the 1960s is to look at the "Index of Formal Powers of the Governorship" first developed by Joseph

Schlesinger,[16] which this author picked up and has continued to update.[17] The Index consists of six different indices of gubernatorial power as seen in 1960 and in 2003. These indices include the number and importance of separately elected executive branch officials, the tenure potential for governors, the appointment power of governors for administrative and board positions in the executive branch, the governor's budgetary power, the governor's veto power, and the governor's party strength in the state legislature. Each of the individual indices is set in a five-point scale with five being the most powerful and one being the least. (See the notes to table 1 for detail on how each of these indices and the overall Index was developed.)

TABLE 1
Governors' Institutional Powers 1960 vs. 2002

Specific Power	Scores		% Change
	1960	2002	
SEP	2.3	2.9	+28
TP	3.2	4.1	+28
AP	2.9	3.1	+ 7
BP	3.6	3.1	−14
VP	2.8	4.5	+61
Totals	14.8	17.7	+20

NOTES:

SEP—Separately elected executive branch officials: 5 = only governor or governor/lieutenant governor team elected; 4.5 = governor or governor/lieutenant governor team, with one other elected official; 4 = governor/lieutenant governor team with some process officials (attorney general, secretary of state, treasurer, auditor) elected; 3 = governor/lieutenant governor team with process officials, and some major and minor policy officials elected; 2.5 = governor (no team) with six or fewer officials elected, but none are major policy officials; 2 = governor (no team) with six or fewer officials elected, including one major policy official; 1.5 = governor (no team) with six or fewer officials elected, but two are major policy officials; 1 = governor (no team) with seven or more process and several major policy officials elected. (*Source: The Book of the States*, 1960–1961 [1960]: 124–25 and 2000–2001 [2000]: 33–38.)

TP—Tenure potential of governors: 5 = 4-year term, no restraint on reelection; 4.5 = 4-year term, only three terms permitted; 4 = 4-year term, only two terms permitted; 3 = 4-year term, no consecutive election permitted; 2 = 2-year term, no restraint on reelection; 1 = 2-year term, only two terms permitted. (*Source:* Joseph A. Schlesinger, "The Politics of the Executive," in *Politics in the American States*, edited by Herbert Jacob and Kenneth N. Vines [Boston: Little, Brown, 1965]: 229; and *The Book of the States*, 2000–2001 [2000]: 31–32.)

AP—Governor's appointment powers in six major functional areas: corrections, K–12 education, health, highways/transportation, public utilities regulation, and welfare. The six individual office scores are totaled and then averaged and rounded to the nearest .5 for the state score. 5 = governor appoints, no other approval needed; 4 = governor appoints, a board, council or legislature approves; 3 = someone else appoints, governor approves or shares appointment; 2 = someone else appoints, governor and others approve; 1 = someone else appoints, no approval or confirmation needed. (*Source:* Schlesinger [1965]: 229; and *The Book of the States*, 2000–2001 [2000]: 34–37.)

Table 1 (*continued*)

BP—Governor's budget power: 5 = governor has full responsibility, legislature may not increase executive budget; 4 = governor has full responsibility, legislature can increase by special majority vote or subject to item veto; 3 = governor has full responsibility, legislature has unlimited power to change executive budget; 2 = governor shares responsibility, legislature has unlimited power to change executive budget; 1 = governor shares responsibility with other elected official, legislature has unlimited power to change executive budget. (*Source:* Schlesinger [1965]: 229; *The Book of the States,* 2000–2001 [2000]: 20–21; and NCSL, "Limits on Authority of Legislature to Change Budget" [1998].)

VP—Governor's veto power: 5 = has item veto and a special majority vote of the legislature is needed to override a veto (three-fifths of legislators elected or two-thirds of legislators present; 4 = has item veto with a majority of the legislators elected needed to override; 3 = has item veto with only a majority of the legislators present needed to override; 2 = no item veto, with a special legislative majority needed to override it; 1 = no item veto, only a simple legislative majority needed to override. (*Source:* Schlesinger [1965]: 229; and *The Book of the States,* 2000–2001 [2000]: 101–103.)

Total—sum of the scores on the five individual indices. Score—total divided by five to keep 5-point scale.

Ambition Ladder for Statewide Elected Officials, 1990–2001

Office	Total Races	Won	Lost	Average
Lieutenant Governor	35	12	23	34%
Secretary of State	12	4	8	33%
State Treasurer	9	3	6	33%
Attorney General	29	4	25	14%
State Auditor	8	1	7	13%
Totals	93	24	69	26%

Source: www.unc.edu~beyle.

Over the four decades involved in the comparison of 1960 and 2003 indices, the overall institutional powers of the governors in the fifty states increased by 12.5 percent. The greatest increase among the individual gubernatorial powers was in their veto power (+61%) as more governors gained an item veto. Further, in 1996 North Carolina voters were finally able to vote on a constitutional amendment giving their governor veto power. For over two centuries the North Carolina state legislature had refused to allow such an amendment to go to the voters as it would have curbed their power. And it was not until November 2002 that the gubernatorial veto was ever used in the state.

The indices measuring the tenure potential of the governor (length of term and ability to seek an additional term or terms), and the number of separately elected executive branch officials showed identical 28 percent increases in favor of the governor. The governor's appointment power over six specific functional area executive branch officials did not increase very much (+7%).[18] In fact, there are still a considerable number of separately elected executive branch officials in addition to the governors across the fifty states, so there is considerable room for reform in this area.

The gubernatorial budgetary power actually declined over the period (-14%). However, we must remember that during this same period state legislatures were also undergoing considerable reform and gaining more power and the ability to work with the governor's proposed budget was one of those reforms sought. Hence, while some states' governors may have seen increased budgetary powers, there were also increased legislative budgetary powers that may have more than balanced out the increases in gubernatorial powers.

Finally, there has been a drop in the gubernatorial party control in the state legislature over the period (-17%). Most of this change can be attributed to the major partisan shifts occurring in the Southern states over the period as the region has been moving from a one-party type of politics to a very competitive two-party type of politics.[19] In 1960, thirteen of the fourteen governors were Democrats, and all twenty-eight state legislative houses were under Democratic control. In 2003, the governorships were split evenly at seven each for Democrats and Republicans, while the Democrats held a seventeen to ten edge in control of the state legislative houses. The North Carolina House, while split evenly between the parties, is run by a coalition of mainly Democrats and a few Republicans—with a "dual speakership" running the House. However, the governors of Alabama, Arkansas, Louisiana, and Virginia face a legislature completely controlled by the opposite party, while the governors of Georgia and Kentucky face a legislature with split partisan control.

WHAT REMAINS TO BE DONE?

To explore the remaining agenda for constitutional reform of the state executive branch, we will look at specific areas that recent events have pinpointed as areas needing attention. In some cases, specific states will be pinpointed as targets of such reforms.

Gubernatorial Tenure

The goal of most states has been to follow the federal model of allowing the executive to serve a four-year term. There are now only two states, New Hampshire and Vermont, that restrict their governors to a two-year term. Recently, constitutional amendments in two other states changed the length of their gubernatorial terms from two years to four years so that the Arkansas governor elected in 1986 and the Rhode Island governor elected in 1994 initiated four-year terms in those states. The argument for a four-year versus a two-year term was succinctly stated by an incumbent governor at a "New Governors' Seminar" run by the National Governors' Association. In your first year, you learn how to become a governor; in the second and third years you are being the governor and getting the business of state done; in the fourth year, you are running for reelection. In a two-year term, those middle two years of being governor are missing.

The second aspect of the gubernatorial tenure question is whether a governor can seek reelection to another term. While eleven states have no limitation on how many terms a governor may serve, thirty-six do limit their governors to two successive terms, while Utah limits their governor to three terms. For some that is an absolute limit, for others it means a two-term governor must vacate the office but could return after someone else serves a term. In Nebraska and Washington governors are limited to serving only eight years in a fourteen- or sixteen-year period. Virginia alone remains as a state that only allows their governor to serve a single term with no consecutive election allowed. Hence, the minute a governor is elected in Virginia and sworn in, he or she is a "lame-duck" as everyone with an interest in the governorship begins to look around to see who might become the next governor.

The goals of reform in terms of gubernatorial tenure are very state specific: New Hampshire and Vermont should join the other forty-eight states in providing their governors with four-year terms, and Virginia should allow its governor a possibility of succession to a second term.

Gubernatorial Elections

Another part of the gubernatorial tenure question concerns the timing of gubernatorial elections in relation to presidential elections. The concern here is the fear or possibility that events at the national and international level tied to the presidential election may prevent state-level candidates from articulating the issues and concerns that voters should be thinking about when voting for state officials. Further, a landslide victory for a presidential candidate can provide presidential coattails for his or her party candidates to win down the ballot. In this situation, it is not clear that the best candidate for the state office would be the winner.

Currently, only eleven states hold their gubernatorial elections at the same time as presidential elections are held, and two of these states are New Hampshire and Vermont, which hold their elections every other even year. Five states hold their gubernatorial elections in the odd numbered years, and thirty-six states hold their gubernatorial elections in the even, nonpresidential year. Again, two of these thirty-six states are New Hampshire and Vermont. A possible reform agenda item here would be for those nine states holding their elections in presidential years to shift them to an off-presidential year so the two sets of elections could be kept separate. This also suggests that if and when New Hampshire and Vermont change their gubernatorial terms to the four-year plan, they also hold them in off-presidential years. While some may argue that there is lower voter turnout in off-presidential-year elections, it is also true that there will be less of a "coattail" effect from the nationwide presidential election both in terms of party line voting and issues. And potentially more attention will be paid to state-level issues by those who do come out to vote.

Separately Elected Executive Branch Officials— The Lieutenant Governor

As already noted, there is still a need to reduce the number of separately elected executive branch officials on any constitutional reform agenda for the states. As of 2000, there were 305 separately elected executive branch officials covering twelve major offices in the states. In addition, ten states also have multimember boards, commissions or councils with members selected by statewide or district elections. To focus on this agenda, let us first look at the office of lieutenant governor, the "heartbeat away" office in most states.

Currently forty-two states elect a lieutenant governor while five states designate a legislative leader as next in line and three designate the secretary of state as the heir apparent. Of the forty-two states with elected lieutenant governors, in twenty-four lieutenant governor candidates run jointly with the governor for election, and in eight other states a joint nomination process is used in selecting the governor and lieutenant governor.[20]

The problems that these arrangements can lead to are often staggering. In one scenario, the separately elected governor and lieutenant governor are of opposite parties, so there is a lack of joint agenda and purpose. Often this can lead to problems when the governor is out of state and the lieutenant governor is the "acting governor" and can take any steps that a governor might consider taking. Some governors of recent vintage have had to rush home to rectify or correct actions of the "acting governor." Even if the two officeholders are of the same party, they may be from different factions of the party and have the same type of political and policy differences. Or, the problem may just be a personality or ego clash that devastates the relationship.

A recent situation in New Jersey indicates another type of problem that can arise if the next-in-line person is a legislative leader. When Governor Christie Whitman, a Republican, resigned the governorship after being named secretary of the federal Environmental Protection Agency in 2001, the President of the New Jersey Senate, Donald DiFrancesco, also a Republican, became "acting governor." There was no change in which party controlled the governorship, but the new "acting governor" could not relinquish his legislative position as that was the basis for his being the "acting governor," thus creating a sort of "prime minister" situation.

The situation in New Jersey reveals some of the difficulties that can arise when a state designates a legislative leader to be next in line should the office of governor become vacant. And it runs against the goal that most reformers have long called for in the various "Model State Constitutions."[21] The reform answer here is clear. The lieutenant governor's office is a legitimate elective position, but it should be handled in the same manner as the office of Vice President, that is, the party's gubernatorial nominee should be the one to select the party's candidate for lieutenant governor, and they should run as a team.[22]

A related concern in the selection of the lieutenant governor involves how vacancies should be filled when the office of lieutenant governor becomes vacant. A vacancy may occur on the resignation, death, disability, or impeachment of the lieutenant governor when the incumbent lieutenant governor succeeds to the governor's chair as the governor has left office due to achieving a higher office, resignation, poor health, death, or removal by impeachment or for conviction of a crime. This midterm succession situation was highlighted in 2001 as the governors of Texas (George W. Bush), Massachusetts (Paul Cellucci), New Jersey (Christie Whitman), Pennsylvania (Tom Ridge), and Wisconsin (Tommy Thompson) all resigned to join the Bush administration in Washington following the 2000 election. On resignation, the lieutenant governor became governor, except as noted above in New Jersey, and thus a vacancy was created in the lieutenant governor's position.

A possible reform in these types of midterm succession situations is to let the new governor select his or her replacement as lieutenant governor, subject to a majority vote confirmation of one or both houses of the state legislature. This most closely approximates the election of the governor and lieutenant governor as a team in the general election, and follows the model used for filling vice presidential vacancies, as spelled out in the Twenty-fifth Amendment to the U.S. Constitution adopted in 1967.[23]

The only examples of this type of midterm succession to the vice presidency occurred during the 1970s "Watergate Era." First, President Richard Nixon selected Congressman Gerald Ford as his appointed vice president when Vice President Spiro Agnew was forced to leave office in 1973. Then, in 1974 when Nixon resigned as president and Ford became president, Ford then selected former New York Governor Nelson Rockefeller as his appointed vice president. Both houses of Congress confirmed the nominations of Ford and Rockefeller to serve as vice president.

Other Separately Elected Executive Branch Officials

Some reformers argue that this is as far as the states need to go in electing state executive branch officials. Once the state begins to move beyond the governor and lieutenant governor being elected officials, several things happen. First, the governor's ability to govern the executive branch is limited by the fact that there are other separately elected executive branch officials who have responsibility over some agencies and departments. Yet, many who vote for a governor feel that they are electing the person who will be in charge of the whole executive branch of state government, not realizing that they are incorrect in this assumption.

Second, when there is an array of state level offices to be filled at election time, the voters often do not know very much about the candidates for these offices, let alone what they might do once in office. Also obscure is just what the responsibilities of some of these offices are. All many voters know is which party the candidates represent. This problem is exacerbated by current trends in the media coverage of state elections, in that coverage of the campaigns for lower-level offices has declined. And the nature of television advertising in the political campaigns for the higher-level offices tends to drown out most information on these other offices and the candidates involved.

One effect of this is that there is considerable "voter falloff" down the ballot—voters do not cast a vote for candidates they do not know about for an office whose role they do not understand. For example, in North Carolina, with ten separately elected executive branch officials, about one out of every ten voters did not vote for several of the so-called lower ballot races in the 1984 to 2000 elections.[24] "If there were a bias in just who those non-voters in particular contests were and a concerted effort by one group or another to affect the outcome of a very close contest, the voting results could be affected."[25] So, democracy is not necessarily served in this situation, but those with a specific interest in one of these lower-level elections, and in who wins these offices may well be. Nevertheless, many states continue to elect various executive branch officials other than the governor and lieutenant governor, and a case can be made in some instances for their selection by someone other than the governor.

Attorney General

Currently forty-three states elect their attorney general. In four states the governor appoints the attorney general subject to the confirmation by one or both houses of the state legislature (Alaska, Hawaii, New Jersey) or the Council (New Hampshire), and in Wyoming the governor appoints the attorney general without any confirmation needed. In Maine, the attorney general is elected by the state legislature, while the state's Supreme Court selects the attorney general in Tennessee.[26]

The attorney general is the state's lawyer initiating suits on the state's behalf and responding to lawsuits filed against the state. When separately elected, this poses no problem as the attorney general has separate elective status to do so, but when appointed by some other elected official or officials, the attorney general's status may be compromised. For example, there may be times when the attorney general must take action against the governor for what he or she has done or not done. If appointed by the governor, this ability would be compromised. This should not affect the governor as every governor's office has or should have a legal assistant whose responsibility is to advise and protect the governor. It is difficult to imagine the potential problems that might arise in a state where the state's Supreme Court selects the attorney general who later would be pressing the state's position on a variety of cases before that same court.

All this suggests that: the attorney general's office can be a legitimate elective position, chosen separately from how other elected executive branch officials are chosen. This does vary from the federal model in which the attorney general is selected by the president with the advice and consent of the U.S. Senate.

Auditor

The officials that perform the state auditing function are selected in a variety of ways. In twenty states the auditor is elected by the public, and in eighteen states the state legislatures select the auditor. Governors and agency heads select the auditor in seven states, and in California, the legislature forwards three nominees to the governor who then appoints one of those nominees to the position. Two other states have a shared method of selecting officials for the position.[27]

The auditing function is critical to the functioning of state government and the credibility of what state government officials do. The governor proposes the budget, the legislature adopts it, and then the budget is back in the hands of the governor and those in the various branches and agencies to use in funding their various responsibilities and activities. Occasionally, questions are raised about how budgeted funds are being used or not used. In more than a few such cases, it is a member of the legislature who raises the issue about how the money approved in the budget has been used. It is usually the auditor's responsibility to investigate such questions and allegations to ascertain whether they are justified or not. Having an auditor chosen by someone other than a governor is important because of the responsibilities that an auditor has.

The reform answer here is not quite as clear as in those offices noted above: the auditor should not be chosen by the governor but can be selected by the legislature or directly by the people. The goal is to ensure that the occupant of the office is free to fulfill the responsibilities of auditing the activities of other officials without being compromised by how he or she arrived in the position.

Treasurer

Currently thirty-seven states elect their state treasurer. In four states the treasurers are elected by the state legislature; in four the treasurers are appointed by the governor with the consent of the legislature; in two they are appointed by the governor with no confirmation needed; and in three they are appointed by an agency head, in one state subject to the approval of the governor.[28]

The treasurer serves as the state's banker, supervising the normal cash flows in and out of the state treasury. The treasurer also serves as the state's investor, investing funds for a variety of purposes from "rainy day funds" to state retirement plans, and is involved in any borrowing the state may undertake. In the latter role, the treasurer is a key actor in making sure the state's credit rating is kept at a high level so interest costs are lower than if the state had a poor rating. So the office of treasurer is of considerable importance for the state's fiscal health.

The reform prescription here is not altogether clear. Since so few state treasurers are gubernatorial appointees, it is clear that earlier reforms wanted to separate the chief executive from the person with access to the state's money. That may very well still be a good idea, as long as those who are elected or appointed by the legislature have the requisite skills in money management.

Secretary of State
Currently thirty-five states elect their secretary of state, and in three other states the elected lieutenant governor serves as secretary of state. In three states the secretary of state is elected by the legislature, and in nine other states the governor appoints the secretary of state and seven of them the appointment must be approved by the legislature.[29]

Secretaries of state have a range of responsibilities tied to elections (chief election official, ballot eligibility, election reports), to various types of registration (corporations, securities, trade names), to custodial duties (state and other records), publications and (manuals, constitutions, laws, rules, and regulations), and some legislative duties. Obviously, the range of responsibilities varies by state, but there is some commonality across the states.[30]

A separately elected official is not necessarily needed for the responsibilities and duties of this position. It would be just as easy to have the governor appoint the person holding this position with or without the consent of the state legislature or let the legislature appoint the person. Since many voters do not know what the office entails or who the candidates are or stand for, this option would seem to make the most sense.

Other Separately Elected Officials

Thus far, we have focused on "process officials"—those separately elected officials who work with the leaders and agencies of state government itself. Now we turn to the third-tier level of elected officials, those who are responsible for running functional agencies providing services to the citizens of the state. These include commissioners or secretaries of agriculture (thirteen states), education (fourteen states), labor (five states), and public utility regulation (seven states), among others. Several states have entire boards elected to run certain agencies.

The direction for reform for these third-tier elected officials heading functional agencies is clear: there is no need to insulate these offices from the governor, as the responsibilities of their offices are those that many will hold the governor accountable for in the first place. Therefore, states need to consider reducing the number of separately elected officials and let the governor be responsible for appointing the officials who run these agencies, with or without the confirmation or approval of the legislature.

The Gubernatorial Ambition Ladder

Before turning to the next item on the agenda of constitutional reform, one additional point needs to be addressed regarding the major separately elected executive branch officials in the states. The officials elected to these offices do have a statewide constituency and they often try to translate that into a run for the governor's chair. In a few words, these elected positions can be used as launching pads for higher office. So, there is an additional political twist involved here—those separately elected officials whose goals include not only serving in the office they have won, but using that office to position themselves for a run for the governor's chair. So trying to change the method of how they are chosen can and often does run directly into individual political goals—and with those goals often come political organizations and supporters who will do everything possible to prevent change in the way things work in the state's political system.

How prevalent is this use of these separately elected state executive branch offices as launching pads to become a governor? To measure this, we look at the last four banks of elections since 1987, with a total of 210 gubernatorial elections being held between 1987 and 2002. We focus specifically on those incumbent or former lieutenant governors, attorneys general, secretaries of state, state treasurers, and state auditors who sought to win the governor's chair. In 101 of these elections, at least one of these separately elected officials was in the race (48%), and in 38 of these 101 races there were two or more of them running (18%).

This underscores that these offices and the officials holding them often are squarely in the middle of a state's political process. Using these separately elected offices as platforms for a gubernatorial race is a political fact of life in almost all states; Maine and Utah are the only exceptions in the last sixteen years of gubernatorial elections.

Gubernatorial Reorganization Authority

Executive branch reorganization was part of the good government movement in the early twentieth century and has been on the reform agenda in most states. As noted earlier, the states are still in the fourth wave of reorganization. Some states attempt a comprehensive reorganization or even a partial reorganization of their state executive branches by creating a commission to study the situation and the problems involved, and to then issue a report on what should be done. After the report is issued, it is up to the governor and legislature to adopt the suggestions in order to have some sort of reorganization occur.

However, nearly half of the states have provided their governors with the authority to reorganize through an executive order.[31] In most of these states, the governor's authority is rather broad and can range across the executive branch of state government, while in a few states it has limitations. These limitations can be that the governor's authority to reorganize by executive order extends only to local governments (New Jersey), is restricted to shifting agencies between cabinet secretarial offices (Virginia), or is limited only to reorganization and does not encompass the creation of agencies (Tennessee). In some states the executive initiatives are subject to legislative review.

There can be several reasons for the need to reorganize. First and foremost has been the drive for "modernization and streamlining of the executive branch machinery, efficiency, economy, responsiveness, and gubernatorial control."[32] When it is the governor making the changes through executive order, with or without legislative review, it would seem more likely that the role of the chief executive would be enhanced. This would lead to the governor becoming more like a chief executive with more extensive control over the executive branch.

But there can obviously be a downside to such authority if the governor is wrong in the assumptions used in issuing the executive order, has some devious or hidden political agenda to further, or goes too far in what is being changed. An example of the latter situation might be the governor who is frustrated by the various problems, situations, and signals emanating from the various educational agencies and organizations of state government. An executive order is issued to bring all of these educational agencies into one superdepartment with a single supersecretary of education in charge of education from kindergarten through professional graduate schools. There are conflicting goals and responsibilities in this new superagency as K–12, community college, and higher-educational goals are pitted against each other. The results can be confusion, loss of direction, and unneeded fights and tensions between the various types of education involved despite the stated goals of the initiative.

The reform prescription here is fairly clear. Governors should be provided with the power to reorganize the executive branches of state government through an executive order process. But this process should include a legislative review and confirmation function that might help reduce problems and build support for the changes being suggested.

Gubernatorial Budget Power

While governors generally have considerable budgetary power in preparing and then executing the enacted state budget, recent events indicate that more thought might be needed on one further aspect of this power. As every state operates under a balanced budget requirement, responsibility often falls on the governor to take steps to cut the budget when there is a revenue shortfall due to a downturn in the nation's or state's economy. There are several types of authority provided governors to make cuts in already enacted budgets. They include: no restrictions on this authority (twelve states); across-the-board authority only (ten states); a maximum percent reduction limit (seven states); required consultation with the legislature (twelve states); and a variety of other steps idiosyncratic to a particular state (twenty-nine states).[33]

From one perspective, the stronger the governor's ability to cut the budget the better; therefore no restrictions on that power of reduction is best. This allows the governor "to reduce spending in short order to balance the budget."[34] But that is thus an unchecked power over the budget process that some question as skewing the separation of powers. Put briefly, "If the power to appropriate money is a legislative function, then the legislature should have some say in reducing the enacted budget."[35]

Having an across-the-board cutting authority would seem to be "the most efficient short-run solution," but it "may not be the best public policy." Why? The impact on "safety-net programs" would hit them with a cut just when these programs are needed most. Some programs are tied to federal matching funds and a cut in state funds would also mean a cut in federal funds—Medicaid, is a prime example. Also, such broad ranging cuts do not distinguish between higher and lower priority programs—all are hit equally.[36]

The message here is that states need to review this "power to cut" they have provided their governors and see if and how it works. Based on the evidence available from the two most recent economic downturns of the 1990s and the early twenty-first century, some states may want to revise this power whether it is in the state constitution or a state statute.

Gubernatorial Veto Power

Since the 1960s governors in the fifty states have gained considerable veto power over legislation passed by the state legislature. Every governor has the ability to veto a bill in its entirety, and forty-three governors have the power to veto particular items in a bill without vetoing the whole bill. Several states have some restrictions on just what types or parts of legislation a governor can use the item veto. State legislatures can override a governor's veto—total or item—by a super majority in forty-six states. That supermajority is either two-thirds of the legislators present and voting, or three-fifths of the legislators elected. The other four states only require a majority of the legislators elected to override the veto. These four states are all in the South, and this obviously reflects the long history of Democratic one-party dominance in those states, now no longer a factor.

The reforms needed here are not too great as so much has been done to provide governors with these powers. Clearly, those seven states that do not allow the governor the power to veto items in bills should consider adding that power to the office. And, those four states allowing just a majority of the legislators elected to override a governor's veto should consider changing the override vote needed to a form of supermajority.

SUMMARY

The agenda items listed above are tied to a very simple premise: a single elected official, the governor should be in charge of what is happening in the state government's executive branch. Based on this premise, the following constitutional or statutory reforms are suggested:

- the need to disconnect gubernatorial elections from national elections;
- the need to provide a governor with the possibility of a second term (and these should be 4-year terms);
- the need to provide for the selection of a lieutenant governor to be elected with the governor, and when the office of lieutenant governor becomes vacant, a process to fill that office involving the new governor and the state legislature;
- the need to reduce significantly the number of other separately elected state executive branch officials;
- the need to provide the governor with the ability to appoint the heads of departments or agencies with or without the approval of the state legislature;
- the need to provide the governor with the authority to reorganize the executive branch of state government by executive order, with the review and consent of the state legislature;
- the need to review the budgetary processes available to a governor to use in the case of financial emergencies; and
- the need to review the governor's veto power to include the item veto potential with a superlegislative majority needed to override a gubernatorial veto.

NOTES

1. Terry Sanford, *Storm Over the States* (New York: McGraw Hill, 1967): 188.

2. Ibid., 187.

3. David McCullogh, *John Adams* (New York: Simon & Schuster, 2001): 220–25.

4. Ibid., 225.

5. Ibid., 222. See also Rob Gurwitt, "The Massachusetts Mess," *Governing* (December 2001): 25.

6. Robert S. Rankin, *The Government and Administration of North Carolina* (New York: Thomas Y. Crowell, 1955): 75.

7. A. E. Buck, *The Reorganization of State Government in the United States* (New York: Columbia University Press, 1938): 7, 12.

8. Ibid., 44.

9. Ibid., 14–28, passim.

10. Sanford, 43.

11. Herbert Kaufman, "Emerging Conflicts in the Doctrines of Public Administration," *The American Political Science Review* v. 50 (December 1956): 1065.

12. Terry Sanford created "A Study of American States" at Duke University with grants from major national foundations. His agenda was to take the lead in developing a multistate Compact for Education to help the states develop nationwide educational policies. Out of this came the establishment of the Education Commission of the States. He also wrote *Storm Over the States* (1967) as an agenda for the states to follow in reforming how state governments operated and set policy goals. Jess Unruh directed the newly formed the Citizens Conference on State Legislatures as an organization that would assist the legislatures of the fifty states bring their structures and processes up to date. This CCSL project was also funded by major national foundations. Change was needed in the states, and these two state leaders were instrumental in helping the states chart their way forward.

13. Larry Sabato, *Goodbye to Good-Time Charlie: The American Governorship Transformed*, 2d ed. (Washington, D.C.: CQ Press, 1983): 57.

14. Keon S. Chi, "State Executive Branch Reorganization: Options for the Future," *State Trends Forecasts* 1:1 (December 1992). South Carolina, which reorganized in the early 1990s, is added to Chi's list.

15. James K. Conant, "In the Shadow of Wilson and Brownlow: Executive Branch Reorganization in the States, 1965 to 1987," *Public Administration Review* 48:5 (September–October 1988): 895.

16. Joseph A. Schlesinger, "The Politics of the Executive," in *Politics in the American States*, 1st and 2d eds., edited by Herbert Jacob and Kenneth N. Vines (Boston: Little Brown, 1965 and 1971).

17. Thad L. Beyle, "The Governors," in *Politics in the American States*, 8th ed., edited by Virginia Gray and Russell Hanson (Washington, D.C.: CQ Press, 2003).

Earlier versions of this Index by the author also appeared in the 4th edition (1983), 5th edition (1990), 6th edition (1996), and 7th edition (1999).

18. The specific functional officials were those directing the following departments or agencies: corrections, K–12 education, health, highways/transportation, public utility regulation, and welfare/social services.

19. The following states are included in this definition of the South: Alabama, Arkansas, Florida, Georgia, Kentucky, Louisiana, Mississippi, North Carolina, Oklahoma, South Carolina, Tennessee, Texas, Virginia, and West Virginia.

20. The Council of State Governments, *The Book of the States, 2000–01*, 33rd ed. (Lexington, Ky.: CSG, 2000): 15–16.

21. The National Municipal League's "Model State Constitution" can be seen in my edited book, *State Government: CQ's Guide to Current Issues and Activities, 1985–86* (Washington, D.C.: CQ Press, 1985): 193–205.

22. In 1987, I revised the National Municipal League's "Model State Constitutional" with the help of some sage state government participants and observers. This version was presented as a "Prototype State Constitution," which can be seen in my edited book, *State Government: CQ's Guide to Current Issues and Activities, 1987–88* (Washington, D.C.: CQ Press, 1987): 195–204. This version called for the joint election of the governor and lieutenant governor.

23. Section 2 of the Twenty-fifth Amendment reads: "Whenever there is a vacancy in the office of the Vice President, the President shall nominate a Vice President who shall take office upon confirmation by a majority vote of both houses of Congress."

24. Thad Beyle, "Voter Falloff Down the Ballot, 1984–2000," *North Carolina Data-Net* #27 (February 2001): 12–13.

25. Ibid., 13.

26. The Council of State Governments, *The Book of the States* 2003 ed., vol. 35 (Lexington, Ky.: CSG, 2003): 201.

27. Ibid., 204.

28. Ibid., 201.

29. Ibid.

30. CSG, *Book of the States*, 2003 ed.: 219–21.

31. Ibid., 190–91.

32. Conant, op. cit.

33. The National Conference of State Legislatures, *Legislative Budget Procedures* (Denver: NCSL, 1997).

34. "The Power to Cut," *State Policy Reports* 19:21 (November 2001): 8.

35. Ibid., 9.

36. Ibid., 8.

Chapter Four

The Judicial Branch

G. Alan Tarr

INTRODUCTION

For almost a century, since Roscoe Pound's famous address to the American Bar Association in 1906 on "The Causes of Popular Dissatisfaction with the Administration of Justice," the reform of state court systems has remained a high-priority item for state constitutional reformers, for national organizations within the legal profession, and for judges and other court professionals.[1] Since 1913, the American Judicature Society has sought to educate the public about the deficiencies of state court systems, especially with regard to judicial selection, and to promote a more efficient administration of justice. The American Bar Association (ABA) has contributed to state court reform by disseminating standards pertaining to court organization, judicial administration, and judicial selection. More recently, the National Center for State Courts and the State Justice Institute have assisted state judicial branches in developing trial and appellate court performance standards and in developing strategic planning processes.

Reformers within the states have drawn on these standards in championing changes in the structure and administration of state court systems and changes in the mode of selection of state judges. In the decades following World War II, these reformers enjoyed considerable success.[2] Several states completely revised their judicial articles or used the occasion of adopting a new constitution to institute major reforms. Other states, although eschewing comprehensive reform, nonetheless introduced changes that took account of the national standards. As a consequence, in contrast with most other articles of state constitutions, the judicial articles of many (but not all) state constitutions have been subject to thorough reexamination and reformulation during the last half century.

This does not mean that all the problems confronting state court systems have disappeared. For one thing, the reformers did not enjoy complete success. For example, although administrative and structural reforms were introduced, the campaign to substitute "merit selection" for election of judges bogged down, and in recent years it has pretty much ground to a halt.[3] For another thing, the success of the reformers is a positive development only if they accurately diagnosed the problems afflicting state court systems and proposed constitutional remedies that in fact solved those problems. Finally, new problems may have arisen that the reformers did not anticipate but that may be susceptible to constitutional resolution. Nevertheless, the reform perspective provides a useful starting point for considering possible changes in state judicial articles.

GUIDING PRINCIPLES

Four concerns should guide the reform of state judicial articles:

- *Judicial Independence:* Judicial independence involves the insulation of judges from undue or improper influence by other political institutions, interest groups, and the general public, so that they can render impartial judgments according to law in the cases they decide. This decisional independence is designed to serve not the parochial interests of judges but rather the interest of the public in even-handed justice. In serving that interest, judicial independence also promotes public confidence in the integrity of the judicial branch.[4]
- *Institutional Independence (Autonomy) of the Judicial Branch:* Complementing decisional independence of the judiciary is institutional independence or autonomy. Separation-of-power principles require recognition of the autonomy of the judicial branch as a coequal partner in state government. This means that the judicial branch, like the other branches of state government, must have the authority to govern and manage its internal affairs, free from undue interference by other branches of government, although not free from the scrutiny of those branches or of the public.
- *Effective Delivery of Judicial Services:* State judicial systems must be structured, organized, and managed so that they ensure access to justice for all citizens and provide for the expeditious and cost-effective administration of justice.
- *Accountability of the Judiciary:* The American system of government embraces the notion of accountability for public officials in order to prevent corruption or other abuses of power and to ensure that governmental policy reflects the values and interests of the community. This underlies the creation of a system of separate institutions sharing power to ensure checks and balances and the establishment of mechanisms for public scrutiny of the performance of government officials.

  Like the other branches of state government, the judiciary too must be accountable. With respect to the judiciary, two different types of accountability can be distinguished. With regard to their decisions, judges must be accountable to the law, i.e., their rulings must be consistent with the law. For trial court judges and lower appellate court judges, this accountability is enforced in part within the judicial branch through appellate review of judicial decisions. For state supreme court justices, this accountability comes from the need to justify decisions in written opinions that are subject to legal and public scrutiny. The courts' interpretation of statutes can be overridden by the enactment of corrective legislation, and their interpretations of the state constitution by constitutional amendment.

With regard to the operation of the judicial branch, the judiciary is accountable to the people and to their representatives through the normal processes of legislation and appropriations.

Among the mechanisms for enforcing judicial accountability are: (a) appellate review of judicial decisions, (b) judicial retention processes, whether electoral or appointive, sometimes guided by judicial performance evaluations, (c) judicial discipline processes enforcing codes of professional conduct, and (d) impeachment.

Two points deserve particular emphasis. First, the principles that should guide the reform of state judicial articles are not ends in themselves. Rather, they are important because they enable state courts to do justice. Second, these principles may be in some tension with one another. Accountability and decisional independence may seem at odds. So too may accountability and institutional independence (judicial-branch autonomy). Such tensions are not unusual—state constitution makers must also balance competing concerns in dealing with the other branches of state government, with the scope of state powers, and with the protection of rights. Moreover, such tensions need not be viewed as negative. Our discussion will both identify those instances in which constitution makers must choose between apparently conflicting principles and highlight those opportunities for reconciling or striking a balance between competing concerns.

THE STRUCTURE OF THE STATE COURT SYSTEM

Trial-Court Consolidation

For much of the nation's history, most state court systems were essentially "nonsystems," characterized by a proliferation of limited-jurisdiction and specialized courts, often with their own distinctive rules of procedure and with overlapping or ill-defined jurisdictions. This led to uneven workloads among courts and to an unnecessary duplication of support personnel and facilities. Judges found their time consumed in hearing jurisdictional rather than substantive arguments and in unnecessary retrials resulting from an erroneous choice of forum. Even more important, the proliferation of courts interfered with the administration of justice. Litigants, unsuccessfully searching for the proper forum to hear their cases, too often were unable to get a ruling on the merits of their claims.

Over the course of the twentieth century, most states recognized the problem posed by multiple trial courts and, following reform prescriptions, consolidated their trial courts into either one-tier or two-tier systems. A two-tier system retains a trial court of general jurisdiction and a separate trial court of limited jurisdiction. Virginia provides an example of a two-tier system. Its District Court is a limited jurisdiction court, while the Circuit Court is a general jurisdiction trial court that also hears appeals de novo from the District Court. Illinois provides an example of a one-tier system. Its Circuit Court is the state's sole trial court, hearing all cases of first instance.

In most states the coherence of the state court system no longer is a pressing issue. However, in some states—including populous states such as Georgia, New York, and Texas—it remains a concern. The experience of the states that have consolidated their trial courts suggests that consolidation has contributed to a more effective administration of justice, although there remains some dispute about how far consolidation and hierarchy should proceed.[5] Thus, those states that have failed to consolidate their trial courts because of political or historical factors should consider seriously the potential gains likely to follow from consolidation. This is an area in which the models developed in other states lend themselves to adoption in states consolidating their courts. In addition, those states that continue to maintain separate courts for law and for equity should reexamine this choice.

In recent years there have been renewed calls for specialized state courts, such as drug courts, family courts, and business courts.[6] Typically, state court systems have responded to calls for such "problem-solving courts" by creating divisions within existing trial courts, by devising special "calendars" or "dockets," or by special assignment of judges. However, some advocates of specialized courts insist that they should not be created as divisions within existing trial courts, because they will not in such circumstances attract the resources and committed judges they need to succeed. The validity of this argument is open to question. But whatever its validity, it does not follow that these specialized courts should be enshrined in the state constitution. Different eras may have quite different views of what specialized courts (if any) are desirable, and giving specialized courts constitutional status may produce undesirable rigidities, empower vested interests, and promote unproductive competition for scarce resources among court constituencies.

This leads to a more general consideration of constitutional provisions relating to the structuring of state court systems.

Constitutionalization of Court Structure

A structural issue on which no consensus has emerged involves the extent to which the structure of the state court system should be constitutionalized. States have adopted a variety of approaches:

- *The Federal Model:* Some state constitutions, following the example of Article III of the Federal Constitution, require the establishment of a Supreme Court but leave it to the Legislature to create and empower all additional courts. For example, the Maine Constitution vests the judicial power in a supreme court and such other courts as the Legislature shall create.[7]

- *The Modified Federal Model:* Some state constitutions establish various appellate and trial courts but allow the Legislature to create and empower additional courts. Illustrative is the Arizona Constitution, which creates the Supreme Court and the Superior Court (the general-jurisdiction trial court) but allows the Legislature to create an intermediate court of appeals and limited-jurisdiction trial courts.[8] Some state constitutions—for example, the Connecticut Constitution—restrict the Legislature to creating additional limited-jurisdiction trial courts.[9] Other constitutions—for example, the Michigan Constitution—grant the Legislature the power to create additional courts but seek to discourage a proliferation of separate courts by requiring an extraordinary majority (two-thirds of the total membership of each house) for the creation of courts.[10]

- *The Full-Articulation Model:* Some state constitutions establish the state's appellate and trial courts and expressly or implicitly prohibit the Legislature from creating additional courts. Thus, the Florida Constitution specifies all state courts and bans the creation of additional courts, while the Georgia Constitution requires that the judicial power be vested exclusively in those courts designated in the Judicial Article.[11]

An advantage of the Full-Articulation Model is that it can ensure a unified court system with clear divisions of jurisdiction and clear lines of authority. (However, in a nonunified system, constitutional specification of the court structure can impede the efforts of reformers to create more unified courts.) The advantage shared by the Federal Model and the Modified Federal Model is that they build in flexibility, allowing states to respond to changing needs and changed perceptions of desirable institutional design. The disadvantage of those latter models is that they encourage special interests to petition the Legislature to create specialized courts, thus undermining the coherence and unity of the court

system. The Michigan requirement of an extraordinary majority for the creation
of additional limited-jurisdiction trial courts has proved an effective safeguard in
that state against an unwise proliferation of courts. States departing from the
Full-Articulation Model should therefore consider emulating Michigan's
approach of requiring an extraordinary majority for the creation of new courts.

Degree of Unification

Another structural issue on which no consensus has emerged involves the degree of consolidation appropriate to a state court system. States that have
adopted the full-articulation model have adopted three alternative approaches
in their constitutions:

- *The Single-Court Model:* Some state constitutions conceive of the
  court system as a single court, with divisions including the supreme
  court, perhaps an intermediate appellate court, the general-jurisdiction trial court, and perhaps a limited-jurisdiction trial court. Thus,
  the Michigan Constitution states: "The judicial power of the state is
  vested exclusively in one court of justice which shall be divided into
  one supreme court, one court of appeals, one trial court of general jurisdiction known as the circuit court, one probate court, and courts of
  limited jurisdiction that the legislature may establish by a two-thirds
  vote of the members elected to and serving in each house."[12]
- *The Multiple-Level Model:* Most state constitutions expressly distinguish a supreme court, an intermediate court of appeals, a trial court of
  general jurisdiction, and (in most states) one or more trial courts of limited jurisdiction. The Indiana Constitution exemplifies this model.[13]
- *The Multiple-Court Model:* Some state constitutions treat each intermediate court of appeals, each trial court of general jurisdiction, and
  each trial court of limited jurisdiction as a separate court.

There is no evidence that these differences in design or designation substantially
affect the operation of state courts or the administration of justice, and state
constitution makers might well retain the existing provisions in their states.

THE JURISDICTION OF STATE COURTS

Closely related to the issue of whether to constitutionalize court structure is the
issue of whether to constitutionalize the jurisdiction of various courts. One possibility is to assign the allocation of jurisdiction to the Legislature—the Alaska
Constitution, for example, mandates that jurisdiction "shall be prescribed by

law."[14] This maximizes flexibility. Another possibility is to allocate the jurisdiction of each court in the constitution. This is problematic, particularly if the Legislature is authorized to create additional courts, as it hampers the reallocation of jurisdiction to those new courts. Many state constitutions grant broad authority to the Legislature to allocate jurisdiction but nonetheless constitutionalize certain choices, particularly as they relate to the jurisdiction of the supreme court, and there are advantages to this approach. More specifically, the following choices may be appropriate for constitutionalization:

- *Are there appeals that the constitution should require be heard by the state's highest court as a matter of right?* Several states mandate in their constitutions that their supreme court hear certain classes of appeals as a matter of right. The Louisiana Constitution, for example, requires that the court hear appeals in capital cases and in cases in which a law or ordinance is declared unconstitutional.[15] Other states have expanded this list. One should be hesitant about expanding the list too much, however, since that may overburden the supreme court and impair its ability to focus on cases with the broadest legal and political significance for the state. In states that have an intermediate court of appeals, that court should have the task of error correction, while the supreme court should focus on the most important issues and on legal development in the state. States that do not have an intermediate court of appeals should consider whether the case pressures on the state's supreme court prevent it from performing its primary role of supervising the development of law in the state.

- *Should the constitution authorize the supreme court to issue advisory opinions or address the constitutionality of bills before their enactment into law?* Federal courts are not permitted to issue advisory opinions. As of 2004, however, the constitutions in seven states authorized their supreme courts to do so.[16] These opinions are precisely what their name indicates, advisory; they are not binding as a matter of law, and they do not preclude constitutional challenges to laws after their enactment. Internationally, the movement has been to empower supreme courts/constitutional courts to rule authoritatively on the constitutionality of bills before they have been enacted into law upon petition from legislators or from the executive (so-called abstract review).[17] State constitutional reformers should contemplate both the state and international experience in determining what state courts should do during the twenty-first century. However, if a state supreme court is given the power to issue advisory opinions or to rule on the constitutionality of bills prior to final passage, it will undoubtedly have major implications for the political process in the state. Thus, it seems reasonable that the citizenry should decide whether or not to grant this power through the process of constitutional amendment or revision.

- *Should the constitution authorize the supreme court (or some other body) to rule on whether proposed initiatives meet state constitutional requirements governing the initiative process before the proposals appear on the ballot?* Eighteen states authorize the citizenry to propose constitutional amendments via the initiative, and twenty-one allow the citizenry to enact laws via the initiative.[18] State constitutions, however, impose restrictions on the changes that can be introduced through initiative. They typically restrict the use of the constitutional initiative to amendment, rather than revision, of state constitutions. Courts in several states have aggressively enforced this restriction, striking down constitutional initiatives.[19] Similarly, courts have enforced against statutory initiatives state constitutional requirements that the titles of laws accurately reflect their contents and that laws deal with only a single subject.[20] Whatever the validity of particular decisions overturning initiatives or upholding them against legal challenges, the fact remains that invalidation of initiatives after their approval by voters is a costly procedure. The costs include those expenditures of time, effort, and money associated with campaigns for and against proposed initiatives. They also include the animosity generated by courts when they invalidate popular measures after their adoption. Finally, the costs include the missed opportunity to remedy constitutional defects in proposals at an early stage in the process, so that only constitutionally valid proposals are submitted to the voters for approval. States can reduce these costs by establishing a procedure for review of the procedural regularity of initiatives before their appearance on the ballot. Should state courts overreach in this area, citizens can amend their constitution so as to reduce the impediments to propositions finding their way onto the ballot.[21]
- *Should the constitution protect against legislative use of its power over jurisdiction to infringe on the autonomy of the judiciary?* This seems a desirable goal in order to maintain the separation of powers. The Idaho Constitution deals with this effectively: "The legislature shall have no power to deprive the judicial department of any power or jurisdiction which rightly pertains to it as a coordinate department of the government."[22] Other states should consider adopting similar provisions.

THE ADMINISTRATION OF THE STATE COURT SYSTEM

Paralleling the movement for structural unification of state courts has been a movement for administrative unification.[23] Administrative unification has been championed as necessary to rescue trial courts from immersion in local politics, to ensure procedural uniformity throughout the state court system, and to encourage better management of the courts—in short, to promote a more efficient and uniform administration of justice. The reforms to achieve these ends included: (1) vesting rule-making authority in the state supreme court in order to encourage uniform procedures throughout the court system, (2) making the chief justice the administrative head of the court system in order to promote a systemwide management perspective, (3) creating and empowering chief judges of trial courts in order to strengthen management at that level, and (4) establishing vertical lines of authority within the court system. We turn now to constitutional provisions relating to specific aspects of judicial administration.

Administrative Authority

Most state constitutions vest administrative authority over the court system in the state supreme court, with the chief justice serving as the chief administrative officer. As the judicial article of the Kansas Constitution succinctly states: "The supreme court shall have general administrative authority over all courts in this state."[24] This power to ensure the efficient and effective delivery of court services typically extends to selection of the administrative director of the courts and other personnel, to regulation of the bar and disciplinary authority over members of the legal profession, and to reassignment of judges from their "home" court in order to allocate workload equitably.[25] This administrative authority may also include rule making over practice and procedure in the courts. It may likewise include preparation of a budget for the entire judicial branch. Finally, the supreme court's responsibility for the operation of the judicial branch may lead to delivery of a "state of the courts" address and to less formalized contacts between the chief justice or his or her staff and members of the executive and legislative branches.

The California Constitution provides the major alternative to vesting administrative responsibility in the supreme court and the chief justice. It creates a Judicial Council comprised of judges from both appellate and trial courts that exercises rule-making authority, oversees the work of the state's courts, reports to the governor and the legislature regarding that work, and makes recommendations for the more effective administration of justice.[26] The aim of the California model is to encourage widespread participation in making major decisions affecting the court system. Such a model may work well in large, populous, and diverse states such as California, but its value is not so limited. Utah, for example, a relatively small and homogeneous state, has had considerable success with its judicial council. Of course, vesting administrative responsibility in the supreme court or the chief justice rather than in a judicial council need not preclude consultation. In fact, ABA Standard 1.32, Administrative Policy, states: "All judges and judicial officers of the court system should share in deliberations and discussions concerning the procedure and administration of the courts."[27] Some states also encourage consultation. The Alaska Constitution creates a Judicial Council of seven members—the chief justice, three attorneys appointed by the state bar, and three nonattorneys appointed by the governor with the concurrence of the legislature—to recommend improvements in the administration of justice.[28] And the Georgia Constitution authorizes the Chief Justice to promulgate rules and record-keeping rules only after consultation with a council of the affected class or classes of courts.[29]

Because not all judges possess the requisite managerial skills or interest in administration, selecting as chief justice a judge qualified to act as the chief administrative officer for the court system is essential. The states currently employ three methods for selecting the chief justice. First, in some states those who select the judges also determine who will serve as chief justice. Thus, in New Jersey the governor appoints for the slot of chief justice when it becomes vacant, and in Alabama candidates run in partisan elections for the office of chief justice. Second, in some states—for example, Georgia and Michigan—the members of the supreme court elect the chief justice, usually for a set term of office. Third, in some states—for example, Louisiana and Kansas—the office of chief justice rotates, often going to the senior justice in terms of service. Although this last method may avoid infighting on the supreme court, it does so at excessive cost. There is no reason to expect that the senior justice on a court has either the interest or ability to manage the courts effectively, and a senior justice may only serve a limited time after assuming the chief justiceship, thus precluding continuity in leadership. Likewise questionable for the same reason is Alaska's ban on the chief justice, who is elected by colleagues to serve a three-year term, serving successive terms. A more extended tenure may give the chief justice the opportunity to develop the skills and knowledge necessary to administer the court system effectively. In addition, a longer tenure may give the chief justice the incentive to undertake long-term reforms by ensuring that he or she will have the opportunity to see them through to completion.

Rule Making

As a concomitant to vesting administrative authority in the supreme court, some state constitutions expressly grant the supreme court the authority to adopt rules governing the administration of the court system. This has typically not occasioned great controversy. In the majority of states whose constitutions do not expressly grant such power, it is generally understood that the power is implicit in the grant of administrative authority to the supreme court. Nevertheless, express recognition of this authority in the state constitution may prevent conflicts from arising and safeguard the separation of powers by helping to secure the appropriate autonomy of the judicial branch.

Considerably more controversial is the decision where to lodge the authority to make rules relating to legal practice and procedure—that is, rules pertaining to the methods and stages whereby cases move from initiation to dis-position. In part, the controversy reflects the natural tension between the leg-islative and judicial branches. In part, too, what fuels this controversy is the difficulty of distinguishing rules relating to practice or procedure, which might be made by the judiciary, from rules relating to substantive law, which should be enacted by the legislature. Conflict has arisen, for example, over whether leg-islative efforts to enact some tort reforms intrude on the rule-making author-ity of the judiciary. Even careful constitutional drafting cannot altogether obviate this difficulty.

Many state constitutions expressly grant the authority to make rules of practice and procedure to the state supreme court, thus ensuring a uniformity of rules within the judicial system. Michigan's provision is exemplary, in that it vests the power in the supreme court and identifies the ends for which the power should be employed: "The supreme court shall by general rules establish, modify, amend, and simplify the practice and procedure in all courts in the state."[30] (As noted, California has chosen an alternative approach, vesting rule-making authority in its Judicial Council.)

During the early twentieth century, legal commentators began to assert that the power to make rules of practice and procedure belonged to the courts as an inherent judicial power. They argued that the judicial branch should de-termine its own procedures and modes of operation, just as do the legislative and executive branches. Some state constitutions, emphasizing a strict sepa-ration of powers, grant the supreme court exclusive rule-making power over procedure and practice. Other state constitutions permit the legislature to adopt rules as well or to alter those rules adopted by the supreme court. The Alabama Constitution, for example, permits court-created "rules to be changed by a general act of statewide application," thus securing uniform rules statewide but not judicial control over rules.[31] Similarly, the Louisiana Con-stitution authorizes rule-making by the supreme court "not in conflict with the law."[32] Such provisions seem incompatible with the idea that each branch of government should govern its own internal operations. Some states (e.g., Florida) permit the legislature to annul rules adopted by the supreme court but only by a two-thirds majority.[33] Although this still involves some intrusion on the judicial branch, the requirement of an extraordinary majority guaran-tees that the power will be used sparingly and makes it less likely that it will be used for narrow partisan purposes.

In recent years legislators in some states have responded to judicial rulings that they opposed by seeking to remove rule-making authority altogether from the judicial branch. Such attempts to penalize the judiciary for disfavored deci-sions run contrary to the principle of judicial independence. It is unwise to base constitutional prescriptions for the allocation of powers on dissatisfaction with particular rulings.

FUNDING AND BUDGETING IN THE STATE COURT SYSTEM

State versus Local Financing?

During the first half of the twentieth century, state courts—especially state trial courts—received almost all of their nonsalary funding from local sources. This reliance on local governments for funds enmeshed the courts in local politics. It also meant that the level of funding enjoyed by a particular court depended in large measure on the wealth and generosity of the local government. In some instances, trial courts generated much of their own funding from the fees and fines that they collected.[34]

State court reformers championed a state takeover of court financing, with all funds flowing from the state's general fund and with local fees and fines paid directly to the state treasury. Advocates of state financing argued that it would ensure a rough parity of funding—and thus of court services—throughout each state. They also believed that it would integrate the state judicial system, because it would facilitate planning and strengthen judicial management at the state level. Without state funding, they argued, it is impossible to secure coherence within the judicial system. Finally, they contended that the level of funding for the courts would increase, because the state had greater resources at its disposal than did local governments.

During the 1970s a gradual shift toward more state funding occurred in many states, driven less by the reformers' arguments than by increasing court costs and by the financial plight of local governments in a period of economic stringency. There is no conclusive evidence either supporting or refuting the reformers' claims of the benefits that would accompany state financing, although this may reflect the difficulty of measuring the long-term effects of state financing.[35] At present, there remains considerable diversity among the states in the level and form of state financing. Some states have increased state-level control through increasing state financing. Others, such as Pennsylvania, have sought to shoulder more of the financial burden without imposing excessive centralization by emphasizing grant financing of local courts.

Because the judicial branch is one of the three coequal branches of state government, states have a responsibility to ensure that it has sufficient funding to carry out its responsibilities. The Institute for Court Management has recommended minimum funding standards to guard against retaliatory budget cuts and to ensure that the judiciary's core functions are not sacrificed in times of financial stringency.[36] Some states have expressly recognized in their constitutions the obligation to maintain adequate funding for state courts. The Alabama Constitution, for example, mandates that "[a]dequate and reasonable financing for the entire unified judicial system shall be provided."[37] The extent to which such mandates are enforceable remains a question. Even in the absence of such constitutional language, state trial courts have on occasion invoked the "inherent-powers" doctrine to order local governments to pay expenses that they deemed necessary to the performance of their judicial functions.[38]

Beyond possible constitutional recognition of the need for adequate financing of the court system, it is likely that decisions about the allocation of funding responsibilities should be made at the subconstitutional level. Even if these decisions are constitutionalized, there is no conclusive evidence that suggests that a particular approach to the funding of courts should be adopted nationwide.

Budgeting

The states differ in the authority that they give the judicial branch over its budget. Many states require that the judiciary submit its budget requests to executive branch officials who review and revise the judiciary's requests and incorporate the revised requests in the overall budget sent by the governor to the legislature.[39] However, from a separation-of-powers perspective, this seems inappropriate: one should not treat the requests of a coequal branch the same as one treats the requests of a (subordinate) executive-branch agency. Consequently, some states either permit the judiciary to submit its budget directly to the legislature or require the governor to transmit the judiciary's budget request without alteration to the legislature. Of course, the legislature is not obliged to fund all judicial requests, any more than it is obliged to fund the requests of the executive branch. And in those states in which the governor exercises an item veto, that veto extends to appropriations to support the activities of all branches, including the judiciary.

The state constitution can expressly protect the autonomy of the judicial branch with regard to budgeting. The New York Constitution provides a model provision: "Itemized estimates of the financial needs . . . of the judiciary, certified by the comptroller, shall be transmitted to the governor not later than the first day of December in each year for inclusion in the budget without revision but with such recommendations as he may deem proper."[40] However, beyond safeguarding the autonomy of the judicial branch, details of the budgeting process should be dealt with not by the constitution but by other forms of legal regulation.

JUDICIAL QUALIFICATIONS AND PROHIBITIONS

All state constitutions impose qualifications for judicial office. These provisions parallel constitutional provisions establishing qualifications for legislators and for executive branch officials. Some states also authorize the legislature to impose additional qualifications by statute.

The constitutionally prescribed qualifications for state judicial office typically include United States citizenship, a minimum age, a minimum number of years as a member of the state bar or in legal practice, and a period of residency in the state (and perhaps in the district or county as well) in which the judge serves.[41] Some states have instituted different judicial qualifications depending on the court on which the judge serves, imposing less onerous requirements on trial-court judges, particularly those serving on trial courts of limited jurisdiction. Some states have established distinctive requirements—for example, Arkansas and Arizona require that judges be of good moral character, and Delaware and Minnesota mandate that they be learned in the law. Nevertheless, there is considerable similarity in the qualifications from state to state.

Many state constitutions also limit off-the-bench activities of judges. The Florida Constitution, for example, requires judges to serve full time and prohibits them from practicing law or from holding a position in a political party.[42] The Michigan Constitution prohibits judges from holding another office during their term of service and for one year thereafter.[43] These requirements might as easily be imposed through codes of judicial ethics, but there is no harm to constitutionalizing them. In fact, their appearance in the constitution may help promote public confidence in the judiciary. One must note, however, that the appropriate limits on off-the-bench activities may vary from state to state. To take an obvious example, a ban on active party membership for judges would be inappropriate in a state in which judges are chosen in partisan elections.

JUDICIAL SELECTION, TENURE, AND REELIGIBILITY

Judicial selection represents the most controversial issue in the state judicial article, because it raises in the clearest fashion the tension between judicial independence and judicial accountability. The federal Constitution provides that federal judges be appointed by the president with the advice and consent of the Senate and hold office during good behavior. However, each state is free to establish its own mode of selection and determine the tenure and reeligibility of its judges. Most states depart from the federal model, providing for fixed terms of office rather than for tenure during good behavior, so the length of tenure and the process for determining whether an incumbent judge should remain in office are likewise important issues.[44] Most states also depart form the federal model and follow ABA Standard 1.24 in providing for a fixed retirement age (usually 70) while allowing retired judges to be recalled to active service on an annual basis at the request of the chief justice. Although there are distinctive features to the selection process in each state, basically five methods are currently used in selecting state judges. These methods include:

1. Merit selection: This system, sometimes called the Missouri Plan after the state in which it was first adopted, emphasizes judicial independence rather than judicial accountability. The key feature of merit selection is a judicial nominating commission, composed of lawyers selected by the state bar and nonlawyers typically appointed by the governor. When a judicial vacancy occurs, the commission nominates three to seven candidates (the number is determined by state law) to fill the position. The governor then selects the judge from that list. After a short period of service on the bench, the judge runs in an uncontested retention election, which allows voters to determine whether the judge should remain in office. If retained, the judge stands for reelection in retention elections periodically thereafter.

2. Election by the legislature: In South Carolina and Virginia the legislature selects state judges. In the former, a nominating screening committee provides a list of candidates for judgeships.

3. Appointment by the governor: In four states the governor appoints judges with the advice and consent of the state senate. (This parallels the system for selection of federal judges.) Judges appointed by the governor typically serve a fixed term of office, so it is necessary to establish a procedure for determining whether they should continue in office. These procedures vary from state to state. In New Jersey, judges serve for seven years, after which, if reappointed by the governor and confirmed by the state senate, they hold office until they reach retirement age. In California, judges run in a retention election at the next general election after their appointment and periodically thereafter at the conclusion of each twelve-year term.

4. Partisan election: This system is the main mode of selection in eleven states. Political parties nominate judicial candidates, and they run with party labels in the general election. Typically, judges under this system must seek reelection in contested partisan elections, although Illinois and Pennsylvania hold retention elections for incumbent judges.

5. Nonpartisan election: Nineteen states conduct judicial elections with no party affiliation indicated on the ballot. Typically, the top two candidates in a nonpartisan primary qualify for the general election. In most states judges elected in nonpartisan elections run for reelection in retention elections.

Legal groups—such as the American Bar Association and the American Judicature Society—have long espoused merit selection, as have reform groups, such as the National Municipal League and the Citizens for Independent Courts, and ad hoc groups, such as the National Summit on Improving Judicial

Selection.[45] Many sitting judges, who do not relish having to participate in political fund-raising and campaigning, have also urged that merit selection replace election. According to its proponents, merit selection encourages judicial independence, promotes informed choice in the selection of judges, and attracts more qualified attorneys to the bench. They insist that popular election of judges, particularly contested partisan elections, undermines judicial independence, injects irrelevant considerations into judicial selection, results in a less qualified bench, and gives the appearance of corruption, in that judges are perceived as beholden to those who support them in their campaigns.[46] In contrast, proponents of judicial elections stress the importance of judicial accountability to the public, especially given the broad effects of judicial rulings on controversial issues. They also deny that merit selection eliminates politics from the selection process, insisting that it is merely a different sort of politics that operates under merit selection.[47]

The evidence supporting these claims is largely anecdotal, and in fact it is hard to understand how, for example, one might prove that merit selection leads to a more qualified bench. During the 1960s and 1970s several states shifted to merit selection, but in recent decades voters have consistently opposed merit selection. In Florida in 2000, voters in every county polled rejected the option available to them to change from nonpartisan election to merit appointment of trial judges. This loss of reform momentum has led groups such as the American Bar Association to seek ways of improving existing modes of selection rather than transforming them, at least in the short run.

In choosing the mode of selection for judges, state constitution makers should take account of three important changes in judicial elections within recent years. One development is the increased contentiousness of judicial elections, as more elections are being contested and interest groups are becoming more heavily involved through campaign contributions and through independent expenditures, often in the form of television or radio ads promoting or opposing particular candidates.[48] A second and related development is the vastly greater sums being spent in judicial elections, both by candidates and by groups interested in the outcomes of the elections.[49] A third is the prospect of more outspoken campaigns for judicial office, as the U.S. Supreme Court has invalidated some traditional restrictions on the speech of judicial candidates.[50]

Tenure and Reeligibility

Likewise important to judicial selection are the issues of judicial tenure and reeligibility. Most state constitutions prescribe longer terms of office for judges than for other public officials and place no limits on reeligibility. The median term of office for general-jurisdiction trial court judges is six years, while the median term of office for appellate judges is longer, at eight years.[51] Proponents of judicial independence have proposed extending the terms of judges, because this will reduce the frequency with which sitting judges must seek reelection or appointment. Thus, the American Bar Association's Commission on the Twenty-First Century Judiciary proposed that in states not employing merit selection, "judicial terms should be as long as possible."[52] Reducing the accountability of sitting judges to the political process would theoretically reduce both the fear of electoral retribution and the temptation to curry the favor of potential supporters, thereby encouraging rulings in accordance with the law.[53]

European countries have developed an alternative approach that is worth considering. For members of their constitutional courts—the functional equivalent of state supreme courts—these countries rely on a system of initial appointment that is frankly political. Once selected, justices serve relatively lengthy terms (9 years in some countries, 12 years in others). However, the justices are limited to a single term. This non-reeligibility eliminates the incentive for judges to decide cases in a way that will enhance their prospects for reelection. It also provides a regular opportunity for the dominant political forces in the state to influence the membership and general orientation of the supreme court. However, it excludes highly qualified sitting judges from providing continued service to the state.[54]

Hybrid Selection Systems

Some states employ different modes of selection depending on the level of courts. For example, South Dakota, Missouri and Florida (among others) use merit selection to choose their appellate judges but elect their trial judges in nonpartisan elections. Many states, as noted, also prescribe shorter terms of office for trial judges than for appellate judges. These hybrid systems suggest that assessments of the appropriate balance between judicial independence and judicial accountability may depend on the function served by the judge—deciding cases of first instance or hearing appeals. In the United States, the tendency has been to hold trial judges more accountable through election and shorter terms of office, presumably thereby ensuring that trial judges more closely reflect community sentiment. In Europe the nonpolitical selection of ordinary judges and political selection of members of constitutional courts suggests a different assessment: those judges whose decisions have the broadest societal impact should reflect (in broad terms) public opinion within the country. State constitution makers should keep these alternatives in mind in determining whether to institute hybrid systems of selection.

Local Option

Closely related to the notion of hybrid systems linked to the level of court (trial or appellate) is the idea of local option. Given the diversity of many states, it is possible that different communities within an individual state will have different ideas about how their trial-court judges should be selected. State constitution makers need to decide whether these differing views should be reflected in constitutional arrangements. They might prescribe a system of selection for state trial-court judges but create a mechanism by which a county (or other jurisdiction, where appropriate) could opt out of that system and adopt an alternative mode of selection. Florida's failed ballot question of 2000, in which counties were invited to replace election with merit selection, provides an example of how a system of local option might be instituted.

JUDICIAL COMPENSATION

If legislatures have the power to reduce the pay of judges to punish them for unpopular decisions, judicial independence is compromised. State constitutions can secure judges against this in a variety of ways:

- *The Commission Approach:* The constitution could vest the power to set judicial salaries in a commission separate from the legislature. Alabama experimented with this approach, but it later amended its constitution so that the Judicial Compensation Commission's recommendations did not take effect unless affirmatively adopted by the legislature. Most states that have commissions follow the Alabama model: commission recommendations must be endorsed by the legislature. An alternative is to have the commission's recommendations have the force of law unless expressly disapproved by the legislature within a prescribed time period after their announcement.
- *The Federal Model:* State constitutions could safeguard judicial independence by prohibiting a reduction of judicial salaries during the judge's tenure in office. This mirrors the approach of Article III of the United States Constitution.
- *The Shared-Burden Model:* State constitutions could safeguard judicial independence by prohibiting a reduction of judicial salaries unless it was part of an across-the-board reduction of the salaries of state officials. A number of states have adopted this approach, which affords the state greater flexibility in dealing with difficult economic conditions.

Some state constitutions include a ban on increasing the salary of sitting judges, as well as on lowering it. This is undesirable, because judges who serve for an extended period will suffer a decrease in their real salaries over time. In addition, such a ban will have the effect of establishing different salaries for judges on a single court, depending on when they ascend the bench. It is appropriate that judges of equivalent rank should receive equal pay.

A distinctive provision in the California Constitution authorizes withholding the salary of judges who do not promptly make decisions after cases are submitted to them.[55] In order to receive their paychecks, judges must submit an affidavit under penalty of perjury that they do not have any submitted matters that have been pending for more than ninety days. Judges have regularly been subject to disciplinary proceedings in those rare instances in which they have submitted false affidavits. However, there may be more effective means of ensuring efficient case management, measures that do not require enshrinement in state constitutions.

JUDICIAL DISCIPLINE, RETIREMENT, AND REMOVAL

Ensuring the quality and integrity of the state bench is a paramount constitutional aim. This goal might be achieved by allowing those outside the judiciary to assess the fitness and performance of sitting judges. The legislature might remove judges by impeachment, and the citizenry might do so either by defeat at the polls or (as in nine states) by the recall of judges. However, there are problems with each of these mechanisms. Impeachment has proved too slow and cumbersome to be an effective check on judicial misconduct. Recall is both cumbersome and susceptible to use against judges who announce unpopular but legally defensible rulings, thus jeopardizing judicial independence. Accountability during reelection campaigns shares the recall's susceptibility to abuse and is only periodically available, given the lengthy terms of office of most judges. Perhaps equally important, all these mechanisms employ the ultimate sanction of removal from office, whereas a range of sanctions, proportionate to judicial transgressions, might be more appropriate.

The limitations of these weapons against judicial misconduct are not necessarily a justification for their elimination. Impeachment in particular is a time-honored, even if rarely employed, check on judicial abuses of office. Nevertheless, the deficiencies of these weapons, plus the judicial branch's concern to police its own personnel, has led to the creation in all states of commissions within the judicial branch for the discipline of sitting judges. These commissions have the authority to receive complaints about judges, to investigate those complaints (or when necessary to initiate their own investigations), to file and prosecute formal charges, and either to recommend sanctions to the state's highest court or to impose sanctions themselves. These sanctions might include: (1) private admonition, reprimand, or censure; (2) public reprimand or censure; (3) suspension; or (4) removal from office. Typically, judicial disciplinary commissions also have authority to recommend the retirement of judges who are incapacitated.

Forty-one states employ a "one-tier" model, under which prosecutorial and adjudicative functions are combined, thereby avoiding duplicative work and promoting a speedier disposition of cases.[56] In such systems, the final disposition of cases rests in the hands of the state supreme court, which has administrative authority over the judicial branch. When a case involves a member of the supreme court, a special tribunal is constituted. Nine states employ a "two-tier" system, under which the prosecutorial and adjudicative functions are separated in order to avoid biased decision-making.[57] Because commissions typically include public members who are neither judges nor lawyers, the "two-tier" system allows the public to be represented in the final disposition of cases. The American Bar Association's Model Judicial Article endorses the "one-tier" model.

State constitution makers may decide whether the constitution should prescribe the one-tier model or the two-tier model. Alternatively, they may merely create the Judicial Discipline Commission and leave the selection, structure, and operation of the Commission to implementing legislation, as does the Kansas Constitution.[58] State constitution makers must also determine what role the public should play in the discipline process. The movement over time seems to be to provide for greater representation for nonlawyers on the Judicial Discipline Commission, although in no state do nonlawyers comprise a majority of members.

CONCLUSION

It is important to emphasize that this chapter confines itself to the problems confronting state judiciaries that can be dealt with through constitutional prescriptions. There are a host of other problems confronting state judiciaries, including ensuring timely and affordable access to justice for all citizens, promoting an even-handed administration of justice, and making courts more responsive to the needs of the community. These problems are important, but they must be dealt with outside the constitution. What the state constitution can seek to provide is a structure that facilitates addressing these problems and a system of judicial selection and discipline that ensures the judicial branch is staffed by highly qualified and committed personnel. This is hardly a negligible contribution in the effort to secure equal justice under law.

NOTES

1. Pound's speech is reproduced in 35 F.R.D. 241 (1964).

2. On the spread of court reform, *see* Larry Berkson and Susan Carbon, *Court Unification: History, Politics, and Implementation* (1978); Frank Munger, "Movements for

Court Reform: A Preliminary Interpretation," in *The Politics of Judicial Reform* (ed. Philip E. Dubois, 1982); and Robert W. Tobin, *Creating the Judicial Branch: The Unfinished Revolution* (1999).

    3. Whereas in 1960 only three states—Alaska, Kansas, and Missouri—employed merit selection in choosing state supreme court justices, by 1980 eighteen did. *See* Joan Goldschmidt, "Merit Selection: Current Status, Procedures, and Issues," 49 *U. Miami L. Rev.* 1, app. A, at 79 (1994). However, since 1998 only Rhode Island has adopted merit selection, and a number of states have considered merit selection only to reject it. Moreover, there is reason to doubt that merit selection will indeed ensure judicial independence, as proclaimed by its proponents, given changes in the political context for even nonpartisan and retention election campaigns. See G. Alan Tarr, "Rethinking the Selection of State Supreme Court Justices," 39 *Willamette L. Rev.* 1445 (2003).

    4. The importance of judicial independence has been recognized by Americans since the Founding. In the Declaration of Independence, one charge against King George III was his interference with judicial independence. Article XIX of the Declaration of Rights of the Massachusetts Constitution states: "It is essential to the preservation of the rights of every individual, his life, liberty, property, and character; that there be an impartial interpretation of the laws, and administration of justice. It is the right of every citizen to be tried by judges as free, impartial and independent as the lot of humanity will admit." For reports focusing on how judicial independence can be secured in the current era, *see* American Bar Association, Division for Public Education, *Judicial Independence* (1999), and American Bar Association, Report of the Commission on the Twenty-First Century Judiciary, *Justice in Jeopardy* (2003). For a valuable comparative perspective, *see Judicial Independence in the Age of Democracy: Critical Perspectives from Around the World* (eds. Peter H. Russell and David M. O'Brien, 2001).

    5. For skeptical perspectives and alternative proposals, *see* Carl Baar and Thomas Henderson, "Alternative Models for the Organization of State-Court Systems," in *The Analysis of Judicial Reform* (ed. Philip Dubois, 1982), and Geoff Gallas, "The Conventional Wisdom of State Court Administration: A Critical Assessment and an Alternative Approach," 2 *Just. Sys. J.* 35 (1976).

    6. For helpful analyses of the assumptions underlying these approaches, *see* Symposium, "The Changing Face of Justice: The Evolution of Problem Solving," 29 *Fordham Urb. L.J.* 1790 (2002); James L. Nolan, Jr., *Reinventing Justice: The American Drug Court Movement* (2001), and Peggy F. Hora, William G. Schma, and John T. A. Rosenthal, "Therapeutic Jurisprudence and the Drug Treatment Court Movement: Revolutionizing the Criminal Justice System's Response to Drug Abuse and Crime in America," 74 *Notre Dame L. Rev.* 439 (1999).

    7. Me. Const., art. VI, § 1.

    8. Ariz. Const., art. VI, §1.

    9. Conn. Const., art. V, § 1.

    10. Mich. Const., art. VI, § 1.

    11. Fla. Const., art. V, § 1, and Ga. Const., art. VI, § 1.

12. Mich. Const., art. VI, § 1.

13. Ind. Const., art. VII, § 1.

14. Alas. Const., art. IV, §1.

15. La. Const., art. V, § 5.

16. These states include Colorado, Florida, Maine, Massachusetts, New Hampshire, Rhode Island, and South Dakota. Alabama and Delaware provide for advisory opinions by statute, and North Carolina by court decision. *See* Note, "The State Advisory Opinion in Perspective," 44 *Fordham L. Rev.* 81 (1975).

17. *See* Carlo Guarnieri and Patrizia Pederzoli, *The Power of Judges* (2002).

18. For a listing of states, see the web site of the Initiative and Referendum Institute at www.iandrinstitute.org. *See also* Gerald Benjamin, "Constitutional Amendment and Revision," in this volume.

19. *See,* for example, *Adams v. Gunter,* 238 So.2d 824 (Fla., 1970), and In re Initiative Petition No. 344, 797 P.2d 326 (Okla., 1990).

20. *See,* for example, *Amalgamated Transit Union Local 587 v. State of Washington,* 11 P.3d 762 (Wash., 2000); *Armatta v. Kitzhaber,* 959 P.2d 49 (Ore., 1998), and *Evans v. Firestone,* 457 So.2d 1351 (Fla., 1984).

21. This was done in Florida following *Adams v. Gunter,* supra note 19. *See Weber v. Smathers,* 338 So.2d 819, 822–23 (Fla., 1976).

22. Ibid. Const., art. V, § 13.

23. For description and evaluation of these efforts to achieve administrative unification, *see* Berkson and Carbon, supra note 4; Tobin, supra note 4; Baar and Henderson, supra note 7, and Gallas, supra note 7. A cautionary note has been voiced by Donald Dahlin: "To fulfill their role in our society, courts must have considerable administrative independence from coordinate branches of government; that to achieve such independence, courts must develop their own administrative capacity and that capacity must be structured in such a way as to provide a strong central authority; but an authority that encourages widespread participation in the making of major decisions and widespread decentralization and delegation in the operation of the court system." *See* Donald C. Dahlin, *Models of Court Management* (1986) 101.

24. Kans. Const., art. III, § 1.

25. *See,* for example, Alas. Const., art. IV, § 16.

26. Calif. Const., art. VI, § 6. The Institute for Court Management has endorsed this approach: "Because of the perceived isolation of the Supreme Court from the problems and dynamics of trial court operation, the preferred vehicle for developing state court policy is a judicial council which represents judges from all levels. Dahlin, supra note 24, at 47.

27. American Bar Ass'n. Commission on Standards of Judicial Administration, *Standards Relating to Court Organization,* Standard 12 (1974).

28. Alas. Const., art. IV, §§ 9–10.

29. Geo. Const., art. VI, § 9.

30. Mich. Const., art. VI, § 5.

31. Ala. Const., art. VI, § 11.

32. La. Const., art. V, § 5.

33. Fla. Const., art. V, § 2.

34. For a review of state court funding and the issues associated with it, *see* Robert W. Tobin, *Funding the State Courts: Issues and Approaches* (1996). According to Tobin (p. 37), as of 1995, thirty-one state court systems were funded primarily from the state general fund.

35. Ibid.

36. Institute for Court Management, Courts and the Public Interest: A Call for Sustainable Resources (May 2002).

37. Ala. Const., § 6.10.

38. *See* Carl Baar, "Judicial Activism in State Courts: The Inherent-Powers Doctrine," in *State Supreme Courts: Policymakers in the Federal System* (eds. Mary Cornelia Porter and G. Alan Tarr, 1982).

39. *See generally* James W. Douglas and Roger E. Hartley, "The Politics of Court Budgeting in the States: Is Judicial Independence Threatened by the Budgetary Process?" 63 *Public Admin. Rev.* 441 (2003); James W. Douglas and Roger E. Hartley, "State Court Budgeting and Judicial Independence: Clues from Oklahoma and Virginia," 33 *Admin. & Society* 54 (2001); and Carl Baar, *Separate but Subservient: Court Budgeting in the United States* (1975).

40. N.Y. Const., art. VII, § 1.

41. For a state-by-state listing of qualifications for judicial office, see *Book of the States* 2000–01, at 135–36, tbl. 4.3.

42. Fla. Const., art. V, § 13.

43. Mich. Const., art. VI, § 21.

44. The only states that award tenure during good behavior are Massachusetts, New Hampshire, and Connecticut. For a summary listing of the tenure of state judges, *see* Roy A. Schotland, "Comment," *Law and Contemporary Problems* 61 (1998): 154–55. For state-by-state listings, *see Book of the States,* supra note 41, at 203–04, tbl. 5.1.

45. National Summit on Improving Judicial Selection, *Call to Action: Statement of the National Summit on Improving Judicial Selection* (expanded ed., with commentary 2002).

46. The case for merit selection and against election of judges can be found in Larry W. Yackle, "Choosing Judges the Democratic Way," 69 *B.U. L. Rev.* 273; in Jona Goldschmidt, "Merit Selection: Current Status, Procedures, and Issues," 49 *U. Miami L. Rev.* 1 (1994); and in Steven P. Croley, "The Majoritarian Difficulty: Elective Judiciaries and the Rule of Law," 62 *U. Chicago L. Rev.* 689 (1995).

47. The case against merit selection and for election of judges can be found in Judith L. Maute, "Selecting Justice in State Courts: The Ballot Box or the Backroom," 41 *S. Tex. L. Rev.* 1197 (2000), and in Philip L. Dubois, *From Ballot to Bench: Judicial Elections and the Quest for Accountability* (1980). The classic study documenting the operation of political factors in the work of a merit commission is Richard A. Watson and Rondal G. Downing, *The Politics of Bench and Bar: Judicial Selection Under the Missouri Non-Partisan Court Plan* (1969).

48. *See* Tarr, supra note 3, at 1449–60.

49. Roy Schotland, "Financing Judicial Elections, 2000: Change and Challenge," 2001 *L. Rev. Mich. St. U. Det. C. L.* 849 (2001).

50. *Republican Party of Minnesota v. White,* 536 U.S. 765 (2002).

51. The terms of office for judges in each state are listed in *Book of the States,* supra note 41, at 203–04, tbl. 5.1.

52. American Bar Association, *Justice in Jeopardy,* supra note 5, appendix A, p. 4.

53. *See* Schotland, supra note 44, and American Bar Association, *Justice in Jeopardy,* supra note 5, for presentations of the case for longer terms.

54. For elaboration of the European model and its possible implications for judicial selection in the United States, *see* Tarr, supra note 3.

55. Calif. Const., art. VI, § 19.

56. For a sample provision, *see* Mich. Const., art. VI, § 30.

57. *See* Kans.Const., art. III, § 15.

58. Ibid.

Chapter Five

Local Government

Michael E. Libonati

INTRODUCTION

Local government in the United States has a rich history of variety, both in type and form. Cities, counties, towns, townships, boroughs, villages, school districts, and a host of special-purpose districts, authorities, and commissions make up the 87,849 distinct units of local government counted in the 2002 Census of Governments. These local units of government have many different forms and organizational structures. Variations in the numbers and forms of local government reflect the unique political cultures and forces that created and shaped local self-government in each state.

Experience with local government, which is shared by all Americans, has rarely given rise to sustained and systematic reflection about the relationship between local government and state government. Instead, the desire for local self-government has been institutionalized in thousands of compacts, charters, special acts, statutes, constitutional provisions, resolutions, ordinances, administrative rulings, and court decisions since the earliest dates of settlement of this country. Among these enactments, state constitutional provisions are singled out for special attention in this chapter. Given this diversity, there is no single model of constitutional arrangements dealing with local government that is appropriate for all states. Nonetheless, the key issue remains the same from state to state, namely, the level of autonomy to be accorded to local governments in the state constitution.

Increasing fiscal pressures on government and rising service expectations by the citizenry make continued controversy and debate over state constitutional treatment of local governments inevitable. As policy makers evaluate proposals for state constitutional change, they should consider six guiding issues before altering the state-local relationship embodied in their state's constitution:

1. Is it desirable to increase or decrease the restrictions, if any, imposed on the power of the state to regulate local government?
2. What degree of autonomy, however defined in the minds of the citizens of a particular state, should be granted to local governments?
3. To what extent should the local electorate have a choice as to the form of local government and its policies?
4. Should all local government units be eligible for local autonomy?
5. To what extent should local governments be authorized to engage in intergovernmental cooperation?
6. What role should courts have in determining issues of local autonomy?

Defining Local Government Autonomy

This section examines the range of state constitutional definitions of local government autonomy. One of the most useful classifications of local self-government is Gordon Clark's principles of autonomy. These principles distinguish between a local government's power of initiative and its power of immunity. By initiative, Clark means the power of local government to act in a "purposeful goal-oriented" fashion, without the need for a specific grant of power from the legislature. By immunity, he means "the power of localities to act without fear of the oversight authority of higher tiers of the state."[1] There are four variations in the exercise of these two components to autonomy: (1) powers of both initiative and immunity; (2) power of initiative but not immunity; (3) power of immunity but no initiative; and (4) neither power of initiative nor immunity.

Powers of Both Initiative and Immunity

Initiative and immunity powers as expressed in state constitutions vary considerably from one state to another. The Colorado Constitution, for example, confers both initiative ("the people of each city and town of this state . . . are hereby vested with, and they shall always have, power to make, amend, add to, or replace the charter of said city or town, which shall be its organic law and extend to all its local and municipal matters") and immunity ("such charters and the ordinances made pursuant thereto in such matters shall supersede within the territorial limits and other jurisdiction of said city or town any law of the state in conflict therewith").[2] These texts both empower the home rule unit to exercise initiative as to all local and municipal matters and immunize the home rule unit from state legislative interference in all local and municipal matters.

Power of Initiative but Not Immunity

Pennsylvania's home rule provision exemplifies how states afford a charter unit the authority to "exercise any power or perform any function not denied by this Constitution, by its home rule charter, or by the General Assembly at any time."[3] It grants initiative but not immunity In this formulation, known as the Fordham-Model State Constitution devolution-of-powers approach to local governance,[4] the state legislature has a free hand in defining and limiting the scope of local initiative.

Power of Immunity but Not Initiative

State constitutions contain several types of provisions conferring immunity, but not initiative, on local government. For example, the Utah Constitution prohibits the legislature from passing any law granting the right to construct and operate a street railroad, telegraph, telephone, or electric light plant within any city or incorporated town "without the consent of local authorities."[5] Thus, a Utah municipality cannot be forced to accommodate certain state-franchised utilities, but may not otherwise have any affirmative regulatory authority initiative over these enterprises.

Virginia's prohibition of state taxation for local purposes does not, for example, provide its political subdivisions with affirmative taxing authority.[6] In several states, the Constitution forbids the legislature from delegating "to any special commission, private corporation, or association, any power to make, supervise, or interfere with any municipal improvement, money, property, or effects . . . or to levy taxes or perform any municipal function whatsoever" without conferring on protected municipalities any correlative power to initiate action in any of the enumerated policy areas.[7] Also, state constitutional prohibitions against special or local laws are aimed at conferring immunity, but not initiative, on local governments.

Neither Power of Initiative Nor Immunity

The Connecticut Constitution illustrates the strict control by the state over its political subdivisions. It states: "The General Assembly shall . . . delegate such legislative authority as from time to time it deems appropriate to towns, cities, and boroughs relative to the powers, organization, and form of government of such political subdivisions."[8] The apparent utility of this type of provision is to defeat challenges to a broad allocation of authority to local governments based on a delegation doctrine or due process claims.

Finally, some state constitutions, such as New Jersey's, are silent on the issue of local government autonomy, leaving the matter to the legislature.

Beyond the Immunity and Initiative Concepts:
Preemption, Intergovernmental Cooperation, and Privatization

Clark's classification of these concepts provides a good starting point for understanding local legal autonomy, but state constitution makers face further significant issues in creating a local government provision. Sho Sato and Arvo Van Alstyne point out these interrelated issues, using the example of the practical, everyday problems of those who gave legal advice about the scope of local government powers:

> From the viewpoint of the attorney—whether he represents a public agency or a private client—the significant issues relating to home rule ordinarily cluster around three distinguishable problems: (1) to what extent is the local entity insulated from state legislative control; (2) to what extent in the particular jurisdiction does the city (and in some states the county) have home rule power to initiate legislative action in the absence of express statutory authorization from the state legislature; and (3) to what extent are local home rule powers limited, in dealing with a particular subject, by the existence of state statutes relating to the same subject?[9]

It is this third aspect of home rule, the preemption question that is equally important in determining the true scope of local government autonomy. For example, in states like Pennsylvania that have adopted the previously mentioned Model State Constitution approach, a home rule unit has the power to act concurrently with the state legislature "unless the power has been specifically denied.[10] The Illinois Constitution speaks directly to this preemption issue when it asserts that "home rule units may exercise and perform concurrently with the State any power or function of a home rule unit to the extent that the General Assembly does not specifically limit the concurrent exercise or specifically declare the State's exercise to be exclusive."[11]

One other question that initiative and immunity models of local government autonomy do not address is the capacity to contract intergovernmentally (among federal, state, and local governments), interjurisdictionally (among counties, cities, and special districts), and with the private sector. The collaborative perspective has undoubtedly influenced the entrenchment of rules concerning interlocal cooperation and transfer of functions in state constitutions. Thus, Article 7, section 10(a) of the Illinois Constitution provides that:

Units of local government and school districts may contract or other-wise associate among themselves, with the State, with other states and their units of local government and school districts, and with the United States to obtain or share services and to exercise, combine, or transfer any power or function in any manner not prohibited by law or by ordinance. Units of local government and school districts may con-tract and otherwise associate with individuals, associations, and corpo-rations in any manner not prohibited by law or ordinance. Participating units of government may use their credit, revenues, and other resources to pay costs and to service debt related to intergovernmental activities.

ANALYZING LOCAL GOVERNMENT AUTONOMY

The task of conferring "discretionary authority" on local governments requires a careful analysis of the components of local government authority. A report of the U.S. Advisory Commission on Intergovernmental Relations (ACIR), *Mea-suring Local Discretionary Authority* (1981), will assist state constitution makers in addressing the range of issues involved. In this report, ACIR defined local discretionary authority as

> the power of a local government to conduct its own affairs—including specifically the power to determine its own organization, the functions it performs, its taxing and borrowing authority, and the numbers and employment conditions of its personnel.[12]

Examining these four dimensions of local government discretionary au-thority—structure, function, fiscal, and personnel—helps citizens and public officials get a clearer picture of local government autonomy and the trends af-fecting it. It enables the observer—whether trained in law, public administra-tion, or political science-to organize and synthesize the otherwise unwieldy universe of state constitutional provisions, and court cases interpreting them, that bear on the question of local autonomy. The four categories of discre-tionary authority described in the ACIR report are reviewed in this section to determine their fruitfulness in serving as the basis for structuring the local gov-ernment article of a state constitution.

Structural Autonomy

There are several elements that affect the degree of structural autonomy pro-vided to local governments.

Barriers to the Enactment of Impermissible State Legislation
Autonomy in the sense of immunity from state legislative interference preceded affirmative grants of local initiative. Many early state constitutions, for example, made the filling of certain local offices the prerogative of local electors. The New Jersey legislature might define the contours of the office of County Sheriff, for instance, but the state constitution of 1776 required that the sheriff be elected by the inhabitants of the county.[13]

Many nineteenth- and early twentieth-century state constitutions sought to immunize local governments from state legislatures enacting local or special laws affecting local government structures and the duties of local officials. Pioneering provisions of the 1851 Indiana Constitution prohibited state regulation of the jurisdiction and duties of justices of the peace and of constables; the election of county and township officers and their compensation; and the opening and conducting of elections of . . . county or township officers and designating the places of voting.[14] Alabama's 1901 Constitution defined a local law as one "which applies to any political subdivision or subdivisions of the state less than the whole" in creating a similar enumeration of impermissible legislative enactments.[15]

It should be noted, however, that prohibitions against local or special legislation create only a permeable barrier to state legislative actions affecting local government decision-making structures. They reach only statutes that do not meet the constitutionally prescribed level of generality and uniformity. The legislature is ordinarily still free to classify local governments by population or some other general criterion. But in Rhode Island, the General Assembly has the power to enact general laws applicable to all cities and towns provided they do not affect "the form of government."[16]

Often, state constitutional provisions governing local or special legislation may provide for flexibility through local choice. For example, home rule governments in New York may opt out of the protection otherwise afforded by the constitutional ban on local or special laws on request of either a supermajority of its legislative body or its chief executive officer with a concurrent legislative majority.[17] The New Jersey Constitution permits private, local, or special laws affecting the internal affairs of a local government on petition of the governing body, with the approval of a supermajority of each house of the state legislature. The law becomes operative only if subsequently adopted by an ordinance of the governing body or a local referendum.[18]

Approval by the Local Electorate as a Check on the State Legislature
State constitutions are sprinkled with provisions that allow state legislative power over a variety of structural issues only with local electoral approval. In North Dakota, for example, the legislature must provide counties with optional forms of government, including the county manager plan, but no optional form may become operative without the approval of 55 percent of those

voting in a local election.[19] Local voters in Montana periodically must be offered an opportunity to review their existing local government structure.[20]

Several state constitutions contain rules requiring that fundamental changes in county government structure, such as consolidation, dissolution, and shifts in boundaries or county seats, must be approved by a majority of voters in each affected county.[21] And, in several states, the structural autonomy of the local decision-making process is protected by a provision forbidding the legislature from empowering "any special commission, private corporation or association" from performing "municipal functions."[22]

Local Voter Initiatives as a Counterweight to State Power

A more robust guarantee of voter choice is found in state constitutions that entrench not only the blocking power of the local referendum but also the power for citizens to initiate municipal or county legislation. The constitutions of Ohio, Oklahoma, and Oregon provide examples of this approach.[23]

Constitutional Restrictions on the Scope of Home Rule Authority

With regard to autonomy in the sense of initiative, no state constitutions limit the ambit of home rule power simply to matters of structure. The constitutions of sixteen states (California, Colorado, Florida, Georgia [cities only], Illinois, Iowa, Kansas, Louisiana, Maine, Michigan [counties only], Ohio, Oregon [counties only], Rhode Island, West Virginia, Wisconsin, and Wyoming) contain terms like "municipal affairs," "municipal matters," and "powers of local self-government," that would appear to convey discretion over the structure and methods of operation of local government.[24] This is confirmed in the case law of California, wherein matters concerning local elections, procedures for enacting and enforcing ordinances, forms of government (e.g., city manager, strong mayor, or weak mayor), and the establishment and operation of local, administrative bodies fall within the ambit of municipal affairs.[25]

The force of these provisions, however, is weakened considerably when the question presented for decision involves a relevant state statute arguably in conflict with a charter provision. Thus, when an agreement entered into by a California home rule city under a state statute providing for the joint exercise of powers was challenged as violating its charter, the state supreme court relied on the state statute and sustained the agreement. It stated, "If the conceivably conflicting charter provisions of all the contracting cities were held to be applicable and relevant, the effect would be to vitiate the statute authorizing joint and cooperative action."[26]

Courts in several jurisdictions where a constitutional grant of home rule initiative is qualified by the adjective "local" or "municipal" have not been shy in holding that the subject matter in question is susceptible to redefinition as a matter of statewide concern when the state legislature has so spoken.[27]

The Louisiana Constitution guarantees structural autonomy by prohibiting the legislature from changing or affecting the structure and organization or the distribution of powers of a home rule entity.[28] The constitutions of Georgia (counties only), Michigan (cities only), New York, and Rhode Island have language that conveys power over matters concerning "property, affairs or government."[29] Maryland, Nebraska, Nevada, Oklahoma, Utah, and Washington each have constitutions that employ the term "its own government" to delineate the scope of local initiative.[30] As in the case of texts using the arguably broader terms of municipal affairs or local self-government, the scope of structural autonomy afforded will be subject to the vagaries of judicial interpretation as well as to the preemptive effect of general state statutes.

The Oregon and Texas constitutions grant eligible cities comprehensive power to formulate the contents of their home rule charters, limited only by the preemptive powers of the legislature.[31] Eleven states (Alaska, Connecticut, Massachusetts, Missouri, Montana, New Hampshire, New Mexico, North Carolina, North Dakota, Pennsylvania, and South Dakota) embrace the devolution-of-powers model, making the extent of powers afforded local governments dependent on state enabling legislation, which may or may not confine the scope of structural autonomy.[32]

Four state constitutions speak unambiguously to the issue of structural initiative. The Colorado Constitution empowers home rule counties to provide for the organization and structure of county government consistent with state statutes.[33] Tennessee authorizes each home rule entity to provide for "the form, structure, personnel and organization of its government."[34] South Carolina grants the power to frame a charter "setting forth governmental structure and organization."[35] But that power is qualified by a provision expressly limiting the authority of South Carolina home rule entities to set aside "the structure and the administration of any government service or function, responsibility for which rests with State Government or which requires statewide uniformity."[36]

Finally, the South Dakota document achieves clarity on the issues of initiative and immunity by stipulating that "[T]he charter may provide for any form of executive, legislative and administrative structure which shall be of superior authority to statute, provided that the legislative body so established be chosen by popular election and that administrative proceedings be subject to judicial review."[37]

Geographic Reach of Local Government Powers

Home rule powers are not generally interpreted to extend beyond the territorially defined boundaries of the home rule unit.[38] Thus, except in Minnesota and Texas, a home rule entity cannot, on its own initiative, change its boundaries.[39] A home rule city in Alaska, however, was dissolved at the behest of the state legislature.[40]

Constraints on Collaborative Action

Express constitutional or statutory grants of power are normally required to allow home rule units to engage in collaborative activities and agreements with other units of government.[41]

Functional Autonomy

Government is not simply a question of form and structure. Functional autonomy encompasses the power of local government to exercise the police powers. The police powers are broadly defined as providing for the safety; preserving the health; promoting the prosperity; and improving the morals, peace, good order, comfort, and convenience of the locality and its inhabitants.

Current Constitutional Approaches

A study of early constitutional home rule provisions indicates that the power to create a charter "for its government" was granted to local governments along with the power to regulate, and the power to provide services.[42] For example, the Michigan and Ohio constitutions resolved the debate over municipal ownership of public utilities by expressly permitting it.[43]

The Bill of Rights provision of the local government article of the New York Constitution includes a compendious grant of regulatory authority over "the government, protection, order, conduct, safety, health and well-being of persons or property," as well as an express power to acquire, own, and operate transit facilities.[44] Under the Florida Constitution, home rule municipalities "shall have governmental, corporate and proprietary powers to enable them to conduct municipal government, perform municipal functions and render municipal services."[45]

Local regulation of private conduct may, of course, be problematic in the sixteen states that employ a qualifying adjective like "local" or "municipal" in conveying discretion to local governments. Thus, a home rule city's power to enact a rent control ordinance was struck down in Florida but sustained in California.[46] In ten states adopting the devolution-of-powers model, the scope of regulatory authority is limited by the charter, state law, or the constitution itself.[47] Home rule regulatory powers are subject to the preemptive effect of state statute in these ten jurisdictions. In California and other states that provide concurrent powers of the state with their local governments, home rule regulatory powers are subject to preemption if the matter in conflict is of statewide concern.[48]

In any event, autonomy in the sense of immunity cannot be completely conferred on home rule regulatory activities because individuals subject to such regulation possess procedural and substantive constitutional rights against governmental regulatory overreach. Local governments, like the state and federal governments, exercise their regulatory authority subject to judicial review. This restriction always applies.

Authority to Provide Service

States have authorized specific functions as responsibilities that local governments may or must undertake. Oklahoma and Arizona empower municipal corporations to "engage in any business or enterprise" that may be engaged in by the private sector.[49] The Arizona Constitution vests special purpose service provision districts "with all the rights, privileges, benefits . . . immunities and exemptions" afforded Arizona municipalities and political subdivisions.[50] Home rule units in South Carolina can undertake to provide gas, water, sewer, electric, and transportation services if the local electorate consents.[51] The Illinois Constitution establishes only two unlimited powers of home rule cities: the power to make local improvements by special assessments and the power to impose taxes for the provision of special services.[52]

Intergovernmental Relations

A survey of the constitutions of California, Florida, Illinois, Missouri, New York, Ohio, Pennsylvania, and Texas reveals contemporary variations in state constitutional law on intergovernmental relations. The Ohio text, unrevised since 1912, is silent on this topic. A series of ad hoc amendments to the Texas Constitution permits specific collaborative projects between counties.[53] The California Constitution speaks only to the issue of whether a county may perform municipal functions.[54] But the California Supreme Court assured a broad competence to collaborate when it characterized a state statute providing for joint exercise of powers as dealing with matters of statewide concern that could, therefore, lawfully override conflicting charter provisions.[55]

The New York Local Government Bill of Rights confirms that local governments have the power, as authorized by the legislature, "to provide cooperatively, jointly or by contract any facility, service, activity or undertaking which each local government has the power to provide separately."[56] Other states have broadly phrased language permitting collaboration in the provision of public improvement, facilities, and services.[57] The Illinois provision is notable in that it extends local government units and school districts the power to "contract and otherwise associate with individuals, associations, and corporations in any manner not prohibited by law or by ordinance."[58]

Thus, state constitution makers are faced with a number of options in considering the issue of interlocal collaboration. These choices range from silence, to specific and limited authorization, to general grants of authority to collaborate with other governmental entities, and, finally, to the permissive Illinois approach that includes collaboration with the private sector as well. The Illinois model is consistent with the broadest grant of home rule authority, but carries with it a policy judgment concerning the controversial question of privatization of governmental functions.

Fiscal Autonomy

Fiscal autonomy, whether in the sense of initiative or immunity, traditionally has not been considered a necessary component of home rule.[59] An ACIR study reveals that, for local government, financial management is a realm of constraint.[60] Forty-eight states, for example, impose debt limits on cities, forty on counties. Other detailed restrictions cover referendum requirements (forty states); maximum duration of bonds (forty-one states); and interest ceilings (twenty-four states). Thirty-eight states impose property tax limits on cities, and thirty-five impose them on counties. Forty-eight states establish the method of property tax assessment for local governments.

Only a handful of states have provisions that directly address the question of fiscal initiative. Nine state constitutions expressly provide autonomy with respect to borrowing and taxation.[61] Tennessee and Iowa expressly preclude additional taxing authority. Massachusetts and Rhode Island do so for both borrowing and taxation.[62]

Vaguer constitutional grants of power couched in terms like "municipal matters" or "local self-government" are unsparingly criticized in the legal literature.[63] Yet such provisions of the California, Missouri, Ohio, and Oregon constitutions have been interpreted by courts to empower home rule units to diversify their portfolio of revenue generating measures beyond the property tax.[64] Despite the success in these four states, courts did not approve municipal income taxes in two states with similar constitutional language, Missouri and Colorado.[65] Also, taxation, like other exercises of home rule powers in states giving substantial local autonomy, even if somewhat vaguely stated, may be preempted by statute on the grounds that the subject is of statewide concern.[66]

The only area of fiscal policy in which some state constitutions have recently constrained state government power over local government units concerns unfunded mandates. The operative definition of unfunded mandates varies from state to state. The New Hampshire Constitution provides a good example:

> The state shall not mandate or assign any new, expanded or modified programs or responsibilities to any political subdivision in such a way as to necessitate additional local expenditures by the political subdivision are fully funded by the state or unless such programs or responsibilities are approved for funding by a vote of the legislative body of the political subdivision.[67]

Michigan not only prohibits the state from requiring new or expanded activities without full state financing but also bars both reducing the proportion of state spending in the form of aid to local governments and shifting the tax burden to local governments.[68] A less sweeping approach is found in Tennessee and Hawaii provisions that require sharing between the state and its political subdivisions.[69]

Antimandate policies entrenched in fifteen state constitutions aim at strengthening accountability for and transparency in state decision-making by linking program creation and expansion to state funding.[70] Opponents stress the loss of flexibility in dividing and funding programmatic responsibility.

Personnel Autonomy

ACIR also delineates the scope of personnel autonomy.[71] Personnel matters include:

1. the hiring, promotion, discipline, and termination of public employees;
2. civil service and the merit system;
3. levels of compensation and entitlement to fringe benefits, such as pensions;
4. collective bargaining; and
5. conflict-of-interest requirements, disclosure requirements, and restrictions on partisan political activity.

This area annually produces a flood of local controversies, few of which turn for their resolution on the home rule status of the public employer.

Constraints Imposed by Federal Law
Autonomy in the sense of immunity is hard to come by in personnel matters, because public employees' claims are increasingly sheltered by statutes and by individual rights provisions of the federal Constitution applicable to all governments, regardless of home rule status. A home rule public employer is just as limited as any other public employer by constitutional strictures forbidding patronage hiring, sex discrimination, or termination for exercising protected freedoms of speech or association. Similarly, a public employee's due process rights to procedural fairness bind all governments in the federal system.

State Judicial Activism
An activist state judiciary may fashion protection for public employees that exceeds the floor provided by federal courts, as for example, in the area of drug or polygraph testing.

Pension and Benefits
Public employee pension and benefit rights also may be protected by an express provision of the state constitution or a judicial interpretation of a provision forbidding the impairment of contracts.[72] In Florida and New Jersey, public

employees are constitutionally guaranteed the right to organize.[73] In Illinois, financial disclosure by public employees and officials is mandated by the state constitution; in California, however, the extent of disclosure by public employees is limited by their state constitutional privacy rights.[74]

Merit Systems

New York became "the first state to constitutionalize a merit system of civil service employment" in 1894.[75] The New York provision, like that in Ohio's constitution, applies to both the state and its political subdivisions.[76]

Limited Immunity

The most recent state to entrench local autonomy over personnel matters in its constitution is Louisiana. Its 1974 constitution renders the appointment and functioning of city civil service commissions impervious to state legislative control.[77] The legislature is also forbidden from enacting laws mandating Aincreased expenditures for wages, hours, working conditions, pension, and retirement benefits, vacation or sick leave benefits of political subdivision employees" unless the governing body of the affected entity approves or the state legislature appropriates and provides the necessary funds.[78]

IMPLEMENTING LOCAL GOVERNMENT AUTONOMY

Organizing State and Local Government Relations: Dillon's Rule to Illinois Home Rule (1868–1968)

Dillon's Rule

The legal doctrine known as "Dillon's Rule" emphasizes the legal subordination of cities to state government. Although some observers believe this doctrine developed only after the Civil War,[79] much of what became Dillon's Rule apparently derives from a line of Massachusetts cases decided before 1820 that elaborated a theory concerning the juridical subordination of corporate entities to the sovereign that is rooted in medieval law.[80] The rule—named for its author, Chief Justice John Dillon of the Iowa Supreme Court—was firmly established in a landmark case in 1868 and ultimately adopted in nearly every state. Dillon wrote:

> In determining the question now made, it must be taken for settled law that a municipal corporation possesses and can exercise the following powers and no others: First, those granted in express words; second, those necessarily implied or necessarily incident to the powers expressly granted; third, those absolutely essential to the declared objects and purposes of the corporation—not simply convenient, but indispensable;

fourth, any fair doubt as to the existence of a power is resolved by the courts against the corporation—against the existence of the power.[81]

Dillon refined his views in subsequent editions of his treatise on the law of municipal corporations, writing:

> The extent of the power of municipalities, whether express, implied, or indispensable, is one of construction. And here the fundamental and universal rule, which is as reasonable, as it is necessary, is, that while the construction is to be just, seeking first of all for the legislative intent in order to give it fair effect, yet any ambiguity or fair, reasonable, substantial doubt as to the extent of the power is to be determined in favor of the State or general public and against the State's grantee. The rule of strict construction of corporate powers is not so directly applicable to the ordinary clauses in the charter or incorporating acts of municipalities as it is to the charters of private corporations; but it is equally applicable to grants of powers to municipal and public bodies which are out of the usual range, or which grant franchises, or rights of that nature, or which may result in public burdens, or which, in their exercise, touch the rights to liberty or property, or, as it may be compendiously expressed, any common-law right of citizen or inhabitant. . . . The rule of strict construction does not apply to the mode adopted by the municipality to carry into effect powers expressly or plainly granted, where the mode is not limited or prescribed by the legislature, and is left to the discretion of the municipal authorities. In such a case the usual test of the validity of the act of a municipal body is, whether it is reasonable, and there is no presumption against the municipal action in such cases.[82]

It is difficult to overestimate the impact of Dillon's Rule on the shaping of state and local government relations. The rule has been applied to the interpretation of both statutory and constitutional grants of power to local governments. It is so deeply entrenched in American juridical culture that more than a dozen states have abolished or modified Dillon's rule by express provisions in the state constitution. Moreover, the initiative stifling consequences of Dillon's Rule provided a grievance that energized the early advocates of municipal home rule.

NINETEENTH-CENTURY STATE CONSTITUTIONAL RESTRICTIONS ON STATE SUPREMACY

The Indiana Constitution of 1851 apparently contained the first state constitutional provision prohibiting local or special legislation. Although the provision did not exclusively address the relationship between the legislature and local government, the Indiana document enumerated several categories involving local government. The broadest of these prohibitions was aimed at local or special laws "regulating county and township business."[83] Prohibitions in this and many other state constitutions on special and local legislation were viewed as aiding "local self-government to this extent, that whatever rights of government or power of regulating its own affairs a community may have can be neither increased nor diminished without affecting in the same way the power or rights of all similar communities."[84]

Another state constitutional innovation affecting the sovereign prerogative of the legislature was the ripper clause, first developed by the 1872 Pennsylvania constitutional convention in response to the legislature's creation of the Philadelphia Building Commission, a state-appointed body that was charged with building City Hall, and vested with nearly unlimited authority to exact taxes to fund its operations. It read:

> The General Assembly shall not delegate to any special commission, private corporation or association, any power to make, supervise or interfere with any municipal improvement, money, property or effects, whether held in trust or otherwise, or levy taxes or perform any municipal function whatsoever.[85]

Like the language of provisions concerning local or special legislation, the ripper clause is significant because these provisions reveal a conscious attempt to distinguish between purely local, internal, or municipal matters and those of statewide concern. The ripper clause soon found its way into the constitutions of seven other states, normally as part of a policy package that included restrictions on special or local legislation concerning the internal affairs of local governments.

State and local borrowing was another area in which the public restricted state-local action, particularly on behalf of private enterprise. The Ohio Constitution of 1851, for example, prohibited the General Assembly from authorizing any county, city, town, or township from either investing in, or borrowing on behalf of, private enterprise.[86] By 1880, 28 of the 38 states had incorporated similar restrictions in their constitutions.[87]

Developing Concepts of Home Rule and Local Government Autonomy

During the twentieth century states sought to develop a workable model for providing local governments with a modicum of local autonomy. From 1875 onward, debate and deliberation in the states began to shift from placing restraints on their legislatures to empowering local citizens with the ability to articulate their preferences over institutional forms and functional powers within their local communities. Some of the best examples of the early development of home rule ideas can be seen in the Missouri Constitution of 1875 and, then, in the models for devolving powers on local government created by California, New York, the American Municipal Association (AMA), New Jersey, and Illinois.

The Missouri Experiment

The shift from constitutional restraints on the state legislature to constitutional local empowerment began with the home rule provisions of the Missouri Constitution of 1875. Faced with legislative corruption and favoritism in managing the affairs of the city of St. Louis, constitutional convention delegates crafted a prohibition of local or special laws changing the charters of cities, towns, or villages, and a procedural provision requiring a three-month notice to the inhabitants of a county or city prior to the passage of any local laws.[88] These rules were designed to curb the legislature's propensity to make changes in the charter and organization of St. Louis that were not endorsed by the people of the city.[89] The convention's most striking innovation, however, was a provision delegating to the people of St. Louis a power previously possessed solely by the Legislature, namely, the power to make a charter.[90] These charter provisions had to be "in harmony with and subject to the Constitution and laws" of Missouri.[91] That is, whatever principle of local self-government was embodied in the constitutional text had neither the scope nor the dignity accorded other constitutional provisions. Local initiatives were subject to challenge and, thereby, judicial scrutiny not only on constitutional grounds but also on the ground that they were not in harmony with general laws. The charter clearly was subordinate, also, to any general law, including those laws that classified cities by population.

To remove any doubts about legislative supremacy, the convention adopted a second saving clause: "Notwithstanding the provisions of this article, the General Assembly shall have the same power over the city and county of St. Louis that it has over other cities and counties of this State."[92] Accordingly, the Missouri Supreme Court held that home rule cities constituted a class concerning which the legislature was free to enact legislation without violating constitutional prohibitions against local or special legislation.

The Missouri Constitution was the first to contain a separate article devoted to local government and its relationship to the state legislature. Although the constitution did not shield charter cities from state legislative intervention, it generally succeeded in providing charter cities with initiative, "the power to act without prior authorization by the state legislature," such that from its adoption until 1905 "the Missouri Supreme Court approved every exercise of municipal initiative . . . which was authorized by charter, did not conflict with a statute, and did not run afoul of a constitutional prohibition," including the power to tax.[93]

The Early Twentieth Century and Home Rule
During the twentieth century, states struggled with decisions about the structure of their relationships to local governments and the powers that should be granted to those political communities. Ultimately, states adopted one of three versions of home rule powers: (1) the city republic; (2) a local government bill of rights; or (3) devolution of powers.

The City Republic: The complex task of creating a framework to express the demand for differentiating between state and local spheres of authority can be traced to a series of amendments to the California Constitution. Between 1894 and 1902, amendments were enacted regarding city county consolidation (1894); county boards of education (1894); county organization (1894); organization of municipal corporations (1896); the contents of corporate charters (1896); local government debt limits (1900); establishment of a decentralized, fiscally autonomous public school system (1902); tax exempt status of state and local government bonds (1902); tenure of municipal officials (1902); and empowering each city of more than 3,500 inhabitants to frame a charter for its own government, subject to approval by the state legislature, the provisions of which shall become the "organic law thereof and supersede . . . all laws inconsistent with such charter" (1902).

Little by little, the importance of local government for its own and the state's sake began to be recognized. Thus, provisions in the California (1905), Colorado (1902), Oregon (1906), and Ohio (1912) constitutions, adopted during a period when the Progressive movement emphasized autonomy for urban communities, can be viewed as a major step forward in establishing local autonomy, however limited.[94] These provisions widened the scope of local initiative over municipal affairs, local and municipal matters, or all powers of local self-government and immunized local charter provisions within the protected sphere of local autonomy from State legislative intervention.

Local Bill of Rights: New York went one step further than Missouri and pursued in greater detail an effort to delineate the respective spheres of responsibility for the state government and its local governments. The state constitution combined a bill of rights for local governments with explicit definitions of the respective roles and duties of the legislature and local governments with regard to local government matters. The bill of rights, for example, guaranteed: (1) popular participation in the selection of local officials; (2) county option in regard to forms of county government; (3) allocations of local government functions as between counties and cities, towns, villages, districts, or other units of government; and (4) the right of people in an affected area to veto annexation by a neighboring local government by withholding majority approval in a referendum.[95] The bill of rights set limits, also, on the legislature's power to regulate public utility operations conducted by local governments. Then, it conferred power on local governments to: (1) "adopt local laws as provided by this article" (Article IX); (2) enter into contracts with other local, state, and federal government agencies; (3) exercise eminent domain, subject to legislative regulations of its exercise outside the local government's boundaries; and (4) apportion the "cost of a governmental service or function upon any portion of its area, as authorized by act of the legislature."[96]

The next section of the constitution required the legislature to provide for the creation and organization of local governments in such a manner as shall secure to them the rights, powers, privileges, and immunities granted to them by the constitution and, "subject to the bill of rights of local government," to enact legislation "granting to local government powers including but not limited to those of local legislation and administration in addition to the powers vested in them by this article."

Those powers, once granted, "may be repealed, diminished, impaired or suspended only by" a statute enacted twice in successive years. The constitution required that legislative action "in relation to the property, affairs, or government of any local government" must be by general law, subject to certain exceptions. Another part of that section gave local governments power to adopt and amend local laws not inconsistent with the provisions of the constitution or any general law relating to its property, affairs, or government. They also may legislate on any of the following subjects:

1. the powers, duties, qualifications, number, mode of selection and removal, terms of office, compensation, hours of work, protection, welfare, and safety of its officers and employees, except that cities and towns shall not have such power with respect to members of the legislative body of the county in their capacities as county officers;
2. in the case of a city, town, or village, the membership and composition of its legislative body;
3. the transaction of its business;
4. the incurring of its obligations, except that local laws relating to financing by the issuance of evidences of indebtedness by such local government shall be consistent with laws enacted by the legislature;
5. the presentation, ascertainment, and discharge of claims against it;
6. the acquisition, care, management, and use of its highways, roads, streets, avenues, and property;
7. the acquisition of its transit facilities and the ownership and operation thereof;
8. the levy, collection, and administration of local taxes authorized by the legislature and of assessments for local improvements, consistent with laws enacted by the legislature;

9.   the wages or salaries, the hours of work or labor, and the protection, welfare, and safety of persons employed by any contractor or subcontractor performing work, labor, or services for it; and

10. the government, protection, order, conduct, safety, health, and well-being of persons or property therein.[97]

Disputes quickly arose over the scope of the powers that local governments had gained. Addressing the issue, Justice McFarland of the California Supreme Court said, "The section of the constitution in question uses the loose, indefinable wild words 'municipal affairs' and imposes upon the courts the almost impossible duty of saying what they mean."[98] Problems emerged even when the constitutional language spoke only to the empowerment question as, for example, the provision of the Washington Constitution conferring on "any county, city, town, or township" power to "make and enforce within its limits all such local police, sanitary, and other regulations as are not in conflict with general laws."[99] In a series of cases between 1901 and 1914, the Washington Supreme Court applied Dillon's Rule to this constitutional grant of powers. It announced that it would review charter provisions for their reasonableness; held that state regulation of a policy arena preempted local regulation; and refused to recognize that powers traditionally associated with sovereignty, such as eminent domain and taxation, were granted to localities.

Insofar as state constitutional provisions sought to shield charter cities from legislative interference, Judge Timlin of the Wisconsin Supreme Court noted in 1912:

> [I]f the legislature could be constantly prohibited from any interference with the so-called home rule charter adopted by the city so far as the same related to municipal affairs, this would substitute the interference of the judicial department of government for that of the legislative department, and every section of the charter and every ordinance must in time come before the courts in order to ascertain whether it related to a municipal affair only and if so whether subject to repeal or amendment by the state legislature.[100]

Simply put, charter cities would be freed from the tutelage of the state legislature only to find themselves subject to the guardianship of the state judiciary. In some instances, judicial home rule resulted, as in Ohio, where courts, on a case-by-case basis, exercised a legislative function of determining what was or was not a permissible power for local governments to exercise, leaving home rule cities in doubt as to the extent of their powers.[101] In others, such as New York, what resulted was a presumption of state responsibility that led to "a precipitous contraction of home rule powers."[102]

The Devolution-of-Powers Approach: The third approach to local home rule, setting out an area of devolved powers, seemed to avoid the difficulties inherent in delineating a constitutional division of powers between the state and local government. This devolved power provided local government with an area in which to operate freely, subject to the ultimate purview of the state legislature. Sometimes referred to as legislative home rule, the devolution of powers is most commonly associated with the model constitutional provision for home rule formulated in 1953 by Jefferson B. Fordham on behalf of the American Municipal Association's Committee on Home Rule.[103] The operative language of the provision states:

> A municipal corporation which adopts a home charter rule may exercise any power or perform any function which the legislature has power to devolve upon a non-home rule charter municipal corporation and which is not denied to that municipal corporation by its home rule charter, is not denied to all home rule charter municipal corporations by statute and is within such limitations as may be established by statute. This devolution of power does not include the power to enact private or civil law governing civil relationships except as incident to an exercise of an independent municipal power, nor does it include power to define and provide for the punishment of a felony.[104]

This home rule model represented a turning away from "the cross-checks and intersecting lines of divided responsibility" of the federal idea in favor of "a simple pyramid" of efficient, rationalized functional administration.[105]

The 1953 American Municipal Association formulation did not represent a complete abandonment of the search for a protected sphere of local autonomy. It did provide that "charter provisions with respect to municipal executive, legislative, and administrative structure, organization, personnel and procedure are of superior authority to statute."[106] Moreover, it squarely addressed the problem of state-mandated expenditures or programs by proposing that legislation requiring increased municipal expenditures would take effect, absent municipal consent, only on a two-thirds vote of the legislature or if the legislature funded the mandated increases.[107] These protective provisions are absent from the recommended local government article in the 1963 edition of the National Municipal League's Model State Constitution, indicating an even sharper retreat from a strong commitment to local immunity.[108]

The devolution-of-powers model has achieved considerable success. For example, both Missouri and Pennsylvania streamlined their constitutional home rule provisions (e.g., "a municipality which has a home rule charter may exercise any power or perform any function not denied by this Constitution, by its home rule charter, or by the General Assembly at, any time"[109]), and North Dakota's provision tracks the language of the Model State Constitution cited above.[110]

This home rule model makes clear that the state legislature has the authority to confer broad powers on local government units, thus precluding a challenge based on nineteenth century delegation-of-power doctrines. Language empowering home rule cities is drafted to leave "a charter municipality free to exercise any appropriate power or function except as expressly limited by charter or general statute." This eliminates the "strict constructionist presumption against the existence of municipal power" associated with Dillon's Rule.[111] It also strips state judges of the doctrine of implied preemption because a home rule entity's powers can be impeded only by express charter or statutory limits. The devolution-of-powers model seems designed almost exclusively with an eye to reducing the role that courts have played in mediating the division of power between state and local government.

New Jersey and Home Rule: The devolution-of-powers approach, however, has brought forth its own difficulties in state-local relations. Questions concerning administrative flexibility and entrenched rights in a state constitution are not fully developed. The New Jersey Constitution exemplifies one approach coping with some of these problems. That constitution has no local government article, with provisions pertaining to local government placed in the articles dealing with the legislative branch and taxation and finance. Three provisions illustrate the New Jersey approach.

First, the prohibition against local or special legislation regulating the internal affairs of individual municipalities and counties is qualified by an exception that allows such legislation to be enacted on petition by the affected governing body and by a two-thirds vote of the state legislature.[112] This provision relaxes the rigidity inherent in the distinction between internal affairs and matters of statewide concern. Flexibility, therefore, is permitted in the constitutionally prescribed division of powers by having both a concurrent majority of the local governing body and the state legislature participate in passing special acts of the legislature.

Second, the New Jersey Constitution provides guidance to policy makers on the reading of constitutional provisions empowering local governments. It states:

> The provisions of this Constitution and of any law concerning municipal corporations formed for local government, or concerning counties, shall be liberally construed in their favor: The powers of counties and such municipal corporations shall include not only those granted in express terms but also those of necessary or fair implication, or incident to the powers expressly conferred, or essential thereto and not inconsistent with or prohibited by this Constitution or by law.[113]

This "liberal construction" of local government powers counteracts the effect of Dillon's Rule and may produce a greater degree of functional autonomy than a more conventional constitutional grant of home rule. In 1973, for example, the New Jersey Supreme Court sustained a municipal rent control scheme under a statutory grant of authority to adopt such ordinances as the local governing body "may deem necessary and proper for the good government, order, and protection of persons and property, and for the preservation of the public health, safety, and welfare of the municipality and its in habitants."[114] The court thus upheld the municipal creation of a rent control board as a power necessary to carry out the regulatory purpose of a rent control ordinance, even where no statute existed authorizing municipalities to establish one. By contrast, a year earlier, the Florida Supreme Court strictly construed a home rule municipality's constitutional authority to "exercise any power for municipal purposes" when it overturned a similar ordinance.[115]

A third key constitutional provision, found in New Jersey's taxation and finance article, makes the delivery of certain services, notably a "thorough and efficient system of free public schools," a state responsibility.[116] This paragraph is read to mandate that the state create a funding scheme for public education that does not shift its financial burdens exclusively to local taxing jurisdictions.[117]

Local or Special Legislation: Prohibitions against local or special legislation, a mainstay of the state legislature's policy repertoire during the nineteenth century, received little attention during the twentieth century. Nonetheless, it may be time to review that neglect. For instance, although the recent elimination of local or special legislation from the South Carolina Constitution has been hailed as part of "the journey toward local self-government,"[118] others have viewed special legislation as "conducive to greater independence and expanded self-rule" and as an "essential means for ensuring flexibility and adaptability."[119] The framers of the Constitution of Virginia apparently thought so when they rejected the constitutional revision commission's recommendations to restrict the General Assembly's authority to devolve powers on local governments by special act.[120] The Virginia system apparently does deliver. In ACIR's index of city discretionary authority, Virginia cities ranked seventh overall. By comparison, such traditional bastions of home rule as Ohio and California placed eleventh and seventeenth, respectively.[121]

Interlocal Collaboration: Another significant response to emerging intergovernmental problems is represented by state constitutional rules governing interlocal collaboration. A 1987 ACIR report identified types of rules that enable local citizens may use to create and modify local governments. These enabling rules include:

1. rules of association that establish processes, such as municipal incorporation, that enable local citizens to create municipalities or other entities endowed with certain governmental powers);
2. boundary adjustment rules that enable local citizens and officials to alter the boundaries of existing units;
3. fiscal rules that determine local revenue raising authority; and
4. contracting rules that enable local units to enter into a variety of mutually agreeable relationships with one another and with private firms.[122]

The departure from conventional thinking called for by these rules casts new light on the significance of inserting into state constitutions such matters as dissolution and annexation, consolidation and separation, joint participation in common enterprises, interlocal cooperation, and intergovernmental relations, as is done in Missouri.[123] It also clarifies rules concerning the formation, operation, and dissolution of special districts, which are embedded in the local government article of the 1974 Louisiana Constitution.[124] Finally, this approach shifts the focus of attention from a preoccupation with conflict to a recognition of the pervasive collaboration through contractual arrangements that obtains in modern state and local government.[125]

Illinois and the Devolution-of-Powers Approach: The text of the local government article of the 1970 Illinois Constitution provides an interesting departure from the devolution-of-powers model. Article VII of the Illinois Constitution illustrates the complex kind of decision rules that must be supplied if the goal of entrenching the rights of local governments and local citizens is to be realized. These decision rules include:

1. the definition of entities eligible for home rule status;
2. the scope of powers afforded these home rule entities;
3. the interpretation of powers granted to them;
4. the basis for dealing with interlocal conflict and collaboration; and
5. the extent of state legislative control over the scope of home rule powers.

Woven throughout the fabric of the article are requirements for local citizen choice.

The complexity of these rules reflects not only the difficulty of coming to terms with the multifaceted roles that local governments play in the division of governmental responsibilities in a modern society but also the differentiated political culture that flourishes in Illinois. Counties, cities, villages, and incorporated towns in Illinois are eligible for home rule status. A self-executing grant of home rule powers to certain counties and to municipalities with a population of more than 25,000 is subject to repeal by referendum. Otherwise, home rule status can be acquired only by referendum.[126]

In contrast to devolution-of-powers constitutions, the Illinois article distinguishes between several kinds of local autonomy: form of government and office holding, functional, and fiscal matters. A home rule unit can adopt, alter, or repeal its currently prescribed form of government subject to referendum approval. Home rule municipalities and home rule counties possess diverse powers with respect to the creation, manner of selection, and terms of office of local officials.[127] Under this article, " [a] home rule unit may exercise any power or perform any function pertaining to its government and affairs." What is pertinent to its government and affairs are defined expressly to include a copious grant of the police power "to regulate for the protection of the public health, safety, morals, and welfare" and "to license." This grant of power expressly includes the power to tax and to incur debt, attributes of fiscal autonomy without which home rule would be straitjacketed in practice.[128]

The Illinois Constitution also addresses and resolves the problem created by Dillon's Rule: How are decision makers to read the empowering text? The blunt answer is that "[p]owers and functions of home rule units shall be construed liberally." Counties and municipalities that are not home rule units "shall have only powers granted to them by law" plus expressly granted constitutional powers over form of government and office-holding, fiscal matters, and providing for local improvements and services. Limited purpose units of local government, such as townships, school districts, and special districts, "shall have only powers granted by law." In addition, the article prescribes rules for resolving conflicts between legislative enactments of home rule cities and home rule counties. It also is sprinkled with provisions aimed at facilitating interlocal cooperation by contract and power sharing.[129]

Finally, the article speaks to the neglected but pervasive question of state preemption of home rule powers. The Illinois home rule provision makes crystal clear that "home rule units may exercise and perform concurrently with the State any power or function of a home rule unit to the extent that the General Assembly by law does not specifically limit the concurrent exercise or specifically declare the state's exercise to be exclusive."[130] There is no room for a doctrine of implied preemption in this language.

The express preemption question is dealt with generally as follows: "[T]he General Assembly may provide specifically by law for the exclusive exercise by the State of any power or function of a home rule unit." When the state chooses to assert a monopoly, a three-fifths supermajority is required to deny or limit a home rule entity's fiscal and other powers. Significantly, only two areas of home rule autonomy are protected against legislative limitation or denial; the power to add to the stock of local capital improvements by special assessment and the power to finance the provision of special services.[131]

Greater Fiscal Autonomy: A tilt toward local fiscal autonomy, proposed in the 1953 AMA proposal and highlighted in ACIR's studies, has come to fruition in recent amendments to several state constitutions concerning the proliferation of state mandates. The 1975 California provision requires the state to reimburse local governments if any new program or higher level of service cost is mandated.[132] Taken in the context of the taxpayer rebellion of the 1970s, the provision's primary objective is to guard against a potential "smoke and mirrors" device that would enable the state legislature to evade tax and spending limits by shifting costs to local governments. Nevertheless, an arguably unintended consequence of the reform creates a protected sphere of local fiscal autonomy. For example, the Missouri Constitution requires not only that the state fund "any new activity or service or any increase in the level of any activity or service beyond that required by existing law" but also that "the state cannot reduce the state financial proportion of the costs of any existing activity or service required of . . . political subdivisions."[133] The Missouri language thus substantially affects two common dogmas of state constitutional law; namely, that the state possesses virtually untrammeled power to impose duties and obligations on local governments; and that state funding of existing programs is a matter of legislative grace.

CONCLUSION

As local government has developed and become more important to the states, which saw their responsibilities balloon in the twentieth century, the states have integrated local government into the complex provision of services to their citizens. To do this, the constitutional relationship between the state and its localities has undergone significant change. These changes included the following:

- the 1875 Missouri constitutional provision that broadly empowered one city, St. Louis, but created no meaningful barrier to state legislative interference with municipal matters;
- California's constitutional revision, on citizen initiative, to bar state legislative meddling with municipal affairs;
- New York's bill of rights on local governments;
- the American Municipal Association's model state constitution making the state legislature the ultimate arbiter of the scope of home rule;
- the Illinois Constitution marking the reemergence of complex rules for outlining the relationship between state and local government; and
- the New Jersey statutory home rule approach.

In appraising these alternative approaches to state-local relations, state constitution makers should bear in mind the following considerations:

1. The Role of Citizen Choice
    State constitutions teach concern not only for the role of institutional actors but also for citizen choice. An exclusive focus on entrenching rules relating to the roles of state and local institutions may divert attention from the claims of local citizens to participation in decisions with respect to structural, functional, personnel, or fiscal matters. Neglect of the citizen choice factor may have triggered the "tax revolt" in California in 1978, as citizens perceived a loss of control over local taxing policy.

    Constitutional authority to frame a home rule charter facilitates citizen choice by shifting the locus of consent concerning the institutional form and functional powers of local government from the state legislatures to the local electorate. The home rule provision may be designed to assure citizen participation in the process of framing and approving the home rule charter. The contents of the home rule charter adopted by the voters may limit as well as expand the locality's preexisting powers.

    Pennsylvania's constitution permits citizens in the affected area to compel local government "to cooperate, delegate, or transfer any function, power, or responsibility" to "other governmental units, the Federal government, any other state or its governmental units, or any newly created governmental unit." Another provision gives the local electorate the right to consolidate, merge or change boundaries "without the approval of any governing body."[134]

    A local government article of the state constitution can also facilitate citizen choice either by specifying the rules for direct citizen participation in local decision-making or by making it clear that the home rule charter can employ any of the devices of direct democracy—referendum, recall, and initiative.

2. Eligibility for Local Autonomy
    State constitutions have extended various forms of autonomy to general purpose units of government. Counties, as well as municipalities, have been recognized increasingly as appropriate candidates for home rule. Special districts, including school districts, have played a significant role in furthering local self-government through collective action. Consideration may be given to constitutionalizing their powers of initiative, as in Arizona, or immunity, as in Virginia.[135]

    There is no question that the statutory powers given to a wide variety of local government units presents serious issues of jurisdictional overlap. State policies concerning the impact of the grant of autonomy to a whole host of political subdivisions need clarification in most states.

3. Intergovernmental Cooperation

Almost as a necessary concomitant to the issue of eligibility, intergovernmental cooperation will become a powerful resource in resolving the questions raised by local government autonomy. Intergovernmental cooperation provides various local governments with options to expand the scope of discretionary authority in a wide range of services provided to the public. As such, it must be reviewed as a possible constitutional fixture in state-local and local-local government relations. It also allows for the consideration of public-private partnerships in service delivery and government organization. Indeed, it is one of the most flexible of tools in meeting the ever-changing demands of a local citizenry.

4. The Role of the Judiciary

Home rule policies in state constitutions are shaped to a significant degree by the judiciary. Because judicial review is an inevitable feature of the American constitutional framework, policy makers must to take into account juridical problems that predictably occur when power is diffused among political subdivisions. These juridical issues include:

    a. How is the constitutional text to be interpreted?
    b. Do political subdivisions have the authority to assert constitutional claims against the state and its agencies?
    c. How are conflicts between state statutes and home rule charters or ordinances to be resolved?

Failure to think through whether or not decisions concerning these recurrent topics are appropriate to include in state constitutions may lead to the kinds of unanticipated consequences that beset the implementation of complex policies.

5. Drafting Considerations

Translating the concepts of local government autonomy into constitutional language will no doubt tax the ingenuity of the drafters because the language must not only articulate agreed-on policy decisions but also must be sensitive to factors concerning the way in which the text will be interpreted. The most important of these are: (1) the clarity of the text; (2) principles of construction; (3) citizen demands to expand, constrict, or clarify existing texts; and (4) official and institutional demands to expand, constrict, or clarify existing texts.

Clarity of the Text

The process of selecting language for incorporation into a state constitution should be based on a careful consideration of the precise effect of that language. Thus, the use of the adjective "local" or "municipal" in the context of empowering local governments invites both a limiting interpretation and a body of interpretive case law focusing on whether the matter in question is of local rather than statewide concern. The elimination of a qualifying adjective, however, incurs the risk that a home rule unit will seek to extend its policy reach to areas generally recognized as falling within the competence of state or national, rather than local, authorities.

The language of the text has to be formulated clearly to facilitate its application within the legal, as well as political, culture of a given state. The task of educating generalist judges is particularly demanding when the local government article expresses a significant policy change from that in a previous constitution, as in South Carolina, which moved from a strict to a liberal rule of construction of local government powers.[136] Judges must recognize that preexisting precedents are no longer binding or authoritative in view of the policy change embedded in the new constitutional language. In such cases, explanatory language in the legislative history of the provision aids in clarifying intent. So, too, does inquiry into the policy context and language of sister state constitutions.

Principles of Construction

State constitution makers should be aware of the role that judicial interpretation plays in determining the success or failure of efforts to implement new understandings of local self-government. Indeed, court decisions have frequently sparked constitutional reform. Thus, the 1896 amendment to the California Constitution that sought to create a protected realm of immunity against state legislative intrusion into the municipal affairs of a charter city was designed to overturn several decisions of the California Supreme Court interpreting the 1879 text.[137]

Twelve states have included a constitutional provision rooting out Dillon's Rule by mandating liberal interpretation of grants of power either to municipalities in general or to home rule units.[138] However, state courts may interpret even cryptic language in a state constitution so expansively that an interpretive provision is superfluous. The Texas Constitution, for example, confers charter-making authority on cities of over 5,000 population "subject to such limitations as may be prescribed by the Legislature and providing that no charter or any ordinance passed under said charter shall contain any provision inconsistent with the Constitution of the State or of the general laws enacted by the Legislature of this State." This 1912 text has been viewed generally by Texas courts as tantamount to a plenary grant of local legislative authority, including the power to expand the boundaries of the home rule city through annexation and the power to tax.[139]

Inserting a rule of liberal interpretation into the constitution is no guarantee of enhanced judicial responsiveness. Gerald Benjamin has summed up the track record of the New York judiciary as follows: "In . . . home rule . . . policies, the role of the State's high court, the Court of Appeals, as a guardian of State sovereignty against City incursions cannot be overstated. Strict interpretation or broad, the court read New York's constitution so as to assure State dominance."[140] But such directives do have an impact on the state judiciary. For example, the Alaska Supreme Court, after floundering about with a local activity rule, finally recognized the force of the liberal interpretation rule.[141] Case law in California and Ohio substitutes liberal (pro-local) for strict construction of home rule powers in light of the recognition of local autonomy by the state constitution.[142]

Citizen Demands to Expand, Constrict, or Clarify Home Rule Provisions
The state constitution is, by definition, the appropriate vehicle for the exercise of constitutional choice by state citizens. As such, citizen demands to expand, constrict, or clarify constitutional provisions for local autonomy have a significant impact on the constitution's contents. This is particularly true in jurisdictions that permit citizens to initiate amendments to the state constitution. California voters, for example, are responsible for the formulation of their particular style of home rule. The state's electorate may shrink local autonomy as well as expand it, as Californians chose to do with respect to property tax rates and assessment practices.[143]

Official and Institutional Demands to Expand, Constrict, or Clarify Home Rule Provisions
Local governments are institutions with continuity and their own agendas of power, which may or may not correspond to the interests of their constituents. Furthermore, local government officials may prefer existing political arrangements instead of constitutional change. Both the Virginia Municipal League and the Virginia Association of Counties, for example, opposed proposals of the Commission on Constitutional Revision that would have empowered any charter city or county "to exercise any power or perform any function not denied to it" by the constitution, its charter, or general law.[144] These organizations preferred the existing regime of special legislation and strict construction to the devolution of powers model recommended by the commission. They were instrumental in excising the contested language from the document submitted to and ratified by the voters.[145] In contrast, the Florida League of Cities sponsored a state constitutional amendment concerning state mandates whose "thrust is to further the 'home rule' movement through which local government has been given increasing autonomy from legislative action."[146] In Illinois, local officials, particularly Chicago's mayor, Richard J. Daley, actively promoted the concept of home rule and shaped its unique language with regard to local revenues and preemption.[147]

Good government is not always good politics, as proponents of Maryland constitutional reform learned when county officials mobilized to defeat a new constitution that would have streamlined county government by eliminating certain elective offices, including sheriffs. The officials to be eliminated, it turned out, were "of considerable importance to the local political structure almost everywhere."[148] On the other hand, inclusion of home rule for Chicago materially assisted the successful campaign for adoption of the Illinois Constitution.[149]

NOTES

This chapter revises and updates parts of a study prepared by the author and published by the United States Advisory Commission on Intergovernmental Relations. See U.S. Advisory Commission on Intergovernmental Relations, *Local Government Autonomy* vii (1993) [hereafter cited as ACIR].

1. Gordon L. Clark, "A Theory of Local Autonomy," 74 *Annals of the Association of American Geographers* 195–99 (1984).

2. Colo. Const., art. XX, § 6.

3. Pa. Const., art. IX, § 2.

4. American Municipal Association, *Model Constitutional Provisions for Municipal Home Rule* (1953). Jefferson Fordham was hired by the National Municipal League to prepare a model state constitution including home rule provisions.

5. Utah Const., art. XII, § 8.

6. Va. Const., art. X, § 10.

7. Pa. Const., art. III, § 20. This kind of provision has been referred to as a "Ripper Clause." *See* David O. Porter, "The Ripper Clause in State Constitutional Law: An Early Urban Experiment," 1969 *Utah L. Rev.* 287, 450 (1969).

8. Conn. Const., art. X, § 1.

9. Sho Sato and Arvo Van Alstyne, *State and Local Government Law* 136 (2d ed., 1977).

10. Pa. Const., art. IX, § 2; National Municipal League, *Model State Constitution* 97 (6th ed., 1963); Ill. Const., art. VII, § 6(i).

11. Ill. Const., art. VII, § 10(a).

12. ACIR, *Measuring Local Discretionary Authority* 1 (1981).

13. N.J. Const., art. XIII (1776).

14. Ind. Const., art. IV, § 22 (1851).

15. Ala. Const., § 110, § 104(5), (6), (11), (15), (21), (22), (23), (24), (29), (31).

16. R.I. Const., art. XXVIII, § 4.

17. N. Y. Const., art. IX, § 2(b)(2)(a).

18. N.J. Const., art. IV, § VII, par. 10.

19. N. Dak. Const., art. VII, § 6.

20. Mont. Const., art. XI, § 9.

21. Tex. Const., art. 3, § 63, § 64; N. Dak. Const., art. VII, § 3, § 4; Nev. Const., art. IX, § 2; Mo. Const., art. VI, §§ 3–5; Mich. Const., art. VII, § 13; Colo. Const., art. XIV, § 3; Cal. Const., art. XI, § 1; Ark. Const., art. XIII, § 2; Kan. Const., art. 9, § 1; Ky. Const., § 64.

22. Cal. Const., art. XI, § 13; Colo. Const., art. V, 35; Mo. Const., art. VI, § 22; Mont. Const., art. V; N.J. Const., art. IV, § VII, par. 9(12); Pa. Const., art. III, § 31; S. Dak. Const., art. III, § 26; Utah Const., art. VI, § 29; Wyo. Const., art. 3, § 37.

23. Ohio Const., art. II, § 12; art. X, § 1, § 3; Okla. Const., art. V, § 5; art. XIII, § 4(a); Ore. Const., Art. IV § 1(5).

24. Cal. Const., art. XI, § 5; Colo. Const., art. VIII, § 1(9) (counties have all powers of local self-government), art. VIII, § 2(b) (cities); Ga. Const., art. IX, § II, par. II (cities); Ill. Const., art. VII, § 6(a); Iowa. Const., art. III, § 38A (cities), and § 39A (counties); Kan. Const., art. 12, § 5(b); La. Const., art. VI, § 5(E); Me. Const., art. VIII, Part Second § 1; Mich. Const., art. VII, § 2; Ohio Const., art. XVIII, § 3; Ore. Const., art. VI, § 10; R.I. Const., art. XXVIII, § 1; W. Va. Const., art. VI, § 39(a); Wis. Const., art. XI, § 3; Wyo. Const., art. 13, § 1(b).

25. Sho Sato, "Municipal Affairs in California," 60 *Cal. L. Rev.* 1055, 1079–81 (1972).

26. *City of Oakland v. Williams*, 15 Cal. 2d 542, 103 P.2d 168 (1940).

27. Connecticut Advisory Commission on Intergovernmental Relations, *Defining Statewide Local Concerns: Can It Be Done and Is It Necessary?* (Hartford, 1989).

28. La. Const., art. VI, pt. I, § 6.

29. Ga. Const., art. IX, § II, par. I(a); Mich. Const., art. VII, § 22; N.Y. Const., art. IX, § 2(c)(i); R.I. Const., art. XXVIII, § 2.

30. Md. Const., art. XI A; Neb. Const., art. XI, § 2; Nev. Const., art. VIII, § 8; Okla. Const., art. XVIII, § (3)(a); Utah Const., art. XI, 5(a); Wash. Const., art. XI, § 10.

31. Ore. Const., art. XI, § 2; Tex. Const., art. II, § 5.

32. Alaska Const., art. X, § 1; Conn. Const., art. § 1; Mass. Const., art. II, § 6; Mo. Const., art. VI, § 19(a); Mont., Const., art. XI, § 6; N.H. Const., art. I, § 39; N.M. Const., art. X, § 6D; N.D., Const., art. VII, § 1; Pa. Const., art. IX, § 2; S.D. Const., art. IX, § 2.

33. Colo. Const., art. XIV, § 15(1).

34. Tenn. Const., art. XI, § 9.

35. S.C. Const., art. VIII, § 11.

36. Ibid.

37. S.D. Const., art. IX, § 2.

38. *City of Pueblo v. Flanders*, 122 Colo. 571, 225 P2d 832 (1950); *Marcus v. Baron*, 57 N.Y. 2d 862, 442 N.E. 2d 437 (1982); Comment, "The Exercise of Extraterritorial Powers by Municipalities," 45 *U. Chi. L. Rev.* 151 (1977).

39. *See* Frank S. Sengstock, *Annexation: A Solution to the Metropolitan Area Problems* (1960); Robert R. Ashcroft and Barbara Kyle Balfour, "Home Rule Cities and Municipal Annexation in Texas: Recent Trends and Future Prospects," 15 *St. Mary's L.J.* 519 (1984); *Independent School District No. 700 v. City of Duluth*, 170 N. W. 2d 116 (Minn., 1969).

40. *City of Douglas v. Juneau*, 484 P.2d 1040 (Alaska, 1971).

41. *See* ACIR, *A Handbook for Interlocal Agreements and Contracts* (1967).

42. Frank J. Goodnow, *Municipal Home Rule*, 253–54 (1895).

43. Ohio Const., art. XVIII, § 4, § 5 (1912); Mich. Const., art. VII, § 24.

44. N.Y. Const., art. IX, § 2(c)(7)(10).

45. Fla. Const., art. VIII, § 2(b).

46. *City of Miami Beach v. Fleetwood Hotel, Inc.*, 261 So. 2d 801 (Fla., 1972); *Fisher v. City of Berkeley*, 37 Cal. 3d 644, 693 P 2d 261 (1984).

47. For example, Pa. Const., art. IX, § 2.

48. *Fisher v. City of Berkeley*, supra n. 46.

49. Ariz. Const., art. XIII, § 5; Okla. Const., art. XVIII, § 6.

50. Ariz. Const., art. XIII, § 7.

51. S.C. Const., art. VIII, § 16.

52. Ill. Const., art. VII, § 6(1)(2),(2).

53. Tex. Const., art. 9, §§ 4–9, 11–13.

54. Cal. Const., art. XI, § 8.

55. *Rider v. City of San Diego*, 18 Cal. 4th 1035, 959 P.2d 347 (1998) (Joint Exercise of Powers Act overrides contrary provision of city charter).

56. N.Y. Const., art. IX, § 1(c).

57. Fla. Const., art. VIII, § 4; Ill. Const., art. VII, § 10; Mo. Const. VI, § 14, § 16, § 30(a); Pa. Const., art. IX, §§ 5–7.

58. Ill. Const., art. VII § 10(c).

59. Richard Briffault, "Local Government and the New York State Constitution," 1 *Hofstra L. and Pol'y Symp.* 79, 90 (1996).

60. ACIR, *State Laws Governing Local Government Structure and Administration* 38–41 (1993).

61. Colo. Const., art. XX, § 6(e),(g); Ill. Const., art. VII, § 6(a); Kan. Const., art. 12, § 5(b)(tax); La. Const., art. VI, § 30; Me. Const., art. VIII, Part Second § 2 (industrial development bonds only); Mich. Const., art. VII, § 2; N.Y. Const., art. IX, § 2(c)(4),(8); Utah Const., art. XI, § 5(a)(d); Wyo. Const., art. 13, § 1(c).

62. Iowa Const., art. III, § 38A, § 39A; Mass. Const., art. II, § 7(2)(3); R.I. Const., art. XXVIII, § 5; Tenn. Const., art. XI, § 9.

63. *See,* for example, Howard Lee McBain, *The Law and Practice of Municipal Home Rule* (1916).

64. *Weeks v. City of Oakland,* 21 Cal. 3d 386, 579 P.2d 449 (1978) (occupation and business tax measured by gross receipts); *St. Louis v. Sternsberg,* 69 Mo. 289 (1879); *Zielonka v. Carrell,* 99 Ohio St. 220, 124 N.E. 134 (1919) (occupation tax); *Multnomah Kennel Club v. Department of Revenue,* 295 Ore. 279, 666 P.2d 1327 (1983) (power to impose business income tax implied out of grant of power over matters of "county concern").

65. *City and County of Denver v. Sweet,* 329 P.2d 441 (Colo., 1958); *Carter Carburetor Corp v. City of St. Louis,* 203 S.W. 2d 438 (Mo., 1947).

66. *California Federal Savings and Loan Ass'n v. City of Los Angeles,* 54 Cal. 3d 1, 812 P.2d 916 (1991); C. Emory Glander and Addison E. Dewey, "Municipal Taxation: A Study of the Preemption Doctrine," 9 *Ohio State L.J.* 72 (1948).

67. N.H. Const., pt. I, art. 28(a).

68. Mich. Const., art. IX § 25.

69. Haw. Const., art. VIII, § 5; Tenn. Const., art. II, § 24.

70. Ala. Const., art. II, § 19; Cal. Const., art. XIII B, § 10; Fla. Const., art. VII, § 18; Haw. Const., art. VIII, § 5; La. Const., art. VI, § 14; Md. Const., art. XI (E)(F); Mich. Const., art. IX, § 2; Mo. Const., art. X, § 21, art. XII, § 2(b); N.H. Const., pt. I, art. 28(a); N. J. Const., art. VIII, § II, par. 5(a); N.M. Const., art. X, § 5; Ore. Const., art. X, § 15; Tenn. Const., art. II, § 24. *See,* Robert M. M. Shaffer, Comment: "Unfunded State Mandates and Local Governments," 64 *U. Cin. L. Rev.* 1057 (1996).

71. ACIR, supra. n. 12.

72. Alaska Const., art. XII, § 7; Ill. Const., art. XIII, § 5; Mich. Const., art. IX, § 24; N.Y. Const., art. V, § 7. *See also Gauer v. Essex County Division of Welfare,* 108 N.J. 140, 528 A.2d 1 (1987).

73. Fla. Const., art. I, § 6; N.J. Const., art. I, par. 19.

74. *City of Carmel-by-the-Sea v. Young,* 2 Cal. 3d 259, 466 P.2d 225 (1970); *Stein v. Howlett,* 52 Ill. 2d 570, 289 N.E. 2d 409 (1972).

75. Peter J. Galie, The New York State Constitution, 114 (1991); N.Y. Const., art. V, § 9 (1894).

76. N.Y. Const., art. V, 6; Ohio Const., art. XV, § 10.

77. La. Const., art. X, § 4, § 10; *Civil Service Commission of New Orleans v. Guste,* 428 So. 2d 457 (1983).

78. La. Const., art. VI, § 14.

79. Gerald Frug, "The City as a Legal Concept," 93 *Harv. L. Rev.* 1059 (1980).

80. Paul Vinogradoff, "Juridical Persons," 24 *Colum. L. Rev.* 594, 600–601 (1924).

81. Clark, *Dodge and Co. v. Davenport*, 14 Iowa 494, 498 (1863); *Merriam v. Moody's Executor*, Iowa 164, 170 (1868).

82. John E. Dillon, Commentaries on the Law of Municipal Corporations, 239 (1911).

83. Ind. Const., art. IV, 22 (1851).

84. Chauncey C. Binney, Restrictions upon Local and Special Legislation in State Constitutions, 7 (1894).

85. Pa. Const., art. II, § 20 (1873).

86. Ohio Const., art. VIII, § 4, § 6.

87. U.S. Department of the Interior, Census Office, Report on Valuation, Taxation and Public Indebtedness in the United States 649 (1884).

88. Mo. Const., art. IX, §§ 20–25(1875).

89. Thomas S. Barclay, *The St. Louis Home Rule Charter of 1876* (1902).

90. Ibid.

91. Mo. Const., art. IV, §§ 20–22 (1875).

92. Mo. Const., art. IX, § 25 (1875).

93. James E. Westbrook, "Municipal Home Rule: An Evaluation of the Missouri Experience," 33 *Mo. L. Rev.* 45, 46–47, 51 (1968).

94. Michael H. Frisch, "Urban Theorists, Urban Reform, and American Political Culture in the Progressive Period," 97 *Pol. Sci. Q.* 295 (1982).

95. N.Y. Const., art. IX, §§ 1–3.

96. N.Y. Const., art. IX, § 1.

97. N.Y. Const., art. IX, § 2(a), (b), and (c).

98. Ex parte Braun, 141 Cal. 204, 213–14 (1903).

99. Wash. Const., art. XI, § 11.

100. *State ex rel. Mueller v. Thompson*, 149 Wis. 488, 517–18 (1912).

101. Jefferson B. Fordham and Joe F. Asher, "Home Rule Powers in Theory and Practice," 9 *Ohio St. L.J.* 18 (1948).

102. James E. Cole, "Constitutional Home Rule in New York: The Ghost of Home Rule," 59 *St. John's L. Rev.* 713, 716 (1985).

103. Kenneth VanLandingham, "Constitutional Municipal Home Rule Since the AMA (NLC Model,) 17 *Wm. & Mary L. Rev.* 1 (1975).

104. American Municipal Association, supra. n. 4, 19.

105. Ibid.

106. Ibid.,19–20.

107. Ibid., 23–24.

108. National Municipal League, supra n. 10, 94–100 (6th ed., 1963).

109. Mo. Const., art. VI, § 19(a); Pa. Const., art. IX, § 2.

110. N. Dak. Const., art. VII, § 1.

111. American Municipal Association, supra. n. 4, 20.

112. N.J. Const., art. IV, § 7, par. 9(13), par. 10.

113. N.J. Const., art. IV, § 7, par, 11.

114. *Inganamort v. Borough of Fort Lee*, 62 N.J. 521 (1973).

115. *City of Miami Beach v. Fleetwood Hotel, Inc.*, 261 So. 2d 801 (1972) (Fla. Const., art. VIII, § 2(b)).

116. N. J. Const., art. VIII, § 4, par. 1.

117. *Abbott v. Burke*, 100 N.J. 269 (1985).

118. James Lowell Underwood, 2 *The Constitution of South Carolina: The Journey Toward Local Government* 177–79 (1989).

119. Jon C. Teaford, *The Unheralded Triumph: City Government in America, 1870–1900* 94 (1984).

120. Report of the Commission on Constitutional Revision, *The Constitution of Virginia* 228 (1969).

121. ACIR, supra n. 12, 59.

122. ACIR, *The Organization of Local Public Economies* 39 (1987).

123. Mo. Const., art. VI, § 5, § 14, § 16, 30(a); see, ACIR, *Metropolitan Organization: The St. Louis Case* (1988).

124. La. Const., art. VI, § 15, § 16, § 18, § 19, § 38, § 43.

125. Joseph F. Zimmerman, *State-Local Relations: A Partnership Approach* (1983).

126. Ill. Const., art. VII, § 4(a), 6(a), (b).

127. Ill. Const., art. VII, § 6(a), (f).

128. Rubin G. Cohn, "Municipal Revenue Powers in the Context of Constitutional Home Rule," 51 *N.W.L. Rev.* 17 (1957).

129. Ill. Const., art. VII, § 6(m); § 7, § 8; § 6(c), § 6(l); § 7(l), § 10.

130. Ill. Const., art. VII, § 6(i).

131. Ill. Const., art. VII, § 6(h), (i), (j), (l).

132. ACIR, *State Mandating of Local Expenditures* (1978); Cal. Const., art. XIII B, § 6.

133. Mo. Const., art. X, § 21; art. XII, § 2(6).

134. Pa. Const., art. IX, § 5, § 8.

135. Ariz. Const., art. XIII, § 7; Va. Const., art. VIII, § 7; *School Board of City of Richmond v. Parham*, 218 Va. 950, 243 S.E. 2d 468 (1978).

136. Underwood supra. n. 123, 177–79.

137. William C. Jones, "Municipal Affairs in the California Constitution," 1 *Cal. L. Rev.* 132, 132–34 (1913).

138. Alaska Const., art. X, § 1; Ill. Const., art. VII(m), § 6; Iowa. Const., art. III, § 38A, § 38B; Kan. Const., art. 12, § 4(d); Mich. Const., art. VII, § 34; Mont. Const., art. XI, § 4(2); N.J. Const., art. IV, VII, par. 11; N.M. Const., art. X, § 6; N.Y. Const., art. IX, § 3(c); S.C. Const., art. VIII, § 17; S. Dak. Const., art. IX, § 2; Wyo. Const., art. 13, § 1(d).

139. Millard H. Ruud, "The Legislative Jurisdiction of Texas Home Rule Cities," 37 *Tex. L. Rev.* 682 (1959).

140. Gerald Benjamin, "The Political Relationship," in Gerald Benjamin and Charles Brecher, eds., *The Two New Yorks: State-City Relationships in the Changing Federal System* 146 (1988).

141. *Liberati v. Bristol Bay Borough*, 584 P.2d 1115 (Alaska, 1978).

142. *City of Grass Valley v. Walkinshaw*, 34 Cal. 595, 212 P. 894 (1949); *Bazell v. City of Cincinnati*, 13 Ohio St. 2d 63, 233 N.E. 2d 864 (1968).

143. David O. Sears and Jack Citrin, *Tax Revolt* (1985).

144. Report of the Commission on Constitutional Revision, supra n. 125, 288.

145. A. E. Dick Howard, 2 *Commentaries on the Constitution of Virginia* 811–12 (1974).

146. Talbot D'Alemberte, *The Florida State Constitution* 11 (1991).

147. Elmer Gertz and Joseph P. Pisciotte, *Charter for a New Age* 248–60 (1980).

148. John P. Wheeler, Jr., and Melissa Kinsey, *Magnificent Failure—The Maryland Constitutional Convention of 1967–1968*, 203 (1970).

149. Gertz and Pisciotte, supra, n. 152, 328.

Chapter Six

Voting and Elections

James A. Gardner

Introduction

A basic function of a constitution in a democratic society is to establish the ground rules of politics. A substantial portion of even the sparest American constitutions is devoted to structuring the political process by distributing the franchise, allocating political control over government officials, establishing electoral rules and practices, and assuring the integrity of the electoral process.

Although constitutional responsibility for structuring the political process is shared at the state and national levels, states shoulder significant responsibility in this area. States possess primary authority to create institutions and processes to implement self-government at the state level, subject to federal constitutional limitations, but they also bear considerable responsibility to structure the processes by which even national politics is conducted by determining qualifications for voting in congressional elections, exercising in the first instance the power to regulate the time, place, and manner of congressional elections, and determining how presidential electors are selected.

The states have a long reformist tradition of using state constitutions as vehicles to remake electoral politics. Indeed, the American record of political reform is written overwhelmingly at the state level. The Jacksonian revolution in expansion of the franchise, for example, was effected entirely at the state level, mainly through elimination of restrictive state constitutional property qualifications. Progressivism brought a host of state constitutional reforms including initiatives and referenda; term limits; recall elections; nonpartisanship in local and judicial elections; and in some cases even proportional representation and unicameralism. Today, the tradition of state constitutional reform of politics continues in the form of novel regulation of political parties; increasing constitutionalization of the regulation of campaign finance; and the movement to establish term limits for elected government officials.[1]

145

State power over politics is nevertheless subject to constraints imposed by the U.S. Constitution and by federal civil rights laws. The federal Constitution drastically restricts the grounds on which the franchise may be withheld, making it illegal to deny the right to vote on the basis of race, color, sex, failure to pay a poll tax, or age when a person is eighteen or over.[2] The Equal Protection Clause implements a rule of one-person, one-vote under which all federal, state, and local legislative districts must be of approximately equal population. The Constitution also prohibits discrimination through "vote dilution" worked through gerrymandering or the use in certain circumstances of at-large voting systems. Principles of free speech and association place significant restrictions on the ability of states to regulate candidates' access to the official ballot, the procedures by which political parties nominate candidates, the spending and donation of money in political campaigns, and the substance and timing of political speech itself.

Additional limitations on state authority are imposed by federal statutes. The Voting Rights Act (VRA) bars racial discrimination in all voting practices and procedures, and prohibits states from conditioning voting on passage of a literacy test. Under section 5, the VRA's most restrictive provision, officials in nine states and portions of seven others may not enact any change to existing voting practices and procedures without advance approval by the United States Attorney General or a federal court. Other federal laws with which states must comply proscribe electoral violence and intimidation; regulate voting eligibility in presidential elections; require states to maintain voter registration procedures for federal elections that are convenient and easy to satisfy (the "motor voter" law); and provide standards governing absentee voting by members of the armed forces.

Notwithstanding this federalization of the regulation of politics, state constitutional drafters should devote careful attention to constitutional provisions dealing with voting, elections, and other aspects of political architecture. In the first place, federal law leaves to the states far more areas of discretion than it forecloses, particularly concerning the design and management of their internal political institutions. Second, federal constitutional law can change, so the fact that states are presently foreclosed from exercising certain kinds of discretion does not necessarily mean that they should refrain from making important constitutional choices.

Third, and most important, state constitutional drafters must pay careful attention to the structure of state political and electoral institutions because they must inevitably decide, in drafting the state constitution, how much authority and discretion to grant the state legislature to regulate the state's political processes. Most state constitutions grant legislatures plenary legislative power, meaning that all questions are left to the legislature except those specifically decided by the state constitution. Drafters must therefore choose whether to allocate decisions on legal rules to the people by constitutionalizing them, or to leave such decisions to the legislature to resolve in the course of ordinary legislative politics. While drafters face this decision in virtually every domain of law, the question of whether to constitutionalize legal rules takes on special significance in the realm of structuring and regulating the political process.

An electoral system must be set up fairly and impartially at the outset. Legislators, however, have an obvious self-interest in the structure of electoral politics, since sitting legislators are always the beneficiaries of whatever political structures and practices got them there in the first place and thus are likely to be predisposed against change. This conflict of interest suggests that more rather than fewer significant decisions about the electoral process should be made at the constitutional rather than the legislative level, and probably explains why the most significant recent reforms have been undertaken at the constitutional level through amendment by popular initiative rather than by legislative action.

Constitutionalization may take several forms ranging from explicit, authoritative constitutional decision-making to mere encouragement of legislative action. The most authoritative and explicit constitutional provisions are complete in themselves, such as provisions criminalizing bribing voters or betting on elections. Less explicit provisions might merely direct the legislature to take some specified action. For instance, the Connecticut Constitution does not identify specific election crimes, but instead directs the legislature to "prescribe the offenses" resulting in a loss of voting eligibility.[3]

A third form of constitutionalization that grants governmental actors even greater flexibility involves establishing a constitutional allocation of authority or responsibility for particular electoral functions. Thus, rather than setting out specifically how election returns are to be canvassed and counted, a state constitution might merely designate a particular entity to perform those functions, such as the secretary of state or a state canvassing board. Finally, at the weakest end of the spectrum, drafters might decide to include a provision that does nothing more than express a commitment to certain political or electoral principles. For example, numerous state constitutions provide that "[a]ll political power is inherent in the people."[4] Although such a provision neither requires nor prohibits any government action, it nevertheless expresses a constitutional commitment to a discrete principle of popular sovereignty in a way that might guide state legislative or executive officials in the performance of their duties, and might even help courts give meaning to other provisions of the state constitution with greater legal "bite."

In making these kinds of decisions, drafters and reformers need to pay close attention to the substantive principles that ought to guide their structuring of

the state's democratic institutions. The discussion that follows suggests that attention ought to be paid to several important questions:

1. What are the characteristics of a fair and just electoral process?
2. What constraints on such a process are imposed by federal law, and
    how is compliance best achieved?
3. How trustworthy is the legislature likely to be in using its authority
    to superintend the electoral process?
4. In view of the answer to the previous question, what aspects of the
    electoral system should be constitutionalized rather than delegated
    to the legislature?
5. What level of detail is desirable in constitutionalized provisions given
    the expected characteristics of the legislature and the anticipated risks
    of rigidity associated with excessive constitutional detail in this area?
6. Given that the legislature must be granted at least some, and perhaps
    substantial, authority to regulate the electoral process, what is the
    best way to secure legislative fidelity to constitutionalized principles
    of electoral democracy?

With these principles and questions in mind, the ensuing sections of this chapter review the main areas of current state constitutional practice and then discuss current issues of interest to state constitutional drafters and reformers.

CURRENT STATE CONSTITUTIONAL PRACTICES

The Occasions for Democracy

Certainly the most obvious and in some ways the most significant question regarding the constitutional structure of electoral institutions concerns when and
how often the public is to be afforded opportunities to exercise democratic control over state affairs. State constitutions routinely provide numerous "occasions
for democracy." For example, every state constitution provides for an elected
legislature and governor, and nearly all provide for the election of other executive branch officials such as an attorney general or secretary of state. The majority of state constitutions also provide for the election of local officials such as
county commissioners, sheriffs, district attorneys, clerks, treasurers, and asses-
sors. Most states also provide for popular election of some or all state judges.

   Besides providing opportunities to elect officials, most state constitutions
afford opportunities for direct popular approval of certain kinds of substantive
measures. About half the state constitutions set out procedures for popular initiatives and referenda, but even state constitutions that lack such procedures

typically provide that some kinds of measures cannot take effect without popular approval. At the state level, for example, seven state constitutions require statewide popular approval before legislative measures increasing tax rates may take effect. Many more such requirements appear at the local level, typically requiring popular approval of taxation and borrowing, alteration of county boundaries, adoption or amendment of county and municipal home rule charters, and changes to the form or organization of local government.

This proliferation of opportunities for popular control has sometimes been viewed as an unadulterated good on the theory that since democracy is good, more democracy must be even better. Today, however, in the light of experience, it seems clear that the multiplication of occasions for democracy carries with it certain democratic costs. Voter turnout in the United States is notoriously low in national elections, and even lower for state and local elections. Low turnout, together with "ballot fatigue"—the tendency of voters to lose interest partway through a lengthy ballot—may cause electoral contests to be decided by an extremely small and often unrepresentative portion of the electorate, paradoxically casting doubt on the democratic legitimacy of decisions that have been submitted to the people precisely for the purpose of enhancing their legitimacy.

Voter Eligibility

Every state constitution contains at least some provisions, and in many cases extensive provisions, regarding eligibility to vote, reflecting a judgment that the most significant questions of voter eligibility should be settled by the constitution rather than left to the legislature. These questions involve two distinct factors: (1) a person's competence, both mental and moral, to be entrusted with the franchise; and (2) a person's entitlement to vote either as a member of the relevant political community, or on account of having a stake in the outcome of the electoral process.

Citizenship

Nearly every state expressly requires that voters be citizens of the United States. Delaware, South Carolina, and West Virginia also require that voters be citizens of the state itself. However, the ubiquitous requirement of state residency is functionally equivalent to a requirement of state citizenship, as the Fourteenth Amendment of the U.S. Constitution provides that all citizens of the United States are also automatically citizens of "the State wherein they reside."[5]

States are not required to exclude noncitizens from the franchise and at various times in the past have granted aliens the vote. Pennsylvania, for example, permitted unnaturalized German immigrants to vote in the mid-eighteenth century, and the United States permitted noncitizens to vote in the western territories as part of a deliberate policy to encourage settlement.[6] More recently, a few localities have attempted to extend the right to vote to noncitizen residents, though no state has done so in modern times.

Age

The Twenty-sixth Amendment to the United States Constitution forbids denial of the right to vote to those eighteen years old or older. States are permitted to set the age limit lower, but none has done so.

Residency

Most state constitutions establish a state residency requirement for voting. Some state constitutions also condition voting on residency in a county, town, or election district. Residency is not a self-defining concept, and state constitutions have attempted to give meaning to the term in several ways. The most common approach is to establish a required residency period. Here, it is relevant that the U.S. Supreme Court has invalidated a durational residency requirement of three months, though it has twice upheld residency requirements of fifty days.[7] Rather than set a firm period, some states have required only that residency be "permanent"[8] or "bona fide,"[9] or have delegated to the legislature the task of defining residency more specifically.

Following widely accepted legal principles of domicile, some state constitutions have unlinked the concept of state residency for purposes of voting eligibility from actual physical presence in the state. One common measure, adopted in thirteen states, provides that no person shall be deemed to have lost state residency merely on account of physical absence from the state while performing military service, conducting private business, serving a prison sentence, attending school, or for certain other reasons.[10] Conversely, eleven state constitutions specifically bar any presumption that mere physical presence within the state for the requisite period may establish the required residency by providing that military service within the state is not enough, by itself, to give a person constitutionally sufficient residence. Such provisions must be drafted with care, however, because the U.S. Constitution forbids states from denying members of the military the right to vote merely because of their membership.

In conformity with federal law, many state constitutions provide for the relaxation of residency requirements for purposes of voting in presidential elections. This assures that otherwise eligible voters who move shortly before a presidential election from one state to another, or within a state from one voting jurisdiction to another, will not thereby lose their eligibility to vote for nationwide offices.

Colorado is the only state to have expanded voter eligibility in a few narrowly defined circumstances to nonresidents of the relevant jurisdiction. The pertinent section provides: "No unincorporated area may be annexed to a municipality unless . . . [t]he question of annexation has been submitted to the vote of the *landowners* and the registered electors in the area proposed to be annexed."[11] This provision permits nonresident landowners to vote on questions of municipal annexation.

Registration

Eighteen states have constitutionally established voter registration as a condition of voting eligibility, and five others have expressly authorized the legislature to make registration a condition of voting eligibility. However, since virtually every state that has not constitutionalized the registration requirement nevertheless has found it necessary to maintain a voter registration system to prevent fraud (only North Dakota maintains no system of voter registration), it is not clear what advantage accrues from constitutionalizing the registration requirement.

Property Qualifications

Twelve state constitutions establish property qualifications as a prerequisite to voting in certain special-purpose elections. For example, Arizona and Michigan limit voting on bond issues and special assessments to real-property-tax payers. New Mexico permits only property taxpayers to vote in local elections seeking approval to incur debt. In Florida, only freeholders may vote on whether to exceed local property tax rate limitations, and in Georgia only owners of affected real property may vote on whether to create a community improvement district. While some of these provisions are of dubious validity under the U.S. Constitution (Arizona's was struck down by the Supreme Court),[12] they reflect on the merits a largely obsolete way of thinking about membership in political communities, and state constitutional drafters and reformers should give serious consideration to eliminating property qualifications on voting.

Early property qualifications for the franchise typically were justified on the ground that the lack of property made individuals unduly dependent on their social and economic superiors.[13] This belief soon was supplanted by Jacksonian notions of equality, and today wealth and property ownership qualifications are generally disfavored under the U.S. Constitution.[14] Nevertheless, some states continue to impose property qualifications for certain highly specialized local government offices, such as agricultural water storage and reclamation districts, and the U.S. Supreme Court has in some cases sustained them.[15]

States typically defend modern property qualifications on the ground that certain government policies are so narrow in scope, and so disproportionately affect property owners, that only property owners have a genuine stake in managing those policies through voting. This argument proves too much. Many government programs such as food stamps or soybean subsidies affect only a narrow and well-defined class of citizens, yet we do not typically delegate control over those programs to specialized officials elected exclusively by food stamp recipients or soybean farmers. Moreover, single-purpose agencies and ballot measures preclude the kind of negotiation and logrolling that occurs in general purpose legislatures, amplifying the power of property owners to establish policies that affect them without the need to consider the interests of other political constituencies. Finally, it is rare that even the most narrowly targeted government functions and programs truly lack any significant spillover effects on nonproperty owners.

A few state constitutions have taken a very different approach to property qualifications by banning them outright. For example, the North Carolina Constitution provides: "As political rights and privileges are not dependent upon or modified by property, no property qualification shall affect the right to vote or hold office."[16]

Disqualification for Mental Incompetence

Thirty-five state constitutions expressly disqualify from voting persons suffering from a serious mental disability. Most affirmatively require disqualification on this ground, although four states merely authorize disqualification by the legislature. As with the disqualification of minors, such provisions reflect a commonplace and fundamentally sound belief that popular political decisions should be well-considered and rational, and that meaningful, rational participation in politics requires some minimal level of mental competence.

Defining the relevant mental disability is a complex task, and no state constitution attempts to do so. Most implicitly leave further definition of the conditions of ineligibility to the legislature by incorporating by reference standard legal concepts of mental disability (e.g., "insane," "non compos mentis") that are within the province of the legislature to define. Oregon's unique provision combines disqualification for mental incompetence with an extension of protection against disqualification to the merely disabled: "A person suffering from a mental handicap is entitled to the full rights of an elector, if otherwise qualified, unless the person has been adjudicated incompetent to vote as provided by law."[17]

Disqualification for Felony Conviction

The constitutions of forty-three states provide for the disqualification from voting of those convicted of serious crimes. Some state constitutions require disqualification on conviction of an "infamous crime,"[18] or a crime of "moral turpitude."[19] Most specify disqualification on conviction of "a felony."[20] Disqualification is usually mandatory, although in eight states the legislature is merely authorized to enact disqualifying legislation. In some states, convicted felons are disqualified from voting only while serving their prison terms; others also disfranchise felons on parole. The state constitutions are almost evenly divided between those that provide for permanent disqualification and those that provide for requalification on formal restoration of civil rights. However, the prospect of restoration of civil rights is widely thought to be illusory because the procedure for restoring civil rights is so difficult and so rarely navigated successfully by convicted felons. Typically, restoration of civil rights requires individualized action by the governor, and most governors grant very few clemency petitions of any kind. Under the Mississippi Constitution, a convicted felon's civil rights may be restored only upon a two-thirds vote of each house of the state legislature,[21] making it just as difficult to restore a felon's civil rights as to amend the state constitution.

The practice of disqualifying those convicted of felonies has a significant impact on voting eligibility around the nation. It is estimated that nearly four million American citizens presently cannot vote as a result of felony convictions, including over one million who have completed their sentences. Largely as a result of the increased severity and stepped-up enforcement of drug laws over the last two decades, the impact of felon disfranchisement provisions has tended to fall increasingly on African-Americans, and particularly on African-American men. Nationwide, approximately 1.4 million African-American males of voting age—thirteen percent of that population group—are currently disfranchised. About 440,000 of that group have completed their sentences.

Felon disfranchisement has unsavory roots in Jim Crow efforts to suppress African-American voting strength. Many late nineteenth- and early twentieth-century felon disfranchisement provisions were added to state constitutions in a deliberate attempt to specify disqualifying crimes that were believed to be committed more often by African-Americans and thus disproportionately to deprive African-Americans of the right to vote. The United State Supreme Court has held that felon disfranchisement provisions added to state constitutions for the purpose of racial discrimination violate the Equal Protection Clause of the U.S. Constitution.[22] However, the Court also has acknowledged that felon disqualification can serve legitimate purposes, and that disqualification provisions adopted for nondiscriminatory reasons are expressly permitted by Section 2 of the Fourteenth Amendment.[23] In addition, some suspect older provisions can be and have been "sanitized" by later nondiscriminatory readoption or amendment.[24]

The best justification for disqualification of felons is that commission of a serious crime constitutes a fundamental breach of the social contract. While this reasoning may justify disfranchisement during periods of criminal punishment, it provides little justification for permanent disqualification. Those who serve out prison terms generally are understood to have "paid their debt" to society. If the social contract is suspended during imprisonment and restored on its conclusion, it is unclear what legitimate purpose is served by permanent disqualification.

Disqualification for Electoral Crimes
Delaware, Kentucky, Maryland, New York, Pennsylvania, Utah, Vermont, and West Virginia provide specifically for permanent disqualification of individuals who commit election fraud by offering bribes to voters to register or to vote, or for the commission of other crimes against the elective franchise. The Maine Constitution provides that disqualification for conviction of election bribery may extend for no more than ten years. A stronger case may be made for permanent disqualification of persons who have committed crimes against the electoral process itself than for those who have committed ordinary crimes against the person or property of another. One who commits election fraud not only has shown a specific disregard for the ground rules of politics established by the social contract, but also may be said to present a threat to the basic processes of self-governance that assure the legitimacy of governmental power. In these circumstances, permanent disfranchisement may constitute both just desert as well as a prudent precautionary measure for the protection of the electoral process.

Political Rights

Every state constitution contains at least some provisions protecting broad classes of individual rights—for example, the freedoms of speech and assembly—that play some kind of role in enabling citizens and voters to participate meaningfully in the political process. Other provisions relate to the structure of popular sovereignty. For example, many state constitutions provide that "[a]ll political power is inherent in the people"[25] or that governments are "founded on their authority."[26] Some provide that governments derive their powers from popular consent or that government officials are trustees or servants of the people, and many provide that the people have a right to change the form of government whenever they wish. Thirteen states specifically enumerate a right of the people to "instruct" their representatives.[27] Many states require that elections be "free,"[28] or "free and equal,"[29] or "free and open."[30]

These declarations may be important statements of principle, but they do relatively little actual work in structuring popular self-government. Those provisions with federal counterparts, such as the freedom of speech, have rarely been construed to provide protection beyond that afforded by the U.S. Constitution. Although some provisions, such as the right to instruct representatives or the provisions requiring elections to be free and equal, seem at first glance to have potentially significant applications to electoral politics, in practice they have been either ignored or interpreted by state courts to have little practical significance.[31] Most recently adopted state constitutions, such as Alaska's and Hawaii's, dispense with elaborate articulations of political rights.

Specific Protections for Voting

In addition to establishing broad political rights, most state constitutions also seek to protect democratic self-government in ways that are more specifically targeted toward voting and the electoral process.

Limitations on Substantive Grounds of Denial of Right to Vote

A few state constitutions provide specific substantive protection for the right to vote, most commonly by limiting the grounds on which it may be denied. For example, various state constitutions prohibit denial of the right to vote on the grounds of race, sex, property qualifications, nonpayment of a tax, and culture or social origin. Some establish due process-style procedural protections for the right to vote by providing that no citizen may be disfranchised "unless by the law of the land."[32] Although these kinds of provisions tend to duplicate protections available under the federal Constitution, they may also provide a basis for establishing state constitutional protections that exceed federal minima.

Protection from Physical Interference

Many states constitutionalize rules protecting elections from violence or physical interference with voting. One provision, found in similar form in fourteen constitutions, provides: "no power, civil or military, shall at any time interfere to prevent the free exercise of the right of suffrage."[33] Twenty-seven state constitutions establish an election-day privilege under which voters engaged in the act of voting, or in transit to or from the polls, may not be subjected to civil legal process or to criminal arrest for any crime less than a felony. A typical provision is Indiana's, which provides: "In all cases, except treason, felony, and breach of the peace, electors shall be free from arrest, in going to elections, during their attendance there, and in returning from the same."[34] Nine states additionally privilege voters from performing state military service on election day except in time of war or danger.

Access to polling places for the physically disabled is required by federal law. However, Kentucky and New Hampshire have constitutionalized specific provisions requiring access for the disabled.

Protection of Secrecy

Another commonly provided protection for the right to vote requires preservation of secrecy in voting. Twenty-eight state constitutions contain such a provision. A typical provision is Wisconsin's, which declares: "All votes shall be by secret ballot."[35]

Election Crimes

A few states also protect the electoral process by constitutionalizing specific election crimes, most commonly bribery. Since states that do not define these crimes at the constitutional level tend to include them in their election codes anyway, the benefits of constitutionalization are unclear.

Direction to Legislature to Enact Protective Legislation

By far the most common kind of state constitutional provision protecting the right to vote directs the legislature to take specific regulatory action, such as enacting certain kinds of laws to protect the electoral process. For example, eight states require the legislature to pass laws prohibiting "all undue influence [on elections], from power, bribery, tumult, and other improper conduct,"[36] and thirteen require it to pass laws to secure the "purity"[37] or the "integrity"[38] of elections.

Because state constitutions tend to grant legislatures plenary power, such provisions are probably unnecessary as grants of regulatory authority, and legislatures in states that lack specific directives to enact these kinds of laws tend to do so anyway. On the other hand, provisions directing legislative action may prove useful, if not always enforceable, by offering guidance to the legislature concerning the scope of its duties or by expressing a constitutional commitment to particular electoral processes.

Election Procedures

In regulating the procedures by which elections are to be conducted, state constitutions generally pursue one or more of three strategies: (1) granting legislative authority to regulate specific areas of election procedure, or specifically directing the legislature to regulate certain subjects; (2) granting authority to specific officials to administer elections; and (3) constitutionalizing specific procedures to be followed in the electoral process.

Grants of Legislative Authority

State constitutions specifically grant legislatures a wide variety of powers to regulate electoral procedures. Some of these grants are extremely broad and unspecific. For example, the Maryland Constitution provides: "The General Assembly shall have power to regulate by Law . . . all matters which relate to the Judges of election, time, place and manner of holding elections in this State, and of making returns thereof."[39] Often these provisions direct the legislature to regulate the electoral process. The Alabama Constitution, for example, provides: "The legislature shall pass laws . . . to regulate and govern elections."[40] Others direct legislative regulatory action with greater specificity, requiring legislatures to set the date for general elections, prescribe methods of voting, establish a system of voter registration, provide for absentee voting, regulate the use of voting machines, and regulate many other aspects of the electoral process.

These specific grants of regulatory authority tend to be superfluous because the legislature is generally deemed to possess plenary power. Furthermore, the more specific the constitutional directive, the less flexibility the legislature retains to respond to changed conditions in the electoral environment. A more flexible approach would be to specify the goals for which electoral regulation should be undertaken rather than the specific kinds of measures to be implemented. For example, rather than require the legislature to establish systems of voter registration, a state constitution might provide that electoral regulation should be undertaken so as to promote accuracy and prevent fraud; rather than require a system of absentee voting, it could require any electoral system to preserve the voting rights of the elderly, physically disabled, homebound, or those absent temporarily from the state.

Allocation of Authority to Administer Elections
Every electoral system requires some authority to implement and administer it. The choice of administrative authority may be important. For elections to serve as vehicles for the expression of popular will, they must be administered fairly and impartially, and there is obvious danger in entrusting to elected officials control over the very apparatus by which they may be ousted from office. These considerations suggest that those who administer elections ought to have some degree of independence from those who have a stake in electoral outcomes.

Perhaps surprisingly, more than half the state constitutions are silent concerning the allocation of authority to administer elections, implicitly leaving the subject to the legislature, or provide only that the legislature is to decide on the process of electoral administration. However, those that expressly address the issue generally pursue one of three different strategies to secure the integrity and independence of electoral administration. One strategy is to allocate the canvassing function to an official who is independently electorally accountable to the public. Louisiana goes the furthest, granting general responsibility for administering elections to the secretary of state, an independently elected official. Six states grant the secretary of state the somewhat narrower authority to oversee the process of canvassing votes for some or all constitutional offices. Connecticut creates a board of canvassers consisting of three independently elected state officials: the treasurer, secretary of state, and comptroller.

A second strategy is to apply constitutional principles of blended power to the allocation of administrative authority by creating canvassing boards consisting of officials from branches of government other than the one whose votes are being counted. Minnesota, for example, creates a hybrid board of canvassers consisting of the secretary of state, two supreme court judges, and two "disinterested" district court judges.[41] Delaware, in which all judges are appointed, and Nevada, in which they are all elected, both provide for vote canvassing to be conducted by courts.

The third and probably weakest strategy is to create an appointed, politically dependent canvassing authority, but to increase its independence by requiring its membership to be bipartisan. Illinois and Oklahoma, for example, require the creation of a bipartisan state board of elections, and Virginia requires bipartisan local election boards; New York authorizes, but does not require, creation of bipartisan election boards to administer state and county elections.

In spite of this constitutional interest in fostering independence in the administration of elections, there is little evidence that election administrators are any less independent in those states where provision for administration is left entirely to legislative discretion.

Threshold of Victory

Although democracy is generally associated with majority rule, virtually every state that has constitutionalized an electoral threshold of victory has chosen to award elections to the candidate who wins a plurality of the votes cast. Only Vermont requires a true majority of votes, in executive branch elections.[42] A typical provision is Missouri's, which states: "[t]he persons having the highest number of votes for the respective offices shall be declared elected."[43]

Requiring only a plurality for election has certain advantages. A winner can nearly always be determined after just one round of voting, reducing the cost of holding elections without any loss of clarity in identifying the winner. Also, when elections require additional rounds of voting, as with the use of runoff elections, voter interest often wanes, leading to lower turnout in the later rounds. The use of a plurality system also makes it easier for independents and minor party candidates to compete successfully. During the 1990s, independent governors such as Jesse Ventura (Minnesota 1998, 38%), Angus King (Maine 1994, 35%), Walter Hickel (Alaska 1990, 39%), and Lowell Weicker (Connecticut 1990, 40%), all were elected with less than an absolute majority of votes cast. The same property is sometimes thought to make the plurality format more congenial to female or minority candidates.

On the other hand, officials who assume office with the backing of less than a majority of those voting sometimes suffer from a perceived lack of legitimacy. Moreover, the very qualities that make the plurality format more congenial to third party candidates also make it more vulnerable to candidacies of undesirable or unqualified candidates. Finally, although a majority vote requirement in a runoff format does not in itself violate the federal Voting Rights Act,[44] it would violate the Fourteenth or Fifteenth Amendments of the federal Constitution if adopted deliberately for the purpose of obstructing the success of candidates backed by racial minorities.

Tie-breaking Procedures
Another widely constitutionalized basic electoral ground rule is a procedure to break electoral ties. Most state constitutions provide that in case of a tie in gubernatorial and other executive branch races, the legislature, meeting in joint session, selects one of the tied candidates by joint vote. In Mississippi, the choice is made by the house of representatives alone. In Illinois and Kentucky, ties are broken by drawing lots.

In legislative races, twenty-eight state constitutions contain a provision much like Rhode Island's, which provides: "Each house shall be the judge of the elections and qualifications of its members."[45] This provision has the disadvantage of appointing the legislature final judge in its own cause, a practice that has traditionally been justified on the ground that lodging final authority over legislative elections in any other organ of government would unduly endanger legislative independence. Two states, however, do not follow this model: Maryland, which holds a new election, and North Dakota, in which ties in legislative races are broken by the secretary of state, who tosses a coin.

Nonpartisanship
Since the Progressive era, proponents of nonpartisanship have argued that party competition is destructive of cooperative political life, as well as unnecessary because most governmental functions require administrative skill rather than policy judgment. On this view, government officials should be chosen for their expertise and personal integrity rather than on the basis of their partisan affiliation. Political scientists, however, have often criticized nonpartisanship for weakening political parties and for increasing the electoral advantage of incumbents.

The highest visibility instance of constitutionally required nonpartisanship in the United States is Nebraska's unique establishment of a nonpartisan (and unicameral) state legislature. Although thousands of municipalities across the nation have adopted nonpartisanship as a matter of local choice, only California constitutionally requires it in county and municipal elections. The constitutions of California, Florida, and West Virginia require local school board elections to be nonpartisan. Hawaii and Nebraska require nonpartisan elections for the state board of education. Massachusetts, Ohio, Rhode Island, and Utah require local charter commissions to be elected on a nonpartisan ticket. Sixteen states, however, constitutionally require some or all judicial elections to be nonpartisan.

Specific Procedural Choices
Finally, many state constitutions approach certain aspects of the electoral process at a much greater level of specificity, constitutionalizing a wide variety of highly specific procedural choices. Among these are provisions setting the date for elections, the location and hours of polling places, the methods of recording votes, the content and presentation of information contained on ballots, details of voter registration, methods of proving eligibility to vote,

requirements for absentee voting, procedures for contesting elections, and many others.

Constitutionalization at a high level of specificity risks obsolescence, and the results are often painfully apparent in state constitutional provisions dealing with elections. For example, in this dawning age of electronic voting, numerous state constitutions still require votes to be cast by "ballot,"[46] one requires voting to be by "written ballot,"[47] and two, in sadly unsuccessful attempts to be more modern, require voting to be by "ballot" or any "mechanical" method.[48] Similarly, at a time when states are experimenting with extending the voting period by using early voting procedures and voting by mail, it makes little sense for a state constitution to specify either the location of polling places or their hours. Again, a better approach, if any constitutionalization is thought necessary, is to specify the values that electoral regulations must advance—accuracy, speed, convenience, and prevention of fraud, for example—rather than the precise procedures to be used.

Apportionment

One of the most important political functions states routinely perform is apportionment—that is, the division of the state and its localities into districts for purposes of electing members of multimember bodies such as legislatures, executive boards and commissions, and courts.

When Apportionment Is Required
The federal Apportionment Act, with which states must comply, requires members of Congress to be elected from districts rather than at large. Art. II, sec. 1 of the federal Constitution leaves to state legislatures decisions concerning how electors are to be selected in presidential contests, and it is well within the legislative discretion to apportion the state into presidential elector districts. As of 2004, only two states, Maine and Nebraska, select presidential electors from districts, though they do not undertake a separate apportionment for that purpose. Instead, one presidential elector is elected from each existing congressional district, and the winner of the statewide popular vote is awarded two additional electors at large.

The main exercise of state discretion in apportionment lies in its choice of how to structure representation in the state legislature, county and municipal legislatures, courts, and various multimember elected boards and commissions, such as boards of education. The choice between representation at large or by district is typically informed by notions of (1) who or what is appropriately represented, and (2) what representation ought primarily to accomplish. Where a jurisdiction is thought to be inhabited by a united polity with substantially similar interests and outlooks, election at large might be the more appropriate choice, although its feasibility is limited to some extent by the size of the jurisdiction and the number of representatives to be elected. Election at large is typically said to produce representatives who possess a jurisdiction-wide outlook rather than an interest in a particular region or neighborhood. Conversely, where a jurisdiction is thought to be inhabited by a collection of predominantly different groups with diverse interests and beliefs, representation by district may be the method of choice, so that representatives can monitor and advance the interests of their particular constituency (although this outlook need not be incompatible with a broader interest in the common welfare). Similarly, if the main function of representatives is thought to be participating in the making of policy for the benefit of the entire jurisdiction, at-large election might be the more appropriate vehicle. If a representative's main function is thought to be providing constituent service, then election by district may secure better constituent access and more efficient service from officials.

Election at large and election by district are not mutually exclusive. A jurisdiction might, for example, elect some representatives at large and others by district, as in Maine and Nebraska's systems for electing presidential electors. It is also possible for a jurisdiction to combine representation by district and at large by creating a mix of single-member and multimember districts, or by the use of "floterial" districts, which are at-large districts created from two or more contiguous single-member districts.[49]

In the aftermath of the Supreme Court's one-person, one-vote rulings and the enactment of the Voting Rights Act, most state constitutions provide either expressly or implicitly for the election of state representatives and senators exclusively from single-member districts. Alaska, for example, provides expressly that the redistricting authority "shall establish forty house districts, with each house district to elect one member of the house of representatives."[50]

The one significant exception to this trend is West Virginia, in which state legislators are elected from a mix of single-member and multimember districts. The West Virginia Constitution expressly provides that "[e]very [senatorial] district shall elect two senators."[51] It also structures the allocation of representation in the house of delegates in such a way as to produce numerous multimember delegate districts; during the 2002 election, for example, Kanawha County, which contains Charleston, elected seven delegates.

About half the state constitutions expressly require the division of the state into judicial districts, most commonly for purposes of allocating and electing lower court judges. Several states expressly prohibit statewide at-large judicial elections. Practices respecting states' highest courts vary: California and Idaho require supreme court judges to be elected at large; Oklahoma requires them to be elected by district; North Carolina authorizes the legislature to choose either method.

State constitutions have much less to say about districting for elections to other offices, with only a handful constitutionalizing requirements for state boards of education, statewide service authority boards, county legislatures, and local charter commissions. Decisions about apportioning local jurisdictions are often left to the relevant localities, at least when they possess home rule authority.

Basis of Apportionment

Although the Equal Protection Clause of the U.S. Constitution requires districts for most offices to contain substantially equal numbers of people, it does not require any particular method of counting represented populations; states are thus free to include or exclude such groups as "aliens, transients, short-term or temporary residents, or persons denied the vote for conviction of crime."[52] The Supreme Court has suggested, however, that the use of registered or actual voters as a benchmark would be prohibited.

How the population of districts is measured has implications for the distribution of political power. A decision to exclude aliens or minors, for example, may disproportionately affect districts containing high concentrations of recent immigrants, a complaint sometimes heard from Latino groups. Similarly, a decision to count disfranchised felons increases the proportionate political clout of eligible voters within a rural prison district without exposing them to political competition from incarcerated populations.

About half the state constitutions do not specify the population basis for apportionment, thereby leaving the decision to the legislature. Of the remainder, most require apportionment based on "population." Ten states use the term "inhabitants." Ohio requires the use of "whole population." Texas uses "qualified electors" in senatorial redistricting. Maine, Nebraska, and New York specifically exclude aliens. Kansas and Washington exclude nonresident military personnel. Kansas also excludes nonresident students, although it includes resident military personnel and students.

Timing of Apportionment

Most state constitutions use the completion of the decennial federal census as the trigger for reapportionment. About half go on to provide that reapportionment is to take place only every ten years, or in some cases not until completion of the next federal census. However, fifteen states provide for the redrawing of districts for some or all offices more frequently than every ten years. Texas, for example, permits reapportionment "as the necessity appears."[53] In practice, however, legislatures generally do not undertake the politically divisive task of reapportionment more often than legally required. Recently, however, state legislatures in Colorado and Texas performed an unusual additional round of congressional redistricting after political control of the legislature changed hands in the 2002 election cycle. The Colorado Supreme Court invalidated the 2002 redistricting under the state constitution and a court challenge is pending in Texas. It is too early to tell whether these redistrictings are merely aberrations or presage a new tolerance for more frequent reapportionment.

Authority to Apportion

State constitutions generally allocate the authority to conduct legislative apportionment either to the legislature itself, or to an independent board or commission. The main problem with permitting a legislature to reapportion itself is, of course, that incumbent officials may assure their own continuance in office, and the continuance in office of other members of their party, through gerrymandering.

It is not clear, however, that allocating redistricting authority to commissions will solve the problem of partisan gerrymandering. The political forces organizing legislatures may well reappear in redistricting commissions, particularly when its members are appointed by partisan officials, as is the case in most commission states. Perhaps more importantly, thanks to computerization, the precise impact of any redistricting criterion that a commission might adopt, even for use in a mechanically applied redistricting algorithm, can be known in advance. This requires redistricting commissions to evaluate any proposed plans, algorithms, or redistricting criteria, and it is unclear how they would do so other than through the exercise of subjective judgment. This, in turn, suggests countervailing dangers of redistricting by commission: unlike legislatures, commissions tend to be anonymous, temporary, and democratically unaccountable. Finally, there is at present no systematic evidence to suggest that incumbency is less of an advantage when commissions rather than legislatures control the redistricting process.

In practice, thirty-six state constitutions opt for legislative apportionment, either through express delegation or omission to provide otherwise, although a substantial minority of fourteen provide for an independent redistricting commission. Such commissions are most commonly bipartisan, composed either of legislative leaders from each party or their designees. Some states combine the two apportionment models by using different methods to redistrict different bodies. For example, Colorado and Missouri designate a commission to redistrict the state legislature, but require the state legislature to conduct congressional redistricting. The picture is further complicated by the fact that the constitutional allocation of redistricting authority to the legislature does not necessarily preclude the legislature from redelegating that authority by statute to an independent commission, as in Iowa.

Another important variable concerns procedures where the primary apportionment authority fails to adopt a plan. In Connecticut, Illinois, Mississippi, Oklahoma, and Texas, the failure of the legislature to adopt a plan triggers appointment of a redistricting commission. In Florida, Iowa, Louisiana, Maine, South Dakota, Vermont, and Washington, and in Mississippi in the case of judicial redistricting, if the legislature fails to adopt a redistricting plan, apportionment authority devolves on the state supreme court. In commission states, failure of the commission to adopt a plan most commonly results in redistricting authority vesting in the supreme court (Michigan, New Jersey, and Oregon).

For nonlegislative offices, the legislature is nearly always chosen to perform the apportionment. For example, nearly half the state constitutions specifically appoint the legislature to divide the state into judicial districts, although North Dakota assigns this responsibility to the supreme court. Methods for county and municipal apportionment are not typically specified, presumably leaving the choice to the legislature. The constitutions of a few states, such as Florida, New Mexico, Tennessee, and Texas, specifically delegate the authority to conduct local apportionment to the relevant local legislature.

Required Qualities of Apportioned Districts

The single most important quality that apportioned districts must possess is demanded by the federally mandated rule of one-person, one-vote: they must be equipopulous. This rule, which overrides all others, is applied strictly to congressional districts: essentially no deviation from exact population equality is permitted.[54] When drawing state legislative districts, redistricters are allowed somewhat greater latitude: the Fourteenth Amendment requires only that such districts be "as nearly of equal population as practicable."[55] In practice, federal courts have applied this requirement so as give states freedom to draw legislative districts that deviate from exact equality by up to 10 percent; greater deviations generally will be sustained only if the state produces a convincing justification. Twenty-nine state constitutions impose their own requirement of population equality in districting for at least some kinds of districts. For example, the Washington Constitution provides: "Each district shall contain a population . . . as nearly equal as practicable to the population of any other district."[56] Colorado and Ohio impose more rigorous requirements than federal law by limiting population deviations between districts in most circumstances to 5 percent. New York provides that population discrepancies between districts may not exceed the population of any town or city block in an immediately adjoining district.

The great majority of state constitutions provide additional criteria to guide the redistricting process, most dealing primarily with the shape and boundaries of election districts. Establishment of these criteria serves two distinct purposes. First, such criteria impose additional constraints on the discretion of redistricting authorities, a tactic meant to further reduce opportunities for successful gerrymandering. However, now that computers can predict the partisan impact of minute changes in district contours with great accuracy, it is unclear how successful such constraints can be. A second purpose of regulating the shape of election districts lies in the belief that such districts demarcate distinct political communities whose citizens share interests, beliefs, and a way of life that ought to be preserved.

Following these principles, thirty-six state constitutions provide expressly that election districts for at least some legislative chambers be "contiguous." State courts have tended to interpret this requirement deferentially, particularly where districts contain or detour around bodies of water.[57] The Ohio Constitution further defines contiguity by providing: "the boundary of each [house] district shall be a single nonintersecting continuous line."[58] Twenty-four states require election districts to be "compact." Colorado is more specific: it requires that "the aggregate linear distance of all district boundaries shall be as short as possible."[59] Michigan, Minnesota, Missouri, New York, Washington, and Wisconsin also require districts to be "convenient," a now archaic term that is sometimes taken to refer to the ability of citizens or candidates to travel easily about the district.[60] Michigan additionally requires certain senatorial districts to be "as rectangular" and "as nearly uniform in shape as possible."[61] It is not clear, however, that provisions restricting allowable district shape have had any appreciable constraining effect on redistricting practices.[62]

Many constitutions require that certain kinds of local government boundaries be respected to varying degrees in drawing legislative districts. A relatively weak provision is Alaska's, which requires only that "[c]onsideration may be given to local government boundaries."[63] At the other extreme, many states expressly prohibit the division of counties, towns, or municipalities. A rule banning entirely the division of a unit as large as a county is extremely difficult to observe without violating the equipopulation requirement, and is likely a relic from an era when representation was allocated explicitly among counties. Between these extremes lie rules such as Nebraska's, which provides that "county lines shall be followed whenever practicable,"[64] or Maine's, which provides that districts "shall cross political subdivision lines the least number of times necessary to establish as nearly as practicable equally populated districts."[65]

Three state constitutions cut more directly to the idea that election districts should be coherent political communities. The Alaska Constitution provides that legislative districts should contain "as nearly as practicable a relatively integrated socio-economic area."[66] The Hawaii Constitution similarly provides: "submergence of an area in a larger district wherein substantially different socio-economic interests predominate shall be avoided."[67] More comprehensively, the Colorado Constitution provides: "communities of interest, including ethnic, cultural, economic, trade area, geographic, and demographic factors, shall be preserved within a single district wherever possible."[68] Delaware, Hawaii, and Washington try to achieve fairness in redistricting even more directly by requiring that districts not unduly favor or discriminate against any person, group, or political party.

Far fewer state constitutions regulate the qualities of districts drawn for nonlegislative state offices and local offices. The one-person, one-vote requirement does not apply to judicial elections,[69] so states are generally free to draw judicial districts, and to assign judges to them, for reasons other than equalization of population. The constitutions of Mississippi, New York, and Ohio, for example, direct the legislature to allocate judges to judicial districts based not only on population, but also on factors such as the district's caseload. A few states require judicial districts to conform to county lines. Nevertheless, nine states independently impose conditions on the drawing of judicial districts that resemble the constraints imposed by the federal equipopulation requirement.[70]

Even fewer state constitutions establish requirements for local government districts. The constitutions of Florida, New Mexico, and Virginia contain an equipopulation requirement for local government districting, and all three require local legislative districts to be contiguous. New Mexico and Virginia also require such districts to be compact.

THE REFORM AGENDA

Reformers have most often been motivated by a desire to address a relatively small number of issues that they have repeatedly identified as problems of American democracy. These include the following:

- insufficient citizen participation in politics, including low voter turnout;
- insufficient voter competence caused by a lack of information, interest, or both;
- insufficient citizen control over elected officials;
- a lack of adequate political virtue in voters, elected officials, or both;
- insufficient representativeness of legislatures;
- political inequality with respect to race, gender, class, geographical region, or other factors.

A wide variety of reformers, from Jacksonians in the early eighteenth century, to Progressives and women suffragists in the early twentieth century, to civil rights activists in the 1950s and 1960s, maintained not only that politics could be reformed through law, but that change at the constitutional level was the most reliable way to achieve it. Although some of these political reform movements were astonishingly successful at achieving constitutional change, none fully accomplished all its goals. In contemplating state constitutional reform of the electoral process, then, a good place to start is with the unfinished business of the major political reform movements of the past. The immediately following section reviews some of the most significant unfulfilled or only partially fulfilled reform proposals of the past, while the final section briefly examines some of the most pressing contemporary reform issues.

Unfulfilled and Partially Fulfilled Agenda Items of Past Reform Movements

Easier and More Convenient Voting

The Progressives were the first to raise systematic complaints about the difficulty of voting, primarily in response to concerns about declining voter turnout during the 1920s. They attributed this problem to the excessive length and complexity of ballots, and largely succeeded in reducing ballot length by lowering the number of elective offices.[71] Today, low voter turnout still is often deemed a problem, and efforts continue to increase turnout by making voting easier and more convenient. The process of voter registration in the United States is among the most onerous in the world, and some reform efforts, such as the federal National Voter Registration Act ("Motor Voter"), aim to lessen the burden. Turnout figures since passage of this law suggest that it has not had the anticipated impact.

Other efforts to make voting easier include improving polling place access for the disabled, and expanding the period during which votes may be cast beyond Election Day itself by providing an "early voting" procedure under which voters who would not otherwise qualify for absentee ballots may mail in ballots in advance of Election Day. It is also possible that the ballot is still too long for many voters, and shortening it by further reducing the number of elective offices might make voting easier.

Pursuit of many of these reforms need not require constitutionalization so long as the legislature possesses authority to enact them on its own, although care should be taken to avoid inadvertently prohibiting legislative experimentation through excessive constitutional specificity. Even the number of local elective offices may be and frequently is left to legislative discretion. Under the Wyoming Constitution, for example, "[t]he legislature shall provide by law for the election of such county officers as may be necessary";[72] the Nevada Constitution grants the legislature "power to increase, diminish, consolidate or abolish" certain county offices.[73]

Alternative Voting Systems

Reformers have long criticized the standard American voting system in which contested offices are awarded after a single round of voting to the candidate winning a plurality of the vote within a single-member district. This system is said to overrepresent the winning majority or plurality coalition, and thus to produce a legislature that is both unrepresentative of, and therefore insufficiently responsive to, public opinion in its full complexity. Also, by allowing voters to vote for only one candidate, the system has been said to be unnecessarily blunt by depriving voters of the opportunity to register either their relative preferences among candidates or the intensity of their preferences.

The Progressive reform agenda frequently included efforts to replace this voting system with a more sensitive one, most commonly proportional representation (PR).[74] In proportional representation, candidates are elected at large from multimember districts, and voters are permitted to vote for multiple candidates and to rank-order their preferences. Votes are then tabulated so as to produce a legislature in which candidates' chances of gaining a seat are proportional to their support in the electorate. This allows for representatives with a greater variety of views that correspond more closely to the distribution of views within the electorate, and greatly increases the possibility that the voice of sizable political minorities will be heard within the legislature.

By 1950, PR had been adopted in about two dozen American cities, most notably in the major cities of Ohio.[75] Although proportional and semiproportional systems are used increasingly around the world (e.g., Ireland, Israel, Germany, and New Zealand), PR eventually fell out of favor in the United States, and is rarely used today. The constitutions of only two states, Oregon and West Virginia, mention PR at all, and then only to authorize the legislature to employ it.[76]

A completely different alternative voting system that reformers have sometimes proposed is instant runoff voting (IRV). IRV is intended to assure that offices are filled only by candidates who have the backing of a majority of voters, but without the need for additional rounds of voting, and the attendant expense and additional campaigning, when no candidate wins a majority on the first ballot. In IRV, voters rank candidates in order of preference. When the first-choice votes are tallied and no candidate earns a majority, a paper runoff is held by dropping the candidate with the lowest number of first-place votes, and substituting the second-choice candidates of voters who had ranked the dropped candidate in first place. This process is continued until one candidate has a majority. Despite its simplicity and uncontested advantages, IRV is used only in San Francisco, Oakland, and a few other municipalities. In 2002, Alaska voters rejected an initiative that would have implemented IRV in most statewide races.

Devolution of Political Authority
Numerous and varied reform movements have contended that political authority should be exercised at the most local level possible. According to these reformers, devolution of political power not only increases the ability of citizens to exercise close control over the most significant decisions made by government, but also improves the quality of political life by giving more people a chance to become meaningfully involved in politics. To some extent, this position has been institutionalized in state constitutions through a largely successful movement for local home rule authority. However, home rule authority varies considerably from state to state, and a great many highly significant decisions are still made at the state level even in strong home rule states. Many

problems, moreover, such as environmental and resource management issues, may be best handled at a regional rather than local level. Very few state constitutions provide for the exercise of regional authority. One of the few is Virginia's, which provides: "The General Assembly shall provide . . . for the organization, government, powers, change of boundaries, consolidation, and dissolution of . . . regional governments."[77]

Direct Democracy
A significant article in the Progressive reform agenda, direct democracy through initiative and referendum has been implemented with considerable success by past generations of reformers. Although provisions for direct democracy have typically been justified as a way of making government more responsive to the popular will, direct democratic lawmaking has rarely been understood to be intrinsically superior to lawmaking through traditional forms of representation. Reformers have generally claimed only that representative democracy periodically becomes perverted by legislative incompetence or corruption, and that direct democracy provides a needed corrective.[78]

About half the state constitutions, mostly of western states, provide procedures for direct democracy at the state level through a process of voter-initiated lawmaking or constitutional amendment. Attempts to introduce similar procedures in older, eastern states have long been successfully resisted. Direct democracy is somewhat more common at the local level. For example, Georgia and South Carolina, which do not provide for statewide direct democracy, nevertheless require local voter approval for the consolidation of counties and municipal governments. Several states that lack statewide direct democracy require local voter approval for certain fiscal measures, such as incurring debt or exceeding local tax rates.

Reform Areas of Recent Interest

While interest persists in many of the reforms supported by political movements of the past, several new kinds of reform have recently pushed their way into public consciousness.

Term Limits
A presidential term limit was added to the U.S. Constitution by amendment in 1951.[79] There has been no serious federal attempt to impose term limits on members of Congress, although numerous states attempted to do so until the Supreme Court ruled in 1995 that congressional term limits could be imposed only by amending the federal Constitution.[80] Since 1990, initiative amendments to state constitutions in more than a dozen states have imposed term

limits on executive and legislative branch officials. Recently, however, efforts to repeal term limits have begun to appear.

Voting Technology

Improving voting technology has gained interest as computers become cheaper and more widely available. Reformers have begun to explore electronic voting as a way to make voting easier by allowing people to vote from locations other than an official polling place, and at times that they prefer. Electronic voting may also allow voters easier access to information that will help them make informed decisions. Some political theorists argue that electronic voting and communication can provide opportunities for participation and meaningful political community that have been lost in modern political life. Interest in electronic voting as a means of improving the accuracy of vote tabulation also grew after the 2000 presidential election, where faulty ballot design may have induced some voters to mark their ballots incorrectly, and where recounting ballots by hand required election officials to make a large number of seemingly contestable judgments about the intent of voters. The federal Help America Vote Act, enacted in 2002, responds in some degree to these concerns, although it has yet to be fully implemented. Moreover, concerns emerged after the 2002 elections about the capacity of electronic voting systems to generate accurate paper trails as a check on voting fraud and error.

By its nature, however, technology changes so fast that constitutional drafters might want to avoid constitutionalizing any particular voting methods or standards. Attention might instead be given to the approach mentioned earlier, in which only the ultimate normative goals of election administration are constitutionally specified (e.g., speed, accuracy, convenience, fairness), and the actual methods of voting are left to legislative discretion.

Party Primaries

States have long regulated the process by which political parties nominate candidates. Interest in the topic has revived recently due to apparently growing dissatisfaction with the candidates routinely put forward by the parties, and attention has focused on tinkering with the nomination process to produce more broadly appealing candidates who would better engage the electorate. The most prominent recent innovation was California's 1996 initiative mandating the use of a "blanket" primary, in which any eligible voter could vote for candidates of any party for any office, regardless of the voter's formal party affiliation. The Supreme Court struck down this measure in 2000,[81] but hinted that an "open" primary might survive constitutional scrutiny. In an open primary, voters are essentially free to vote in any party's primary, but they must choose only one party's primary in which to vote and may not switch party allegiance from office to office, as they may in a blanket primary.

Whether to constitutionalize such reforms presents a difficult question. State constitutions generally contain few provisions regulating political parties. Most such provisions merely direct the legislature to provide for and regulate primary elections. The North Dakota Constitution is typical, providing only that "[t]he legislative assembly shall provide by law for . . . the nomination of candidates."[82] Only a handful of state constitutions address the specific format of a primary election. Arizona, for example, provides for a semi-open primary in which registered independents may vote in party primaries.[83] Florida specifies an open primary when only one party fields candidates and the winner will run unopposed in the general election.[84] For the most part, however, regulation of political parties is left to the legislature.

On the other hand, there are good reasons to be suspicious of legislative regulation of political parties. There is an obvious risk that the party in power will use its regulatory authority to its own advantage, or that the major parties will strike undemocratic agreements of mutual advantage. This is probably why recent innovations in party regulation have been accomplished more often by initiative than by legislative action. In either case, however, care must be taken to comply with extensive federal constitutional restrictions on the kinds of regulations that may be imposed on parties.

Campaign Finance
Perhaps the most controversial and legally difficult area of state constitutional reform of the political process concerns campaign finance. Public support for reform apparently is high, yet the federal Constitution greatly restricts the ability of government to regulate the use and transfer of money in the political process. Moreover, legislatures seem to have great difficulty enacting campaign finance reform measures, as illustrated by the long struggle in Congress to enact the Bipartisan Campaign Reform Act (BCRA).

The constitutions of nine states—Arizona, Colorado, Florida, Hawaii, Minnesota, Nevada, Oklahoma, Oregon, and Rhode Island—contain provisions regulating campaign finance. About half of these were enacted by initiative amendment. The least controversial, and legally the least vulnerable to challenge, are provisions requiring disclosure of campaign contributions or spending. The Florida Constitution, for example, provides: "all elected public officers and candidates for such offices shall file full and public disclosure of their campaign finances."[85] Oregon's is more specific, requiring disclosure of all contributions exceeding $500, and all subsequent contributions of any amount from the same donor.[86]

Systems of public financing for elections also raise manageable issues under the U.S. Constitution, so long as participation in the system, and any restrictions on contributions and spending associated with participation, are genuinely voluntary. Florida, Hawaii, and Rhode Island require the legislature to establish some system of public financing. In Florida, the system must cover statewide offices; in Hawaii, state and local elections; and in Rhode Island, gubernatorial elections and any other "general officers" the legislature may specify.[87]

Restrictions on campaign contributions enter trickier constitutional territory. The U.S. Supreme Court has ruled that regulatory restrictions on contributions to candidates raise severe constitutional issues, although is has upheld state-imposed contribution limits of as low as $250 for certain offices. The constitutionalization of a specific figure seems of dubious desirability, however, since the cost of campaigning will fluctuate over time. The Supreme Court's 2003 decision upholding most aspects of BCRA may give states additional latitude to regulate contributions to state political parties.

Limitations on campaign spending by candidates and their supporters are flatly prohibited under the federal Constitution, yet the Hawaii and Minnesota Constitutions require the legislature to enact limits on campaign expenditures. An initiative amendment to the Oregon Constitution prohibiting the expenditure of funds donated by nonresidents of the relevant election district was invalidated.[88] Such defects are more common among proposals in this area that have been generated through the initiative process.

State constitutional provisions regulating campaign finance clearly deal with an important problem, and frequently seem to do so in novel ways, raising possible questions about both their efficacy and their constitutionality under federal law. They also seem to respond to a suspicion that the legislature cannot be counted on to address the problem adequately. Resort to the initiative process, however, is not always the most reliable way to make sound constitutional policy, particular in areas of great legal delicacy.

NOTES

1. Not all of these reforms have been successful. The Supreme Court has invalidated some regulations of parties. Term limits have been held illegal for Congress, but legal for states. Subsequent state attempts to achieve term limits indirectly, through ballot notations with slanted wording, were also invalidated.

2. U.S. Const., amends. XV, XIX, XXIV, XXVI.

3. Conn. Const., art. VI, § 3.

4. For example, Tex. Const., art. 1, § 2; Wyo. Const., art. 1, § 1.

5. U.S. Const., amend. XIV, § 1.

6. See Gerald M. Rosberg, "Aliens and the Right to Vote," 75 *Mich. L. Rev.* 1092 (1977), and Jamin B. Raskin, "Legal Aliens, Local Citizens: The Historical, Constitutional and Theoretical Meanings of Alien Suffrage," 141 *U. Pa. L. Rev.* 1391 (1993).

7. *Dunn v. Blumstein*, 405 U.S. 330 (1972); *Marston v. Lewis*, 410 U.S. 679 (1973) (per curiam); *Burns v. Fortson*, 410 U.S. 686 (1973) (per curiam).

8. Fla. Const., art. VI, § 2.

9. Conn. Const., art. VI, § 1.

10. For example, Haw. Const., art. II, § 3; Maine Const., art. II, § 1; N.D. Const., art. II, § 1.

11. Colo. Const., art. II, § 30 (1) (emphasis added).

12. *City of Phoenix v. Kolodziejski,* 399 U.S. 204 (1970). See also *Hill v. Stone,* 421 U.S. 289 (1975) (invalidating Texas property qualification in municipal bond election).

13. Robert J. Steinfeld, "Property and Suffrage in the Early American Republic," 41 *Stan. L. Rev.* 335 (1989).

14. *Harper v. Virginia State Board of Elections,* 383 U.S. 663 (1966); *Kramer v. Union Free School District No. 15,* 395 U.S. 621 (1969).

15. *Salyer Land Co. v. Tulare Lake Basin Water Storage District,* 410 U.S. 719 (1973); *Ball v. James,* 451 U.S. 355 (1981).

16. N.C. Const., art. I, § 11.

17. Ore. Const., art. II, § 3.

18. For example, Tenn. Const., art. I, § 5; Wash. Const., art. VI, § 3.

19. For example, Ala. Const., amend. 579; Ga. Const., art. II, § 1 ¶ 3.

20. For example, Kan. Const., art. 5, § 2; Mont. Const., art. IV, § 2.

21. Miss. Const., art. 12, § 253.

22. *Hunter v. Underwood,* 471 U.S. 222 (1985).

23. *Richardson v. Ramirez,* 418 U.S. 24 (1974). This result stands in interesting contrast with a recent decision of the Supreme Court of Canada, in which it invalidated under the Canadian Charter of Human Rights a federal law providing disfranchisement as a punishment for certain crimes. *Sauvé v. Canada* (Chief Electoral Officer), [2002] 3 S.C.R. (4th) 519.

24. *See,* for example, *Cotton v. Fordice,* 157 F.3d 388 (5th Cir.), cert. denied, 525 U.S. 893 (1998).

25. For example, Idaho Const., art. I, § 2; Utah Const., art. I, § 2.

26. For example, Ky. Const., § 4; S.D. Const., art. VII, § 26.

27. For example, Cal. Const., art. I, § 3; N.C. Const., art. I, § 12.

28. For example, Neb. Const., art. 1, § 22; Va. Const., art. I, § 6.

29. For example, Del. Const., art. I, § 3; Ill. Const., art. III, § 3.

30. For example, Colo. Const., art. II, § 5; S.C. Const., art. I, § 5.

31. *See,* for example, Matthew C. Jones, "Fraud and the Franchise: The Pennsylvania Constitution's 'Free and Equal Election' Clause as an Independent Basis for State and Local Election Challenges," 68 *Temple L. Rev.* 1473 (1995).

32. Haw. Const., art. I, § 8; N.Y. Const., art. I, § 1.

33. Mont. Const., art. II, § 13.

34. Ind. Const., art. 2, § 12.

35. Wis. Const., art. III, § 3.

36. Conn. Const., art. VI, § 4. *See also,* for example, Ala. Const., art. I, § 33; Cal. Const., art. VII, § 8.

37. For example, Mich. Const., art. II, § 4; Wyo. Const., art. 6, § 13.

38. For example, Ill. Const., art. III, § 4.

39. Md. Const., art. III, § 3.49.

40. Ala. Const., amend. 41.

41. Minn. Const., art. VII, § 8.

42. Vt. Const., ch. II, § 47.

43. Mo. Const., art. IV, § 18.

44. *Butts v. City of New York,* 779 F.2d 141 (2d Cir., 1985), cert. denied, 478 U.S. 1021 (1986).

45. R.I. Const., art. VI, § 6.

46. For example, Tex. Const., art. 6, § 4; Wyo. Const., art. 6, § 11.

47. Maine Const., art. II, § 1.

48. Mo. Const., art. VIII, § 3; Utah Const., art. IV, § 8.

49. A floterial district is one that is overlaid on two or more other districts for the same body and thus resembles a limited at-large district. Voters within a floterial district vote for two representatives: one representative who represents exclusively their "regular" district, and another, floterial representative who represents their own district as well as one or more adjoining districts. Floterial districts sometimes are drawn to comply with the one-person, one-vote requirement by raising the fractional representation of a discrete geographical region without the need to rearrange existing district lines within the region.

50. Alaska Const., art. VI, § 4.

51. W. Va. Const., art. VI, § 6–4. The provision creates an exception for multi-county senatorial districts, which must be partitioned.

52. *Burns v. Richardson,* 384 U.S. 73, 92 (1966).

53. Tex. Const., art. 5, § 7a(f).

54. *Karcher v. Daggett,* 462 U.S. 725 (1983).

55. *Mahan v. Howell,* 410 U.S. 315, 324 (1973), quoting *Reynolds v. Sims,* 377 U.S. 533, 577 (1964).

56. Wash. Const., art. II, § 43(5).

57. *See,* for example, In Re Constitutionality of House Joint Resolution 1987, 817 So.2d 819 (Fla. 2002); *Wilkins v. West,* 571 S.E.2d 100 (Va., 2002).

58. Ohio Const., art. 11, § 7(A).

59. Colo. Const., art. V, § 47(1).

60. For example, In re Livingston, 160 N.Y.S. 462, 469, 96 Misc. 341, 351 (N.Y. Sup. Ct., 1916); *People ex rel. Smith v. Board of Supervisors,* 42 N.E. 592 (N.Y., 1896). Today, the requirement of easy travel around a district is more often subsumed under the requirements of contiguity or compactness. *See,* for example, *Wilkins v. West,* 571 S.E.2d 100, 109 (Va., 2002); *Prosser v. Elections Board,* 793 F. Supp. 859, 863 (W.D. Wis., 1992).

61. Mich. Const., art. IV, § 2.

62. One well-known study describes them as "largely ineffective." Richard H. Pildes and Richard G. Niemi, Expressive Harms, "'Bizarre Districts,' and Voting Rights: Evaluating Election-District Appearances after Shaw v. Reno," 92 *Mich. L. Rev.* 483, 528 (1993).

63. Alaska Const., art. VI, § 6.

64. Neb. Const., art. III, § 5.

65. Maine Const., art. IV, pt. 1, § 2.

66. Alaska Const., art. VI, § 6.

67. Hawaii Const., art. IV, § 6(8).

68. Colo. Const., art. V, § 47(3).

69. *Wells v. Edwards,* 347 F. Supp. 453 (M.D. La., 1972), summarily aff'd, 409 U.S. 1095 (1973). The federal Voting Rights Act, however, does apply to judicial districting. *Chisom v. Roemer,* 501 U.S. 380 (1991).

70. Illinois and Mississippi specifically require certain judicial districts to contain approximately equal populations. Nebraska and South Carolina require judicial districts to be contiguous. Kentucky, Montana, Nebraska, Ohio, South Carolina, South Dakota, and Wisconsin require judicial districts to be compact.

71. *See,* for example, Alexander Keyssar, *The Right to Vote: The Contested History of Democracy in the United States* (New York: Basic Books 2000), at 232.

72. Wyo. Const., art. 12, § 5.

73. Nev. Const., art. 4, § 32.

74. *See,* for example, George H. Hallett, Jr., *Proportional Representation—The Key to Democracy* (National Home Library Foundation, 1937)

75. Kathleen L. Barber, *Proportional Representation and Election Reform in Ohio* (Columbus: Ohio State University Press, 1995).

76. Ore. Const., art. II, § 16; W.Va. Const., art. VI, § 6–50.

77. Va. Const., art. VII, § 2.

78. Thomas E. Cronin, *Direct Democracy: The Politics of Initiative, Referendum, and Recall* (Cambridge, Mass: Harvard University Press 1989).

79. U.S. Const., amend. XXII.

80. *U.S. Term Limits v. Thornton,* 514 U.S. 779 (1995).

81. *California Democratic Party v. Jones*, 530 U.S. 567 (2000).

82. N.D. Const., art. II, § 1.

83. Ariz. Const., art. VII, § 10. A challenge to this provision on federal constitutional grounds is pending. *See Arizona Libertarian Party, Inc. v. Bayless*, 351 F.3d 1277, (9th Cir., 2003).

84. Fla. Const., art. VI, § 5(b).

85. Fla. Const., art. II, § 8(b).

86. Ore. Const., art. II, § 24.

87. R.I. Const., art. IV, § 10.

88. *Vanatta v. Keisling*, 899 F. Supp. 488 (D. Or., 1995), aff'd, 151 F.3d 1215 (9th Cir., 1998), cert. denied, 525 U.S. 1104 (1999).

Chapter Seven

Constitutional Amendment and Revision

Gerald Benjamin

Because the authors of constitutions are neither infallible nor prescient all constitutions must anticipate the need for change. Indeed, the process of altering the basic arrangements for governance may itself be salutary for citizens in a democracy. As Thomas Jefferson wrote in 1816, "Each generation [has] . . . a right to choose for itself the form of government it believes most promotive of its own happiness."[1]

Constitutional change in democracies occurs in two ways: by altering the meaning of the document through interpretation, or by altering the text of the document through amendment or revision. For the United States Constitution, change through interpretation predominates. For state constitutions textual change is far more common. This chapter focuses on methods for achieving textual change, or "formal" change, in American state constitutions. It begins with seven basic principles that should guide constitutional change. There follows an exploration of the experience in the states with legislative proposal of constitutional amendments, and amendments proposed by initiative or the use of a commission, two methods that bypass the legislature, in the light of these principles. Constitutional revision by convention is then considered. Finally, we derive a series of guidelines for constitution makers that might guide their design or reform of provisions for constitutional change.

BASIC PRINCIPLES

Experience suggests that constitutional change should be guided by seven fundamental principles:

1. Because constitutional amendment and constitutional revision are not the same, provisions for each should be separate and distinct.

177

2. Constitutions should provide for at least two means for *amendment;* one through governmental institutions established by the constitution, and one that bypasses the existing institutions.
3. Constitutional *revision* may be initiated by the legislature or without the legislature, but once started revision should proceed in a manner entirely distinct from the legislative process.
4. Sufficient constitutional detail is required defining amendment and revision methods that bypass the legislature to assure that these will be truly available and effective when used.
5. Whether achieved through the legislature or without its participation, procedural requirements for changing the constitution should be more demanding than those for passing ordinary legislation.
6. Constitutional change processes should be all treated in the same location in the state constitution.
7. Because all constitutional change should be subject to popular ratification, necessary information must be provided in understandable form to inform public choice.

1. Amendment and Revision: Analysts distinguish between textual change of constitutions by amendment and by revision. Amendment is "the alteration of an existing constitution by the addition or subtraction of material." Revision is "replacement of one constitution by another."[2] "Revision" is specifically referenced in the constitutions of twenty-three states.[3] The language of many state constitutions is not as precise as is desirable regarding this distinction between amendment and revision.

2. Proposing *Amendments* Through or Without the Legislature: All states constitutions permit amendments to be formally proposed by state legislatures and most constitutional change is accomplished in this manner. However, as beneficiaries of the political and governmental status quo legislators frequently resist change in the structure and process of the state government. Twenty-five state constitutions therefore expressly provide methods for amendments to be proposed without legislative participation: by popular petition (the constitutional initiative), state constitutional commission, or constitutional convention.[4]

3. Constitutional *Revision*: Broader scale constitutional revision is likely to require the calling of a state constitutional convention, though at least six states allow constitutional revision through the legislature, and at times "sets of amendments" passed simultaneously have "substantially altered the character of state government."[5] Forty-one state constitutions explicitly provide for conventions to be called by state legislatures. Courts in other states have found in their constitutions an implied power to call a convention.[6] Perhaps to avoid this, Missouri's document states explicitly that "This constitution may be revised and amended only as therein provided."[7] North Carolina's constitution also expressly limits change methods to those specified in it.[8] Recognizing that legislatures may be the target of revision and therefore resistant to calling a convention, fourteen state constitutions provide for automatic periodic placement on the ballot of the question of whether a constitutional convention should be held.[9] Additionally, the Florida and Montana constitutions explicitly provides for the calling of a convention by the use of initiative and referendum.[10]

State legislatures are created by and subordinate to state constitutions. Constitutions that have originated in the legislature without specific constitutional authorization or the calling of a convention have engendered controversy. In Georgia, Idaho, and Kentucky courts have permitted legislatures to seek ratification of constitutions they have drafted without explicit constitutional authority to do so.[11] An attempt to revise the Oregon constitution through the initiative was invalidated in the courts.[12]

4. The Necessity for and Disadvantages of Detail: State constitutions are often criticized for being excessively detailed. Provisions for constitutional change that bypass the legislature are frequently a locus of considerable of this detail, and for good reason. Specificity is a means of protection from legislatures' often manifest hostility to the prospect of being bypassed in the restructuring of state government. There is ample experience that legislatures, either through action or inaction, raise barriers to constitutional processes that might produce results contrary to their interests.[13] To avoid being stymied by legislative hostility, constitution makers seek to make these provisions for amendment or revision "self-executing," that is, operable without any need for legislative action.[14] The goal is to set out in detail in the constitution, beyond the easy reach of the legislature, when, how and by whom these amendment processes are to be made to work.

Yet detailed specification of the processes for amendment and revision used to bypass the legislature may have unintended consequences. One effect is to specially empower state high courts—already the key sources of constitutional change through interpretation—in the textual change process. When detailed procedures are embedded in the constitution these courts say not only what the constitution means, but what the constitutional change process requires. Another effect may be to block rather than facilitate change efforts. A constitutional provision designed in one era to bypass barriers to change—for example, the New York provision making the pay for a convention delegate equal to that of a legislator—might itself become a barrier in a later era, in a very different political context. Finally, detail in the constitution does not bar further detail and process specification through legislation. The resulting combined effect of constitutional provisions, added statutory requirements and court interpretations may add to the complexity, and therefore the relative difficulty, of constitutional change without legislative participation.[15]

5. Difficulty of Change Compared to Passing State Law: Whatever means is used, the process for proposal of constitutional amendment or revision in the states is structured to make constitutional change more difficult than the adoption ordinary legislation. Moreover, the difficulty is enhanced by the requirement of an additional step for ratification (in all states but Delaware). This is as it should be, for constitutions are fundamental law. Moreover, protections that constitutions afford minorities would mean little if they were as easily changeable by majorities as is ordinary law.

Formal state constitutional change is far more frequent than formal change at the national level for at least three reasons.

- First, the U.S. Constitution has importance as a symbol of national unity. Amendment is therefore approached with enormous caution.
- Second, the formal national amending process is far more difficult than that of any state; at minimum, it requires supportive action by thirty-nine separate governments (the national government and thirty-eight state governments). Within the states there has been a general evolution over the nineteenth and twentieth centuries to a "more flexible" amending process.[16] The result is more frequent amendment, and greater constitutional length.
- Third, the inclusion in state constitutions of much detail (often of matter that some might not regard as "constitutional") invites—even requires—more frequent amendment for the effective operation of state government.[17]

What is true for amendment is also true for revision. The process provided in the U.S. Constitution for revision has never been used. In contrast, state constitutional revision has been relatively frequent. There have been more than 230 constitutional conventions in the United States, and 146 state constitutions adopted.

6. Constitutional Location of Change Processes: Modern drafters usually include provisions for legislatively initiated constitutional amendment or revision, or for the calling of constitutional conventions, in a separate article in the document devoted to constitutional change.[18] Some constitutions, however, place provisions for amendment in the legislative article, or in a general or omnibus article. Provisions for popularly initiated amendment or revision are variously including in the article on the amending process, the legislative article, or in separate articles providing for initiative and referendum.[19] To reduce complexity and assure full understanding of available options, there is virtue in a single constitutional location for all means for formal constitutional change available to the polity.

7. Democratic Theory Requires Popular Ratification: The first American state constitutions explicitly or indirectly emphasized popular authority.[20] Relatively early in the nation's history state constitutions came to created through special processes—conventions elected for the explicit, singular purpose of drafting and proposing them—with the results of their work subject to public ratification.[21] This gave the final word on the structure of governance to the sovereign people. At the beginning of the twenty-first century the adoption of a formal constitutional change in all states but Delaware required a popular vote. Since the highest authority in democracy, the sovereign people, is the source of state constitutions, it follows that this same authority must also authorize alterations to them: thus the requirement for popular ratification of constitutional amendments or revisions. Because of the necessity of popular ratification, constitutional assurance that understandable unbiased information be provided to inform the public is essential.

Proposal and Adoption of Amendments

Through the Legislature

Over the course of American history about 90 percent of state constitutional amendments have been proposed through state legislatures. Between 1992 and 2000, 862 constitutional amendments were proposed in American state legislatures, and 664 adopted, for an adoption rate of 77 percent.[22] Generally, amendments offered through the legislature have been far more likely to be ratified by the voters than those offered by popular initiative, though the rate of approval for those offered as the result of the constitutional initiative have increased in recent years.[23] But they have enjoyed a lower success rate than those offered by conventions.[24] Research on New York demonstrated that amendments proposed by the legislature "rarely deal with the distribution of power in state government, and those that do are not designed to limit or constrain the principle political institutions or actors.

There are three approaches in state constitutions for proposal for constitutional amendment through the legislature.[25]

- Nine states use single passage by simple majorities of members elected to both legislative chambers.
- Fifteen states require passage in two successive sessions, with some requiring an intervening general election. Simple majorities at each passage are required in twelve of these states. In Massachusetts this is a simple majority of the two chambers sitting together. In Delaware (where no popular ratification is required) two-thirds majorities of each house must pass an amendment twice for it to be adopted. Tennessee requires first passage of an amendment by majorities in both houses; second passage, however, requires two-thirds majorities. In Vermont in partial contrast, the proposal of an amendment requires a two-thirds

majority in the Senate and a simple majority in the House on first passage. Second passage requires a simple majority in both chambers. In South Carolina, two-thirds of each house is needed to propose an amendment. Unlike in other states, the second legislative vote follows popular ratification; for it, simple majorities in each house are required.

- Twenty-nine states require extraordinary majorities in each house to propose amendments. In ten of these a three-fifths majority is required. In eighteen, the requirement is two-thirds. And in one, Connecticut, it is three-quarters.

Note that the number of methods for proposing a constitutional amendment exceeds the number of states, because Connecticut, Hawaii, New Jersey, and Pennsylvania—four states with relatively recently adopted constitutions—offer their legislatures alternatives: simple majorities with dual passage, or extraordinary majorities with single passage (though in Pennsylvania, only for emergencies). Provisions for size of majority and frequency of passage are often linked. Single passage appears with extraordinary majority required; passage twice appears with simple majority required.

Research has shown that when a simple majority is used to propose an amendment, requiring double passage does not make the amending process substantially more difficult. However, requiring extraordinary majorities does make amendment significantly harder to achieve. And requiring extraordinary majorities and double passage raises very substantial barriers to the possibility of constitutional amendment.[26] However another study has shown that "States with more onerous procedures have yearly adopted LCA [legislative constitutional amendment] . . . rates that are as great or greater than those with less onerous procedures." They conclude also that "States that make it more difficult to pass LCAs out of the legislature tend to have the highest LCA success rates."[27]

Process

Amendments may generally be introduced by any member in either house. In some states a minimum passage of time or a number of readings is specified before the legislature may act. The New Jersey Constitution requires a public hearing before a legislative vote on an amendment. Where a second passage in a following session is required, an elapsed time before second passage is also often indicated. Most constitutions require that the results of the legislative vote on an amendment be properly recorded in the journal of each house. Failure to follow a constitutionally specified recording procedure caused at least one state high court to invalidate an amendment after passage.[28] The Illinois Constitution specifies that a majority of the legislature that proposes an amendment may withdraw it (though three-fifths are required to submit it). California provides for withdrawal by the same majority as passage.

Responsibility of Other State Officials

Locating responsibility for elements of the amending process in a specific official helps to assure that these tasks are performed and builds accountability. Some state constitutions charge the secretary of state with receiving proposed amendments after passage, assuring that they are properly considered by the electorate and proclaiming the results. In those states, the secretary of state is usually also responsible for preparing the form of the ballot question, sometimes within constitutionally prescribed guidelines requiring impartiality. Alternatively, as in Alaska, the task may fall to the lieutenant governor. In Alabama and Vermont the governor must timely "give notice" of or "proclaim" an election on a constitutional amendment. In Ohio responsibility for preparing ballot language (with an explanation of proposed amendments and arguments in favor and against) is given to a board that includes the secretary of state and four others, no more than two of whom may be in the same political party. The sole constitutional responsibility of the Attorney General in New York is "to render an opinion in writing to the senate and assembly as to the effect of . . . [an] amendment or amendments" within twenty days after it is filed.

Limits

Constitutional limits on the amending process through the legislature seek to assure that the ratification process is manageable for voters, and that they have the unbiased information they need about proposed amendments so that they may vote intelligently.

Number of Amendments Offered by One Session: In Arkansas the legislature may propose to the voters no more than three amendments in any one year. In Kentucky the limit is four; in Kansas five. The Illinois legislature may propose to amend no more than three articles of the constitution in any one year. The Colorado legislature is limited to seeking alteration of six articles in any one session.

Single Purpose: Amendments are generally limited to a single purpose (or in Louisiana, "object"), though a number of state constitutions specifically allow a number of articles to be altered by an amendment pursuant to a single purpose.[29]

Election Timing: In most states, amendments may be considered at either general or special elections. A few—Connecticut, Kentucky, and New Hampshire are examples—require submission at a general election only. In West Virginia, if a special election is used for consideration of constitutional amendments it may not be used for another purpose.

Separate Vote: State constitutions generally provide for a separate vote on each proposed amendment. In Oregon, however, an amendment submitted by the initiative and one submitted by the legislature may be framed as alternatives in a single question so that "one provision will become a part of the Constitution if a proposed revision is adopted by the people and the other provision will become a part of the Constitution if a proposed revision is rejected by the people."

Limits on Resubmission: If an amendment proposed by the legislatures of New Jersey fails, neither it nor a similar change may be submitted again to the voters until two general elections have passed. In Pennsylvania, five years must pass before resubmission.

Time for Consideration, Publicity, and Information: Most constitutions specify a minimum period of time that must pass after legislative approval (three months is common) before a vote on an amendment may occur. During this time publication of the text, a summary description and other information about the amendment or amendments is often required. The Missouri constitution requires publication in "two newspapers of different political faiths" in each county. In Georgia, a summary of any proposed amendment must be prepared by the attorney general, the legislative counsel, and the secretary of state and published throughout the state. Idaho specifically requires publication of arguments for and against each amendment. As noted, Ohio has a similar requirement. A unique provision in New Mexico requires publication in both English and Spanish, with the legislature also making "reasonable efforts" to communicate the substance of proposed constitutional amendments in indigenous languages and minority language groups.

Court Challenges
The Ohio Constitution establishes deadline is established for court challenges to a proposed amendment. The state supreme court is given original jurisdiction. Amendment language may be invalidated only if found likely to "to mislead, deceive, or defraud the voters." The Ohio Constitution also provides that "An election on a proposed constitutional amendment submitted by the general assembly shall not be enjoined nor invalidated because the explanation, arguments, or other information is faulty in any way."

Home Rule
In Georgia constitutional amendments must have "uniform and general applicability throughout the state." The Louisiana constitution requires amendments that affect five or fewer parishes to be passed by both statewide and parishwide majorities to become effective. Similarly, in Maryland if an amendment is found by the legislature to affect just one county or the city of Baltimore, it must pass with a majority in the potentially effected locality as well as

one statewide. The California Constitution prevents the legislature from passing amendments that "Include or exclude any political subdivision of the State from the application or effect of its provisions based upon approval or disapproval of the measure, or based upon the casting of a specified percentage of votes in favor of the measure," within a jurisdiction.[30]

Substantive Limits or Special Majorities

Several examples are illustrative. A provision in the Alabama Constitution that the legislature may not amend the constitution to change the basis of legislative representation from population dating to 1901 anticipated the current requirements of federal law.[31] The constitution of New Mexico requires higher popular majorities to change provisions on franchise and education than to pass other amendments. Support of two-thirds voting on the question in Florida is needed if an amendment imposes a new tax or fee.[32]

Ratification[33]

In Delaware no popular ratification is required to amend the state constitution. The vast majority of states (forty-three) require a majority of those voting on the question to ratify amendments proposed by the legislature. To deal with the problems of "dropoff" of voters on ballot questions or low turnout, in Hawaii this number must also equal 50 percent of those voting in a general election, or the equivalent of 30 percent of those registered if a special election is used. In Nebraska the majority for an amendment must also exceed 35 percent of those voting in the election.

New Hampshire requires a two-thirds favorable vote on the question to adopt an amendment. Passage of amendments requires support of a majority of those voting in the election in Minnesota and Wyoming. In Tennessee adoption requires backing by the number of voters equal to a majority voting in the gubernatorial election. In Illinois support is required by either a majority in voting in the election or three-fifths voting on the question.

Effective Date

Most state constitutions specify an effective date for amendments once they are ratified. Clarity on this matter is importance. Litigation in Wisconsin in 2002 established that a constitutional amendment there did not take effect until the canvass of the vote adopting it was completed.[34]

Without Legislative Participation

Twenty-five states provide expressly for a means of constitutional amendment that bypasses the legislature. The constitutional initiative is the means most commonly used. Amendment may be also achieved through convention. The constitutional commission has also been adopted in a limited number of jurisdictions.

Constitutional Initiative

Tax limitation and legislative term limitation, the two most far-reaching structural reforms in state government of the late twentieth century, were achieved largely through the use of the constitutional initiative.[35] Sixteen states, most in the Midwest and West, permit direct access to the ballot for constitutional amendments proposed by popular initiative.[36] In one of these (Illinois), however, the use of the initiative for constitutional revision is confined to the legislative article only, perhaps because this is the area of the constitution in which the legislature is likely to be most self-interested, and therefore least likely to initiate change.

An additional two states, Massachusetts and Mississippi, allow the use of the indirect initiative to propose amendments.[37] In Massachusetts, an amendment may not reach the ballot unless passed in two consecutive sessions by one-quarter of the legislature sitting jointly. On first consideration, but not thereafter, an initiative proposal may be amended by three quarters of the legislature. The legislature may simultaneously present a substitute proposal with an initiative measure it passes. In Mississippi a constitutional initiative may reach the ballot without legislative action. If a proposal sent to it as a result of the indirect initiative is amended by the legislature both the original and the amended versions are placed on the ballot.[38]

The indirect initiative has not yet been used in Mississippi, and is rarely successful in Massachusetts. However, one study shows that "many initiatives that fail to pass the legislature succeed in prodding the legislature to take action on an issue."[39]

The use of the initiative process to achieve constitutional change is hotly debated. Critics argue that it is insufficiently deliberative, overly demanding on voters, excessively susceptible to manipulation by moneyed interests, inconsiderate of minorities, and, therefore, ultimately undermining of republican government. Defenders, with greater faith in the capacity of referendum voters to make reasonable choices, argue the legitimacy of direct action by citizen majorities and the utility of this mechanism for constraining entrenched self-interested elected officials. Resultant policies, they say, are no more subject to special interest influence than those made by legislatures, nor are they, in general, substantively less defensible.[40]

Both constitutional and statutory provisions are used in the states to define and delimit the constitutional initiative process. In reaction to the more extensive use of the initiative, legislatures in several states have sought by law or constitutional amendment to place more limiting procedural requirements on the initiative process. Considerable litigation has ensued, much of it focused on the freedom of speech and equal protection implications of these actions under the United States constitution. This review focuses on procedural requirements for the initiative process that are included in state constitutions.

Administration of the Process
Because of their general responsibility for administering elections, Secretaries of State are typically charged in state constitutions with administering the constitutional initiative. In some states the Attorney General is constitutionally required to receive petitions, put them in proper form and prepare an official title and summary. It is important that the locus of responsibility for effecting this or any constitutional change process be clearly identified in the document to assure accountability and avoid proposed changes being blocked through passive resistance by those in office who might oppose them.

Correction of Error
If he or she finds an error or errors in an initiative petition, the North Dakota Constitution requires the Secretary of State to allow petitioners a period of twenty days to correct it.

Timing
State constitutions often require that complete initiative petitions advancing a constitutional amendment be filed by a specified date (for example, 4 months in Arkansas, 90 days in Nevada) before the question is scheduled for a vote.

General or Special Election
Selection of the election at which a question will be considered is one key factor affecting the size of the electorate that will consider it. Most states allow proposed constitutional amendments to be voted on at the next scheduled general election or, with legislative authorization, at a special election. However, Michigan, Montana, Nebraska, Nevada, and Ohio specify a general election. Colorado allows constitutional change through initiative to be considered at the regular biennial general election only. Florida requires a three-quarters vote in each legislative house to permit a special election, and restricts its use to a single amendment question.

Signature Gatherers
The North Dakota Constitution specifies that petitions be circulated only by electors. Oregon requires that signature gatherers be registered to vote in the state. The use of paid signature gatherers in initiative campaigns is widespread. Massachusetts specifically empowers the legislature, if it chooses, to bar paid signature gathers from circulating petitions. Oregon in 2002 constitutionally barred payment on a per signature basis to paid gatherers. *Statutory* limitations on the signature gathering process (most are statutory, not constitutional)— including bans in Colorado on paid gatherers and requirements there that petition circulators disclose their identities and be registered voters—have been invalidated as violations of the First Amendment to the United States

Constitution. This brings into question the validity of similar state constitutional provisions elsewhere.[41]

Time Parameters for Gathering Signatures
One study found that three-quarters of the initiative states allowed petitioners at least one year to gather signatures.[42] Oklahoma allows the least time, ninety days; Florida allows the most, four years. Under the Illinois Constitution, signatures advancing a constitutional amendment by initiative must be gathered within twenty-four months of the election date at which the matter will be placed on the ballot. The Nevada constitution requires the person who intends to circulate a petition to file a copy with the secretary of state before beginning circulation and not earlier than September 1 of the year before the year in which the election is to be held.

Public Information
Citizens are the ultimate authority for making constitutional change. Informed citizens presumably are likely to make wiser choices. State constitutions therefore commonly include requirements that voters get neutral information on a question before it is brought to a vote, but also in at least one case while it is being circulated. Requirements are common that the text of amendments proposed through the initiative be published in newspapers of general circulation throughout the state at a specified time or during a specified period prior to the general vote. In Colorado the legislative research and drafting staff review proposed amendments and must comment on them in a public meeting within two weeks of their being filed with it. This same nonpartisan staff is required to prepare and publishes a voter information pamphlet thirty days prior to the vote on a constitutional initiative question. No publication or information requirements yet require the use of television, the Internet, or interactive technologies.

Signature Requirements
Paralleling the higher threshold for legislative action to propose formal constitutional change, petitions proposing amendments to state constitutions generally require more signatures than those proposing ordinary law. Greater percentage differences between the signature requirement for placing a statutory change and advancing a constitutional change through the initiative seemed to diminish the proportion of constitutional changes proposed.[43]

The Base: The signature requirement is universally stated as a percentage of a base. The selection of the base is critical; a base election with higher turnout elevates the signature requirement. Most commonly, the base is the vote in the previous gubernatorial election. Other bases used are voters in the previous election for secretary of state (Colorado), for presidential electors (Florida), for the state office receiving the highest number of votes (Oklahoma), or those who voted in the entire state (Nevada). North Dakota does not use an election as the base for determining the petition signature requirement, but the population of the state.

The Percentage: Percentages required vary from a low of 3 percent (Massachusetts) to a high of 15 percent (Arizona), with 8 percent or 10 percent most common.

Geographic Distribution: In nine states a geographic distribution of signatures (e.g., in Nebraska, signatures equal to 10 percent of the gubernatorial vote in the last election must include at least 5 percent of that vote in two-fifths of the counties) or a maximum proportion of signatures from a specified geographic location (e.g., in Mississippi, no more than 20 percent from any one congressional district) may add to the demands of the signature gathering process. In 2002 Montana amended its constitution to require that an initiative petition proposing a constitutional amendment be signed by 10 percent of voters in the last gubernatorial election in at least half the state's counties, not (as before) two-fifths of the legislature's house districts. A geographic distribution requirement does assure that support for a proposal is not concentrated in a single large population center. States in which the initiative is most used—Oregon, California, Arizona, Colorado, and Washington—have no geographic distribution requirement.[44] In 2001 a Federal District Court judge in Idaho, saying it gave "rural voters preferential treatment," struck down the geographic distribution requirement there as a violation of the equal protection clause of the United States Constitution.[45]

The Number: Percentage-based requirements of course result in the need to gather greater numbers of signatures in larger states. The number of signatures required also shifts with voting participation, which itself is partly a function of population growth. Massachusetts sets an absolute minimum of 25,000 for the signature requirement.

Petition Form or Format: Some state constitutions (e.g., Colorado, Nevada) constitutionally specify petition form or format.

Procedural and Substantive Limitations
Half of the states that provide for constitutional amendment through the initiative process place no restrictions on the subject matter they may address.[46] Massachusetts bars the use of the initiative for matters concerning religion, judicial tenure, judicial decisions, abolition of courts, local matters, appropriations, and protected rights. In California the initiative cannot be used to name a person to office or designate a private entity to perform a function or exercise

a governmental power or duty. In Missouri, appropriations through the initiative process are bared. The Mississippi Constitution bars the use of the initiative process to modify the state Bill of Rights, to amend or repeal statutory or constitutional provisions relating to the state public employee retirement system, to repeal the constitutional "right to work" provision, or to modify the initiative process itself.[47]

Single Subject or Single Article and Clear Identification of the Amendment Subject in the Title: A constitutional limitation of each amendment to a single subject, or a single article, is common for constitutional amendments advance by popular initiative. These rules are similar to those that constrain the ordinary legislative process in most states. Such limitations have often been the subject of litigation.[48]

Question Form: In some states (Arkansas, Massachusetts, Missouri), the general form of initiative petitions or ballot questions is specified in the constitution.

Financial Impact: The Mississippi Constitution requires that a fiscal analysis of proposed amendments be prepared by the chief legislative budget officer and be included on the ballot. A proposal offered by the Florida legislature and accepted at the polls in 2002 requires the for the provision of an economic impact statement to prior to any vote on an amendment of the Florida Constitution proposed by initiative.

Conflicting Outcomes: If two conflicting amendments are passed in a single election, some state constitutions provide that the one that gained the most votes must prevail. In Hawaii, if an amendment proposed by a convention and one proposed by the legislature conflict, and both pass at referendum, the former prevails.

Resubmission: The Nebraska Constitution bars the resubmission by the initiative of the same question (in form or substance) more than once in every three years. In Mississippi, a provision that fails at the polls must be off the ballot for two years before it is offered again to the voters.

Vote to Ratify: In Illinois ratification requires three-fifths voting on the question or a majority voting in the election. Arizona, Michigan, and Wyoming require amendments to be passed by a majority of those voting in the election. (A proposal by the Wyoming legislature in 2002 that amendments to the state constitution be submitted to the electors of the state without prior presentment to the governor for his approval or disapproval received 52.7 percent of the votes cast on the question but failed because it did not gain a majority of those voting in the election.) Nebraska requires that the vote of a successful initiative amendment be a majority on the question and at least 35 percent of the total vote cast at the election. In Nebraska, amendments must be ratified by majorities on the question in two successive elections. In the Mississippi indirect process an initiative or legislative alternative must receive a minimum of 40 percent of the total votes cast. Moreover, if an initiative proposal and a legislative alternative are presented, voters most vote twice: first for approval of either measure or against both measures, and then for one or the other measure.

Effective Date: It is common for state constitutions to specify an effective date for an amendment offered by this method, once it is adopted.

The Constitutional Commission

As an alternative means of bypassing the legislature to achieve constitutional change, the Florida constitution provides for two commissions. These commissions may place proposals directly on the ballot. They are constitutionally required to convene automatically every ten years, no more than thirty days after the close of the legislative session.[49] The Constitutional Revision Commission, which may consider the entire document, has thirty-seven members, with no single political actor controlling a majority: fifteen are appointed by the governor, nine by the speaker of the House; nine by the president of the Senate, and three by the chief justice of the Supreme Court. The chair is designated by the governor. The Taxation and Budget Reform Commission acts only on matters concerning the state's fiscal policies and budgetary processes. It has twenty-nine members. Eleven are selected by the governor, seven by the majority leader, and seven by the speaker. Legislators may not be among these twenty-five. However, two from each house—one from the major and one from the minority party—are appointed by the speaker and majority leader to participate as nonvoting members. The group chooses its own chair, who not be a sitting legislator.

The commission process in Florida has resulted in considerable constitutional change. This is an effective method of bypassing the legislature to make reforms in state government structure or processes that are not in accord with the interests of incumbent power holders. A legitimacy issue arises concerning commission proposals because most commission members, unlike legislators and constitution convention delegates, are not popularly elected. But the commission mechanism was popularly ratified, most commissioners are appointed by elected officials, and their work—like that of all sources of constitutional change proposals—is subject to popular ratification. Moreover in 1980, Florida votes rejected an amendment proposed by the legislature that would have abolished the revision commission process.[50]

There is a concern that commissions that come into existence on a fixed schedule rather in response to a felt political need. However, analysts of successes in 1997–98 emphasized the dependence of commission success on extensive preparatory work, outreach in agenda formation, a self-imposed supermajority rule for decision making and effective communication prior to the vote.[51]

The addition of the commissions to the legislative and initiative amending processes gives Florida three means of constitutional amendment. This increases the possibility that changes offered by one means might be at odds with those proposed by another, or that one process might be used in reaction to try to undo the results of another. It may also raise the degree to which constitutional change politics is routinely intertwined with legislative politics.

The New Mexico constitution provides for an "independent commission established by law" that might propose constitutional changes to the legislature.[52] In Utah such a commission is not constitutionally based but established by statute.[53] As a result of the prestige of its members and careful attention to its agenda, the Utah Commission has had some success in initiating constitutional changes that have gained legislative approval. Because neither the New Mexico nor the Utah Commission is provided direct ballot access to present their proposals these are not effective mechanisms for bypassing the legislature to make constitutional changes opposed by those in control of the state government.

Revision by Convention

Constitutions in all but nine states explicitly specify processes for calling constitutional conventions.[54] They provide that state constitutional conventions may be proposed or called by legislatures, or be called as a result of automatic call provisions, or through use of the initiative.

Proposed by the Legislature
In Illinois and Nebraska three-quarters of the legislators elected must support a convention for a referendum on the matter to be authorized. South Dakota also requires three-quarters, but no following popular vote is needed. Two-thirds of the members elected are required to authorize a convention in an additional twenty states; in five of these, no popular referendum must be held. (In Maine the two-thirds majorities must be concurrent.) Finally, in sixteen states majorities elected to both houses may put a convention question on the ballot for voter approval. In Louisiana, these majorities must be obtained in two successive legislatures.[55] In Alabama a vote to call a convention may be repealed only by a vote at the same legislative session, requiring the same majority as when called.

Proposed Through the Initiative
The Florida Constitution provides for calling a convention only through use of the initiative. In South Dakota the initiative may be used to call a convention in the same manner as it is used to amend the state constitution.

Automatic Convention Call
Fourteen states provide that the people be automatically asked periodically whether they wish to hold a constitutional convention. In eight of these the period is twenty years, and in four ten years. Michigan has a convention question vote every sixteen years, and Hawaii every nine years.[56] In 2002, votes were negative by wide margins on the automatic convention question in Alaska, New Hampshire, and Missouri. Rhode Island's convention in 1985 was the most recent called by use of the automatic question. Between 1970 and 2002 the outcome of votes on the automatic convention call was positive four times (Rhode Island, Hawaii [1976] and New Hampshire [1972, 1982]) and negative twenty-five times.[57] Recent history notwithstanding (and as is demonstrated below [table 1]) constitutional conventions have been more frequently called in states with automatic call provisions.

Referendum Election Timing
Constitutions generally require the referendum on a convention to be held in a general election year. Connecticut specifies a general election in an even numbered year. In Oregon and Oklahoma the question may be put at either a general or special election.

Preparation for the Convention Vote
The Rhode Island constitution requires the legislature to create a nonpartisan commission to inform voters of potential constitutional issues prior to a vote on whether to call a convention.

Popular Vote Requirement
Of those states that call for popular ratification of a legislatively proposed convention before it is called, most (twenty-one) require the majority to be of those voting *on the question.* Two of these also specify a minimum required vote: one-quarter of those voting in the last general election in Kentucky, and at least 35 percent of the vote in the general election in which the referendum is held, in Nebraska. Ten states require support of a majority of those voting *in the election* for a convention to be called. (Alternatively in Illinois a convention may be authorized by three-fifths voting on the question.) Six of the ten states with the more demanding popular vote requirement also mandate extraordinary legislative majorities to propose a convention.[58] Finally, three states—Arizona, Oklahoma, and Oregon—are silent on the base of the popular majority required to call a constitutional convention.

For automatic periodic referenda, a majority vote on the proposal is generally required for calling a convention. In Hawaii in 1996 an automatic convention call was supported by a majority of those voting on the question, but the measure failed because a majority of those voting in the election was required.[59]

Limited or Unlimited Convention

The Kansas Constitution is most specific in providing for calling a constitutional convention with a limited agenda. Both the North Carolina and Tennessee constitutions also allow limited conventions. In Tennessee the legislature can limit a convention's substantive reach, but not how it may act on a specified subject one it is called.[60] A convention called in Pennsylvania in 1967 was limited to consideration of some specified matters and barred from taking up others.[61] An attempt to use the indirect initiative to call a limited convention was blocked by the Supreme Judicial Court in Massachusetts in 1970.[62]

In contrast, the Montana Constitution specifies that a convention called through the use of the initiative be unlimited. The Alaska Constitution refers to the power of a convention as "plenary," and says "No call for a constitutional convention shall limit these powers of the convention." Nine automatic referendum states specify the ballot question in their constitutions.[63] This precludes a limited convention resulting from this process. Inability to limit a convention if one is called, and the possibility of the calling of an unlimited convention resulting opening a "Pandora's Box," has been an argument used against calling a convention.[64] This argument is effective because powerful groups in state politics—for example, labor unions, tax limitation advocates, and public employees—often have won inclusion in state constitutions of provisions that protect their interests. They do not wish to see these put at risk of change or removal, however remote the political risk may be. The possibility of a limited convention may remove or reduce this source of opposition.

Staffing, Convening, Structuring, and Operating a Convention

State constitutions vary enormously in the degree of detail with which they deal with the specifics of staffing, convening, structuring, and operating a constitutional convention once it is called. There are three general approaches: minimal detail, maximum detail, and reliance on the legislature with constraining detail.

Minimal Detail: In those states in which legislatures control calling conventions constitutional provisions regarding conventions tend to be relatively simple and flexible. For example, the California Constitution provides that: two-thirds majorities in both houses of the state legislature may schedule a vote on whether to call a convention, if one is called that it should be scheduled within six months, and that delegates should be voters elected from districts as equal as possible in population.[65] Even more simply, the Wisconsin Constitution says:

> If at any time a majority of the senate and assembly shall deem it necessary to call a convention to revise or change this constitution, they

shall recommend to the electors to vote for or against a convention at the next election for members of the legislature. And if it shall appear that a majority of the electors voting thereon have voted for a convention, the legislature shall, at its next session, provide for calling such convention.[66]

Provisions like these leave the legislature free, through enabling statutes dealing with such matters as delegate election and convention structure and operations, to allay fears that commonly arise about these venues for constitutional change being "seen as distant from the general populace, another forum in which elite reformers and entrenched interests compete for political power."[67] Moreover, because ballot language for a convention call is not specified, there is even room in these provisions to test whether the agenda of a convention may be limited in the legislative call presented to the electorate. But this flexibility means little, because history shows that legislators rarely call conventions.

Politicians in power will rarely create a forum they may not control that might seriously alter the power relationships in the polity they govern. It is instructive that only three of the sixteen nonsouthern states in which the legislature has sole control over calling a constitutional convention have had more than one constitution in their history.[68] The average constitution's longevity in these states is significantly higher, and the number of constitutions adopted lower, than for nonsouthern states with an automatic referendum provision or that make no provision at all for calling a convention. (See table 1.)

TABLE 1

Convention Call Provisions, Mean Number of Constitutions, and Average Constitution Longevity (Nonsouthern States Only)

Revision Provision	Number of States	Mean Number of Constitutions	Average Longevity (in years)
Periodic Automatic Referendum*	14	3.0	54.5
No Provision†	6	2.5	79.9
Legislative Call Only‡	19	1.5	94.2
Total	39	2.2	80.3

*Alaska, Connecticut, Hawaii, Illinois, Iowa, Maryland, Michigan, Missouri, Montana, New Hampshire, New York, Oklahoma, Ohio, and Rhode Island.

†Indiana, New Jersey, North Dakota, Pennsylvania, Massachusetts, and Vermont.

‡Arizona, California, Colorado, Delaware, Idaho, Kansas, Kentucky, Maine, Minnesota, Nebraska, Nevada, New Mexico, Oregon, South Dakota, Utah, Washington, West Virginia, Wisconsin, and Wyoming.

Source: Calculated by the author from data in Council of State Governments, Book of the States, 2000–2001 (Lexington, Ky.: The Council, 2000), tables1.1 and 1.4, pp. 3 and 8.

Maximum Detail: In states in which legislatures may be bypassed to call conventions—those with periodic automatic convention referenda—constitutional change provisions tend to be highly detailed. This complexity arises from an effort to make the election of delegates and the organization and operation of the convention as minimally dependent as possible on legislative support.[69]

One example is the New York constitutional provision concerning calling a convention. Not dissimilar from that of a number of other automatic call states, it is more than six times as long as that of Wisconsin. It specifies the ballot question to be used for a convention call by the legislature or as the result of the state's automatic referendum provision; indicates the necessary majority for calling a convention; details the districts to be used for the election of delegates; identifies the time and place the convention will first meet and its duration; provides for the compensation of delegates; establishes the convention's quorum rule; enumerates many of its powers, processes, internal procedures, and required majority for acting; makes provision for filling delegate vacancies; and indicates when its work is to be submitted and how it is to be approved.[70]

The automatic convention call on a twenty-year cycle was added to the New York Constitution in 1846. In a referendum vote required by this provision, the state's voters approved a convention in 1886. However, partisan difference between the Republican state legislature and a Democratic Governor blocked the election of delegates until 1893 and the convening of this convention until 1894. In reaction to this experience, delegates at this convention added detail to New York's provision for constitutional amendment and revision to assure that a convention, once called, would be staffed, and then could meet and do its work in a timely manner, the partisan circumstances in state government notwithstanding.[71]

In 1997, the requirements of these self-executing provisions were used as arguments against a convention when the automatic question provision again required a referendum. One of several possible examples illustrates the point. The New York Senate has been Republican controlled for almost the entire post–World War II period. Senate districts are redesigned every decade by incumbents to assure continuing GOP control of this body. Given this history, the use of these districts for delegate selection as required by the constitution, it was argued by opponents, would likely produce a Republican bias in any potential convention. Moreover, the employment of Senate districts as multimember districts and the election of fifteen convention delegates at-large, both required by the constitution, raised voting rights concerns under federal law, and almost certainly assured litigation if a convention was authorized.[72] Thus a provision added in 1894 to expedite the convening of a convention if it was called came, a century later, to be the basis of arguments against one being called in the first place. The 1997 automatic convention question in New York was decisively defeated at the polls. This outcome was typical. Since 1970 only four of the twenty-five referenda held in states with periodic automatic call provisions have had positive outcomes, the last in 1984.[73]

Reliance on the Legislature, With Some Constraining Detail: A third approach is to rely on the legislature to actually effect a convention if one is called, but direct its activity or build in constraints in specified areas where difficulties might be encountered. Thus, the Colorado Constitution provides that the the general assembly may place a convention call on the ballot by a two-thirds vote of both houses. A majority of those voting is needed to authorize a convention, with delegates elected from state Senate districts numbering twice the membership of that body. Those who seek to serve in the convention must meet the same qualifications as state Senate candidates; vacancies are filled in the same manner as those in the legislature. The convention must begin within three months of delegates' election, and must report between two and six months after adjournment. Most other details are left to the legislature.[74]

The difficulty of this and similar approaches (and even the most detailed approaches), of course, is that they may fail to anticipate all the means in which a state legislature, if hostile, might thwart the holding of a convention.

Specific Areas of Detail
A further review of specific areas of detail in state constitutional provisions concerning conventions reveals the concerns of drafters as they reacted to historic experience and drew lessons from the record in other states.

Frequency of Conventions: The Tennessee Constitution limits the state to no more than one constitutional convention every six years.

Size of the Convention: Delaware's constitution calls for a convention of forty-one delegates. But generally when the size of a convention is constitutionally specified, it is with reference to the size of the state legislature. In Idaho the convention is to be twice the size of the most numerous legislative house; in Colorado twice the size of the Senate. A convention in Kentucky has the same number of members as the Assembly. In Maryland its total membership is equal to the combined membership of the legislative houses.

Districting for Delegate Elections: California requires that delegates be selected from "districts that are as nearly equal in population as may be practicable." Georgia has a similar requirement. Legislative districts are frequently specified for use in delegate selection. In Illinois, for example, two delegates are to be selected from each legislative district. Delaware uses representative districts, augmented by "two . . . from New Castle County, two from Kent County and two from Sussex County." Provisions for using multimember districts for electing convention delegates may raise voting rights concerns under federal law.[75]

Election of Members: Ohio specifies nonpartisan election of convention delegates. In Missouri nonpartisan election is specified for at-large members. A limited nomination and voting system within Senate districts used to elect two delegates each there is used to assure that the two major parties will be equally represented from these districts.

Qualification to Serve: Because legislators fully control the legislative route for proposing amendments, some argue that they should not be permitted to participate in the alternative route (designed to bypass the legislature) as convention delegates. Such a ban should be extended, some think, to all government elected officials and employees, because those in public service should not design the document that creates their jobs, and empowers them. The contrasting view is that such bans are tantamount to "barring doctors from the operating room," excluding the most knowledgeable and interested from convention service.

The Kansas Constitution specifies that legislators may serve as convention delegates. In direct contrast, Missouri bars from service as convention delegates (with a few minor exceptions) persons "holding any other office of trust or profit" in the state. The Hawaii Constitution provides that "any qualified voter of the district concerned shall be eligible" to serve in the convention. Somewhat similarly, the Illinois constitution provides that "To be eligible to be a delegate a person must meet the same eligibility requirements as a member of the General Assembly."

Filling Vacancies: It is common for vacancies in delegate positions to be filled in the same manner as those for one or the other house of the legislature. In Hawaii the governor fills vacancies with "a qualified voter from the district concerned." In Missouri, the governor must appoint to any vacancy a person of the same party, from the same district as the person vacating the post.

Time and Place of First Convening: It is common for constitutions to specify a date on which or by which by which a convention must first meet. The state capitol is often designated as the location of that meeting. With legislatures now in session for far longer than they were when most constitutional amendment and revision provisions were written, there arises the possibility that both the legislature and the convention will have need of the use of the capitol chambers simultaneously.

Leadership, Rules, and Process: Where details are provided, state constitutional conventions are generally charged with selecting their own leadership, adopting their own rules, hiring and compensating staff, keeping a record of their proceedings, and being judge of the qualifications of their own members. Quorum rules and similar procedures appear similar to those constitutionally specified for state legislatures.

Compensation of Delegates: The Delaware and Hawaii constitutions require that the rate of pay for delegates to a constitutional convention be set by statute. The Missouri Constitution sets delegate pay at $10 per day, plus mileage. In New York, delegates must receive the same salaries and be reimbursed for expenses at the same rate as state legislators. As a result of this provision, and because there was no bar to service by legislators as convention delegates, many New York legislators who were elected as delegates to the 1967 constitutional convention—to great public consternation about "double dipping"—were paid two salaries and gained double pension benefits.

Finance: Constitutions often contain general directives that the state legislature provide necessary support for a convention. The Alaska Constitution specifies that "The appropriation provisions of the . . . [convention] . . . call shall be self-executing and shall constitute a first claim on the state treasury."

Time for Consideration and Publicity: Timely submission of the work of a convention, while also allowing enough time for voters to consider it, is an apparent concern in some revision provisions. For example, the Illinois Constitution requires that the work of a convention "shall be submitted to the electors in such manner as the Convention determines, at an election designated or called by the Convention occurring not less than two nor more than six months after the Convention's adjournment." The Georgia Constitution imposes the same obligations to publicize its results on a convention as it does on the legislature to publicize any amendments it proposes. Regarding publicity, the Hawaii Constitution requires that the text of convention recommendations be available at least thirty days prior to their submission to voters at every public library, office of the clerk of each county, and through the chief election officer. The Hawaii document also says that "The convention shall, as provided by law, be responsible for a program of voter education concerning each proposed revision or amendment to be submitted to the electorate." As is the case with legislatively initiated amendments, more recently developed electronic technologies are not specified in constitutions for publicizing convention results.

Submission of Results: Conventions are almost always left discretion regarding the form in which they submit their work to the public. This may be in a single question or in multiple questions. Decisions about the form of submission of convention results may be very important in determining outcome. The submission of the work of the 1967 convention in New York as a single question is widely regarded as a major reason for the draft constitution's failure at the polls.[76]

Ratification: In Missouri and South Dakota ratification of convention proposals must be sought at a special election. The general election must be used in

Florida, Missouri, and New Hampshire (where ratification must also be in an even numbered year). Twenty-one states require a majority voting on the question or questions for ratification of constitutional convention proposals. In Michigan three-fifths support on the proposal is required, and in New Hampshire two-thirds. In Colorado the majority must be of those voting in the election. In Hawaii the requirement is at least 50 percent of those voting in a general election, or in a special election, the equivalent of 30 percent of those registered. In other states ratification majorities are not constitutionally specified. Such specification is desirable to avoid ambiguity, and potential litigation.

Conflict: If both pass and are in conflict, revisions proposed by a convention are given precedence in Hawaii over those proposed by the legislature.

Gubernatorial Veto: The Alabama, Hawaii, and Georgia constitutions specifically bar gubernatorial veto of convention proposals.

Effective Date: As for amendments adopted by various means, most constitutions specify an effective date for constitutional revisions proposed by conventions that receive popular support.

GUIDELINES FOR DEVELOPING A CONSTITUTIONAL CHANGE PROCESS: A CHECKLIST

These guidelines are derived from the foregoing consideration of state provisions for constitutional change, and experience in the states with constitutional change with these provisions, in light of the seven principles identified as fundamental to the change process.

GENERAL

1. POPULAR RATIFICATION—To assure legitimacy, all constitutional changes should be popularly ratified. Ratification is best done by a majority of those voting on a proposal for revision or amendment. Provision that a higher turnout election be used for this vote (a general election in an even numbered year) or—less desirable—that this majority also be a specified proportion, but not a majority, of those voting in the election assures that the change will not be pushed through by a very small proportion of the eligible electorate. Because significant proportions of voters in any election commonly fail to vote on propositions, requiring that a ratifying majority be of all those voting in an election is a high

barrier to change, as is requiring special majorities for amendments concerning specific subject matter (e.g., tax increases).

2. A SINGLE ARTICLE—To reduce complexity and assure full understanding of available options and the possible interactive effects of alternative approaches, there should be a single constitutional location for all means for formal constitutional change available to the polity.

3. AMENDMENT AND REVISION—The constitution should define the difference between amendment and revision and distinctly detail the processes for each.

4. BOTH THROUGH AND WITHOUT THE LEGISLATURE—Both amendment and revision should be achievable without legislative participation, as well as with it.

5. RESPONSIBLE PARTIES—To assure that constitutional requirements are actually effected, accountability for implementation of specific aspects of the change process should be located by the constitution in a specified official or officials (e.g., the Secretary of State, the Attorney General).

6. TIME—Sufficient time should be allowed to accomplish crucial elements of the change process (e.g., signature gathering, correction of error, informing the public of potential constitutional changes). Many states allow one year for signature gathering. Twenty days may be given for error correction. Many states require at least three months to pass after an amendment is proposed or the results of a convention are presented before a vote is taken.

7. CLARITY AND UNDERSTANDABILITY—Ballot language for all proposed constitutional changes should be vetted through a prescribed procedure to assure that it is understandable to a state's citizen with the average level of education for that state. One possible approach is review and certification of the language by the state's highest-ranking Education Department official.

8. VOTER INFORMATION—Provision should be made for informing voters about a proposed change neutrally, as early as practicable, and in a manner that may engage them in an interactive and deliberative process. Options available as the result of the development of new or emerging communications technologies might be anticipated.

9. RESUBMISSION AND RECONSIDERATION—If a constitutional change fails of ratification, a time period should pass before it may be resubmitted. The passage of at least two general election before reconsideration may be reasonable.

10. EFFECTIVE DATE—Clear provision should be made for an effective date for adopted constitutional changes.

AMENDMENT PROCESSES

1. SINGLE SUBJECT—Amendments are best limited to a single subject or object.

2. IMPACT ON EXISTING CONSTITUTION AND INTERPROVISION RELATIONSHIPS—The Attorney General or another responsible state official should be charged with timely assessment and public reporting regarding the effect of a proposed amendment on existing constitutional provisions.

3. HOME RULE—Constitutional changes with specific impact on a single place or class of places within a state should be effective only with its or their specific request or consent.

4. CORRECTION OF ERROR—An alternative procedure to litigation should be constitutionally provided for the identification and correction of error in a proposed amendment before certified for the ballot.

5. LEGISLATIVE PROPOSAL—Constitutional change through the legislature should be more difficult than the passage of ordinary legislation. Extraordinary majorities should be required: two-thirds of those elected to each house is common; three-fifths is an alternative.

6. THE INITIATIVE
   a. The percentage of signatures required to qualify a constitutional initiative should be based on a high turnout statewide race, for example, the previous election for governor.
   b. This percentage should be one and a half to two times as great as for a statutory initiative; between 8 percent and 10 percent are commonly used for constitutional change in the states.
   c. A requirement that assures that signatures are gathered from across the state is desirable.
   d. Provision should be made for expedited judicial review of procedural or substantive challenges to constitutional initiatives made at any stage of the initiative process.
   e. Qualification of an initiative should immediately trigger a neutral process for public information at public expense, including forums, hearings, publications, and the use of the range of available information technology.
   f. Limitations on the reach of the constitutional initiative should be clearly specified in the constitution. (e.g., prohibitions on diminishing individual rights through the initiative).

7. THE COMMISSION—A commission on the Florida model, automatically called to life at specified intervals, should be considered to directly propose to citizens amendments to the constitution's legislative article and to other specified constitutional provisions that directly engage the self-interest of sitting legislators.

CONSTITUTIONAL REVISION

1. REVISION BY CONVENTION—Constitutional revision should be done by a convention authorized by a majority of voters, at the time and in the manner outlined above, and explicitly convened for this purpose.
2. LEGISLATURE AUTHORIZES BUT IS NOT ITSELF A CONVENTION—The legislature should be explicitly empowered to request that the voters call a constitutional convention, but the legislature is not itself a constitutional convention and should be barred from functioning as a convention.
3. AUTHORIZATION OF A CONVENTION WITHOUT THE LEGISLATURE—A means is necessary for bypassing the legislature to place the question of whether to call a constitutional convention before the voters, either use of the initiative to advance the question, or the automatic periodic constitutional convention ballot question.
4. AUTOMATIC BALLOT QUESTION—If the provision is adopted, responsibility should be directly and clearly placed in a specified official to assure that it is asked as constitutionally provided.
5. LIMITED OR UNLIMITED CONVENTION—Whatever the origin of the convention ballot question, the constitution should explicitly authorize both limited and unlimited conventions.
6. SELF-EXECUTING—To the greatest degree practicable, provisions for convening a convention without legislative participation should be self-executing.
7. CONSTITUTIONAL COMMISSION—Concomitant with the authorization of a constitutional convention vote, a publicly financed and professionally staffed nonpartisan commission appointed by multiple appointing authorities (e.g., the governor, legislative leaders from both parties, other statewide elected officials, the chief justice of the state high court) should be established to study and publicize potential constitutional issues before the state. If a convention is authorized, this commission would continue to further engage the public and do necessary preparatory work.
8. DELEGATE ELECTION—The number of convention members and the manner of their election should be constitutionally specified. Nonpartisan elections are desirable. Public financing of these elections should be considered.
9. ELIGIBILITY TO SERVE—Persons holding federal or state elected office should not be eligible to serve as constitutional convention delegates.
10. FIRST MEETING—The time and place of the convention's first meeting should be specified.
11. ORGANIZATION—The convention should judge the qualifications of its members, provide for filling vacancies, select its own

officers, retain staff, and adopt its own rules and generally govern its own proceedings.

12. RESOURCES AND STAFFING—Provision should be made to assure that the convention is adequately staffed and supported in its work.

13. TIME FOR DELIBERATION—The convention should have adequate time for deliberation before reporting, but should place the results of its work on the ballot no later than the second general election day after it first convenes.

14. DELEGATE COMPENSATION—Delegates should be compensated at a level equivalent to the average compensation for a state worker at the date of the convening of the convention, and receive reimbursement for expenses in accord with normal state practice for state workers. Persons should be compensated either as delegates or be provided paid leave from other employment while acting as delegates, but should not be compensated twice while delegates.

15. PUBLIC ENGAGEMENT—The convention should be explicitly charged with assuring public engagement during the course of its work through public hearings and forums, publications, the use of electronic media, and other methods of outreach.

16. BALLOT QUESTIONS—The convention should have discretion in offering its work to the public in a single question or series of questions.

NOTES

1. Adrienne Koch and William Peden (eds.), *The Life and Selected Writings of Thomas Jefferson* (1944), p. 575.

2. G. Alan Tarr, *Understanding State Constitutions* (Princeton: Princeton University Press, 1998), p. 23. Writing in 1987, Michael Colantuono noted that six state courts had established "nonrevision requirements" limiting the scope of state constitutional change permissible through amendment. He cites as the leading case *McFadden v. Jordan*, 32 Cal. 2d. 330, 196 P. 2d 787 (1948) which dealt with whether an amendment made by initiative could revise rather than amend. See his "The Revision of American State Constitutions: Legislative Power, Popular Sovereignty, and Constitutional Change," 75 *California Law Review* 1473, at 1478 and note 27. *See also Raven v. Deukmejian* 801 P. 2d 1077 (Cal., 1990) and *Adams v. Gunther* 238 So. 2d 824 (Fla., 1970).

3. Alaska, Alabama, California, Colorado, Florida, Hawaii, Idaho, Illinois, Kansas, Louisiana, Michigan, Missouri, Montana, Nevada, New Hampshire, North Carolina, Oklahoma, Oregon, Rhode Island, South Carolina, South Dakota, Utah, and Virginia.

4. *See* Gerald Benjamin and Melissa Cusa, "Constitutional Amendment Through the Legislature in New York," in G. Alan Tarr (ed.), *Constitutional Politics in the States* (Westport, Conn.: Greenwood Press, 1996), table I, p. 50.

5. These six states are California, Florida, Hawaii, Georgia, North Carolina and Oregon. *See* Colantuono (1987), note 33, and Tarr (1998), p. 24.

6. *See* Colantuono (1987), p. 1480 and notes 25 and 34.

7. Art. XII, § 1.

8. Art. XIII, § 2.

9. *See* Gerald Benjamin. "The Mandatory Constitutional Convention Question Referendum: The New York Experience in National Context," 65 *Albany Law Review* 1117 (Vol. 65, 2002), pp. 1017–50.

10. Art. XI, § 4.

11. Colantuono (1987), p. 1480. For detail on Georgia *see* Joseph Zimmerman, *The Referendum: The People Decide Public Policy* (Westport, Conn.: Praeger, 2001), pp. 73–74, citing *Wheeler v. Board of Trustees of Fargo Consolidated School District*, et al., 200 Ga. 323, 37 S.E. 322 (1946).

12. *Holmes v. Appling* 237 Ore. 546, 392 P. 2d 636 (1964) cited by Colantuono (1987) at note 42.

13. *See* Benjamin (2002) and Albert L. Sturm, *Thirty Years of State Constitution Making: 1938–1968* (New York: National Municipal League, 1970), pp. 23–24.

14. In fact the Alaska Constitution seeks, as far as practicable, to make the entire document self-executing. *See* art. 12, § 9, cited in Zimmerman (2001), p. 74, note 25.

15. The constitutionality of statutory provisions in Colorado attendant to the initiative process were addressed in *Buckley v. American Constitutional Law Foundation, Inc.* 525 U.S. 182 (1999) and discussed in T. J. Halstead, *State Regulation of the Initiative Process* (Washington, D.C.: Congressional Reference Service, February 16, 1999. RL30067). *See also* Garriga, "Initiative and Referendum . . ." for a discussion of a statutory scheme in Mississippi that, the author argues, combined with a detailed constitutional provision renders the Mississippi indirect initiative extremely difficult to actually employ.

16. John Dinan, "The Earth Belongs Always to the Living Generation": The Development of State Constitutional Amendment and Revision Procedures," *The Review of Politics* (Vol. 62, No. 4, 2000), pp. 645–74.

17. This point is explored in detail in Christopher W. Hammond, "State Constitutional Reform: Is It Necessary?," *Albany Law Review* (Vol. 64, 2001), pp. 1333–34.

18. Five early American state constitutions, New York's among them, lacked amending clauses. Tarr (1998), p. 35. *See also* Burton C. Agata, "Amending and Revising the New York Constitution," in Gerald Benjamin, *The New York State Constitution: A Briefing Book* (Albany: The Temporary State Commission on Constitutional Revision, 1994), p. 42.

19. Formal Change Provisions for State Constitutions: Alabama §§ 284–287; Alaska, art. XIII; Arizona, art. 21; Arkansas, § 22; California, art. 18; Colorado, art. XIX; Connecticut, arts. XII, XIII; Delaware, art. XVI; Florida, art. XI; Georgia, art. X; Hawaii, art. XVII; Idaho, art. XX; Illinois, art. XIV; Indiana, art. 16; Iowa, art. X; Kansas, art. 14; Kentucky, §§ 256–263; Louisiana, art. XIII; Maine, art. X; Maryland, art. XIV; Massachusetts, art. XLVIII; Michigan, art. XII; Minnesota, art. IX; Mississippi, art. 15, § 273; Missouri, art. XII; Montana, art. XIV; Nebraska, art. CXV; Nevada, art. 16; New Hampshire, art. 100; New Jersey, art. IX; New Mexico, art. XIX; New York, art. XIX; North Carolina, art. XIII; North Dakota, art. III, § 9, art. IV, § 17; Ohio, § 16; Oklahoma, art. 24; Oregon, art. XVII; Pennsylvania, art. XI; Rhode Island, art. XIV; South Carolina, art. XVI; South Dakota, art. XXII; Tennessee, art. XI, § 3; Texas, art. 17; Utah, art. XXII; Vermont, § 72; Virginia, art. XIII; Washington, art. XXIII; West Virginia, art. XIV; Wisconsin, art. XII; Wyoming, art. 97–20.

20. Tarr (1998), pp. 73–74.

21. John Alexander Jameson, *The Constitutional Convention: History, Powers and Modes of Proceeding* (New York: Charles Scribner and Company, 1867), chapter VII.

22. Council of State Governments, *Book of the States, 2000–2001*, Vol. 33 (Lexington, Ky.: The Council, 2000), calculated by the author from table 1.6, p. 11.

23. Council of State Governments (2000), table 1.6, p. 11.

24. Lutz. "Patterns . . ." (1996), p. 40.

25. Council of State Governments (2000), summarized from table 1.2, p. 5.

26. Lutz (1996), table 2.8, p. 41.

27. Bruce E. Cain, Sara Ferejohn, Margarita Najar, and Mary Walther, "Constitutional Change: Is It Too Easy to Amend Our State Constitution?," in Bruce E. Cain and Roger G. Noll (eds.) *Constitutional Reform in California* (Berkeley: Institute of Governmental Studies Press, University of California, 1995), pp. 273 and 276.

28. *State ex. rel. Stevenson v. Tufly* 19 Nev. 391 (1887).

29. Generally on the single subject rule see Martha J. Dragich, "State Constitutional Restrictions on Legislative Procedure: Rethinking the Analysis of Original Purpose, Single Subject, and Clear Title Challenges," *Harvard Journal on Legislation*, Vol. 38 (Winter, 2001), pp. 103–67.

30. Art. 4.8.5 (a).

31. But *see* Opinion of the Justices, 81 So. 2s 881 (Ala. 1955). By a 4–3 majority the Alabama Supreme Court, reasoning that no state constitution could be immune from amendment by the people, said that an amendment offered by the legislature would be acceptable that repealed the provision on representation. The minority wrote that such an amendment might be made by a constitutional convention only.

32. *See* the discussion of "Home Rule" ratification provisions, above.

33. *See Book of the States, 2000–2001* (2000), pp. 5–6, table 1.2.

34. *State v. Gonzales* 645 N.W. 2d. 264 (Wis., 2002). *See* Robert Williams and Frank Grad, *State Constitutions for the Twenty-first Century*, Vol. 2 (Albany: State University of New York Press, 2005).

35. G. Alan Tarr summarized developments in the use of the constitutional and statutory initiative in the states during the 1990s thusly: "[D]uring the 1990s, voters in twenty-one states established term limits for state legislators, and in five states they placed such limits on executive branch officials as well. California complemented its attack on incumbency with the adoption of Proposition 140, which prohibited legislators from earning state retirement benefits and required major reductions in legislative agencies and staff. Other states have amended their constitutions to authorize the recall of state elected officials. Minnesota in 1996 brought the number of states employing this device to eighteen. Initiatives in three states have required a supermajority in the legislature to enact tax increases. Initiatives in two other states have tied increases in spending to the rate of inflation and to population increases. Additionally, a Colorado initiative has required voter approval for all new taxes. Indeed, the proliferation of constitutional initiatives itself suggests a profound skepticism about whether the institutions of state government can be relied on to enact good policy. "The State of State Constitutions," *Louisiana Law Review* (Vol. 62, Fall 2001), pp. 3ff. (footnotes deleted). See also Harry N. Scheiber, "The Direct Ballot and State Constitutionalism," *Rutgers Law Journal* (Vol. 28, 1997), pp. 787ff.

36. For a brief but very valuable analysis of the debates in several states on adopting the constitutional initiative *see* John Dinan, "Framing a People's Government: State Constitution Making in the Progressive Era," *Rutgers Law Journal* (Vol. 30, 1999), pp. 979–84.

37. http://www.inadrinstitute.org/factsheets/.

38. This is similar to the provision in the *Model State Constitution*. Art. XII, §§ 12.01–12.02 (New York: National Municipal League, 1968).

39. CCL Task Force (2002), p. 9. For frustrations connected with the Massachusetts process in 2002 *see* Justin Pope, "Voter Initiatives Die at the Statehouse Door in Massachusetts, the Cradle of Liberty," Associated Press, Friday, August 2, 2002.

40. *See* David Magleby, *Direct Legislation: Voting on Ballot Propositions in the United States* (Baltimore: Johns Hopkins, 1984); Thomas Cronin, *Direct Democracy: the Politics of Initiative, Referendum and Recall* (Cambridge: Harvard University Press, 1989); Shaun Bowler and Todd Donovan, *Demanding Choices: Opinion, Voting and Direct Democracy* (Ann Arbor: University of Michigan Press, 2000); and David S. Broder, *Democracy Derailed: Initiative Campaigns and the Power of Money* (New York: Harcourt, 2000).

41. See Zimmerman (2001), pp. 84–87, citing *Meyer v. Grant* 108 S. Ct. 1886 (1988) and *Buckley v. American Constitutional Law Foundation, Inc.* 119 S. Ct. 636 (1999). For a history of the use of paid signature gatherers *see* Richard J. Ellis, "Signature Gathering in the Initiative Process: How Democratic Is It" (typescript, files of the author, 2002), pp. 14–17.

42. Ellis (2002), p. 12.

43. Ellis (2002), p. 12. Montana requires 5 percent of those voting in the imme-diate preceding general election to propose a statutory change by initiative, and twice that to propose a constitutional change. Oregon's signature requirement for a statutory change was 6 percent of those voting in the last gubernatorial election; for a constitutional change it was 8 percent.

44. Ellis (2002), p. 13.

45. *Idaho Coalition United for Bears v. Pete T. Cenarrusa*, Civ. No. 00-0668-BLW cited in Ellis (2002), pp. 58–59.

46. Todd Donovan and Shawn Bowler. "An Overview of Direct Democracy in the States," at http://www.inandrinstitute.org/ filed under "In Depth Studies."

47. Art. 15, § 273.5.

48. *See*, for example, "Developments in State Constitutional Law," *Rutgers Law Journal* (Vol. 32, Summer, 2001), p. 1549ff.

49. Art. XI, §§ 2 and 6.

50. Robert Williams, "The Role of the Constitutional Commission in State Con-stitutional Change," in Gerald Benjamin (ed.), *The New York State Constitution: A Brief-ing Book* (Albany: New York State Commission on Constitutional Revision, 1994), p. 78.

51. Robert Williams, "Is Constitution Revision Success Worth Its Popular Sov-ereignty Price?" *Florida Law Review* (Vol. 2, No. 2, April 2000), pp. 249–73; Rebecca Mae Salokar, "Constitutional Politics in Florida: Pregnant Sows or Deliberative Revi-sion?" Paper given at the Annual Meeting of the American Political Science Associa-tion, San Francisco, California, August 30, 2001. For a range of opinions on the Florida experience *see* other essays in the above cited April 2000 symposium issue of the *Florida Law Review*.

52. New Mexico Constitution, art. XIX, § 1.

53. Utah—Statutes 63.54.1–4, at 63-54-3a,b,c.

54. Those that do not provide for calling conventions are Arkansas, Indiana, Massachusetts, Mississippi, New Jersey, North Dakota, Pennsylvania, Texas, and Ver-mont. *Book of the States* (2000), p. 8, table 1.4.

55. Council of State Governments, *Book of the States* (2000), p. 8, table 1.4. The Alaska majority is drawn from an internal constitutional reference to following proce-dures for the 1955 convention, but is not explicitly specified. In the Hawaii Constitution the majority is not specified.

56. Benjamin (2002), pp. 1018–19, and footnote 12.

57. Benjamin (2002), p. 1044.

58. They are Minnesota, Nevada, South Carolina, Utah, Washington, and Wyoming.

59. Benjamin (2002), p. 1044. Election outcomes for all mandatory constitutional convention referenda between 1970 and 2000 are given on page 1044.

60. Zimmerman (2001), p. 80 citing *Cummings v. Beeler* 189 Tenn. 151, 223 S.W. 2d. 913 (1949) and *Snow v. City of Memphis* 527 S.W. 2d. 55 (1975).

61. Zimmerman (2001), pp. 121–22.

62. Zimmerman (2001), p. 75, citing *Cohen v. Attorney General* 357 Mass. 564, 259 N.E. 2d. 539 (1970).

63. Benjamin (2002), p. 1021, footnote 31.

64. *See* Peter Galie and Christopher Bopst, "The Constitutional Commission in New York: A Worthy Tradition," *Albany Law Review* (Vol. 64, 2001), p. 1285ff.

65. Art. 18, § 2.

66. Art. XII, § 2.

67. Tarr (2001), p. 12.

68. These states are California, Nebraska, and West Virginia. The other states in this group are: Arizona, Colorado, Idaho, Kansas, Maine, Minnesota, Nevada, New Mexico, Oregon, South Dakota, Washington, Wisconsin, and Wyoming. This analysis is confined to nonsouthern states because secession, reconstruction and reunification resulted in an extraordinary level of constitutional change in for the eleven states in the south that joined the Confederacy.

69. A number of other states, Delaware, for example, also have detailed provisions. Two automatic call states, Iowa and Maryland are exceptions. They have very simple revision articles that rely entirely on the legislature for implementation. Iowa's reads: "in case a majority of the electors so qualified, voting at such election, for and against such proposition, shall decide in favor of a convention for such purpose, the general assembly, at its next session, shall provide by law for the election of delegates to such convention, and for submitting the results of said convention to the people, in such manner and at such time as the general assembly shall provide," art. X, § 3.

70. Art. XIX, § 2.

71. Agata (1994), pp. 45–46.

72. *See* Benjamin (2002) passim for a detailed discussion of the 1994–1997 experience in New York.

73. Benjamin (2002), p. 1020.

74. Art. XIX, § 1.

75. Richard Briffault, "The Voting Rights Act and the Election of Delegates to a Constitutional Convention, in Temporary New York State Commission on Constitutional Revision," *Interim Report: The Delegate Selection Process* (Albany: The Commission, 1994), pp. 53–84.

76. Henrik N. Dullea. *Charter Revision in the Empire State: The Politics of New York's 1967 Constitutional Convention* (Albany: the Rockefeller Institute of Government, 1997), chapter 13. In contrast, the 1938 convention in New York submitted its work to the voters in nine questions. Six passed, incorporating fifty-eight proposals for change. *See* Dullea, p. 30.

Chapter Eight

State and Local Finance

Richard Briffault

INTRODUCTION

Nearly all state constitutions give considerable attention to questions of state and local public finance. The typical state constitution devotes at least two articles to state and local taxation, borrowing, and spending. They limit the purposes for which states and localities can spend or lend their funds, and they expressly address specific spending techniques. Nearly all states also impose significant substantive or procedural restrictions or both on state and local borrowing, and on state and local taxation. Some constitutions limit expenditure levels as well.

This state constitutional focus on government finance differs sharply from the federal Constitution's relative indifference to public finance. The Constitution simply authorizes Congress "to lay and collect taxes, duties, imposts, and excises to pay the debts and provide for the common defense and the general welfare of the United States" and "to borrow money on the credit of the United States."[1] Beyond those brief statements, the Constitution imposes two minor procedural constraints on federal spending and taxation: All bills for raising revenue must originate in the House of Representatives,[2] and no money may be drawn from the Treasury "but in consequence of appropriations made by law; and a regular statement and account of the receipts and expenditures of all public money shall be published from time to time."[3] There are also a handful of substantive constitutional constraints on federal taxation: "All duties, imposts, and excises shall be uniform throughout the United States."[4] Taxes and duties on exports are barred;[5] so, too, direct or capitation taxes are barred unless apportioned among the states according to population.[6] The apportionment requirement, however, was modified by the Sixteenth Amendment to authorize federal taxation on incomes without regard to apportionment. There are no constitutional limits on federal borrowing at all.

Where the federal Constitution primarily empowers Congress to raise and spend money, the state constitutions operate to limit state and local government financial support for private sector activities, and to protect state and local taxpayers from the burdens of state and local debt and taxation. In effect, they constitutionalize both the separation of the public from the private sector and the norm of financially limited government.

Or at least they would if they were honored according to their apparent terms. But one of the most striking aspects of the state constitutional law of state and local finance is the enormous gap between the written provisions of state constitutions and actual practice. The public purpose requirements that ostensibly prevent state and local spending, lending, and borrowing in aid of private endeavors are largely dead letters. The substantive and procedural debt limitations have, to a significant degree, been evaded by a host of financial instruments that the courts have held to be beyond the scope of these rules. The constitutional constraints on state and local taxation have been more effective, but their impact, too, has been cushioned by judicial determinations that certain revenue-raising devices are not taxes subject to limitation. Moreover, courts have held that many special-purpose governments are beyond the scope of the constitutional tax and debt limits. As a result, these limits have contributed to the byzantine structure of state and local governance. This chapter will discuss the texts, background, and evolving judicial interpretations of the principal fiscal provisions of state constitutions; and will then consider, in light of the troubled history of these fiscal limits, their place in contemporary state constitutional design.

PUBLIC PURPOSE LIMITS

Constitutional Provisions

By one recent count, forty-six state constitutions contain provisions that expressly limit the authority of their states or local governments to provide financial assistance to private enterprises and, in some cases, public enterprises.[7] The remaining states appear to rely on judicial doctrines that similarly require that state or local taxpayer funds be spent only for public purposes. The New York Constitution is typical in providing that "[t]he money of the state shall not be given or loaned to or in aid of any private corporation or association or private undertaking,"[8] and that "[n]o county, city, town, village or school district shall give or loan any money or property to or in aid of any individual, or private corporation or association, or private undertaking."[9]

Many state constitutions supplement this general "public purpose" requirement with further restrictions on specific forms of financial assistance, such as the prohibition on the state or locality giving or lending its credit to private firms, or the ban on the state or local government becoming a shareholder in a public or private corporation.[10] In addition, public purpose requirements typically apply to state and local borrowing, so that debts may be incurred only to support public purpose projects.

History

Public purpose limitations date back to the middle decades of the nineteenth century, and reflect the disastrous consequences of the states' extensive investments in and assistance to private firms in the 1820s and 1830s. The enormous success of the Erie Canal, which opened in 1825, in energizing New York's economy inspired a massive program of state support for turnpikes, canals, and railroads over the next two decades. Many of these projects blurred public and private lines, with states in partnership with private firms, lending or giving funds to private firms, or providing loan guarantees to firms. The states frequently obtained the funds they used to aid private firms by borrowing. Fueled by interstate competition for economic development, this era of state-supported infrastructure finance was marked by waste, overbuilding, and mismanagement. The Panic of 1837 led to a contraction in economic activity and eventually to an economic crisis. Many firms that had borrowed from the states were unable to repay their loans, and many infrastructure projects failed to generate projected revenues. The states had great difficulties meeting their obligations to their creditors; nine defaulted on interest payments and four states—Arkansas, Florida, Michigan, and Minnesota—repudiated all or part of their debts.

In reaction, the states in the 1840s and 1850s engaged in a wave of constitutional revision. To limit state financial support for private firms, state constitutions were amended to require that state spending or lending be for a public purpose; to bar the gift or loan of state credit except for a public purpose; and to ban direct state investment in business corporation obligations. Initially, these provisions applied only to the activities of state governments. As a result, they could be circumvented by state legislation authorizing local governments to provide assistance to private firms, especially railroads. Another round of waste, overbuilding, and economic crisis followed, and in the late nineteenth century most states amended their constitutions to apply the public purpose and aid limitations to local governments.

Changing Interpretations

The public purpose requirement was never a complete bar to all government financial assistance to the private sector. In the leading mid-nineteenth-century case of *Sharpless v. Mayor of Philadelphia*,[11] the Pennsylvania Supreme Court held that aid to a privately owned railroad could serve a public purpose. "The public has an interest in such a road" even if privately owned, because a railroad provides "comfort, convenience, increase of trade, opening of markets, and other means of rewarding labor and promoting wealth." Most nineteenth-century courts, however, treated their states' public purpose requirements as significant barriers to programs that would provide state or local assistance to private firms or individuals.[12]

Starting in the 1930s, state courts began to widen the definition of public purpose. In 1938, the Mississippi Supreme Court upheld a state program of issuing bonds to finance the construction of factories and the acquisition of machinery and equipment for long-term lease to private firms willing to relocate to the state; such an industrial development program was held to serve a public purpose.[13] Over time, as state industrial and economic development initiatives spread, courts came to broaden the notion of public purpose to include increased employment and tax base growth, and to approve programs that provided assistance to individual firms. Initially, many of these programs were funded by revenue bonds, that is, by bonds backed solely by new revenues to be generated by the firms receiving assistance, so that courts could find that taxpayer dollars were not at risk.[14] Other courts did not distinguish between programs financed by revenue bonds and programs backed by treasury funds.[15] Some courts resisted the general trend and continued to invalidate public financial assistance to private businesses.[16] In some states where courts were reluctant to permit direct state assistance to private firms, the state constitutions were amended to permit some forms of industrial development assistance.

By the end of the twentieth century, virtually every state supreme court had concluded that economic development, job creation, and augmentation of the state or local tax base are public purposes justifying programs that provide aid to the private sector, including direct assistance—cash grants, low-interest loans, tax breaks—to individual firms.[17] Courts have specifically rejected the argument that significant benefits to one or a small number of profit-making firms cause a program to violate the public purpose requirement.[18] Landmark decisions include *Common Cause v. Maine*,[19] in which the Maine Supreme Court upheld the state's plan to commit $15 million in taxpayer funds to improve the facilities of the Bath Iron Works in order to persuade the company to remain in the state, and *Hayes v. State Property & Buildings Commission*, in which a closely divided Kentucky Supreme Court upheld a package of inducements—with direct costs estimated at between $125 and $268 million—to persuade Toyota Motor Corporation to open a plant in the state.[20]

Some courts have continued to police economic development programs, invalidating some—such as those aimed at aiding nonindustrial economic activities like hotels and restaurants.[21] More generally, courts have taken a posture of extreme deference to state legislatures, finding that a broad range of goals fall under the rubric of public purpose, and that legislative determinations that a spending, loan, or tax incentive program will promote the public purpose are to be accepted as long as they are "not . . . irrational,"[22] and will be rejected "only if it is clear and palpable that there can be no benefit to the public."[23] As one dissenting North Carolina justice observed, lamenting the state supreme court's

1996 decision to uphold a new economic development program that would permit taxpayer dollars to be used, inter alia, to pay for spousal relocation assistance when private firms move to the state, there was nothing in the court's decision that would prevent the use of public funds for country club memberships for corporate executives if that would entice firms to relocate to the state.[24]

The decline of the public purpose doctrine as a limit on state spending has had some impact on other state constitutional restrictions on public aid to the private sector. In some states, the restriction on lending of credit does not apply if the assistance is provided for a public purpose.[25] In those states the expansion in the scope of public purpose has eroded the lending of credit ban.[26]

In other states, however, lending of credit remains an additional restriction. Even if a program constitutes a public purpose, the technique of lending the state's or locality's credit may still be proscribed. Most state courts find that a lending of credit has occurred when a state serves as a surety or guarantees a loan made by another lender.[27] The constitutional provision, thus, protects against the tendency of legislators to discount the risks posed by standing surety when the state is not required to directly commit any funds at the time the suretyship obligation is assumed. A few state courts have gone further and found that a proscribed lending of credit occurs when a state borrows money and provides the proceeds to another entity.[28] For the most part, however, state courts have distinguished lending of credit from borrowing followed by the provision of public funds to a private recipient, and have limited the lending of credit ban to the former situation.[29]

In addition to public purpose and lending of credit requirements, a number of state constitutions prohibit state investment in business corporations. This ban may apply even if the investment is for an economic development purpose.[30] These provisions appear to be a direct response to the nineteenth-century practice of state subscriptions to canal or railroad company stock. As a result, a state may be able to give or lend money to a private firm on a public purpose theory, but may be barred from taking an equity position in the firm that would enable it to share in any appreciation in the firm's value. These provisions have generated relatively little litigation.

BORROWING AND DEBT LIMITATIONS

Constitutional Provisions

The vast majority of state constitutions impose some limitation on the ability of their states and local governments to incur debt. These constitutional limitations take a variety of forms. Some bar state debt outright.[31] Others impose very low limits on the amount of debt a state may incur.[32] Some cap state debt

or debt service at a fraction of taxable wealth or revenues.[33] Tying the debt limit
to a fraction of property wealth or revenue is a particularly widespread way of
limiting local government debt.[34] This approach suggests an attempt to limit
debt to the "carrying capacity" of the state or locality, so that new borrowing
does not result in burdensome taxation or cuts in existing services.

Most commonly, state constitutions rely on a procedural restriction: state
or local debt may not be incurred without the approval of a majority (or supermajority) in the legislature, of voters in a referendum, or of both.[35] A legislative supermajority or voter approval requirement may also be combined with a
substantive cap on the amount of state or local debt.[36]

For state governments, the procedural requirements are often the real restrictions on debt. As state constitutions can be amended, an absolute prohibition or a low dollar limit on debt can be circumvented by a constitutional
amendment authorizing a specific bond issue. As a result, the legal requirements for a constitutional amendment—typically, a combination of a legislative
supermajority and voter approval in referendum—also become the requirements for issuance of debt. Thus, although the Alabama Constitution flatly
bars state debt, as of the early 1990s, it contained thirty-three amendments authorizing specific bond issues.[37]

Background

Like the public purpose requirements, the state constitutional debt limitations
date back to the turnpike, canal, and railroad boom of the 1820s and 1830s, the
Panic of 1837, and the resulting wave of tax increases to pay off the state debts
blithely assumed in prior years. The first constitutional limits were adopted in
the 1840s, and by 1860, nineteen states had adopted debt limitations. Most of
the reconstructed southern states and the western states admitted to the Union
after the Civil War included debt limitations in their constitutions. When state
legislatures turned to local governments to borrow funds to aid private firms,
particularly railroad companies, and localities found themselves overcommitted
in the aftermath of the economic crisis that began in 1873, most states amended
their constitutions to limit local government borrowing as well.

Apart from the specific historical background, constitutional restrictions
on debt may be justified as a means of reconciling the conflict between short-
term and long-term interests that debt generates. When a government finances
a capital project—a bridge, a school building, a prison—that has long-term
benefits, it is appropriate to spread the costs of the project over the project's
useful life. Borrowing the money and repaying the debt over a period of
decades spreads the cost to the future generations who will benefit from the

project. But the ability to shift the costs into the future may also induce elected officials to incur too much debt. The benefits of the project financed by the debt will be received immediately while the costs of paying off the debt are deferred into the future. As a result, current elected officials may be tempted to approve projects that are not fully cost-justified. After all, they can get the credit for the new project, but the blame for the additional taxes needed to pay off the debt will be borne by their successors. A central justification of constitutional limits on debt is to offset the temptations that can cause elected officials, and the current generation they represent, to burden future generations with unnecessary debt. The constitutional control can provide a constraint likely to be missing from the ordinary political process.

Evasions of the Limits

Like the public purpose requirements, the state debt limitations have not had quite the effect their terms suggest. State constitutions typically require the state or locality to pledge its "full faith and credit" in support of its debt. This means that such a debt is a "general obligation" of the state or locality backed not by a particular revenue source but by the full revenue-raising capacity of the borrowing government. Debt limitations clearly apply to such debt. But today most state and local borrowing does not involve general obligation debt and avoids the pledge of full faith and credit.

Revenue Bonds
Stimulated in part by the desire to avoid the substantive caps and voter approval requirements of their constitutions, states and localities have developed financial instruments that enable them to borrow without pledging their full faith and credit. Instead, the debt is backed only by a specific revenue source. As a result of state judicial interpretation, or in some states, constitutional amendment, such "nonguaranteed" or "revenue bond" debt is not subject to the constitutional limitations that apply to general obligation debt.

Initially, the only revenue bonds exempt from the debt limitations were self-liquidating project finance bonds, for example, bonds issued to finance a project whose revenues would be used to pay off the debt incurred to finance the project. For example, to build a bridge, the state might issue a bond, promise the bond buyers to impose a toll on the bridge financed by the bond, and pledge the revenues generated by the bridge toll to repay the bonds. State courts found that as long as the state limits its payment obligation to the "special fund" generated by the project the debt does not pose a risk to future taxpayers and, thus, is not "debt" within the meaning of the state constitutions.

Over time, however, the revenue bond concept spread well beyond debts backed solely by charges imposed on the use of the facilities financed by borrowing. One extension involves bonds backed by taxes on activities that benefit from the project financed by the bond. Many courts have held that bonds to finance highway construction are not "debt" in the constitutional sense if they are backed solely by taxes on motor fuels and vehicle license fees. In theory, the new highways so financed will generate the additional auto usage and the additional fuel tax and fee revenues that will pay off the debt and thus do not pose a risk to future taxpayers.[38] Similarly, a bond issued to finance a convention center might not be "debt" within the meaning of the constitutional constraint if it is backed by taxes on hotel occupancy, on the theory that the convention center would promote hotel use, generate the necessary new hotel tax revenues, and thus not threaten future taxpayers.[39] The cases are not always consistent,[40] but the trend has been to loosen the nexus required between the project financed by the bond and the revenues committed to paying off the obligation in order to justify avoidance of the debt limitation.[41]

Lease Financing

Lease financing extends the revenue bond concept—and the exemption from debt restrictions—from the creation of new revenue-generating infrastructure to the construction of new government facilities. In a lease-financing scenario, a private firm or a public authority issues the necessary bonds and builds the facility. Private debts are certainly not subject to constitutional debt limits, and virtually all state courts have held that the debts of public authorities are not debt in the constitutional sense since the authorities lack the capacity to impose taxes or pledge the full faith and credit of the state or a locality. To finance the bond, the state or a local government enters into an arrangement with the bond issuer to lease the facility for a period of time, with the government's lease payments covering the annual debt service. So long as the government's commitment to make payments is contingent on its use of the facility and is subject to annual legislative appropriation, most courts have found that the commitment is not "debt" in the constitutional sense. [42]

Subject-to-Appropriation Debt

The closing decades of the twentieth century witnessed the emergence of a new form of revenue bond that dramatically expands the opportunities for evasion presented by the leasing-financing bond. Under this scenario, the debt is issued by an entity, typically a public authority or special district not subject to constitutional restriction, which uses the borrowed funds to undertake some project for the state or a constitutionally restricted locality. This need not involve the construction of a leaseable facility or the payment of rent. Rather the state or locality that benefits from the debt simply contracts with the issuer to make an annual payment to cover the annual debt service. So long as the contract is subject to annual appropriation—and any duty to make an annual appropriation is clearly disclaimed—most courts that have considered this financing scheme have held that the government's commitment to make a debt service payment is not a legally binding obligation and thus not debt within the meaning of the state constitution.[43]

Subject-to-appropriation debt is a relatively recent development and a particularly blatant evasion of the constitutional debt limitations. It closely resembles so-called moral obligation debt, which loomed large in municipal finance in the 1960s and 1970s. Under the moral obligation scenario, a public authority issued a bond that would be backed by authority revenues, typically, revenues to be generated by the facility to be financed by the bond. If the authority, or potential investors, were uncertain whether the facility so financed would be able to produce the necessary revenues, the state would make a nonbinding commitment of state funds to cover debt service in the event that revenues from the bond-financed projects fell short. The state's moral obligation provided an important safety net for public authority bond issues for moderate-income housing, hospitals, universities, and mental institutions. State courts generally concluded that the legislature's mere "moral" obligation to appropriate debt service did not constitute a debt triggering the constitutional debt limitations.[44] The moral obligation device, however, came under a cloud in the mid-1970s when New York State had to come to the rescue of its Urban Development Corporation and make good on its moral obligation to support the UDC.

In one sense, appropriation clause debt is less troubling than moral obligation debt since states did not make any initial appropriation to the authorities issuing the moral obligation bonds. The state's role was only to serve as a safety net. But that may have created the illusion that moral obligation debt was cost free to the state, and may have led states to take on such debt too easily. Contemporary subject-to-appropriation obligations dispense with the illusion that they involve no cost to the state. Rather, from the beginning, they involve the expenditure of public funds, and they thus can be factored into budget projections and counted as part of regularly recurring government costs. Yet, by treating subject-to-appropriation obligations as part of baseline expenses and treating them like debt from the very beginning, the new device only heightens the tension with the constitutional debt restrictions.

Appropriation-clause debt has become increasingly common in recent years. According to a 2001 statement issued by Standard & Poor's, a leading bond rating agency, "this type of debt issuance is now common in at least 33 states." Default levels have been comparable to those of full faith and credit general obligation bonds. "[W]hile appropriation-backed bonds are not considered debt under a strict legal definition, Standard & Poor's considers all appropriation-backed bonds of an issuer to be an obligation of that issuer and a failure to appropriate will result in a considerable credit deterioration for all types of debt issued by the defaulting government."[45]

Indeed, in upholding subject-to-appropriation debts, many state courts have candidly acknowledged that the state or locality behind the obligation will do its best to assure that the annual appropriations are made, since failure to make the annual payment would surely have a sharply negative impact on the state's own bond rating. As the California Supreme Court has stated, "we are not naive about the character of this transaction."[46] Courts have repeatedly acknowledged but then rejected the argument that the "practical consequences" of nonpayment will compel states and localities to treat nonbinding appropriation clause debt as binding debt.[47] Instead, courts have relied on the disclaimers of any state legal obligation to pay debt service as conclusively establishing that the dangers for future taxpayers of long-term financial commitments that were the driving force behind the debt restrictions are not presented by appropriation-clause debt.[48]

Not all courts have been happy with this development. Many of the cases in which state supreme courts accepted appropriation-clause debt have been marked by close votes and sharp dissents, with the dissenters decrying the evisceration of the constitutional debt limitations and calling for a "common sense" or realistic interpretation that would recognize that these borrowings are binding in practice.[49] In a dramatic move, the New Jersey Supreme Court recently called into question its acceptance of appropriation clause debt. In its 2002 decision in *Lonegan v. State*,[50] the Court threatened to reverse itself and hold that public authority debt backed solely by state contracts subject-to-appropriation is debt in the constitutional sense. *Lonegan* involved $8.6 billion in bonds for repairing and constructing new public schools—the "largest, most comprehensive school construction program in the nation."[51] The bonds were to be issued by a state authority, and backed by a state subject-to-appropriation contract. The voter approval constitutionally required for new state debt had been neither sought nor obtained. The Court expressed serious doubt about the propriety of the appropriation contract device, but ultimately concluded that since the school construction program involved the "provision of constitutionally required facilities"[52] and was itself a response to the orders of the Court in New Jersey's long-standing school funding litigation, it did not violate the state's debt limitation provision.[53] The Court then set down for reargument the broader question of the constitutionality of subject-to-appropriation debt outside the school construction context.[54]

It is not clear if *Lonegan* will signal a change in the highly deferential approach most state courts have taken to state debt, whether the courts will return to much older practices of limiting the revenue bond to self-liquidating or revenue-generating projects, or whether the lease-financing exemption will be narrowed to require that lease payments reflect fair market rentals rather than debt service. Certainly, the general trend across the country in recent decades has been one of broad toleration for state and local evasion of constitutional limits so long as the full faith and credit of a government restricted by the state constitution has not been pledged.

Indeed, as a result of these various evasive techniques, approximately three-quarters of all state debt and two-thirds of city and county debt is not subject to the panoply of substantive limitations and procedural requirements found in state constitutions. Debt limits have plainly affected the form of state and local debt, but it is far from clear whether they have affected the total amount of debt. Moreover, evading state constitutions has costs. In order to avoid falling into the category of constitutional debt, these instruments avoid pledging the full faith and credit of the state or locality, and they limit the recourse of lenders seeking principal and interest payments to certain funds. As a result they present a slightly greater risk to investors, and thus usually carry a slightly higher interest rate than general obligation bonds. They also involve greater administrative and legal costs than general obligation debt since issuers not pledging full faith and credit have to provide lenders with other forms of security. Over time, as the bond market has grown familiar—and comfortable—with these debts, the interest rate differential between the guaranteed and nonguaranteed obligations of the same jurisdiction has narrowed, but some distinction usually continues, and the higher administrative costs of issuing these bonds remains.

In addition, as the discussion indicates, public authorities play a major role in the evasion of state constitutional debt limits. Unless the state constitution specifically provides otherwise, state courts have generally found that as public authorities lack the power to impose taxes or to pledge the full faith and credit of their states public authority debt is not subject to constitutional debt limits.[55] In many states public authorities have become conduits for the "backdoor financing" of appropriation-backed debt.[56] Debt avoidance has played an important role in explaining the rise of public authorities and their significant role in state and local governance today.

TAXATION AND EXPENDITURE LIMITATIONS

Background

State constitutional provisions concerning state and local taxation are marked by far greater state-to-state and intrastate variation than the public purpose requirements and the borrowing and debt limitations. State constitutions have traditionally given their greatest attention to the property tax. Like many other features of state constitutions, this is an artifact of history. When states first began to amend their constitutions to address questions of taxation, the property tax was the dominant mode of taxation for state and local government. As late as 1902, the property tax accounted for 82 percent of total state and local tax collections—including 53 percent of state tax dollars and 89 percent of local tax dollars. Over the course of the twentieth century, the role of the property tax declined. The states generally turned the property tax over to local governments, and came to rely on other revenue sources, primarily sales and income taxes, for state funds. Today property taxes generate no more than 2 percent of state revenues and in many states the property tax generates nothing for the state government at all. The property tax remains the leading source of local revenues—about 75 percent of local tax dollars—although with the rise of other local taxes, intergovernmental assistance, and especially, local nontax revenue sources, the property tax generates only about 30 percent of all local revenues.

State constitutional provisions concerning taxation have two primary strands: (1) equality or uniformity requirements; and (2) substantive and procedural limitations on levels of taxation. These provisions are addressed primarily, but not exclusively, to the property tax.

Uniformity

Almost all state constitutions contain some provisions for uniform or equal taxes.[57] In some states, the uniformity requirement applies to all taxes.[58] In other states, the uniformity or equality requirement is focused on the property tax.[59] The uniformity requirement may apply to tax rates; to the measure of the value subject to tax; or to the determination of the persons or activities subject to a tax. The uniformity requirement appears intended to promote equal treatment of taxpayers. It also presumes that taxation ought to function as a broad and general means of raising revenues from the community, rather than as a policy tool for subsidizing certain programs, for imposing differential burdens on different parts of the community, or for redistribution. The uniformity requirement, thus, poses a challenge for certain common forms of taxation. "A graduated income tax by its very nature lacks the uniformity of taxation typically required by the state constitutional restrictions. A controversy that raged throughout the country, as states enacted income tax levies, was whether the income tax constituted a property tax that violated the uniformity provisions."[60]

As noted, many states limit the uniformity requirement to the property tax, but uniformity has posed challenges even for that tax. Many local governments have long imposed higher property taxes on commercial and industrial properties, which can pass their taxes along to consumers, than on residential property. Typically, in tacit deference to the uniformity requirement, this was accomplished by assessing industrial and commercial property at a higher percentage of value and by assessing residential property at a lower percentage of value. Courts long tolerated such de facto variations in assessments, but in the latter part of the twentieth century they more vigorously enforced uniformity rules and analogous provisions requiring property to be assessed at full value. Constitutional controversies concerning assessments have also been triggered by state laws that seek to cushion the burden of property taxes on certain uses, like agriculture or open space, by permitting such property to be assessed at a lower percentage of value or according to "current use value" rather than fair market or exchange value. Some state constitutions now expressly authorize differential tax rates or assessments by providing for the "classification" of property into commercial, industrial, residential, and other classes and requiring uniformity of tax treatment only within a class. Some state constitutions also authorize, or require, the exemption of certain property (educational, charitable, religious) from taxation. Even in states that authorize classification or exemption, issues continue to arise concerning the definition of classes, whether a property falls within a particular class, or whether the provision of other tax preferences violates uniformity. As a result state courts may be more involved in reviewing the constitutionality of tax differentials and tax preferences than their federal counterparts.

Substantive Limitations on Local Taxation

Most state constitutions impose some substantive limitations on local taxation. Until recently, reflecting the historic primacy of the property tax in state and local finance, these were focused almost exclusively on that tax. Limitations "first appeared in state statutes in the 1870s and 1880s and were later incorporated in many state constitutions." These were aimed at holding down government spending and protecting property owners. A "second round of constitutional tax limitations appeared during the Depression of the 1930s. They were aimed at forcing tax reductions, thereby stemming the tide of tax delinquencies and tax foreclosures of residential property."[61] A third wave of constitutional limitation of taxation began with California's adoption of Proposition 13 in 1978, and continues to some degree to this day.

These tax limitations have taken a variety of forms, including: (1) limitation on the tax rate; (2) limitation on assessments of particular parcels; (3) limitation on the rate of increase in assessment or the rate of increase in tax due from a taxpayer; (4) limitation on the total levy from the locality as a percentage of the community's assessed valuation; (5) limitation on the rate of increase in the community's total levy.

California's Proposition 13 focuses on limiting tax rates, assessments, and assessment increases. Massachusetts's Proposition 2½, adopted in 1980, addresses the community-wide levy, by limiting the total property tax yield to

2.5 percent of total assessed valuation, and limiting the increase in total revenue raised by the property tax in each locality to 2.5 percent per year.[62] Many older limits also capped local property tax levies as a percentage of local assessed valuation.[63] These different forms of tax limitation can have different incentives for community land use practices, and on local capacity to finance services.

Voter Approval Requirements

Some of the older tax limitations permitted local overrides, and higher rates or levies, if authorized by a local referendum. Proposition 2½ similarly permits local voters to override the 2.5 percent limit on the rate of local property tax revenue increase (but not the 2.5% total levy cap). The round of tax limitations that began with Proposition 13 has given new prominence to the role of the electorate in taxation. Several state constitutions—for example, those of California, Colorado, Michigan, and Missouri—make new local taxes or tax increases subject to voter approval. Similar measures were adopted by voters in Montana and Washington, though the supreme courts of these states held the initiatives violated state constitutional single-subject requirements.[64] Efforts to require voter approval of new taxes or tax increases have also been underway in Arizona, Florida, and Oregon.[65] These go beyond the traditional constitutional focus on the property tax and apply to all local taxes. Indeed, the Missouri measure applies to licenses and fees,[66] although the state's courts have struggled over the application of the voter approval requirement to nontax revenues.[67]

Limitations on State Taxation and Expenditures

In the post–Proposition 13 wave of tax limitation, many states amended their constitutions to constrain state taxation, not just local taxes or the property tax, which were the traditional targets of constitutional regulation. Proposition 13 prohibits any increases in state taxation without approval of two-thirds of each house of the California legislature.[68] The constitutions of a dozen states now require a legislative supermajority (ranging from 60% to 75%) for new or increased state taxes.[69] A number of states have also adopted constitutional or statutory measures that cap either state revenues or state appropriations. Generally, these measures seek to limit any increase in revenues or expenditures to the growth in state personal income, growth in state population, growth in the cost of living, or some combination of these measures, relative to a baseline year.[70]

Michigan's Headlee Amendment is illustrative. In addition to limiting local taxes, the measure establishes a state revenue limit "equal to the product of the ratio of Total State Revenues in fiscal year 1978–79 divided by the Personal

Income of Michigan in calendar year 1977 multiplied by the Personal Income of Michigan in either the prior calendar year or the average of Personal Income of Michigan in the previous three calendar years, whichever is greater."[71] The state legislature is prohibited from imposing "taxes of any kind which, together with all other revenues of the state, federal aid excluded, exceed the revenue limit." In any fiscal year in which total state revenues exceed the revenue limit by 1 percent or more "the excess revenues shall be refunded pro rata based on the liability reported on the Michigan income tax and single business tax (or its successor tax or taxes) annual returns filed following the close of such fiscal year. If the excess is less than 1 percent, this excess may be transferred to the State Budget Stabilization Fund."[72] This limit can be exceeded only if the governor's declaration of emergency is confirmed by two-thirds of the members of each legislative house.[73] Missouri's Hancock Amendment is very similar.[74]

Effects

Empirical research on tax and expenditure limitations (TELs) has found several broad effects, although the effects vary considerably from state to state according to the terms of the specific restrictions.

Reduced Role of the Property Tax
TELs have contributed to the reduction in property taxes as a percentage of personal income and in the role of property taxes in funding local government. Nationwide (including the many states that did not adopt TELs), the property tax share of personal income dropped from 4.1 percent in 1978 to 3.2 percent in 1982, rebounded to 3.7 percent in 1992, and dropped modestly after that. In California, which adopted one of the most stringent property tax limits in the country, the share of county revenue from the property tax dropped from 33.2 percent in 1977–78 to 11.6 percent in 1995–96; the role of the property tax in funding cities and special districts dropped as well.[75]

Increased Role for Nontax Revenue Sources
TELs appear to have contributed to an increase in the role of assessments, fees (including development impact fees) and user and service charges in funding local governments. One study found that for California cities the percentage of current revenue from service charges rose from 25 percent in 1977–78 to 41 percent in 1999–96.[76] Nationwide, by the early 1990s, fees and charges accounted for 14.6 percent of total local revenues and 23 percent of local own-source revenues.[77]

This development has involved both greater state and local efforts to fund public programs out of fees, charges, and assessments imposed on service users and the immediate beneficiaries of government spending—rather then rely on more redistributive general taxation—and a greater state judicial willingness to expand the notion of what constitutes an assessment, fee, or charge, rather than a tax.

Traditionally courts have ruled that fees and assessments are not taxes—and therefore outside the scope of constitutional tax restrictions—for one of two reasons.

1. In the case of a fee or charge, payment was not coercive but contingent on the payer's decision to use a service, or was intended to offset a cost imposed by the feepayer's activity. Either way, by foregoing the service or the activity, the payer could avoid the fee. So, too, where the size of the fee is based on the amount of the service used, or the extent of the activity triggering regulation, the payer could reduce its liability by reducing its usage or activity. As a result, the payment was considered voluntary, not coercive—with coercion the hallmark of a tax.[78]

2. In the case of assessments, these were traditionally used to fund new government infrastructure—like a street, sidewalk or utility hookup—directly adjacent or connecting to the payer's property. As a result, the payer was provided with a benefit worth at least as much as the assessment. Although the assessment was still coercive—a property owner could not choose to avoid the assessment by declining to have his sidewalk paved—the provision of a special benefit directly to the property owner enabled courts to conclude that the assessment was not a tax in the constitutional sense.[79]

In recent years, many state courts have come to embrace a broader view of the permissible uses of fees and assessments. Some state courts have validated regulatory fees without tying a particular firm's fee to the costs attributable to that firm—thereby reducing the ability of the firm to use changes in its behavior to control its fee and thus undermining the "voluntary" nature of the fee.[80] So, too, many state courts have sustained a dramatically expanded use of the assessment to finance traditional municipal services and programs that provide diffuse benefits to relatively large areas, with the payer's assessment calculated based on his property value. Despite the close resemblance to the property tax, courts have upheld such assessments when the area benefited is less than the entire municipality.[81]

Combining the assessment and fee concepts, many state courts have upheld development impact fees, which require developers to pay in advance for a host of municipal services and improvements—including new roads, new schools, and expansions of water supply and sewage systems—required by the population growth attributable to the development. These charges are based on property, impose costs that are presumably passed along in increased property prices to new home buyers, and pay for traditional municipal services. But viewed as assessments or fees they are not subject to state constitutional constraints on taxation.[82]

To be sure, some courts have attempted to police the fee/tax line more closely and have required that to avoid treatment as a tax the fee must be truly voluntary and calibrated according to the payer's use or the cost the payer imposes.[83] Moreover, some fairly recent state constitutional amendments explicitly impose voter approval requirements on fees and special assessments.[84]

Nevertheless, it appears that much as the debt limitations stimulated the proliferation of new forms of public borrowing that avoid the constitutional "debt" label, the tax limitations have spawned a host of revenue-raising devices that avoid the constitutional "tax" label. As with debt, a significant share of state and local revenue is now raised by devices not subject to tax limits, although, unlike the case with debt, most state and local revenue is still raised by constitutional taxes. Like the debt limits, the tax limits have also added to the complexity of local government structures by inspiring states and localities to create special districts and other limited-purpose governments that are not subject to constitutional restrictions.[85]

Moreover, the rise of nontax revenue sources has reduced the ability of states and especially local governments to engage in redistributive programs. The key to the exemption of fees, charges and assessments from the label of "tax" is that they provide the payers with a benefit at least equal to their payments (or to the social costs imposed by the payer's behavior). By definition, this precludes the use of fees and assessments to finance broadly redistributive activities. Assessments and fees enable those willing and able to pay for higher levels of service for themselves to do so, but the poor remain dependent on the votes of the community as a whole to approve the taxes necessary for the services that benefit them.

Shift in Power to the States

TELs imposed on local governments may have contributed to a shift in power to the states. The fiscal limits on local governments are typically more stringent than those imposed on the states, and they have made local governments more dependent on state aid. For California counties, for example, the share of revenue from intergovernmental transfers rose from 50.6 percent in 1977–78 to 64.1 percent in 1995–96.[86] With limits on local property taxation, the state also now plays a greater role in allocating local property revenues among competing local governments.

Reduction in Local Revenue Growth

Even with the growth in intergovernmental aid, new taxes, and nontax local revenues, TELs appear to have reduced local revenue growth. To be sure, the impact of the TELs has varied from state to state, according to the stringency of the limits, changes in the economy, and subsequent state legislative or constitutional action. But for the most part, revenues in states with TELs have grown more slowly than in states without them.[87] To that extent, then, state constitutional limitations on taxation have succeeded where the state limitations on debt appear to have failed. But this poses more directly the question of whether this is an appropriate goal for state constitutions.

THE REFORM AGENDA

Initial Considerations

Two initial considerations ought to shape the general question of what public finance restrictions ought to be in state constitutions. First, what matters need to be constitutionalized, that is, placed beyond the day-to-day control of the political process and instead entrenched in the fundamental structure of the states? Second, even if in theory a rule or principle ought to constrain ordinary politics and be protected from politics rather than subject to politics, is constitutionalization an effective means of obtaining that goal? Considering these considerations in light of the purposes, history, and contemporary applications of the state public finance provisions leads to two paradoxical outcomes.

First, there is much to be said in theory for constitutionalizing the public purpose requirement and restrictions on debt. The fundamental purpose of government—the purpose that justifies the coercive taxation that enables government to pursue its spending and lending programs—is the promotion of the public good. Public purpose is essential to all government action. Moreover, it would be desirable to adopt a constitutional rule limiting the ability of the states and localities to dedicate public funds to private ends. State and local spending presents the classic problem of concentrated benefits for the politically influential few at the expense of costs diffused across the broad polity of taxpayers. Special interest groups have the incentive to lobby and the means to reward legislators who provide them with benefits. But the general public is unlikely to be sharply affected by any one interest group giveaway and lacks both the incentive and the means to police closely spending programs. Thus, there is a case for a public purpose limit on government spending.

So, too, it may be difficult for the public to effectively control debt through ordinary electoral control of state and local officials. As already noted, debt involves a combination of immediate gain followed by a cost at some point in the future. That cost will be felt by future taxpayers who can respond only by punishing future officeholders—who quite often will not be those who voted to incur the debt in the first place. Future debts are likely to be current campaign issues, and concern about debt may be offset by the benefits from debt-funded programs. Debt limits are justified by the lack of effective political controls over the borrowing decision.

Yet, constitutional public purpose and debt limitations have been largely ineffective. Courts have expanded the notion of public purpose to the point where it encompasses virtually all forms of government activity. If direct assistance to individual private firms can be justified as promoting employment, then the constitutional public purpose requirement can no longer limit government spending. For the most part the courts have held that determining public purpose is a job for the political branches, not the courts. If that is the case, then a constitutional public purpose requirement is purely rhetorical.

The courts have been almost as tolerant of devices that evade debt limits, repeatedly indicating that arrangements that abide by the letter of the law—albeit barely—but not its spirit are constitutional. As several courts have stated, "it is never an illegal evasion of a constitutional provision or prohibition to accomplish a desired result, which is lawful in itself, by discovering or following a legal way to do it."[88] Indeed, the courts have praised debt evasion as a tribute to "the modern science of government" and a "constitutionally acceptable device of modern day progressive government."[89]

Second, limits on aggregate taxation or expenditures seem to have little justification. New or increased taxes, or increased spending levels that must be sustained by new or increased taxes, are immediately apparent to and felt by the voters. As the political power of the antitax movement has demonstrated in recent decades, the public is ready, willing, and able to make its sentiments on taxation known to elected officials. There is little need for constitutional limits to supplement public political control. Yet, such limitations are widespread and have to a considerable degree (at least compared with the debt limits) been enforced by the courts. While they have accepted some evasive devices, courts have been far more protective of the tax limits than the debt limits.[90]

As a result, the limitations that are most defensible in terms of the role of the constitution in addressing defects in the political process have been generally abandoned by the courts, while the limitations that have little constitutional justification have been somewhat more vigorously enforced. This both shapes and complicates the appraisal of the proper role of the state constitution in regulating state and local finance.

Public Purpose

The Public Purpose Requirement

The general public purpose requirement is a dead letter today and probably incapable of constitutional resuscitation. The courts are correct in noting the broad expansion over the course of the twentieth century of what constitutes a legitimate public purpose. In particular, there is general political acceptance of the belief that government has some responsibility to promote economic development and, especially, employment. Today, the definition of what are the public purposes of government is a deeply political one, which may appropriately be left to the political process, not the courts.

The closer question involves the degree to which a particular program advances the stated public purpose of economic development, and what to do about public programs that provide large benefits to specific private firms as part of promoting the public purpose. Should courts strictly scrutinize the fit between the public end and the means chosen, or the balance between the public and private benefits? The courts have largely concluded that such review is beyond their capacity, and that the question of means as well as ends is a political question, not a judicial one.

Direct public aid to the private sector is a controversial economic development strategy. Most studies indicate that government financial assistance and tax breaks are relatively minor factors in corporate location decisions.[91] Moreover, corporations have proved adept at playing off competing localities against each other in order to extract government payments or tax exemptions. Even when companies do create new jobs in response to a government incentive, the payments may be short term and the firm may pull up stakes a few years later.[92] Given the difficulties of judicial policing of constitutional limits on economic development programs, a better strategy for promoting the public purpose might be statutory reforms that provide for better recordkeeping and public disclosure of the benefits that economic development programs produce so that the ongoing political debate over these programs may be better informed.

Lending of Credit and Subscriptions of Stock

Two specific constitutional limitations on aid to the private sector—the bans on the lending of credit and the limits on public subscriptions of private stock—have fared better. The ban on the lending of credit makes sense. Lending credit in the sense of suretyship generates the fiscal illusion that it is cost-free. Government officials may persuade themselves that the contingent liability will never come due. Given that there is no initial out-of-pocket cost, voters may have little incentive to police these arrangements either. For that very reason, constitutional restriction is appropriate. On the other hand, the stock subscription ban seems to make little sense. Today, the principal effect of the ban is to preclude the government from taking an equity interest in the firms it is assisting, thus eliminating the possibility that the public might gain directly from its investment. It is difficult to see why it is permissible for the government to give public money away but not to get some of it back.

Debt Limitations

As already noted, there is a reasonable case for constitutional limits on debt obligations, yet the courts have been complicit in widespread evasion of these restrictions. The courts seem to be quite sympathetic to the programmatic spending goals—roads, dams, schools, power plants, convention centers, sports arenas, and economic development aid—that the debt limits would thwart. From this perspective, the debt limits appear to get in the way of good government in the era of the modern activist state, not to promote it.

Substantive Limitations

One reason for this lack of judicial sympathy for debt limitation may be the archaic nature of many of the constitutional debt provisions. Absolute debt prohibitions, laughably low dollar limits that date back to the nineteenth century, even carrying capacity percentage limits that are much lower than contemporary debt levels are completely out of step with the needs of modern government. Such provisions inspire, if they do not justify, evasion. One possible reform of the debt limits thus might look to simultaneously raising the level of the debt limit while redefining the limit to include all debts that would be repaid with public funds.

The difficulty would be to decide what is the appropriate debt level. Effective debt limitations require debt ceilings that are appropriate in light of the current ability to finance debt and current needs for debt-funded projects. Thus debt limits ought to be determined by setting debt service as a percentage of revenues, or as they are in some states, as a percentage of a moving average of revenues in recent years.[93] Determining the appropriate ratio of debt service to revenues is more difficult. There does not appear to be any theoretical basis for determining carrying capacity in theory or any consistency in practice among the states that take this approach. At best, any future debt limit is likely to proceed from a baseline of current debt levels. In so doing, however, such a debt limit ought to be based not just on the state's or locality's outstanding general obligation bonds, but on debt service payments for revenue bond, lease-financing, appropriation-backed debt and other obligations ultimately covered by state or local revenues.

Determining the appropriate level for a debt cap would also require adequate definition of the revenues that would be called on to pay these debts. In most states the local debt limit is defined as a percentage of local assessed valuation. Yet non-property-tax revenues play a considerable role in financing many localities. The local government debt cap ought to look to all local revenues, not just assessed valuation or property tax payments.

In short, if debt limits were modernized—and liberalized—to permit borrowing at levels adequate to the needs of today's state and local governments while still protecting the public from unduly burdensome future obligations, the courts might be more willing to enforce the restrictions and less inclined to wink at evasions than has been their practice in recent decades.

Voter Approval and Special Voting Rules

Separate from the question of substantive limitations is the role of voter approval and special legislative voting rules in authorizing debt. Some states subject debt to both substantive limitations and legislative supermajority and/or voter approval requirements; others rely on substantive limits or voter approval alone. Supermajority requirements and voter approval certainly provides an additional hurdle for elected officials who may be too quick to incur debt. The case for voter approval, however, is uncertain. It is not clear that today's voters will do a better job of representing tomorrow's taxpayers. Moreover, if politicians are too tempted to approve new debt, voters may be insufficiently attentive to the potential long-term benefits of the program the debt would finance. Low voter participation in most bond issue elections may reflect a lack of interest in or understanding of the cost and benefit questions that bond issues pose, and the voters who do participate may be unrepresentative of the electorate as a whole.

Still, debt—with its binding long-term nature—bears some resemblance to a constitutional amendment. Both commit future generations to a long-term course of action. Indeed, debt may be more binding since constitutional provisions may be repealed while debt creates interests protected by the federal Contracts Clause from subsequent state impairment. Most states have long required legislative supermajorities, voter approval, or both for both constitutional amendments and bond issues. It may thus be appropriate to continue to have a similar requirement for debt.

However, it makes little sense to have both a debt cap and a voter approval requirement for borrowing that falls beneath the cap. That would just reinstate the incentive to evasion. So, too, voter approval requirements without substantive limitations have given rise to evasion and judicial acceptance of evasive techniques. A better approach might consist of relying primarily on a substantive cap set by tying annual debt service to a percentage of a moving average of annual revenues, with that percentage based on the current debt service/revenue ratio (including all forms of current debt) and then permitting a jurisdiction to go beyond the limit with the approval of the voters. Referendum voters, thus, would have the ultimate authority over whether debt should exceed the constitutional cap, but debt within the constitutional cap would be treated as an ordinary political matter.

Taxation and Expenditure Limitations

Uniformity

The uniformity requirements are intended to promote the equal treatment of taxpayers but they also reduce the ability of states and localities to take into account the differential effects of similar tax burdens, and to use taxation as a policy-making tool and not just a revenue-raising device. Indeed, in many states uniformity requirements have been modified with provisions for classification and exemptions, thereby shifting questions of tax preferences and tax policy back to the political process. Uniformity of taxation, subject to some form of classification, seems to be a well-accepted constitutional norm.

Limitations

The tax limitation provisions are more controversial. Tax limits, like debt limits, suppose that the level of taxation is a constitutional matter, rather than one for resolution by current elected officials. But whereas the long-term consequences of debt obligations provide some support for treating debt as a quasi-constitutional matter, tax rates may easily be changed, and politicians who enact high taxes may be punished by the voters in the next election. Certainly as the last two decades have demonstrated, antitax forces are well represented in the political process. It is not clear why further constitutional protection needs to be superimposed on the protections provided by the ability of the voters to vote out of office elected officials who raise taxes.

State constitutional limitations on local taxation seem particularly inappropriate. Local government actions may be more transparent than state decisions and many local governments are subject to effect monitoring, participation, and political control by grassroots taxpayers. Local taxation is further constrained by the vigorous interlocal competition for mobile taxpayers. Given the existence of both significant exit and significant voice opportunities it is unclear what constitutional need state tax limits on localities serve. Moreover, substantive constitutional limits on local taxation seem in tension with local autonomy since they preclude localities where the people are willing to support tax increases from taking such action. Holding all local governments to the same limit seems inconsistent with the recognition of interlocal variation and diversity that animates home rule.

Whatever the theoretical difficulties with constitutional limitations on state and local taxation they are widespread and appear to enjoy considerable popular support. Indeed, whereas the public purpose requirements and debt restrictions largely date back to the nineteenth century—with some twentieth century revisions—many of the tax and expenditure limitations, including some of the most rigorous provisions, are recent developments. Tax limitations are here to stay.

If we are to have tax limitations, are some constitutional provisions preferable to others? As noted, there is considerable variety in the type of tax limitation, including rate caps, levy caps, levy increase caps, and caps on increases in individual taxpayer liabilities. And, of course, within each category, there is interstate and intrastate variation in the number or percentage of the cap.

There is certainly something to be said for limits that aim at protecting taxpayers from sharp swings in their liabilities—swings that result from appreciations in the unrealized value of their homes but not from increases in their current incomes. This is the focus of California's Proposition 13. On the other hand, limiting tax liability increases can result in two different owners of properties of similar values paying very different amounts of tax.

Limitations on tax rates or on the aggregate levy as a percentage of local wealth are more widespread and seem to reflect a desire to impose a constitutional norm of financially limited government. This is a substantive value choice of a state's votes. Levy limits would be more effective in attaining their end, however, if they were targeted not solely on the property tax—as many of them are—but on all revenue sources, or at least on all own-source revenues (not counting intergovernmental assistance). Localities derive a large and growing share of their revenues from taxes other than the property tax and especially from nontax revenue sources like fees and assessments. Indeed, the current tax limitations may very well be at least partially responsible for that fiscal shift. Limitations would be more effective in attaining the goal of limiting the share of local wealth devoted to government and in avoiding the distortions caused by the desire to evade the "tax" label if the limits were more encompassing.

On the other hand, as with debt, one reason for the widespread shift to revenue sources that evade the limitations is the recognition that the programs today's state and local governments maintain require more revenue than the constitutionally limited taxes allow. If tax limits were made more encompassing, the limits as a percentage of local wealth would have to be raised. Perhaps, as with the proposal for debt limits, the best approach would be to take current revenue levels, including revenues from fees and assessments as a baseline and cap increases from that level by requiring that they be tied to factors that drive up the costs of government, such as population, the rate of inflation, or changes in personal income

Voter Approval

The most recent trend in the state constitutional treatment of taxation is the requirement of voter approval for new taxes or tax increases. Voter approval may be a more flexible means of controlling taxes than a specific limit carved into the constitution. Particularly for state constitutional limits on local taxes, voter approval rather than a substantive limitation is preferable—assuming there is to be some limit—since with voter approval the locality at least as some possibility of lifting the limit if local voters so choose. A move from substantive limits to voter approval would be a move in the direction of home rule.

State voter approval requirements are more problematic. These appear to reflect the view that taxation is a fundamental decision and therefore should have direct popular consent. Yet, unlike debt, tax levels have no long-term binding consequences. A tax raised in one year can be lowered in the next. Certainly, given the political salience of tax decisions and the ability of voters to oversee—

and eject—elected officials who vote for tax increases, a voter approval requirement cannot be grounded in the theory that is needed to correct for structural
defects in the ordinary political process that would support. Moreover, to the
extent that the referendum electorate is smaller than and demographically different from the general electorate, adding a voter approval requirement could
make the final result less democratic, not more so.

Ultimately, voter approval rules, like substantive limits on taxation, are
based not on the role on the constitution in correcting political process failures
but on a substantive commitment to making it difficult to impose or increase
taxes. Although procedural in form, the voter approval requirements are substantive in effect. As a result, the decision whether to have such a requirement
will reflect the substantive views of the state community on taxation rather than
on any theory of the appropriate balance of responsibilities between a state constitution and state and local governments.

NOTES

1. U.S. Const., art. I, § 8.

2. U.S. Const., art. I, § 7.

3. U.S. Const., art. I, § 9.

4. U.S. Const., art. I, § 8.

5. U.S. Const., art. I, § 9.

6. Ibid.

7. Dale F. Rubin, "Constitutional Aid Limitation Provisions and the Public Purpose Doctrine," 12 *St. Louis U. Pub. L. Rev.* 143, 143 n. 1 (1993).

8. N.Y. Const., art. VII, § 8.

9. N.Y. Const., art. VIII, § 1.

10. *See*, for example, Colo. Const., art. XI, §§ 1, 2; N.Y. Const., art. VII, § 8, art.
VIII, § 1.

11. 21 Pa. 147 (1853).

12. *See*, for example, *Allen v. Inhabitants of Jay*, 60 Me. 124 (1872) (invalidating aid
to factories); *Lowell v. Boston*, 111 Mass. 454 (1873) (financial assistance to private residential housing development violated public purpose requirement); Opinion of the Justices, 291 Mass. 567 (1935) (use of tax revenues to insure banks against loss on home
mortgages not within "public purpose" limitation).

13. *Albritton v. City of Winona*, 178 So. 799, app. dis. 303 U.S. 627 (1938).

14. *See*, for example, *Basehore v. Hampden Industrial Devel. Auth.*, 248 A.2d 212
(Pa., 1968).

15. *See,* for example, *State ex rel Beck v. City of York,* 82 N.W.2d 269 (Neb., 1957).

16. *See,* for example, *Village of Moyie Springs v. Aurora Mfg Co.,* 353 P.2d 767 (Idaho, 1960); *Mitchell v. North Carolina Indus. Devel. Fin. Auth.,* 159 S.E.2d 745 (N.C., 1968).

17. *See,* for example, *WDW Properties, Inc. v. City of Sumter,* 535 S.E.2d 631, 635–36 (S.C., 2000); *Delogu v. State,* 720 A.2d 1153 (Me., 1998); *Maready v. City of Winston-Salem,* 467 S.E.2d 615 (N.C., 1996); *Libertarian Party of Wisconsin v. State,* 546 N.W.2d 424 (Wis., 1996).

18. *See,* for example, *WDW Properties, Inc. v. City of Sumter,* 535 S.E.2d 631, 635–36 (S.C., 2000); *King County v. Taxpayers of King County,* 949 P.2d 1260, 1266 (Wash., 1997).

19. 455 A.2d 1 (Me., 1983).

20. 731 S.W.2d 797 (Ky., 1987).

21. *See,* for example, *Holding's Little America v. Board of County Comm'rs,* 712 P.2d 331 (Wyo., 1985); *Purvis v. City of Little Rock,* 67 S.W.2d 936 (Ark., 1984). But *see Hucks v. Riley,* 357 S.E.2d 458 (S.C., 1987) (public interest in tourism development provides public purpose for use of state funds to finance privately owned and operated lodging and restaurant facilities).

22. *Delogu v. State,* 720 A.2d 1153, 1155 (Me., 1998).

23. *Jackson v. Benson,* 578 N.W.2d 602, 628 (Wis., 1998).

24. *See Maready v. City of Winston-Salem, supra.*

25. *See,* for example, Alaska Const., art. IX, § 6; Ill. Const., art. VIII, § 1.

26. *See* also *Brower v. State of Washington,* 969 P.2d 42 (Wash., 1998) (lending of credit restriction does not apply if loan advances a "fundamental purpose" of government).

27. *See,* for example, *Barnhart v. City of Fayetteville,* 900 S.W.2d 539 (Ark., 1995).

28. *See,* for example, *Washington Higher Educ. Facilities v. Gardner,* 699 P.2d 1240 (Wash., 1985).

29. *See,* for example, *State of Florida v. Inland Protection Financing Corp.,* 699 So.2d 1352 (Fla., 1997).

30. *See,* for example, *Utah Technology Finance Corp. v. Wilkinson,* 723 P.2d 406 (Utah, 1986). *See also West Virginia Trust Fund, Inc. v. Bailey,* 485 S.E.2d 407 (W.Va., 1997).

31. *See,* for example, Ind. Const., art. X, § 5 (prohibiting state debt except "to meet casual deficits in revenue," repel invasion, suppress insurrection or provide for state defense); W. Va. Const., art. X, § 4 (same).

32. *See,* for example, Ariz. Const., art. IX, § 5 (total state debt limited to $350,000); Ky. Const., § 49 (state debt limited to $500,000); Ohio Const., art. VIII, § 1 (state debt limit of $750,000); R.I. Const., art. VI, § 16 (total state debt limited to $50,000).

33. *See*, for example, Ga. Const., art. VII, § IV, par. II (debt service on state debt limited to 10% state revenue); Hawaii Const., art. VII, § 13 (debt service on state debt limited to 18½% of the average state general fund revenues in the three prior fiscal years; local government debts limited to 15% of total assessed value of real property in each political subdivision); Nev. Const., art. IX, § 3 (aggregate state debt limited to 2% of assessed valuation of property in state); Wash. Const., art. VIII, § 1 (debt service on aggregate state debt limited to 9% of average of state revenues over the three prior fiscal years).

34. *See*, for example, Ind. Const., art. XIII, § 1 (municipal debt capped at 2% of assessed valuation); Ky. Const., § 158 (permissible local government debt set at between 2% and 10% of local assessed valuation, with debt limit varying according to population of city; county and taxing district limits set at 2% of assessed valuation); Mich. Const., art. VII, § 11 (county debt limit set at 10% of assessed valuation); Nev. Const., art. IX, § 23 (state debt capped at 2% of assessed valuation); N.Y. Const., art VIII, § 2-a (debt limits for New York City and Nassau County set at 10% of assessed valuation; debt limit for other large cities is 9% of assessed valuation; debt limit for other cities and counties, and for towns and villages is 7% of assessed valuation).

35. *See*, for example, Cal. Const., art XVI, § 18 (local government debts require approval of two-thirds of local electorate); Mich. Const., art. IX, § 15 (state long-term debt requires approval of two-thirds of members of each house of the legislature and a majority of state voters in referendum); S.C. Const., art. X, § 13 (new state general obligation debt requires approval of either two-thirds of each legislative house or popular referendum).

36. *See*, for example, Ga. Const., art. X, § V, par. 1 (county and municipal debt limited to 10% of assessed valuation; voter approval required); Wash. Const., art. VIII, § 1 (state debt service limited to 9% of average of state revenues for past three years; three-fifths majority vote in each house of the legislature required before debt may be incurred).

37. *See* William H. Stewart, *The Alabama Constitution: A Reference Guide* 115–16 (1994).

38. *See*, for example, In re Oklahoma Capitol Improvement Authority, 958 P.2d 759 (Okla., 1998).

39. *See*, for example, *Convention Center Authority v. Anzai*, 890 P.2d 1197 (Hawaii, 1995).

40. *See*, for example, *Eakin v. State ex rel Capital Improvement Board of Marion County*, 474 N.E.2d 62 (Ind., 1985) (holding bond used to finance a convention center and backed by taxes on hotels, motels, and retail food business is "debt" within meaning of debt limit).

41. The special fund exemption may not be available if the state is dedicating a preexisting revenue source to pay off a bond, rather than creating a new tax or increasing the amount to be paid under an existing tax. *See*, for example, Opinion of the Justices, 665 So.2d 1357, 1362–63 (Ala., 1995); *State of West Virginia ex rel Marockie v. Wagoner*, 438 S.E.2d 810 (W.Va., 1993).

42. *See*, for example, *Bulman v. McCrane*, 312 A.2d 857 (N.J., 1973); *Department of Ecology v. State Finance Committee*, 804 P.2d 1241 (Wash., 1991); *Dieck v. Unified Schl. Dist. of Antigo*, 477 N.W.2d 613 (Wis., 1991). *Contra Montano v. Gabaldon*, 766 P.2d 1328 (N.M., 1989).

43. *See*, for example, *Carr-Gottstein Properties v. State*, 899 P.2d 136 (Ak., 1995); In re Anzai, 936 P.2d 637 (Hawaii, 1997); *Wilson v. Kentucky Transp. Cabinet*, 884 S.W.2d 641 (Ky., 1994); *Employers Insurance Co. of Nevada v. State Bd. of Examiners*, 21 P.3d 628 (Nev., 2001); *Fent v. Oklahoma Capitol Improvement Authority*, 984 P.2d 200 (Okla., 1999); *Dykes v. Northern Virginia Transportation District Comm'n*, 411 S.E.2d 1 (Va., 1991); *Schulz v. State of New York*, 639 N.E.2d 1140 (N.Y., 1994).

44. *See*, for example, *Steup v. Indiana Housing Finance Authority*, 402 N.E.2d 1215 (Ind., 1980); *Utah Housing Finance Agency v. Smart*, 561 P.2d 1052 (Utah, 1977); *State ex rel Warren v. Nusbaum*, 208 N.W.2d 780 (Wisc., 1973).

45. Richard J. Marino and Colleen Waddell, "Revised Lease and Appropriation-Backed Debt Rating Criteria," Standard & Poor's Rating Services, June 13, 2001.

46. *Rider v. City of San Diego*, 959 P.2d at 358.

47. *See*, for example, *Employers Insurance Co. of Nevada v. State Bd. of Examiners*, 21 P.3d 628, 632 (Nev., 2001) (expressly rejecting argument from "realism"); *Wilson v. Kentucky Transp. Cabinet*, 884 S.W.2d at 644 ("Practical, moral or righteous claims do not pass the test of contract or constitutional law").

48. *See*, for example, *Wilson v. Kentucky Transp. Cabinet*, 884 S.W.2d at 644 (appropriation bonds "do not create the evil which the constitutional provision was designed to prevent"); *Department of Ecology v. State Finance Committee*, 804 P.2d 1241, 1246 (Wash., 1991); *Aneroid v. New Jersey Bldg. Auth.*, 448 A.2d 449, 456 (N.J., 1982).

49. *See Wilson v. Kentucky Transp. Cabinet*, supra; *Fent v. Oklahoma Capitol Improvement Auth.*, supra; *Department of Ecology v. State Finance Comm.*, supra.

50. 809 A.2d 91 (N.J., 2002).

51. Ibid. at 104.

52. *See* Ibid. at 105.

53. Ibid. at 104–07.

54. *See* Ibid. at 109.

55. *See*, for example, *Albuquerque Metropolitan Arroyo Flood Control Auth. v. Swinburne*, 394 P.2d 998 (N.M., 1964); *Rider v. City of San Diego*, 959 P.2d 347 (Cal., 1998); *Ragsdale v. City of Memphis*, 70 S.W.2d 56, 68 (Tenn. Ct. App., 2001).

56. *See*, for example, *Rider v. City of San Diego*, 959 P.2d 347 (Cal., 1998); *Fent v. Oklahoma Capitol Improvement Auth.*, 984 P.2d 200 (Okla., 1999); *Dykes v. Northern Va. Transp. Dist. Comm's*, 411 S.E.2d 1 (Va., 1991); *Schulz v. State of New York*, 639 N.E.2d 1140 (N.Y., 1994).

57. *See*, for example, J. R. Hellerstein and W. Hellerstein, *State and Local Taxation: Cases and Materials* 34 (6th ed. 1997).

58. *See*, for example, Ga. Const., art. VII, § 1 ("all taxation shall be uniform upon the same class of subjects within the territorial limits of the authority levying the tax,"); N.H. Const., pt. I, art. 5 ("all taxes [shall] be proportionate and reasonable, . . . equal in valuation and uniform in rate, and just").

59. *See*, for example, Ind Const., art. X, § 1 ("uniform and equal rate of property assessment and taxation"); Me. Const., art. IX, § 8 ("all taxes upon real and personal estate . . . shall be apportioned and assessed equally").

60. Hellerstein and Hellerstein, supra, at 36.

61. M. David Gelfand, Joel A. Mintz, and Peter A. Salsich, Jr., *State and Local Taxation and Finance* 38 (2d ed., 2000).

62. Proposition 2½ is a statutory initiative, not a constitutional amendment.

63. *See*, for example, N.Y. Const., art. VIII, § 10.

64. *See* Kirk J. Stark, "The Right to Vote on Taxes," 96 *Nw. L. Rev.* xxx (2001).

65. Ibid.

66. Mo. Const., art. X, § 22(a).

67. *See Beatty v. Metropolitan St. Louis Sewer Dist.*, 867 S.W.2d 217 (Mo., 1993).

68. Cal. Const., art. XIIIA, § 3.

69. W. Valente, D. McCarthy, R. Briffault, et al., *State and Local Government Law* 536 (5th ed., 2001).

70. Ibid. at 537.

71. Mich. Const., art. IX, § 26.

72. Ibid.

73. Mich. Const., art. IX, § 27.

74. *See* Mo. Const., art. X, §§ 16–18. The Colorado Constitution takes a slightly different approach. Pursuant to a voter initiative adopted in 1992, it sets a "maximum annual percentage change in state fiscal year spending" equal to "inflation plus the percentage change in state population in the prior calendar year, adjusted for revenue changes approved by voters after 1991," Colo. Const., art. X, § 20(7).

75. *See* Terri A. Sexton, Steven M. Sheffrin, and Arthur O'Sullivan, Proposition 13: Unintended Effects and Feasible Reforms, 52 *Nat'l. Tax J.* 99 (1999).

76. *See* Valente, McCarthy, and Briffault, supra 537.

77. Ibid. at 560.

78. *See*, for example, *Trent Meredith, Inc. v. City of Oxnard*, 170 Cal. Rptr. 685 (Cal. App., 1981).

79. *See*, for example, *County of Fresno v. Malmstrom*, 156 Cal. Rptr. 777 (Cal. App., 1979) (special assessment not subject to Proposition 13); *Zahner v. City of Perryville*, 813 S.W.2d 855 (Mo., 1991) (Missouri constitution's requirement of voter approval for tax increases does not apply to assessments).

80. *See*, for example, *Sinclair Paint Co. v. State Board of Equalization*, 937 P.2d 1350 (Cal., 1997); *Nuclear Metals, Inc. v. Low-Level Radioactive Waste Management Bd.*, 656 N.E.2d 563 (Mass., 1995). *See also City of Huntington v. Bacon*, 473 S.W.2d 743 (W.Va., 1996) (sustaining a municipal fee imposed on all building owners to cover costs of fire and flood protection services).

81. *See*, for example, 2nd *ROC-Jersey Associates v. Town of Morristown*, 731 A.2d 1 (N.J., 1999); *City of Boca Raton v. State*, 595 So.2d 25 (Fla. 1992); *Knox v. City of Orland*, 841 P.2d 144 (Cal., 1992); *Grais v. City of Chicago*, 601 N.E.2d 745 (Ill., 1992).

82. *See*, for example, *Home Builders Ass'n of Dayton v. City of Beavercreek*, 729 N.E.2d 349 (Ohio, 2000); *Home Builders Ass'n of Central Arizona v. City of Scottsdale*, 930 P.2d 993 (Az., 1997); *St. Johns County v. Northeast Florida Builders Ass;'n Inc.*, 583 So.2d 635 (Fla., 1991); *Holmdel Builders Ass'n v. Township of Holmdel*, 583 A.2d 277 (N.J., 1990).

83. *See*, for example, *Bolt v. City of Lansing*, 587 N.W.2d 264 (Mich., 1998); *Emerson College v. City of Boston*, 462 N.E.2d 1098 (Mass., 1984).

84. *See,*, for example, Mo. Const., art. X, § 22(a); Cal. Const., art. XIII D.

85. *See*, for example, *Los Angeles Co. Transp. Comm. v. Richmond*, 643 P.2d 941 (Cal., 1982). But *cf. Rider v. County of San Diego*, 820 P.2d 1000 (Cal., 1991).

86. Ibid. at 537–38.

87. *See* John Kirlin, "The Impact of Fiscal Limits on Governance," 25 *Hastings Const. L.Q.* 197, 200 (1998).

88. *See*, for example, *New Jersey Sports & Exposition Auth. v. McCrane*, 292 A.2d 545 (N.J., 1972); *Dieck v. Unified School Dist. of Antigo*, 477 N.W.2d 613, 619–20 (Wisc., 1991).

89. New Jersey Sports Auth., supra 292 A.2d at 557, 559.

90. *Compare Rider v. County of San Diego*, 820 P.2d 1000 (Cal., 1991) (cracking down on the ability of California counties to evade Proposition 13 by creating special districts) with *Rider v. City of San Diego*, 959 P.2d 347 (Cal., 1998) (upholding use of special districts to avoid debt limits).

91. *See*, for example, Peter K. Eisinger, *The Rise of the Entrepreneurial State: State and Local Economic Development Policy in the United States* 200–24 (1988).

92. *See*, for example, *Charter Township of Ypsilanti v. General Motors Corp.*, 506 N.W.2d 556 (Mich. Ct. App., 1993).

93. *See*, for example, Hawaii Const., art. VII, § 13 (debt service on state debt limited to 18½% of the average state general fund revenues in three prior fiscal years); Wash. Const., art. VIII, § 1 (debt service on state debt limited to 9% of average of state revenues over three prior fiscal years).

Chapter Nine

Education

Paul L. Tractenberg*

INTRODUCTION

Education is undeniably one of our most important public functions. Indeed, it is widely considered to be the most important function of state governments, which have primary responsibility for it. In a July 2002 statewide public opinion survey conducted in Florida, respondents were asked to identify the most important issue facing their state. Thirty-seven percent identified the education system; the next highest issues—the environment and terrorism—were identified by 6 percent each.[1] This is hardly a new perception. From the earliest days of the republic, some state constitutions singled out education, sometimes alone among the many important public services provided by state government, as worthy of special recognition. During the nineteenth and early twentieth centuries, as additional states entered the union, this trend accelerated. Today, every state constitution contains an education provision (and that has been true for some time).[2] For at least the past thirty years, these education clauses have been at the heart of enormously important and controversial litigation in the courts of most states aimed at ensuring funding equity and educational adequacy for all students, especially those in poor urban and rural school districts. At the same time as this litigation underscores the centrality of current clauses to twentieth-century education reform, it also raises questions about their sufficiency to provide for education in the twenty-first century.

This chapter will draw on that long and important history, and the pervasiveness of education provisions in state constitutions, to explore:

- How these provisions have evolved overtime
- The extent to which they seem adequate or appropriate to meet current needs

---

*With appreciation to Jung Kim, a 2003 graduate of Rutgers School of Law–Newark for her extraordinarily able and diligent research on the entire project, and to G. Alan Tarr and Robert Williams for their patience and support.

- Whether there are recognized "best practices" in existing state constitutional education provisions or in the literature
- How one might approach the task of developing "model" education provisions for a state constitution

A Historical Overview

The evolution of education provisions in state constitutions has not proceeded in a precise stage-by-stage sequence, each separate and clearly identifiable. Rather, the evolutionary landscape is chaotic, characterized by overlapping developments among, and even within, the states. Partly this is because, although states have sometimes mimicked one another's constitutional provisions,[3] important differences in history, demographics, geography, and political and social orientation have tended to rise to the surface and limit such similarities. One of the most telling differences is the time at which, and the circumstances under which, a state entered the union. As a consequence, important differences persist in state education provisions regarding such central matters as the nature and extent of the commitment to education, state-local relationships, the structure of state education systems and bureaucracies, and funding mechanisms.

Nonetheless, it may be useful to sketch four broad stages through which education provisions have passed, and a rough approximation of the time period occupied by each of those stages.

The introductory stage (1776–1834) reflected a substantial degree of uncertainty about constitutionalization of education with states dividing relatively evenly between those with education clauses and those without them. The initial state constitutional provisions tended to recognize the importance to society of an educated citizenry, either by exhortations about the virtues of learning and knowledge or by charges to state legislatures to establish schools. During the latter part of this introductory period, a number of state constitutional provisions began to impose a more specific obligation on state legislatures—to provide for a general system of free public education, equally open to all.

The second, or foundational, stage (1835–1912) as a period during which the number of states doubled, and most of those entering the union had constitutions with education clauses. Additionally, most of the other states without education provisions in their constitutions added them. This period, clearly the most active one for state education provisions, was dominated by provisions that placed far more explicit responsibility on states and their legislatures regarding the establishment, funding, and administration of free common school systems.

The third stage (1913 and extending to the middle of the twentieth century) was a period of relative quiescence with only limited, sporadic constitutional activity. Mainly, this involved elaboration of the fiscal and administrative structures put in place during the prior stage. Finally, the fourth stage (from the mid-twentieth century to the present) is more notable for its responses to legal or other advocacy efforts of the period, beginning with the desegregation efforts of *Brown v. Board of Education*[4] and extending to the funding equity and educational adequacy litigation of the past thirty years. Many of the education provisions of this period reflect acceptance of the premise that state education clauses afford students enforceable rights and seek to define, or to extend or narrow, those rights.

Stage 1 (1776–1834)—Introduction and Uncertainty

The period between 1776 and 1834 was a period of educational uncertainty.[5] Of the twenty-four states, eleven had no education clauses in their state constitutions;[6] the other thirteen either entered the Union with a constitutional education provision, or included one in a subsequently adopted constitution. The education provisions of that period were generally of two types: hortatory clauses exalting the virtues of learning and knowledge; and obligatory clauses requiring state legislatures to establish schools.[7] This pattern may have reflected uncertainty about the state's role regarding education.

As an example of the hortatory approach, the Massachusetts Constitution of 1780 provided: "Wisdom and knowledge, as well as virtue, . . . being necessary for the preservation of [the people's] rights and liberties . . . it shall be the duty of legislatures and magistrates, in all future periods of this commonwealth, to cherish the interests of literature and the sciences."[8] The Massachusetts Supreme Court interpreted this provision to give "the legislature discretion to act as it saw fit," rather than to confer a right to education.[9] A number of later state constitutions followed the Massachusetts language; for example, the 1802 Ohio Constitution set forth in its Bill of Rights: "religion, morality and knowledge being essentially necessary to good government and the happiness of mankind, schools and the means of instructions shall forever be encouraged by legislative provision."[10]

The obligatory provisions, by contrast, more specifically mandated legislatures to establish schools. For example, the 1776 Pennsylvania Constitution required that: "A school or schools shall be established in each county by the legislature, for the convenient instruction of youth, with such salaries to the masters paid by the public, as may enable them to instruct youth at low prices."[11] Similarly, the Georgia Constitution of 1777 provided that "[s]chools shall be erected in each county and supported at the general expense of the State, as the legislature shall hereafter point out."[12] The 1786 Constitution of Vermont even more specifically provided that: "a competent number of schools ought to be maintained in each town for the convenient instruction of youth; and one or more grammar schools be incorporated, and properly supported in each county."[13]

Some states eventually combined the hortatory and obligatory language in their state constitutions. For example, the Indiana Constitution of 1816 prefaced the legislative duty to provide a general education system and maintain public school lands with the recognition that "[k]nowledge and learning generally diffused, through a community, [is] essential to the preservation of a free Government, and spreading the opportunities, and advantages of education through the various parts of the Country [is] highly conducive to this end."[14]

Regardless of their precise content, the earliest education provisions tended to emphasize the importance of schooling and education, but to leave unaddressed more specific educational matters, such as the ages or other characteristics of students to be educated, the types of schools to be established, the means by which those schools would be funded, and the entities that would be responsible for administering the schools and overseeing the educational system. Thus, while these state constitutions did recognize the value of education to the citizenry and to the state itself, they did not reflect a concrete vision of the state's role in education.

Some of the nineteenth-century education clauses did, however, begin to reflect several more specific educational values: first, that "[t]he purpose of public education was to train upright citizens by inculcating a common denominator of non-sectarian morality and non-partisan civic instruction," and, second, that "[t]he common school should be free, open to all children and public in support and control."[15] The idea of a "common school . . . is a manifestation of the social contract."[16] Education provisions, thus, began quite early to include equality provisions, and broad statements about those who must receive the benefits of public schools. Some of the equality provisions foreshadowed the funding equity litigation of the 1970s since they provided for equitable distribution of funding within districts and from district to district. Of course, these provisions often were honored in the breach. The Ohio Constitution of 1802, for example, contained an explicit equality provision with respect to participation by the poor in schools supported by federal funds.[17] The 1818 Connecticut Constitution also provided that the interest of the school fund "shall be inviolably appropriated . . . for the equal benefit of all the people."[18] In 1816, Indiana mandated that its education system be "equally open to all."[19]

This emerging state constitutional tendency to require legislatures to provide for a general system of free public education, equally open to all, formed the basis of the next evolutionary stage.

Stage 2 (1835–1912)—Clarification and Stabilization

The period between 1835 and 1912 was a period of clarification and stabilization[20] in the evolution of state constitutional education clauses. Indeed, it is easily the period of the most concentrated constitutional activity. Twenty-four new states entered the Union, most with education provisions. Although states rarely have identical provisions, as this large number of new states entered the Union, doubling its size, substantial similarities in constitutional language emerged.[21] During this lengthy period, there also was evolution from relatively simple to much lengthier and more detailed education provisions, roughly corresponding to the pre– and post–Civil War and Reconstruction Period. Hence, "[w]hereas the eight new state constitutions written between 1841–60 contained an average of 6.3 educational provisions, the seven approved by Congress between 1881–1900 had an average of 14.0."[22] This increased detail reflected an effort to clarify the states' educational role as they gradually enlarged their authority and control.[23] The increase in bureaucratic detail also significantly, but not entirely, supplanted "republican rhetoric."[24] Some education clauses of this period still began with hortatory, or purposive, language, harking back to the earliest state constitutions, stressing that an educated citizenry was necessary for a stable republican government. Typical of such provisions was the Mississippi Constitution, which stated that "the stability of a republican form of government depends mainly upon the intelligence and virtue of the people,"[25] and the Arkansas Constitution, which referred to "[i]ntelligence and virtue being the safeguards of liberty and the bulwark of a free and good government."[26] These statements of purpose in education clauses, however, no longer stood alone. They were buttressed by provisions clarifying the state's role regarding education and educational institutions, and stabilizing the structure of state school systems.[27]

This second evolutionary stage saw the emergence of provisions assigning responsibility, usually to the legislature, for establishing and maintaining schools within the state,[28] creating specific state agencies or officers to administer common school funds and to supervise schools on a state level,[29] and creating regional or local agencies or officers to supervise their schools.[30] In fact, by the 1880s, practically all states provided by constitutional provision or legislation for at least some of the following: a state board of education, a state superintendent, a common school fund, school taxes, teacher credentials and a school age range.[31] Yet state control was not unfettered, as local entities, sometimes themselves creatures of state education clauses, consistently resisted its growth.[32] Ultimately, despite any surface similarities, vast differences in the composition of the states, demographically and politically, led to variations in the implementation and specifics of education provisions, such as the level of local control and whether state education officials would be elected or appointed.[33]

Despite these variations in detail and specificity, however, most state constitutional education provisions increasingly assured a state system of free common or public schools,[34] and sought to clarify what state provision of education entailed; in other words, how this system of free public schools was to work.

As this period of "clarification and stabilization" proceeded, education provisions relating to centralization and structuring became "more detailed and bureaucratic," incorporating more specific requirements regarding the administration and oversight of public education.[35] The increased inclusion of bureaucratic detail in state constitutions "suggest[s] that as schooling became more institutionalized, structure became more urgent than philosophy."[36] This trend toward increased bureaucratic detail has continued throughout much of the ensuing history of education clauses.

Furthermore, education clauses of this period explicitly stated who was to benefit from public schools, and who was not. For example, beyond equal access mandates, some state constitutions specified the age range of students.[37] Many states prohibited both the use of state funds for religious or sectarian schools and sectarian instruction in public schools.[38] Provisions both mandating segregated schools and prohibiting discrimination in public schools also appeared during this period.[39]

Another important clarification in state constitutional education provisions was the specification of the kind or quantum of education to be offered by the state. Representative of the language used, many clauses provided for a "general and uniform" system of education,[40] or a "thorough and efficient" free public school system.[41] Washington declared it "the paramount duty of the state to make ample provision for the education of all children residing within its borders."[42]

More specifically, there were provisions requiring minimum school terms,[43] dealing with whether or not mandatory attendance laws could be enacted,[44] specifying what levels of education,[45] and even what specialized kinds of education,[46] were to be provided. Some education clauses included provisions regarding textbooks[47] and teachers.[48]

The stabilization of education as a state function also was reflected by the inclusion of provisions relating to funding and investment of funds, including the establishment of "inviolate" common school funds,[49] local taxation to support public schools,[50] and federally granted school lands.[51] A few education clauses of this era even contained enforcement or accountability provisions, under which a school district would lose funding if it failed to maintain a school as required. For example, the California Constitution provided that a "school [shall] be kept up and supported in each district at least three months in every year," to be enforced by depriving "any school [district] neglecting to keep and support such a school . . . of its proportion of the interest of the public fund during such neglect."[52]

Detailed education provisions of these sorts reflected the entrenchment of public education as a primary function and responsibility of the states, and provided mechanisms by which state governments would fulfill that role. Although states continued to alter or refine details about the supervision, administration and funding of public schools throughout the twentieth century,[53] the mid-nineteenth-century through early twentieth-century period could be seen as the time during which the foundations for today's education provisions and systems were laid.

Stage 3 (1913–1954)—Quiescence and Preoccupation

Although there were some modest and intermittent efforts to build on the clarification and stabilization of the prior stage, especially the centralization and bureaucratization that dominated its later years,[54] for the most part the third stage was characterized by quiescence and preoccupation. After all, it was a time in which the nation had to deal with two World Wars, the Great Depression and the aftermaths of all three. There could hardly have been time, attention or resources to invest in serious state constitutional activity regarding education.

Stage 4 (1954 to the present)—Educational Rights and Entitlements

The effort to find more efficient and effective ways of governing state public school systems resumed in this last evolutionary stage and continues to the present,[55] but it was joined by a new emphasis on educational rights and entitlements. This has involved both an effort to define, or to expand or limit, already recognized rights, and to accommodate newly emerging rights. To a great degree, these emerging rights resulted from advocacy efforts through the courts, a phenomenon of this period.

The United States Supreme Court's decision in *Brown v. Board Education*[56] was an educational and social policy landmark that led to fundamental changes in the way we think about and provide education, as well as other public services. Directly and indirectly it has had profound effects on state, as well as federal, constitutional law. Obviously, any state education clauses that authorized or required segregated schools had to fall before *Brown*. Interestingly, though, *Brown* did not lead to the wholesale adoption of state education provisions that embraced or extended its teachings. Less than one-third of all state constitutions have provisions expressly barring segregation or other forms of discrimination in the schools, and some of those provisions predated *Brown* and others were adopted substantially after *Brown*. For example, New Jersey's antisegregation provision dated from 1947 and Michigan's antidiscrimination provision was adopted in 1963.[57] Much later, in 1996, California amended its constitution to address race and other factors, but in order to preclude affirmative action.[58]

The *Brown* decision may have had a more substantial indirect effect on state constitutions, however. Many commentators believe that it paved the way for the funding equity and educational adequacy litigation of the past three decades, and these issues have increasingly found their way into state constitutional amendments. Indeed, by the middle of the twentieth century, a variety of school finance issues, including voter approval of tax increases and educational assistance to students and parents in the form of guaranteed loans or tuition credits, as well as adequate and equitable funding, had begun to be a focus of state constitutional amendments.

Illustrative of state constitutional provisions relating to school funding were those amendments mandating minimum expenditures on public education. For example, a Colorado amendment requires that public school spending increase "at least by the rate of inflation plus an additional one percentage point."[59] An Oregon amendment requires not only legislative appropriation of "money sufficient to ensure that the state's system of public education meets quality goals established by law," but also that the legislature "publish a report that either demonstrates the appropriation is sufficient, or identifies the reasons for the insufficiency, its extent, and its impact on the ability of the state's system of public education to meet those goals."[60] The Oregon Constitution also was amended to recognize any "legal obligation it [the Legislative Assembly] may have to maintain substantial equity in state funding, . . . establish[ing] a system of Equalization Grants to eligible districts for each year in which the voters of such districts approve local option taxes."[61] Ohio and Georgia amended their constitutions to provide parents and students with direct educational funding assistance.[62]

By contrast, several major states adopted constitutional amendments during this period that effectively limited educational funding, typically by capping property tax rates. The most prominent of these is California's Proposition 13, adopted in 1978.[63]

State constitutional amendments during this period also related to other heavily litigated and highly charged issues, such as affirmative action, state aid to religious schools, and school safety.[64] Most recently, state constitutional amendments are reflecting growing public concern about educational quality, probably best exemplified by Florida's recent activity.

In 1998 and 2002, Florida adopted seven constitutional amendments, most of which relate to educational quality issues.[65] The 1998 amendments involved a large-scale overhaul of Florida's education provision.[66] They declared education a "fundamental value,"[67] characterized the state's duty to provide education as "paramount"[68] and defined an adequate education as being all of the following: (1) uniform; (2) efficient; (3) safe; (4) secure; and (5) high quality.[69] Key 2002 amendments required reduced class size[70] and provided for voluntary universal prekindergarten to every four-year-old.[71]

These Florida amendments have not yet been reflected in a more expansive trend, however, somewhat surprising given the degree of educational ferment that has been precipitated largely by state court litigation during the past three decades. The Florida amendments may signify, though, that the confluence of the following will lead inevitably to much wider state constitutional activity in this area: continuously expanding judicially imposed or inspired educational mandates; increased political implications of educational policy decisions, partly at least due to the enormous state and local costs of education; more effective targeted lobbying; and an ever-growing public perception about the importance of quality education.

ADEQUACY OR APPROPRIATENESS OF EDUCATION PROVISIONS TO MEET CURRENT NEEDS

To try to provide a definitive assessment of whether education provisions of state constitutions, generally or in individual cases, adequately and appropriately meet current needs is beyond the scope of this chapter. It implicates fundamental questions of constitutionalism and one's view of the proper role of the various branches of government. It also is confounded by the extent to which education provisions can fairly be given credit for educational success or blame for educational failure in a particular state or locale.

Depending on one's view, the extraordinary body of state court litigation over the past thirty years, still developing at a substantial pace, that deals with interacting issues of educational equity, access and quality, is either a sign that state education provisions are admirably serving their purposes, or that they have led us badly astray. What is indisputable, though, is that the education funding systems, and perhaps also the education structures, of the nineteenth and early twentieth centuries are inadequate to meet late twentieth- and early twenty-first-century educational needs and expectations.

Consequently, this chapter would not be complete without some discussion of this issue, and the extensive litigation over whether education financing and delivery systems violate state education or equal protection provisions provides important insights because it has raised fundamental questions about the role of state education provisions. In these cases, waged in forty-five states during the past thirty years, courts have been divided over whether the judiciary should or could invalidate legislative structures for funding and managing the public schools, with about 58 percent of the courts sustaining constitutional challenges.[72] Virtually every court that has had to confront this question, however, regardless of its final decision, has found that the way states finance and provide education is deeply flawed. Depending on how they view their proper role in the resolution of this problem, state courts have either ordered, and perhaps insisted upon and even supervised,[73] changes by the other branches or simply implored those other branches to act.

Whichever judicial role one prefers, presumably if there were state education provisions that led courts to regularly assume that role, those provisions would be deemed more "adequate" or "appropriate." The problem is that the commentators' analyses of state education provisions do not strongly suggest that typology predicts judicial result. In particular, "strong" education clauses have not necessarily led to strong judicial action, any more than they necessarily have led to strong public schools. A substantial discussion of this issue appears later in the chapter.

IDENTIFYING "BEST PRACTICES" IN EXISTING STATE EDUCATION PROVISIONS OR THE LITERATURE

Because education has been so consistently rated the most important public service provided by state governments, it is tempting to conclude that "best practices" would be represented by the "strongest" education provisions, as identified by the commentators. However, that assumption is questionable, largely because there is growing agreement that the categorization has failed to meet a basic pragmatic test—strong provisions have not correlated with strong public education systems or with strong judicial rulings in support of educational rights. Therefore, "strong" education clauses are not necessarily better, let alone representative of "best practices."

That does not mean, however, that the large and growing body of education clause litigation is devoid of "best practices" lessons. As with all best practices, though, the lesson to be learned is closely related to the constitutional drafter's goals. If, for example, a goal is to minimize the prospects of lengthy, contentious and costly litigation, certain judicial interpretations of state education clauses will be the focus. If, conversely, the goal is to assure that a particular kind or quality of education is provided, or a particular set of educational outcomes is achieved, then other judicial decisions may provide the "best practices."

Of course, litigation about the meaning of educational quality standards is hardly the only source of "best practices." Another approach would be to establish a much broader set of criteria and to apply them systematically to all extant education provisions. In a sense, the next section of this chapter, by identifying a broad array of issues to be considered in the drafting of "model" education provisions and providing examples for each drawn from existing provisions, may be a major step in that direction. By itself, however, it stops short of being a statement of "best practices."

Another, quite self-evident way is to consider the efforts made over the years to develop model state constitutions, which sometimes include education provisions.[74] The best known is the National Municipal League's *Model State Constitution*, first published in 1921 and last revised in 1968.[75] Its public education provision is hardly path-breaking, however.[76] Drawing heavily on existing state constitutional provisions, the model clause requires the legislature to "provide for the maintenance and support of a system of free public schools open to all children in the state," and authorizes, but does not require, the legislature to "establish, organize and support such other public educational institutions, including public institutions of higher learning, as may be desirable."

A more recent model state constitution includes, under an article dealing with "Miscellaneous Subjects," a more expansive education clause.[77] It adds a hortatory preamble, two qualitative descriptors of the state's "system of public schools" ("general and uniform," and "thorough and efficient"), and requires that the legislature make provision "by taxation or otherwise as will secure a thorough and efficient system of public schools throughout the state."

This model clause is also derived from existing constitutional provisions, but it seems a considerable hodgepodge. Viewed through the prism of equity/adequacy litigation, it is hard to know how a court might construe its two sets of qualitative descriptors, in terms of their meanings or their relationship to one another. A legislature seeking to implement this clause might have similar problems.

Even more recently, two surveys of state education clauses included useful checklists for a model state constitutional framework, although neither purported to be a statement of best practices. In conjunction with the Hamilton Fish Institute's *Review of State Constitutions: Education Clauses*, its special counsel identified the following possible elements of a model provision:

- Preamble & Statement of Purpose.
- Guarantee of free and public schools: types of schools, scope of education, age requirements.
- Reference to funding, including requirements related to uniformity, equity, and source.
- Statement of non-sectarian control.
- Definition of requirements of local agencies, if any.
- Establish right to education and right to safe and secure educational environment.
- Compulsory attendance provision.
- Statement of non-discrimination.[78]

In its updated survey of State Constitutions and Public Education Governance, the Education Commission of the States listed four common elements that appear in state education provisions: "1) Establishing and maintaining a free system of public schools open to all children of the state; 2) Financing schools (in varying degrees of detail); 3) Separating church and state, often in at least one of the following two ways: forbidding any public funds to be appropriated or used for the support of any sectarian school, and requiring public schools to be free from sectarian control; 4) Creating certain decision-making entities (e.g., state board of education, state superintendent of education, local board of education, local superintendent of education); although most state constitutions require at least some of these entities to be in place, they usually do not specify their qualifications, powers and duties."[79]

Still other possible sources of "best practices" include what the states say about their education provisions or their constitutions generally (admittedly a rather self-serving source), and what the states' most recent practices have been regarding constitutional amendments. A number of states routinely claim that their constitutions, but not necessarily their education provisions, are models, sometimes because they are based on the National Municipal League's model and sometimes for other reasons. Prominent among them are Alaska, Montana, and Florida.

Alaska's claim is rooted in the fact that its constitution is relatively recent, and, therefore, was drafted in light of the experience of other states.[80] Whatever one might say about the rest of its constitution, though, the education clause is hardly distinctive. Like the National Municipal League model, it obliges the legislature to establish and maintain, by general law, "a system of public schools open to all children of the State," and authorizes, but does not require, the legislature to provide for "other public educational institutions." It adds provisions assuring no sectarian control of public schools and no public funding of private schools, religious or otherwise, as well as regarding establishment and operation of a state university.

Montana's constitution actually is more recent than Alaska's, having been adopted by a constitutional convention and ratified by the people in 1972. Its education provisions are substantially more expansive than Alaska's, occupying ten sections of an article entitled "Education and Public Lands." The first and main section, entitled "Educational goals and duties," has a few elements reminiscent of other state constitutions, but a number of unique attributes.[81] It begins with an unusually ambitious goal—"to establish a system of education which will develop the full educational potential of each person"—and adds for each person a guarantee of equality of educational opportunity.[82] However, in the more operational third paragraph of this section, the scope of the state's educational mission seems to have been curtailed, or at least made more ambiguous. The legislature is required to "provide a **basic** system of free **quality** public elementary and secondary schools," and is authorized to provide other educational institutions and programs.[83] The legislature also is required to "fund and distribute in an **equitable** manner to the school districts the state's share of the cost of the **basic** elementary and secondary school system."[84]

Florida's claim to being a "best practices" state is based on its seven recent education amendments. As indicated previously, four were adopted in 1998 as a result of a constitutional convention; three were adopted last year as a result of initiative petitions. The purport of these amendments and the extent to which they might constitute best practices is best considered, however, in a broader context.

Recent efforts of states, including Florida, to amend their education provisions can provide important insights about emerging best practice possibilities. This is especially the case because in recent years there have been great public turmoil about, and interest in, schooling. Since 1996, fifty-four proposed amendments to state education provisions have appeared on ballots in twenty-four states.[85] Of those, by far the greatest number—thirty-six, or 66.7%—have related to fiscal matters, some quite technical, others far-reaching. Other topics have included higher education governance (five, or 9.4%), elementary and secondary education governance (four, or 7.5%), teaching and instruction (four, or 7.5%), educational quality (two, or 3.8%), race (two, or 3.8%), and parental authority over their children's education (one, or 1.9%).

Of the fifty-four amendments proposed, thirty-six (66.7%), in eighteen states, were successful. Twenty-four of those successful amendments (66.7%) dealt with fiscal issues, many in a relatively technical manner.[86] However, some interesting best practices directions emerged. Arkansas and Colorado required minimum tax levies for education; conversely, Missouri and South Dakota capped, or made it more difficult to increase, tax rates. Four states allocated funds from other sources to education—Oklahoma from a tobacco settlement fund, and Georgia, South Carolina, and Virginia from state lotteries. Hawaii took a different fiscal direction, authorizing state bonding to assist not-for-profit private schools and universities. Of even greater contemporary relevance, Louisiana authorized the State Board of Elementary and Secondary Education to oversee and even manage an elementary or high school determined to be failing, and to use available state and local funds. Finally, and perhaps most interestingly, Oregon required the legislature to provide sufficient funding to meet state education quality goals and to report publicly whether or not it had been able to do so.

Two successful amendments dealt with racial issues—California's Proposition 209 barring most affirmative action programs[87] and Kentucky's egregiously overdue repeal of a provision requiring segregated schools and permitting poll taxes.[88] Four dealt with university governance issues.[89] The other six amendments dealt with educational quality and K–12 program or administrative issues, and all were adopted in Florida.[90]

On the negative side of the constitutional ledger, also since 1996, eighteen amendments of education provisions, in eleven states, five of them states that also had successful amendments, failed. Twelve of the failed proposals (66.7%) related to fiscal matters, but these tended to be somewhat more substantive and less technical than the successful fiscal amendments.[91] Of note, three of the unsuccessful proposals sought to assist nonpublic schools directly by voucher-style payments (California and Michigan) or indirectly by tax credits (Colorado). A fourth sought to prohibit using property taxes to support public schools (South Dakota).

The other six unsuccessful amendments related, one each, to English language instruction, educational quality, educational administration, institutions of higher education, teacher pay and retention, and parental authority over their children's education.[92] Three of these failed proposals also are of note. A Colorado proposal provided for the inalienable right of parents to direct and control the upbringing, education, values, and discipline of their children. A Nebraska proposal, predating Florida's 1998 amendments, sought to make each of a "quality education," a "fundamental right," and a "thorough and efficient education" a "paramount duty" of the state. An Oregon proposal would have measured a teacher's job performance partly on the extent to which his or her students' appropriate knowledge increased.

Looking at this recent amendatory history on a state-by-state basis, immediately suggests that the activity is not widely and evenly spread across the country. Although almost half the states had ballot proposals, two-thirds of the proposals came from seven states, an average of five per state. Thus, Florida had seven proposed education amendments, South Dakota six,[93] Colorado,[94] Oklahoma,[95] and Oregon[96] five each, California four,[97] and Hawaii three.[98]

The extent of amendatory activity in these states might signal that they were loci for education clause best practices, but there also could be quite different explanations.[99] At least as to Florida, though, as indicated, the number of successful amendments does justify its status as a best practice state.

Florida's recent amendatory activity clearly is the nation's most distinctive. Twice in the past five years, Florida has considered a number of major amendments to its state constitutional education provisions and has adopted all of them, although not always in the form proposed or favored by education advocates.

Of Florida's four 1998 amendments, three are not serious candidates for "best practices,"[100] but the fourth is. Prior to the 1998 amendment, section 1 of Florida's education provision was limited and similar to many nineteenth-century education clauses, committing the state to make "[a]dequate provision . . . for a uniform system of free public schools." The amendment added several important, and seemingly ambitious, elements. First, it added two sentences at the beginning of the section that read as follows:

> The education of children is a fundamental value of the people of the State of Florida. It is, therefore, a paramount duty of the state to make adequate provision for the education of all children residing within its borders.

Second, it added to the required attributes of the public education system that it be "efficient, safe, secure and high quality." Finally, it added that such a system should "allow . . . students to obtain a high quality education."[101]

Without doubt, these modifications of Florida's core education provision make it a strong best practice candidate. That is true even though some Florida advocates have expressed keen disappointment at some watering down of their proposals.[102] Another possible concern is that the Florida education clause, as amended in 1998, also bears some similarity to one of the model constitutions in that it combines two qualitative standards—in Florida's case, "adequate" and "high quality"—thereby potentially creating confusion about the precise extent of the constitutional goal or mandate. On the other hand, the 1998 amendments make very clear the primacy of education to Florida.

Two of Florida's three 2002 amendments also are noteworthy. Both add text to the core education provision whose 1998 amendment has just been discussed. One explicitly does so in response to the broad educational mandate of the 1998 amendment to section 1, and the other may implicitly do so. The first requires the legislature to make "adequate provision" for (that is to say, fund) reduced class sizes, to be phased in between the 2003 and 2010 school years. The stated purpose is "[t]o assure that children attending public schools obtain a high quality education."[103] This amendment was hotly debated and divided the electorate. It was adopted by a 52.9 percent to 47.1 percent vote, easily the most closely contested of the three 2002 education amendments. Many major educational and public interest groups opposed the amendment because of concerns about its fiscal impact, the uncertain availability of sufficient numbers of qualified teachers, and of most relevance to this chapter, the inappropriateness of imbedding in a constitution detailed class size requirements. Indeed, within a year, the Florida State Board of Education voted unanimously to support a constitutional amendment that would sharply scale back the class size mandates.[104]

The other noteworthy 2002 amendment requires the state to provide free, high-quality prekindergarten learning opportunities for all four-year-olds, to be in place by the 2005 school year and to be funded by "new" money.[105] Although this amendment also has substantial cost and instructional capacity implications, it passed easily (apparently because of widespread public outrage over the legislature's prior repeal of the statutory authority for prekindergarten instructional opportunities). It also raised fewer concerns about incorporating inappropriate detail into the constitution.

DEVELOPING "MODEL" EDUCATION PROVISIONS FOR A STATE CONSTITUTION

In considering the development of "model" education provisions,[106] this chapter makes two assumptions: first, that the constitutional drafters have the advantage of the accumulated history and experience recounted earlier; and second, that the drafters are unfettered by the particular political and fiscal constraints of any given state. At least the second assumption might be criticized for divorcing this chapter from reality, but that seems an inevitable attribute of any effort to produce a "model," especially one designed to be of use throughout the country.[107]

This section, then, focuses on two kinds of issues regarding the drafting of state constitutional education provisions. First, there is a set of broad, threshold considerations, followed by a much longer and more detailed set of substantive inquiries. In connection with both, models drawn largely from existing state constitutional provisions are cited. The end result is not a single recommended model education clause or set of education provisions; rather, this chapter seeks to offer a series of informed choices about various education elements that might be incorporated into a state constitution by a thoughtful drafter sensitive to local needs and desires.

There are six threshold issues that tend to subdivide into two categories, one relating to the comprehensiveness and specificity of an education clause, and the other to its enforceability.[108] As to the former category, constitutions often are said to be "written for the ages." Accordingly, their provisions should be relatively general and open-ended, rather than detailed and prescriptive. Details and prescriptions, under that model, are left to statutes and regulations. However, the easier it is to amend a particular constitution, the more feasible (or, at least, the more tempting) it may become to incorporate greater detail into the constitution itself. Thus, this first category contains three interrelated issues—the ease of amendment, comprehensiveness, and degree of detail or specificity.

The second category—relating to enforceability—also raises three interrelated issues: is the clause intended to be mandatory or hortatory, is it intended to be self-executing or does it require legislative or executive action, and does it create individual rights or merely vest the state with an obligation or discretion.

Beyond these threshold issues, the chapter reviews a comprehensive list of substantive issues to be considered in drafting education provisions (or evaluating existing ones). The list is culled from state constitutions, current and historical, and from secondary sources, as are the illustrative provisions set out for many of the issues. The list is designed to be an inclusive checklist, not a recommendation of what should be included in an education clause. As indicated, the illustrative provisions set out are designed as options for a drafter, not definitive recommendations. Although some issues are treated in greater detail than others, this should not be understood to mean that the former are necessarily more important than the latter in any individual state.

Comprehensiveness and Specificity

As indicated previously, there has been a historical trend toward more detailed education provisions in state constitutions, but this has hardly affected every state. A review of current constitutions reveals strikingly different approaches. To some degree, the trend toward greater detail in education clauses is mirrored in state constitutions generally. It seems that states that have engaged in piecemeal amendment from time to time, rather than substantially revising their constitutions at one time, have lengthier documents. Moreover, the time at which the constitution was adopted makes a big difference. The oldest and newest constitutions tend to be the shortest and the ones in between, perhaps reflecting Victorian prolixity, are the longest.[109]

One variable that may help to explain these differences is the ease of constitutional amendment. California has become notorious in that regard because of its liberal approach to initiative and referendum.[110] Florida, on the other hand, presents a mixed picture. It has both initiative and referendum and a Constitution Revision Commission, appointed by the governor, speaker of the house and president of the senate, whose proposed constitutional changes are placed directly on the ballot for public acceptance.[111] The Commission only convenes every twenty years, however. Although its proposals led to the major 1998 education clause amendments discussed previously, it has not been a vehicle for frequent constitutional amendment in years past. Indeed, its proposed Revision 8 in 1978 was rejected by Florida's voters. That revision "would have added [a] statement of purpose to the existing guarantee of a uniform system of free public schools: 'to develop the ability of each student to read, communicate and compute and to provide an opportunity for vocational training.'"[112] It also "proposed to strip the governor and cabinet of the collegial power to act as the 'state board of education' and to transfer the function and name to a nine person board appointed by the governor and confirmed by the senate . . . [and] to elevate the state university system to constitutional status and to provide it with a nine person governing board whose members would have been appointed by the governor and confirmed by the senate."[113]

The bottom line about comprehensiveness and specificity, supported by the substantial weight of expert opinion, however, is that less is more—relatively concise education provisions are preferable to elaborately detailed ones.[114]

Enforceability

Sometimes as a result of their own terms[115] and sometimes as a result of judicial construction,[116] sharp differences have emerged regarding the enforceability of state education provisions. To some extent, the differences turn on whether the constitutional claim is being advanced by an individual student, parent, teacher or other arguably affected person, or by a large class or an educational entity; to some extent, they turn on the nature of relief sought.[117] A review of the school funding/educational adequacy litigation of the past thirty years, by far the most comprehensive body of state constitutional education litigation, suggests that in most states courts have found that, at least in appropriate cases, their education provisions are mandatory, self-executing, and enforceable by citizens or their representatives.[118]

Possible Elements of a "Model" State Education Clause

This section will first provide a comprehensive list, without discussion, of possible elements that might be included in a state's constitutional education provisions and then a relatively brief discussion of some of those elements. For the most part, examples and references will be left for the endnotes. Since there are ten categories of elements and more than forty specific items grouped under those categories, an education clause that incorporated a substantial portion would be long and detailed. Whether that should be the case, obviously, is a threshold question for any drafter.

The Comprehensive List

1. Statement of the state's educational purpose or commitment.
2. Scope of the provisions' coverage in terms of:

    a. age;
    b. educational levels (e.g., early childhood education or higher education);
    c. response to educational disadvantage (e.g., disability, socioeconomic status, or upbringing);
    d. extent to which education is provided "free";
    e. provision for compulsory attendance;
    f. provision for the length of the school day and school year; and
    g. provision for class size limits.

3. Specification of an educational quality standard in terms of:

    a. quantum or level provided for or required; and
    b. whether it is defined by input, process/opportunity or outcome measures.

4. Specification of an educational equality standard in terms of:

    a. freedom from segregation or other discrimination based on race, ethnicity and religion, and possibly, gender, socioeconomic status, disability, and native language;[119]
    b. guarantee of diversity, or racial or other balance;
    c. guarantee of access to comparable schools, programs, and funding; and
    d. whether it is defined by input, process/opportunity or outcome measures.

5. Funding assurances in terms of:
    a. guaranteed sources of state funding (generally or for specific, categorical programs/needs);
    b. relative priority among state services;
    c. extent of reliance on local funding;
    d. state's role in assuring equality or adequacy of total funding;
    e. taxpayer equality;
    f. limitations or caps on taxing or spending levels; and
    g. state support of higher education, including scholarship funding.

6. Prohibitions or limits in terms of:
    a. segregation or other discrimination in the public schools;
    b. sectarian instruction;
    c. sectarian or private school funding;
    d. funding level for public schools;
    e. tax rate; and
    f. judicial role.

7. Provision for specific services and materials in terms of:
    a. pupil transportation;
    b. textbooks; and
    c. teachers.

8. Specification of the locus and form of governmental responsibility for education in terms of:
    a. the "state";
    b. the legislature;
    c. state education officials, and whether they are to be appointed or elected;
    d. state education agency;
    e. county or regional superintendents;
    f. local school districts; and
    g. constitutional or statutory status of items c through f above.

9. Specification of the role of parents and families in terms of:
    a. school choice;
    b. home schooling; and
    c. funding and taxation issues relating to non–public school education.

10. Provision for enforceability in terms of:
    a. creation of individual rights; and
    b. role of courts.

Discussing Some Key Elements

1. *The state's purpose or commitment.* This chapter's description of the historical evolution of state constitutional education provisions clearly suggests that the broad statement of the state's purpose or commitment regarding education has reflected several predominant patterns. Initially, most clauses either were hortatory, exalting the virtues of learning and knowledge, or obligatory, requiring state legislatures to establish schools. Over time, some states combined the two elements into a single clause. Beginning in the latter half of the nineteenth-century, many states added a qualitative standard to their education clauses, often some variation on the "thorough and efficient" theme. Much more recently, especially in reaction to the expansive school funding and educational quality litigation of the past thirty years, some states have begun to consider and adopt more individualized, and sometimes more definitive, qualitative standards. Of course, given the impetus for these recent amendments, the legislative and public debate has focused on the legal, as well as educational and fiscal, implications of various formulations.

This has led to serious consideration of a number of interrelated issues. First, what terminology should the state use to define its educational undertaking? Should it adopt a qualitative term with clear legal implications, such as "fundamental?"[120] Should it link education to specific outcome indicators, such as effective citizenship, ability to compete in and contribute to the economy, or other societal values? Should it describe education as a "paramount" right or duty, thereby quite possibly suggesting the primacy of education over other public services?[121] How clearly and definitively should the constitutional drafters indicate whether the educational undertaking is a goal or a mandate of the state?[122]

Of course, especially during a time of fiscal constraints, these sorts of questions could be answered in a manner that would narrow rather than enlarge the commitment and consequent obligations of the state, and the concomitant rights of its citizens. In fact, for many years narrowing amendments have been proposed periodically, often in direct response to expansive court decisions.[123] Seldom, however, have such narrowing amendments been adopted.

2. *Scope of coverage.* The extent of the state's commitment and its citizens' correlative rights has a variety of other, even more specific dimensions. One of those is the scope of the education provisions' coverage. In the main, this involves two interrelated aspects—the age of students afforded education and the education levels to be

provided. As to both, many, but not nearly all, state constitutions make provision, and their treatments are quite different.

Regarding age, six is the most common entry level, but that is likely to change in light of the substantial emerging evidence of early childhood education's benefits, especially for disadvantaged students, and twenty-one is the most common exit age.[124]

Regarding educational levels, a significant difference among the states relates to whether or not higher education is covered by the constitutional education clauses. The most common approach is to require that education be provided through secondary school, but some states authorize or even require it to be provided beyond.[125] In those states that make constitutional provision for higher education, a related question is the extent to which it should be provided free of charge, and the approaches vary.[126]

As suggested above, pressure is likely to build to amend state education provisions to include early childhood education beginning at age four, or even at age three.[127] This is partly because of the success of state court litigation, mainly New Jersey's *Abbott v. Burke*, which has resulted in a mandate that well-planned, high-quality early childhood education be made available to all three- and four-year-old children in the state's thirty poor urban school districts.[128]

Another kind of scope-of-education provision has made its way into a few state constitutions, but is dealt with primarily by statute. That is the matter of compulsory education—the flip side of educational entitlement. A few state education provisions directly compel attendance;[129] a somewhat larger number authorize legislative action.[130]

3.   *Educational quality standards.*   This element was touched on preliminarily in the discussion of the state's commitment to education. It certainly is true that qualitative statements usually appear in the first section of a state's education provisions as part of the foundational statement. But a separate discussion is warranted by the centrality of educational quality standards to the school funding and educational adequacy litigation movement.

Increasingly, as equal protection doctrine has receded and education clauses have come to the forefront, school funding/education adequacy litigation is premised on a provable gap between what those clauses require of the state and what, in reality, the state education system affords its students. In one form or another, the law suits seek to close or eliminate that gap.

Although the educational quality standards embedded in state constitutions fall into several general categories, they vary considerably from state to state. Moreover, state courts have construed similar, or even virtually identical, clauses quite differently. Several leading commentators have written detailed articles cataloging and evaluating state education clauses, focusing on them mainly from the perspective of their education quality standards.

One commentator, in particular, has focused on the "strength" of education clauses, primarily evaluated through the lens of their qualitative standards.[131] William Thro identified four categories:

- Category I (the weakest) includes eighteen state education clauses that "merely mandate a system of free public schools" without imposing any quality standard;[132]
- Category II (somewhat stronger, but still relatively weak) includes twenty-one state education clauses that "impose some minimum standard of quality, usually thorough and/or efficient, that the statewide system of public schools must reach;"[133]
- Category III (substantially stronger) includes six state education clauses that have a "'stronger and more specific educational mandate' such as 'all means,' and a 'purposive preamble;'"[134] and
- Category IV (the strongest) includes five state education clauses that "make education an important, if not the most important duty of the state."[135]

Tempting as it is to engage in this sort of categorization, Thro's effort has proven to be of limited value. Partially, that may be a result of his approach. Thro's strong-to-weak continuum ignores many, more subtle, and at least equally important, dimensions of constitutional education provisions, such as their treatment of the state-local relationship.[136] Additionally, even with regard to his strong-to-weak continuum, contrary to some statements in his article, Thro seemed to base his categorization entirely on the plain language of the education clauses.[137]

Despite the fact that Thro's linguistic distinctions have not been significant in school finance litigation thus far, Thro suggests that the language of state education clauses should and will be decisive in the future.[138] Categorization aside, though, there is absolutely no question that state constitutional education clauses have come to play a hugely important role during the past thirty years.

Thro was hardly the first to predict an important role for state constitutional provisions, however. Much earlier, Justice Brennan had suggested that state constitutions can be a "font of individual liberties,"[139] and this may be particularly true in the realm of education.

Since 1971, plaintiffs in forty-five states[140] have challenged the constitutionality of their states' public school finance systems, arguing violations of the Fourteenth Amendment of the U.S. Constitution, the "equal opportunity clause" of their state constitution or the state constitution's education provision.[141] However, given the differences among them,[142] there is little uniformity in how courts interpret state education provisions.[143]

In addition to the linguistic categorization of education clauses, some commentators, Thro included, have sought to divide these school finance reform challenges into a sequential "three wave model."[144] During the first "wave," which is said to have begun with the California Supreme Court decision in *Serrano v. Priest*[145] in 1971, plaintiffs argued that wide disparities in educational funding were a denial of equal protection under the Fourteenth Amendment.[146] However, in 1973, the United States Supreme Court effectively ended this wave with its 5–4 decision in *San Antonio Independent School District v. Rodriguez*.[147] As a result, the most successful challenges have been based on state constitutional provisions, which some commentators have divided into two categories: "equity claims" and "minimum standards claims."[148]

Like the first wave, the second wave of school finance reform litigation focused on equity claims, but under state constitutional theories.[149] In 1973, in *Robinson v. Cahill*,[150] the New Jersey Supreme Court first gave major significance to a state education clause, declaring the state school finance system unconstitutional solely because it violated New Jersey's education provision.[151] Like many other second wave cases, *Robinson* had included state equal protection claims, which were relied on by the trial court but ultimately rejected by the state supreme court,[152] as the courts often denied claims that districts were constitutionally entitled to equal spending.[153] Since then, according to proponents of the "wave theory," there has been a gradual shift from "equality suits" to "quality suits," leading to the so-called third wave.[154] Third wave suits rely on the premise that children are constitutionally entitled "to an education of at least a certain quality."[155] This wave was said to have commenced in 1989 with successful suits in Kentucky, Montana, and Texas,[156] and has continued in New Jersey with *Abbott v. Burke*.[157] In truth, though, both educational adequacy and funding equity issues have been integral components of litigation challenges styled as second or third wave cases, so both elements must be considered in drafting a constitutional education clause.

From the perspective of this huge body of state court litigation, time clearly has not been kind to Thro's 1993 categorization, at least if "strong" education provisions should lead to strong judicial and other constructions of those provisions, entitling students to high-quality education. In fact, there almost seems to be an inverse correlation—the weak and relatively weak provisions have led to more expansive interpretations than the relatively strong and strong provisions. A common Category II education quality standard—"thorough and efficient"—has led to a series of court decisions and educational mandates in New Jersey that many consider the most ambitious in the country. Since its 1990 decision in *Abbott v. Burke,* the New Jersey Supreme Court has successively ratcheted up the comprehensiveness and specificity of its orders in response to the failures of the other branches of state government to respond effectively.[158] According to the Education Law Center, legal representative of the 350,000 student plaintiffs, the *Abbott* legal framework includes:

- standards-based education driven by state content standards and supported by per-pupil funding equal to spending in successful suburban schools;
- education program comparability with suburban schools to emulate their "recipe for success";
- required and needed supplemental ("at-risk") programs "to wipe out student disadvantages," including well-planned, high quality preschool education for all three- and four-year-olds;
- comprehensive educational improvement to deliver the *Abbott* programs and reforms at the school site;
- new and rehabilitated facilities to adequately house all programs, relieve overcrowding, and eliminate health and safety violations; and
- state assurance of adequate funding and full, effective and timely implementation in districts and schools.[159]

This comprehensive framework evolved from the New Jersey Supreme Court's initial determination that "thorough and efficient" education requires "'a certain level of educational opportunity, a minimum level that will equip the student to become a citizen and . . . a competitor in the labor market.'"[160] Of other states with a "thorough and efficient" education standard,[161] West Virginia had a major, expansive court decision[162] and Ohio's case invalidated the state's school finance law and initially resulted in a strong judicial enforcement order, from which the state supreme court recently retreated.[163]

Another weak standard—"efficient" education[164]—resulted in a Kentucky Supreme Court decision that, in a way, was even more ambitious than New Jersey's. The court basically invalidated Kentucky's entire education code and required the legislature to start over.[165] In doing so, the court ruled that an "efficient" education required students to possess at least seven capabilities:

- sufficient oral and written communication skills to enable students to function in a complex and rapidly changing civilization;
- sufficient knowledge of economic, social, and political systems to enable students to make informed choices;
- sufficient understanding of governmental processes to enable students to understand the issues, which affect their communities, state, or nation;
- sufficient self-knowledge and knowledge of their mental and physical wellness;
- sufficient grounding in the arts to enable each student to appreciate his or her cultural and historical heritage;
- sufficient training or preparation for advanced training in either academic or vocational fields so as to enable each student to choose and pursue like work intelligently; and
- sufficient level of academic and vocational skills to enable public school students to compete on favorable terms with their counterparts in surrounding states, in academics or in the job market.[166]

Most recently, in New York a clause that Thro ranked in his weakest category led to a strong plaintiffs' victory in the state's highest court.[167] Without an explicit educational quality standard, the court still found that New York City students were entitled to a meaningful high school education, one that would equip them with the skills to be capable civic participants and productive workers in the twenty-first-century economy. According to the website of the Campaign for

Fiscal Equity, the nominal plaintiff, the state was given until July 30, 2004, to reform the current state funding system under a three-part remedial directive that requires the state to:

- ascertain the actual cost of providing a sound basic education in New York City;
- ensure that every school has the resources necessary for providing the opportunity for a sound basic education; and
- ensure a system of accountability to measure whether the reforms actually provide the opportunity for a sound basic education.[168]

By contrast with New Jersey, Kentucky, and New York, several states with "strong" educational quality standards, at least in the sense that they incorporate explicitly ambitious language, have not had successful litigation mandating improved education.[169] This is not because the other branches of government in those states had implemented substantial educational reforms without judicial goading. Florida's relatively recent addition of strong education clause language may provide an interesting new test of whether or not there is evidence of any significant positive linkage between strong educational quality standards and strong education reforms, whether court inspired or otherwise.[170] Beyond that, Florida's amended education provisions have been touted as a model. By declaring education a "fundamental value," characterizing the duty of providing it as "paramount," and defining it to include uniformity, efficiency, safety, security, and high quality,[171] Florida's constitutional amendment process considered and resolved many of the issues contemplated by this section, but not necessarily as others would do.

Of course, those who have identified a "new" wave of education litigation focusing on educational adequacy and based on state education clauses[172] are not completely wrong. Litigation emphasizing educational adequacy and education clauses has largely supplanted the much earlier litigation emphasizing equitable funding and equal protection doctrine.[173] They are wrong, however, in two respects— the degree to which they slough off very early cases, such as *Robinson v. Cahill*,[174] which were decided solely on the basis of state education clauses, and the degree to which they seek to bifurcate educational equity, or funding, and educational adequacy. All the successful cases have combined both aspects, although their emphases and legal theories may have been different.

This body of state education litigation has important implications for constitutional drafters. Although state courts hardly have been uniform in their interpretative approaches, and although decisions in one state lack authoritative precedential value in other states, still the accumulating body of case law provides a resource to drafters. In considering a particular qualitative standard, drafters must be aware and mindful of the judicial interpretations of that standard. If the interpretations, more often than not, have produced results that the drafters desire, then that constitutional formulation may be promising. Of course, the drafters can always incorporate language whose purpose is to assure a specific interpretation or mode of implementation by legislators and judges, but one lesson from Thro's experience may be that there are no guarantees how even the most directive language ultimately will be construed.

A final question to be dealt with in connection with an educational quality standard is whether the provision itself should specify how constitutional compliance would be determined. In other words, once a quality standard is identified, should compliance be measured by inputs, opportunity or outcomes. Most existing constitutional education provisions do not specify how compliance is to be measured. However, some contain fiscal, or input, mandates that occasionally are very specific.[175] Others focus on equality of educational opportunity, an opportunity or process approach.[176]

Where state educational clauses leave compliance unaddressed, state legislatures, departments of education and, ultimately, courts have been left with a substantial measure of discretion in that regard. Their responses, predictably, have varied. Some, especially those focusing on fiscal equity, have tended to emphasize an input-oriented approach, with dollar input or fiscal capacity as the prime criteria.[177] Others have emphasized educational opportunities, sometimes defining those in programmatic terms.[178] A few have opted for outcome measures. New Jersey may provide the best example. Even during the earliest stages of its litigation, when fiscal equity was still a dominant theme, the state courts were indicating that the measure of compliance with the "thorough and efficient" clause was whether students were receiving an education that would equip them to be effective citizens and competitors in the contemporary labor market—outcome standards.[179]

4. *Educational equality standard.* As with the educational **quality** standard, there is an issue about how educational **equality** should be measured and whether the constitutional provision itself should

specify. The most common approach, adopted by several state education provisions, is to opt for an opportunity measure.[180]

A set of other, interrelated issues relate to the content and coverage of the equality standard. Does it stress freedom from discrimination, equal access to schools and programs, or both? Does it protect specific categories of students from specified inequalities or is it more open-ended? Does it extend its protections beyond students?

In spite of the United States' history of de jure school segregation, only a surprisingly small number of state constitutions expressly bar segregation in the schools, typically as part of broader antidiscrimination provisions rather than education provisions.[181] A number of other state constitutions do provide in their education provisions that the schools will be "open to all."[182] Still others prohibit discrimination or guarantee access to students without regard to one or more of the following characteristics: race, color, caste, creed, religion, national origin, sex, or political beliefs.[183]

A number of state constitutions expressly extend their equality protections beyond students to teachers.[184]

5. *Educational funding.*   From the earliest days of state constitutional education clauses, public funding of the schools has been a major focus. The funding provisions raise a number of different types of issues, including: the degree to which they should expressly dovetail with, or implement, the educational quality or equality standards; the extent to which the locus of revenue-raising responsibility should be state or local; whether equality of tax burdens should be assured; and whether provision should be made for scholarships or other higher education assistance.

As to the relationship between funding and educational quality or equality provisions, in a number of state constitutions the education clauses actually are placed in the finance articles, suggesting a substantial interrelationship.[185] Some education clauses set forth the relationship or the funding level in general terms;[186] others are quite specific.[187] There also are a number of provisions that deal with the equitable nature of school funding,[188] minimum funding levels,[189] and proportional distribution of funding.[190]

As to the locus of fund-raising responsibility, only Hawaii can claim to be a full-state-funded jurisdiction; the rest rely on a combination of state and local revenue, although the respective proportions differ greatly.[191] A few state constitutions make the shared responsibility explicit;[192] most do not.[193] Many state constitutions provide for the establishment and perpetuation of permanent, protected endowments or trust funds for public schools, either at the state or local level or both,[194] often accompanied by specifications regarding funding sources,[195] investments,[196] and use.[197] If the fund is depleted, especially by an unconstitutional act, the provision may require that the legislature approve a special appropriation or assume the amount deducted as a debt to be paid back into the fund.[198]

As to equality of tax burdens, despite the virtually universal acceptance of the proposition that education is a state function and the existence of tax uniformity provisions in many state constitutions, taxpayer complaints about unequal tax burdens from district to district have usually fallen on deaf judicial ears. Illustratively, in New Jersey's first school funding decision, an early trial court opinion, the finance system was found to be in violation of the state's tax uniformity provision, but the state supreme court quickly overruled.[199] Interestingly, in several states local taxpayers did succeed in challenging school funding equalization efforts that included state recapture of some locally raised school tax revenue.[200]

As to higher education financial assistance, a number of state constitutions make some provision.[201]

6. *Educational prohibitions/limits.* One relatively common prohibition has already been discussed—the prohibition against segregation or other invidious discrimination in the public schools. A second one, far more common, is the prohibition against sectarian instruction in the public schools, the use of public funds for sectarian purposes, or both. Nearly every state constitution contains such a prohibition, either as part of its education provisions or elsewhere.[202]

Because of the age and pervasiveness of these provisions, until recently they were seldom challenged or seriously at issue. However, that has begun to change as a result of the United States Supreme Court's recent decision in the *Zelman* case.[203] With some commentators interpreting *Zelman* as a broad validation of education vouchers under the federal constitution, the focus is shifting to state constitutions and their prohibitions of public funding of private and sectarian schools.[204] Some have argued that state prohibitions might even run afoul of the newly articulated federal doctrine. Obviously, this issue is closely related to another issue— the scope of parental and student rights to educational choice— still to be discussed.

7. *Provision of ancillary educational services, materials, and teachers.* The most common state constitutional clauses in this area involve textbooks. Some simply authorize the provision of free textbooks.[205] Others either provide for, or proscribe, state-created textbook lists.[206]

8. *Locus of responsibility for education.* In every state, education ulti-
    mately is a state function and responsibility. Therefore, education
    provisions typically repose constitutional power and duty in either
    the "state"[207] or its legislature.[208] Beyond such threshold provisions,
    however, some state constitutions deal with the administration of
    public education, both at the state and local levels. At the state
    level, a significant number of constitutions provide for the election
    or appointment and membership of a state board of education,[209]
    and for its powers and duties.[210] A much smaller number of states
    make constitutional provision for a state superintendent of educa-
    tion or public instruction.[211]

    Some states also give constitutional status to local school dis-
    tricts and boards of education. They do so in several different ways,
    however. Some authorize, but do not require, the establishment of
    county or local boards.[212] Others mandate the establishment of
    local districts and boards, but do not specify their powers and du-
    ties.[213] Still others both mandate the establishment and specify the
    powers and duties of county or local boards.[214] A few even provide
    for the appointment of county or local superintendents.[215]

    A final issue regarding the locus of educational responsibility
    has not yet found its way directly into state education provisions,[216]
    but must now be considered. It has to do with the role of parents
    and families in the education of their children. Under the federal
    constitution, parents have long been accorded the right to choose to
    educate their children outside of the public schools, despite com-
    pulsory education statutes.[217] As previously indicated, the *Zelman*
    decision has further expanded parental rights, albeit in a specialized
    context.[218] Similarly, the federal No Child Left Behind Act has en-
    dorsed parental choice, primarily in the public schools.[219]

    In some quarters, momentum surely is building for even more
    expansive parental choice in education, and state constitutional
    amendments are one vehicle for accomplishing that. The effort
    might involve repeal or judicial invalidation of long-standing state
    constitutional prohibitions against public funding of private or
    sectarian schools. It might alternatively or additionally focus on
    the adoption of amendments expressly recognizing parental
    choice in education. In states such as New Jersey, the picture is
    complicated by strong judicial pronouncements about the consti-
    tutional inviolability of urban education reform mandates.[220] If
    expanded school choice were determined to be incompatible with
    thoroughgoing reform of urban schools, a clear constitutional ten-
    sion would be created.

9. *Enforceability of education rights.* In the spirit of constitutions being written for the ages, most state education provisions do not specify whether they are intended to accord students or others with positive rights to a certain quantum of education that can be enforced through the courts. This fundamental interpretive question, therefore, has been left to the courts, and, from state to state, the answer has differed both about judicial enforceability itself and about the quantum. In a few cases, when the courts' answer aroused sufficient opposition, and the constitutional amendment process was relatively easy, changes were effected, usually to limit the judicial role or authority.[221] Interestingly, there has been no broad-based effort to overturn by constitutional amendment court decisions finding no judicially enforceable educational rights. Florida's 1998 educational amendments may constitute an exception, though, since they were, at least in part, a response to a judicial decision that the state's constitution did not specify an educational quality standard. Additionally, after an Illinois court rejected challenges to that state's school finance system, the Governor's Commission on Education Funding presented a plan for education funding reform, which included "a proposal to amend [the Illinois] constitution by setting an education funding foundation level and mandating that the state pay 50 percent of this amount."[222] The entire report was rejected almost immediately by the state legislature.[223]

The drafter of any education clause will have to decide whether the current state of affairs in this regard, with its attendant uncertainty and unpredictability,[224] is preferable to imbedding in the state constitution express language designed to answer difficult and controversial questions such as the following:

- Should an enforceable right to a certain level of education or educational funding be created?
- If so, for whom should such a right be created?
  - Parents?
  - Students?
  - Taxpayers?
- How should such a right be enforced?
  - What role, if any, should the judiciary play in enforcement?
  - How much deference should be shown to the legislature's judgment of adequacy or constitutional compliance?
  - What remedy should be available to successful litigants?

CONCLUSION

It is tempting to say that a major problem of the past thirty years is that state governments overwhelmingly have sought to use ninetheenth-century education clauses to deal with twentieth- and twenty-first-century education problems, and that it would be preferable to have more current and more responsive provisions available. That presupposes, of course, that clauses work better if they are specifically devised to address contemporary education issues. It exalts specificity over the "constitution for the ages" ideology. It assumes that state constitutions can and will be amended, as necessary, to address new issues or new variations of old issues. It assumes that we have the ability to embody in a constitutional clause workable solutions to complex, multifaceted educational, and often social, problems. It assumes that those responsible for implementing such constitutional clauses do so fully and effectively, or can be forced to do so if they fail to act of their own volition.

The risks of such an approach are plentiful, however. Constitutions can become cluttered with solutions de jour, and prove more resistant to change than expected. Perhaps we will need to develop the constitutional equivalent of software designed to purge your computer of outmoded old programs. Or, we might discover that specificity is more appealing in principle than in practice, and that specific "solutions" turn out to create more problems than they solve.

Perhaps, after we have gone through the process outlined in this chapter of identifying, consulting and applying education clause "best practices," we can decide with some confidence how best to proceed. Of two things, however, we can be certain—the future will hold no fewer challenges than the past 200 years and the importance of providing American students with high-quality education will continue to be of paramount concern to state and national governments, whether or not they incorporate those words into their state constitutions.

NOTES

1. Herbert, Adam W., "The 2002 Florida Elections: Implications for Public Education" 1, ECS Governance Notes (Jan. 2003), available at http://www.ecs.org/clearinghouse/42/10/4210.htm. An even more recent survey canvassed respondents about national priorities, and education topped the list with 55 percent, almost double the percentage of "terrorism and security." Public Education Network and Education Week, "Demanding Quality Public Education in Tough Economic Times: What Voters Want from Elected Leaders" 3 (2003).

2. In addition, for the sixteen newest states, education provisions were mandated for entrance into the Union. Matthew H. Bosworth, *Courts as Catalysts: State Supreme Courts and Public School Finance Equity* 34 (2001).

3. David Tyack, Thomas James, and Aaron Benavot, *Law and the Shaping of Public Education, 1785–1954*, 55 (1987).

4. 347 U.S. 483 (1954).

5. *See* Frank S. White, *Constitutional Provisions for Differentiated Education* 9–27 (1950).

6. The eleven states were South Carolina, Virginia, Maryland, New York, Kentucky, Tennessee, Louisiana, Illinois, Virginia, Rhode Island, and New Jersey.

7. *See* John C. Eastman, "When Did Education Become a Civil Right? An Assessment of State Constitutional Provisions for Education 1776–1900," 42 *Am. J. Legal Hist.* 1, 3 (1998). However, during this early period, no state legislature actually established common schools in accordance with its constitution. Ibid. at 8. Beginning early in the nineteenth century, two other types of education provisions began to appear in state constitutions: federal land grant provisions and provisions establishing state public school funds.

8. Mass. Const. of 1780, chap. V, § 2. *See also* N.H. Const. of 1784, art. 83.

9. Eastman, supra note vii, at 6–7 (citing *Roberts v. The City of Boston*, 59 Mass. (5 Cush.) 198 (1849)).

10. Ohio Const. of 1802, art. VIII, § 3. *See also* Miss. Const. of 1817, art. VI, § 16 ("Religion, morality and knowledge being necessary to good government, the preservation of liberty, and the happiness of mankind, schools, and the means of education, shall forever be encouraged. in this state.")

11. Pa. Const. of 1776, § 44.

12. Ga. Const. of 1777, art. LIV.

13. Vt. Const. of 1786, art. XXXVII.

14. Ind. Const. of 1816, art. IX, § 1. *See also* Cal. Const. of 1849, art. IX, §§ 1–4.

15. Education Commission of the States, "The Invisible Hand of Ideology" 4 (1999), available at http://www.ecs.org/ecsmain.asp?page=/search/default.asp.

16. Kern Alexander, "The Common School Ideal and the Limits of Legislative Authority: The Kentucky Case," 28 *Harv. J. on Legis.* 341, 356 (1991).

17. Ohio Const. of 1802, art. VIII, § 25 ("That no law shall be passed to prevent the poor in the several counties and townships, within this State, from an equal participation in the schools, academies, colleges and universities within this State, which are endowed, in whole or in part, from the revenue arising from donations made by the United States, for the support of schools, academies and universities, shall be open for the reception of scholars and students and teachers, of every grade, without any distinction or preference whatever, contrary to the intent for which said donations were made.").

18. Conn. Const. of 1818, art. VIII, § 2. Substantially later in the nineteenth century, this theme was embraced by a number of other states. For example, the Nebraska Constitution of 1875 stated that "[p]rovisions shall be made by general law for an equitable distribution of the income of the fund set apart for the support of the common

schools among the several school districts of the State." Neb. Const. of 1875, art. VIII, § 7. Similarly, the 1868 Constitution of Mississippi provided that "all school funds shall be divided pro rata among the children of school ages." Miss. Const. of 1868, art. VIII, § 10. *See also* Fla. Const. of 1885, art. XII, § 11 ("The fund raised . . . may be expended in the district where levied for building or repair in school houses, for the purchase of school libraries and textbooks, for salaries of teachers, or for other educational purposes, so that the distribution among all the schools of the district be equitable.").

19. Ind. Const. of 1816, art. IX, § 2.

20. *See* White, supra note v, at 29 .

21. *See* Tyack, James, and Benavot, supra note 3, at 57.

22. Ibid. at 57.

23. Ibid. at 55.

24. Ibid. at 57.

25. Miss. Const. of 1868, art. VIII, § 1.

26. Ark. Const. of 1874, art. 14, § 1.

27. For example, Minnesota stated: "The stability of a republican form of government depending mainly upon the intelligence of the people, it is the duty of the legislature to establish a general and uniform system of public schools." Minn. Const. of 1857, art. XIII, 1. This section continued: "The legislature shall make such provisions by taxation or otherwise as will secure a thorough and efficient system of public schools throughout the state." *See also* Tex. Const. of 1876, art. 7, § 1 ("A general diffusion of knowledge being essential to the preservation of the liberties and rights of the people, it shall be the duty of the Legislature of the State to establish and make suitable provision for the support and maintenance of an efficient system of public free schools"); Miss. Const. of 1868, art. VIII, § 1; Ind. Const. of 1851, art. 8, § 1.

28. *See,* for example, Tenn. Const. of 1869, art. XI, § 12 ("The General Assembly shall provide for the maintenance, support and eligibility standards of a system of free public schools."); Mich. Const. of 1835, art. X, § 3 ("The legislature shall provide for a system of Common Schools"). *See also* Miss. Const. of 1868, art. VIII, § 1; Nev. Const. of 1864, art. 11, § 2 ("The legislature shall provide for a uniform system of common schools); Fla. Const. of 1885, art. XII, § 1 ("The Legislature shall provide for a uniform system of public free schools").

29. *See,* for example, Ga. Const. of 1877, art. VIII, 1877 (state school commissioner); Mich. Const. of 1835, art. X, § 1 (superintendent of public instruction); Miss. Const. of 1868, art. VIII, §§ 2, 3 (superintendent of public education and board of education); Nev. Const. of 1864, art. 11, § 1 (superintendent of public instruction); Cal. Const. of 1849, art. IX, § 1 (superintendent of public instruction); Ind. Const. of 1851, art. 8, § 8 (state superintendent of public instruction); Tex. Const. of 1876, art. VII, § 8 (board of education); Fla. Const. of 1885, art. XII, §§ 2, 3 (superintendent of public instruction and state board of education); Utah Const. of 1895, art. X, § 8 (state board of education and superintendent of public instruction).

30. *See,* for example, Miss. Const. of 1868, art. VIII, § 4 (superintendent of public education in each county); Cal. Const. of 1879, art. IX, § 3 (providing for the election of a superintendent of schools for each county); Colo. Const. of 1876, art. IX, § 6 (county superintendent of schools).

31. Tyack, James, and Benavot, supra note 3, at 58.

32. See Ibid. at 62–63.

33. Ibid. at 60.

34. *See,* for example, Neb. Const. of 1875, art. VIII, § 6; Cal. Const. of 1879, art. IX, § 5 ("The legislature shall provide for a system of common schools by which a free school shall be kept up and supported in each district.").

35. Tyack, James, and Benavot, supra note iii, at 55. Some provisions not only created state-level education entities, but also specified many details. For example, regarding state boards of education, clauses dealt with the number of members, how they were to be selected, their terms of years, and their powers and duties. *See* John Mathiason Matzen, State Constitutional Provisions for Education 5–12 (Teachers College, Columbia University, Contributions to Education No. 46, 1931) (chart detailing state constitutional provisions from 1857 through 1912).

36. Tyack, James, and Benavot, supra note 3, at 57.

37. For example, the 1868 Constitution of Mississippi mandated the establishment of "a uniform system of free public schools . . . for all children between the ages of five and twenty-one years." Miss. Const. of 1868, art. VIII, § 1. *See also* Ala. Const. of 1868, art. XI, § 6; Neb. Const. of 1875, art. VIII, § 6; and Colo. Const. of 1876, art. IX, § 2 ("between the ages of six and twenty-one").

38. For example, New Hampshire amended its education clause in 1877 to provide "that no money raised by taxation shall ever be granted or applied for the use of the schools or institutions of any religious sect or denomination." N.H. Const., art. 83. The 1851 Ohio Constitution prohibited "religious or other sect or sects [from] ever hav[ing] any exclusive right to, or control of, any part of the school funds of this State." Ohio Const. of 1851, art. VI, § 2. New Hampshire and Ohio are two of thirty-eight states that have adopted provisions prohibiting public aid to religious schools. The Colorado Constitution more severely proscribed the mingling of church and state, explicitly prohibiting any "religious test or qualification . . . as a condition of admission into any public educational institution of the State, either as teacher or student." Colo. Const. of 1876, art. IX, § 8. Nebraska's Constitution also prohibited "sectarian instruction . . . in any school or institution supported in whole or in part by the public funds set apart for educational purposes. Neb. Const. of 1875, art. VIII, § 11. *See also* Nev. Const. of 1864, art. 11, § 2.

39. The 1868 Alabama Constitution mandated segregated schools, Ala. Const. of 1875, art. XIII, §§ 1, 11, and that provision was carried forward to the 1901 Alabama Constitution, Ala. Const. of 1901, art. XIV, § 256. Since then, it has been altered, but, amazingly, its segregatory language has not yet been abandoned. In the aftermath of the *Brown* decision, Amendment 111 altered section 256 by effectively eliminating

Alabama's public education system in favor of a system under which parents could opt for "private" single-race schools. More than forty years later, that aspect of section 256 was struck down by the Alabama Supreme Court in a school funding case, Ex Parte James, 713 So.2d 869 (Ala., 1997). In 2002, however, the Alabama Supreme Court partially repudiated its 1997 opinion, Ex Parte James, 836 So.2d 813 (Ala., 2002), 2002 WL 1150823 (May 31, 2002), leaving the status of section 256 in some doubt. A bill to remove section 256's segregatory language, Ala. HB587, as amended, was adopted by both houses of the Alabama legislature during the spring of 2003, but a majority of the state's qualified electors must approve the constitutional amendment for it to take effect. Voter approval cannot be assumed, however. In September 2003, Alabama voters overwhelmingly rejected a $1.2 billion tax increase designed, in part, "to catapult the state's school system from among the nation's worst to one of the best." See David M. Halbfinger, "Alabama Voters Crush Tax Plan Sought by Governor," New York Times (Sept. 10, 2003). See also Ga. Const. of 1877, art. VIII, § 1; Tex. Const. of 1876, art. VII, § 7; Fla. Const. of 1885, art. XII, § 12. In contrast, the Colorado Constitution of 1876 prohibited the "distinction or classification of pupils . . . on account of race or color." Colo. Const. of 1876, art. IX, § 8. Washington's 1889 Constitution prohibited "distinction or preference on account of race, color, caste, or sex." Wash. Const. of 1889, art. IX, § 1.

40. See, for example, Ind. Const. of 1851, art. VIII, § 1; Minn. Const. of 1857, art. XIII, § 1; Nev. Const. of 1864, art. 11, § 2; and Miss. Const. of 1868, art. VIII, § 1.

41. For example, both the 1851 Ohio Constitution and the 1857 Minnesota Constitution mandated "a thorough and efficient system" of common and public schools, respectively. See Ohio Const. of 1851, art. VI, § 2 ("through and efficient system of common schools"); Minn. Const. of 1857, art. XIII, § 1 ("thorough and efficient system of public schools throughout the state."). The 1867 Maryland Constitution and an 1875 amendment to the New Jersey Constitution called for the establishment of "a thorough and efficient system of free public schools." See Md. Const., art. VIII, § 1 and N.J. Const., art. VIII, § 4, par. 1 (originally adopted as art. IV, § 7, par. 9). The 1874 Arkansas Constitution called for "a general, suitable and efficient system of free public schools." Ark. Const. of 1874, art. 14, § 1. See also Del. Const. of 1897, art. X, § 1 ("general and efficient system of free public schools"); Idaho Const., art. IX, § 1 ("general, uniform and thorough").

42. Wash. Const. of 1889, art. IX, § 1.

43. Tyack, James, and Benavot, supra note iii, at 58. See, for example, Calif. Const. of 1879, art. IX, § 5 (six months); Colo. Const. of 1876, art. IX, § 2 (three months); Mich.Const. of 1835, art. X, § 3 (three months).

44. Colo. Const. of 1876, art. IX, § 11 ("every child of sufficient mental and physical ability [may be required to] attend the public school"). See also Nev. Const. of 1864, art. 11, § 2; Idaho Const. of 1890, art. IX, § 9; Va. Const. of 1970, art. VIII, § 3 ("The General Assembly shall provide for the compulsory elementary and secondary education of every eligible child of appropriate age, such eligibility and age to be determined by law.").

45. For example, the California Constitution of 1879 stated: "The public school system shall include primary and grammar schools." Cal. Const. of 1879, art. IX, § 6. See

also Wash. Const. of 1889, art. IX, § 2 ("The public school system shall include common schools, and such high schools, normal schools, and technical schools as may hereafter be established."). Showing that education clauses did not develop uniformly and according to neat time frames, Indiana had adopted a similar provision in 1816, calling for "a general system of education, ascending in a regular gradation, from township schools to a state university." Ind. Const. of 1816, art. IX, § 2. Indiana was ahead of its time in extending the concept of state education to the university level, but other states caught up. *See,* for example, Utah Const. of 1895, art. X, § 2 ("The Public School system shall include kindergarten schools; common schools, consisting of primary and grammar grades; high schools; an Agricultural College; a University and such other schools as the Legislature may establish."); Pa. Const. of 1776, § 44 ("all useful learning shall be duly encouraged and promoted in one or more universities"); Tex. Const. of 1876, art. VII, § 10 ("[t]he legislature shall as soon as practicable establish, organize and provide for the maintenance, support and direction of a University . . . for the promotion of literature, and the arts and sciences, including an Agricultural, and Mechanical department"); Tenn. Const. of 1869, art. XI, § 12 ("The General Assembly may establish and support such post-secondary educational institutions, including public institutions of higher learning, as it determines.").

46. For example, the Mississippi Constitution of 1868 required "the Legislature to encourage, by all suitable means, the promotion of intellectual, scientific, moral, and agricultural improvement." Miss. Const. of 1868, art. VIII, § 1. *See also* Nev. Const. of 1864, art. 11, § 4 ("The Legislature shall provide for the establishment of a State University which shall embrace departments for Agriculture, Mechanic Arts, and Mining.").

47. *Compare* Colo. Const. of 1876, art. IX, § 16 ("Neither the General Assembly nor the State Board of Education shall have power to prescribe text books to be used in the public schools.") *with* Cal. Const. of 1879, art. IX, § 7 ("The local boards of education [and other applicable authorities] . . . shall adopt a series of text books for the use of the common schools within their respective jurisdictions.").

48. *See,* for example, Nev. Const. 1875, art. 11, § 5 (requiring teachers and professors "to take and subscribe to" a prescribed oath."); Cal. Const. of 1879, art. IX, § 7 (giving local boards "control of the examination of teachers and the granting of teachers certificates within their several jurisdictions").

49. *See,* for example, Ohio Const. of 1851, art. VI, § 1. The 1844 New Jersey Constitution also protected the school fund, providing that "[t]he fund for the support of free schools . . . shall be securely invested and remain a perpetual fund . . . [and] shall be annually appropriated to the support of public schools, for the equal benefit of all the people of the State, and it shall not be competent for the legislature to borrow, appropriate, or use the said fund, or any part thereof, for any other purpose under any pretence whatever." N.J. Const. of 1844, art. IV, § 7, par. 6. *See also* Ind. Const. of 1851, art. 8, §§ 2–7; and Idaho Const. of 1890, art. IX, § 3.

50. The 1851 Constitution of Ohio mandated legislative "provisions by taxation, or otherwise . . . [to] secure a thorough and efficient system of common schools throughout the State." Ohio Const. of 1851, art. VI, § 2.

51. *See*, for example, Ind. Const. of 1816, art. IX, § 1; Ala. Const. of 1819, art. VI; and Mo. Const. of 1820, art. VI, §§ 1–2.

52. Cal. Const. of 1849, § 3. *See also* Colo. Const. of 1876, art. IX, § 2; Nev. Const. of 1864, art. 11, § 2; and Miss. Const. of 1868, art. VIII, § 5.

53. Among the most common changes were those relating to whether a state superintendent would be elected or appointed, the number of years in a term, the composition of state and local boards of education, and funding details. For example, Michigan changed its manner of selection of the state school superintendent from gubernatorial appointment, included in its education article (Mich. Const. of 1835, art. X, § 1), to vote of qualified electors, included in its state officers article (Mich. Const. of 1850, art. VIII, § 1). Virginia changed its constitutional provision from election by the general assembly in joint ballot (Va. Const. of 1872, art. VIII, § 1) to election of the superintendent, "who shall be an experienced educator . . . by the qualified voters of the State at the same time and for the same term as the Governor." Va. Const. of 1902, art. IX, § 131. Virginia amended its provision again in 1928 to provide for gubernatorial appointment of the superintendent. Va. Const. of 1902, art. IX, § 131 (1928).

54. *See* Matzen, supra note xxxv, at 33.

55. *See*, for example, Mich. Const. of 1963, art. VIII, §§ 3–7; Va. Const. of 1970, art. VIII, §§ 4–7 (established state board of education, superintendent of public instruction, and local school boards, and specifically delineated state board's powers and duties); and Miss. Const., art. XIII, § 202 (1982 amendment changed superintendent of public education from elected office to position appointed by state board of education).

56. 347 U.S. 483 (1954). The fiftieth anniversary of the first *Brown* decision in 2004 will be the occasion for many commemorative events, most extolling it, but some questioning or even deploring it. For information about one of the major commemorations, *see* http://www.nyu.edu/education/metrocenter/brownplus/home.html.

57. N.J. Const. of 1947, art. I, par. 5 (prohibits segregation "in the public schools, because of religious principles, race, color, ancestry or national origin"); Mich. Const. of 1963, art. VIII, § 2 ("every school district shall provide for the education of its pupils without discrimination as to religion, creed, race, color or national origin"). For another, more general constitutional amendment long after *Brown, see* Mont. Const., art. X, § 1 (provision adopted and ratified in 1972 guarantees "[e]quality of educational opportunity . . . to each person of the state").

58. Cal. Const., art. I, § 31.

59. Colo. Const., art. IX, § 17.

60. Ore. Const., art. VIII, § 8.

61. Ore. Const., art. VIII, § 8. Arkansas also amended its constitution in 1996, stating that "to provide quality education, it is the goal of this state to provide a fair system for the distribution of funds." Ark. Const., art. XIV, § 3 (amended, not yet codified). Arkansas "established a uniform rate of ad valorem property tax . . . to be used solely for maintenance and operation of the schools." Ark. Const., art. XIV, § 3 (amended, not yet codified).

62. Ohio added a provision "guarantee[ing] the repayment of loans made to residents of this state to assist them in meeting the expenses of attending an institution of higher education." Ohio Const., art. VI, § 5. Georgia amended its constitution in 1983 to authorize the expenditure of public funds for educational assistance to students and parents of students. Ga. Const., art. VIII, § 7.

63. Cal. Const., art. XIIIA (Proposition 13). Largely as a consequence of its adoption, California's spending on education has plummeted, as has the quality of its schools and performance of its students. For an analysis, *see* Paul L. Tractenberg, "A Tale of Two States: Comparing California's and New Jersey's 30-Year School Funding Wars" (1996) (unpublished manuscript). *See also* Mich. Const., art. 3 (1995 amendment).

64. *See*, for example, Cal. Const., art. I, § 28(c) ("All students and staff of public primary, elementary, junior high and senior high schools have the inalienable right to attend campuses which are safe, secure and peaceful.").

65. Interestingly, Florida is generally considered to have the most easily changed constitution in the country. *See* Robert F. Williams, "Is Constitutional Revision Success Worth Its Popular Sovereignty Price?," 52 *Fla. L. Rev.* 249, 250 (2000).

66. *See* John Mills and Timothy McLendon, "Setting a New Standard for Public Education: Revision 6 Increases the Duty of the State to Make 'Adequate Provision' for Florida Schools," 52 *Fla. L. Rev.* 329, 332 (2000).

67. Fla. Const. art. IX, § 1 (1998). Apparently because of litigation concerns, its framers were careful not to assign it the status of a fundamental "right." *See* Joseph W. Little, "The Need to Revise the Florida Constitution Revision Commission," 52 *Fla. L. Rev.* 475, 489 (2000).

68. Fla. Const., art. IX, § 1 (1998). *See* Mills and McLendon, supra note lxvii, at 368.

69. Fla. Const., art. IX, § 1 (1998). *See* ibid. at 369–76. Through numerous challenges to state funding of education, these terms have taken on meaning beyond their common usage. Indeed, courts have scrutinized these terms to varying degrees to determine what their respective education clauses mandate. For example, in *Pauley v. Kelly*, 255 S.E.2d 859, 874 (W.Va., 1979), the court used both contemporaneous and modern dictionaries, prior case law and also looked at the framers' statements "to define the words 'thorough,' 'efficient,' and 'education' to ascertain the boundaries of the legislature's constitutional mandate." Jonathan Banks, "State Constitutional Analyses of Public School Finance Reform Cases: Myth or Methodology?," 45 *Vand. L. Rev.* 129, 146, and notes 105–09 (1992). In the Florida context, the Florida Supreme Court had held in 1996 that Florida's long standing constitutional mandate that 'adequate provision' be made for a 'uniform system of free public schools' did not provide a juridical basis to review the adequacy of the amount of school funding provided by the Legislature." *See* Little, supra note lxviii, at 489 (citing *Coalition for Adequacy and Fairness in School Funding, Inc. v. Chiles*, 680 So.2d 400 [1996]). Little surmised that Revision 6 was "apparently intended to provide a constitutional standard to which the judiciary may hold the Legislature accountable." Ibid.

70. Fla. Const., art. IX, § 1, par. a (as amended 2002).

71. Fla. Const., art. IX, § 1, par. b (as amended 2002).

72. For an up-to-date, state-by-state review of the litigation, see the Campaign for Fiscal Equity's ACCESS project website, http://www.accessnetwork.org (last visited Jan. 13, 2004). According to CFE's latest tally, plaintiffs have prevailed in twenty-five states and defendants in eighteen, with a number of cases in process, including several in states with prior decisions. Only five states—Delaware, Hawaii, Mississippi, Nevada and Utah—have never had a case filed. For discussions of decisional trends, *see*, for example, Kelly Thompson Cochran, "Beyond School Financing: Defining the Constitutional Right to an Adequate Education," 78 *N.C.L. Rev.* 399, n. 2 (2000), for a list of school finance cases in the various states. "Nearly every state has faced at least one round of school financing litigation." Ibid. "[M]ost of the school financing cases recognizing a right to a substantive level of education have been decided in the last decade." Ibid. at 401. For an earlier set of "summary descriptions, state by state, of the significant post-Rodriguez state court decisions that address the constitutionality, on either equality or adequacy grounds, of educational finance systems that rely on variable local revenue sources," *see* Peter Enrich, "Leaving Equality Behind: New Directions in School Finance Reform," 48 *Vand. L. Rev.* 101, 185–91 (1995).

73. New Jersey presents perhaps the strongest example of a state supreme court maintaining a persistent judicial role in school finance reform. *See* Paul L. Tractenberg, "The Evolution and Implementation of Educational Rights Under the New Jersey Constitution of 1947," 29 *Rutgers L.J.* 827 (1998), for an exploration of "the origins and evolution of the 1947 Constitution's provision relevant to public education," state constitutional educational rights, and a thorough review of school finance litigation in New Jersey. *See also* Charles S. Benson, "Definitions of Equity in School Finance in Texas, New Jersey, and Kentucky," 28 *Harv. J. on Legis.* 401 (1991) (reviewing successful school finance litigation in Texas, New Jersey and Kentucky and finding that "the remedies demanded in the three states set new and higher standards for equity in school funding," while specifically commending the *Abbott v. Burke* decision by the New Jersey Supreme Court as "offer[ing] strong hope that the courts will make a concerted effort to correct our gravest educational deficiencies."). *Cf. City of Pawtucket v. Sundlun*, 662 A.2d 40 (R.I., 1995) (commenting that "the absence of justiciable standards could engage the court in a morass comparable to the decades-long struggle of the Supreme Court of New Jersey that has attempted to define what constitutes the 'thorough and efficient' education specified in that state's constitution.") The broader, linked issues of whether litigation and judicial intervention are appropriate means of resolving complex educational policy and political issues, and what the impact of such cases has been, have spawned a huge body of literature. *See*, for example, John Dayton, "Examining the Efficacy of Judicial Involvement in Public School Finance Reform," 22 *J. Educ. Fin.* 1 (1996); Michael Heise, "The Effect of Constitutional Litigation on Education Finance: More Preliminary Analyses and Modeling," 21 *J. Educ. Fin.* 195 (1995); Sheila E. Murray, William N. Evans, and Robert Schwab, "Education Finance Reform and the Distribution of Education Resources," 88 *Am. Econ. Rev.* 789 (1998).

74. A model state constitution primarily designed to press for proportional representation in legislative bodies, which is widely circulated on the internet, does not include an education provision. *See* http://www.cooperativeindividualism.org/law_constitutional state.html.

75. National Municipal League, *Model State Constitution* (6th ed., 1963; rev'd 1968).

76. Ibid. at 18, 101 (art. IX, Public Education).

77. Campaign for Responsible Government, Model State Constitution for Responsible Government, art. XI, Miscellaneous Subjects, § 1 (1998) (available at http://www.geocities.com/responsegov/stateconst.html). This model constitution also contains clauses prohibiting aid to sectarian schools, ibid. at art. XI, § 2, regulating a permanent school fund, ibid. at art. VIII, Taxation, § 8, and regulating a permanent university fund, ibid. at art.VIII, § 9.

78. Kirk A. Bailey, *Summary-Education Clauses in State Constitutions* 2 (Oct. 31, 2000) in conjunction with Hamilton Fish Institute, *Review of State Constitutions: Education Clauses* (Oct. 31, 2000).

79. Education Commission of the States, *State Constitutions and Public Education Governance* 1 (ECS State Note, Oct. 2000).

80. Alaska's constitution dates from 1956. By contrast, according to Professor Tarr, "American state constitutions tend to be 'old'—the average state constitution has been in operation for over a century." G. Alan Tarr, Keynote Address (available at http://www-camlaw.rutgers.edu/statecon/keynote1.html).

81. The remaining nine sections deal with quite detailed aspects of the funding and governance of both lower and higher education, with the prohibition of aid to sectarian schools, and with nondiscrimination in education. Mont. Const., art. X, §§ 2–10 (2001).

82. Ibid. at § 1 (1). In § 1 (2), Montana "recognizes the distinct and unique cultural heritage of the American Indians," and commits itself (at least as a goal) to preserve their cultural integrity, another distinctive provision.

83. Ibid. at § 1 (3) (emphasis added).

84. Ibid. (emphasis added).

85. Of course, many proposals for constitutional amendment never succeed in reaching the ballot stage. Usually, that is because of insufficient public or legislative support. In a less common circumstance, a proposed 1996 Arkansas amendment, which would have created a state-run lottery and established an education trust fund with the proceeds, was excluded from the ballot by court injunction.

86. *See* La. Const., art. VIII, § 3(A) (2003) (state board empowered to manage and operate failing schools, and to use state and local funds for that purpose); Ariz. Const., art. IX, § 21 (2002) (specifies how income from public lands is to be used for educational purposes and relates to school and community college district expenditure limitations); Haw. Const., art. X, § 1 (2002) (authorizes the state to issue bonds to financially assist private schools and to use the bond proceeds to assist not-for-profit private schools and universities); Utah Const., art. X, § 5 (2002) (repeals a provision requiring a portion of the interest earnings from the State School Fund be kept in the Fund as a protection against the effects of inflation and allows dividends from the Fund's investment to be spent to support the public education system); Ore. Const., arts. XI–L (2002) (allows the state to issue general obligation bonds for seismic rehabilitation of public education buildings); Ore. Const., art. VIII, § 8 (2000) (requires the legislature to

provide enough funding for schools to meet state education quality goals, or publish a report explaining why it was unable to do so); Colo. Const., art. IX, § 17 (2000) (increases per pupil funding by at least the rate of inflation plus one percentage point for the next ten years, and by at least the rate of inflation thereafter); Okla. Const., art. X, §§ 9, 10 (2000) (allows individual school districts to eliminate annual votes on school levies with approval from local voters); Okla. Const., art. X, § 40 (2000) (creates the Tobacco Settlement Endowment Trust Fund, the earnings of which may be expended for education); S.C. Const., art. XVII, § 7 (2000) (allows state lottery to benefit education); S.D. Const., art. VIII, § 15 (2000) (permits legislature to establish multiple classes of agricultural property for school taxation purposes); S.D. Const., art. VIII, § 2 (2000) (allows state to invest permanent school funds in stocks and similar investments with relatively high levels of risk); Cal. Const., art. XVI, § 8, and art. XIIIA, § 1 (both sections were amended pursuant to Proposition 39; authorizes bonds for repair, construction or replacement of school facilities, classrooms, if approved by 55 percent local vote for projects evaluated by schools, community college districts, county education offices for safety, class size, and information technology needs); Idaho Const., art. IX, § 4 (2000) (changes the name of the Public School Fund to the Public School Permanent Endowment Fund; allows proceeds from the sale of public school endowment lands to be deposited into a Land Bank Fund to buy other lands within the state for the benefit of public schools); Va. Const., art. X, § 7-A (establishes a Lottery Proceeds Fund, wherein all net revenues from any state-run lottery must be placed, to be distributed among localities to be spent locally for public education); Mo. Const., art. X, § 11 (prohibits the school board from setting an operating levy higher than $2.75 without a vote; requires levy to be set up to $6.00 for voter approval by simple majority; requires levy to be set above $6.00 for voter approval by two-thirds); Ore. Const., art. XI–K (1998) (allows the state to guarantee the payment of general obligation bonds issued by qualified school districts, community college districts and education service districts; to pay the guaranteed indebtedness by using available state funds, borrowing from the Common School Fund or issuing state bonds; and to issue bonds to reimburse moneys borrowed from the Common School Fund); Okla. Const., art. X, § 15 (1998) (provides exception regarding use of certain public facilities; modifies restrictions related to investment of public funds); Ark. Const., art. XIV, § 3 (1996) (establishes a uniform minimum property-tax rate to benefit schools; requires a minimum 25-mill levy for maintenance and operation in all school districts of the state); Colo. Const., art. IV, §§ 3, 9, 10 (changes state board of land commissioners and refocuses mission of panel from maximizing income to managing lands for loans and bonds; allows schools to tap school-trust-land funds for loans and bonds); Ga. Const., art. I, § 2 (limits the purposes and programs for which state lottery funds may be spent, by specifically providing that lottery proceeds go to: (1) tuition, grants, and loans, (2) voluntary prekindergarten, (3) educational shortfall reserves, (4) K–12 teacher training in computer technology and distance learning, and (5) capital outlay projects for education facilities); Haw. Const., art. VII, § 11 (1996) (allows the state to grant funds under the special school-facilities program for periods longer than 3 years); S.D. Const., art. VIII, § 11 (1996) (grants the state investment council authority to invest money from the permanent school fund and other school funds); S.D. Const., art. XI, § 14 (1996) (requires two-thirds majority of the legislature to increase taxes).

87. *See* Cal. Const., art. I, § 31 (1996).

88. *See* Ky. Const., § 187 (1996) ("In distributing the school fund no distinction shall be made on account of race or color."); § 180 (1996).

89. *See* Ala. Const., amend. 670 (2000) (details composition of the Board of Trustees of Auburn University); Okla. Const., art. X, § 23 (2000) (allows state colleges and universities to make contracts with presidents for more than one year, but not more than three years); Haw. Const., art. X, § 6 (2000) (grants the University of Hawaii authority and power of self-governance in matters involving only internal structure and operation of the university); Fla. Const., art. IX, § 7 (2002) (creates "a single state university system comprised of all public universities" as well as a "board of trustees [to] administer each public university and a board of governors [to] govern the state university system.").

90. *See* Fla. Const., art. IX, § 1 (1998) (declaring public education to be a "fundamental value" and making it "a paramount duty of the state to make adequate provision for the education of all children residing within its borders"; mandating "[a]dequate provision . . . for a uniform, efficient, safe, secure, and high quality system of free public schools that allows students to obtain a high quality education"); Fla. Const., art. IX, § 2 (1998) (providing for membership, appointment and term of state board of education, and its authority to appoint commissioner of education); Fla. Const., art. IX, § 4 (1998) (specifying that electors of each school district shall vote for its local school board "in a nonpartisan election"); Fla. Const., art. IX, § 5 (1998) (amending language to delete the gender-specific pronoun "he" in referring to school superintendent position); Fla. Const., art. IX, § 1 (2002) (providing for "[e]very four-year old child . . . a high quality pre-kindergarten learning opportunity in the form of an early childhood development and education program which shall be voluntary, high quality, free, and delivered according to professionally accepted standards," to be "implemented no later than the beginning of the 2005 school year through funds generated in addition to those used for existing education, health, and development programs"); Fla. Const., art. IX, § 1 (2002) (mandating reduced class size).

91. *See* Louisiana, Constitutional Amendment 8 (2002), available at http://www.sec.state.la.us/elections/2002-ca.htm (proposed to authorize institutions of higher education or their management boards to invest in stocks up to 50% of certain funds received from gifts, grants, endowments and other funds); Nevada, Question 7 (2002), available at http://sos.state.nv.us/nvelection/2002_bq/bq7.htm (proposed to extend the debt limit for the purposes of school construction or improvements); Oklahoma, State Question 684 (2000) (proposed to change how the state may use the permanent school fund); California, Proposition 26 (2000), available at http://primary2000. ss.ca.gov/VoterGuide/Propositions/26text.htm (proposed to lower the voting requirement for passage of local school bonds); California, Proposition 38 (2000), available at http://vote2000.ss.ca.gov/VoterGuide/text/text_title_summ_38.htm (proposed to authorize annual state payments of at least $4,000 per pupil for private and religious schools phased in over four years); Michigan, Proposal 00-1 (2000), available at http://www.michigan.gov/sos/0,1607,7-127-1633_8722_14689-31515—,00.html (proposed to eliminate the ban on direct support of students attending nonpublic schools through tuition vouchers, credits, tax benefits, exemptions or deductions,

subsidies, grants or loans of public monies or property, and to require teacher testing on academic subjects in pubic schools and nonpublic schools redeeming tuition vouchers); Colorado, Amendment 17 (1998), available at http://www.state.co.us/gov_dir/leg_dir/lcsstaff/ballot/text-17.htm (proposed to create a state income tax credit for parents of students in private and public schools, and students educated at home, and to prohibit the state from using the measure to increase regulations on private schools); South Dakota, Constitutional Amendment A (1998) (proposed to prohibit using property taxes for public school purposes); South Dakota, Constitutional Amendment F (1998) (proposed to permit an unlimited number of classes of agricultural property for school taxation purposes); Oregon, Measure 59 (1998) (proposed to prohibit using "public funds" to collect or assist in collecting "political funds"); Arkansas, Amendment 7 (1996) (proposed to allow for the creation of a state-run lottery and to establish the Arkansas Education Trust Fund, to be funded with some gaming proceeds); Nebraska, Measure 412 (1996) (proposed to allow limits on property-tax rates).

92. *See* Colorado, Amendment 17 (2002), available at http://www.state.co.us/gov_dir/leg_dir/96bp/amd17.html (proposed to amend art. II, § 3 of the Colorado Constitution to include as an inalienable right the right of parents to direct and control the upbringing, education, values, and discipline of their children."); Colorado, Amendment 31, available at http://www.rmpbs.org/campaign2002/i_a31.html (proposed to require that all public school students be taught in English); Oregon, Measure 95 (2000) (proposed to add a provision to change the method by which all public school teachers, whether or not in a collective bargaining unit, are paid and laid off, and to define job performance as the degree to which the appropriate knowledge of the teacher's students increased while under that teacher's instruction); North Dakota, Constitutional Measure 1 (1998) (proposed to remove references to the names, locations, and missions of the institutions of higher education); Nebraska, Measure 411 (1996) (proposed to make "quality education" a fundamental right and the "thorough and efficient" education promised in the state constitution the paramount duty of the state); Montana, Amendment 30 (1996) (proposed to replace the state board of education, board of regents and commission of higher education with one state education dept and a single education commissioner).

93. All of South Dakota's amendments, four adopted and two rejected, were fiscal in nature. Two were of some note, one successful—requiring a two-thirds legislative vote to increase taxes—and one unsuccessful—seeking to prohibit the use of property taxes for education. *See* notes lxxxviii and xciii supra.

94. Two of Colorado's five proposed amendments, both fiscal in nature, were adopted, and one was of note, requiring a minimum increase in educational funding. The three amendments rejected suggest an interesting educational perspective since they proposed English-only instruction, an inalienable parental right to educate, and a tax credit for education that could not be used to increase state authority over private schools. *See* notes lxxxviii and xciv supra.

95. Four out of five proposed amendments in Oklahoma passed. They related to higher education administration and to fiscal matters, and one was noteworthy, allowing individual school districts to eliminate annual votes on school levies with approval from local voters. The failed amendment also was fiscal in nature. *See* notes lxxxviii, xci and xciii supra.

96. Three of five proposed amendments in Oregon passed. They were all fiscal in nature, and one was especially noteworthy, requiring the legislature to provide enough school funding to meet state education quality goals, or to publish a report explaining why it was unable to do so. One of the failed amendments also was of special interest; it would have changed the method by which public school teachers are paid and laid off—to have student learning determine teacher pay and to have teacher qualifications, not seniority, determine retention. *See* notes lxxxviii, xciii, and xciv supra.

97. Two out of four proposals in California passed. One successful amendment was fiscal and the other barred most affirmative action programs. Both failed measures also were fiscal, one relating to school vouchers and state funding of private schools. *See* notes lxxxviii, lxxxix, and xciii supra.

98. All three of Hawaii's proposed amendments passed. Two were fiscal, one relating to issuance of bonds to provide financial assistance to private schools, and the third related to higher education governance. *See* notes lxxxviii and xci supra. Nebraska and Arkansas, with two proposals each, were the only other states with more than a single proposed amendment. Both of Nebraska's proposed amendments in 1996 failed, and both were interesting, if inconsistent, responses to equity/adequacy litigation. Measure 411, like Florida's 1998 amendments, would have made "quality education" a fundamental right, and the constitutionally required "thorough and efficient" education a paramount duty of the state. Measure 412, like California's infamous Proposition 13, would have allowed limits on property tax rates. *See* notes xciii and xciv supra. Ironically, Arkansas voters passed a proposal, which was the converse of Nebraska's failed Measure 412, to establish a uniform *minimum* property tax rate to benefit schools. Its other proposed amendment, seeking to create a state-run lottery and establish the Arkansas Education Trust Fund, to be funded with gaming proceeds, was judicially excluded from the ballot. *See* notes lxxxviii and xciii supra.

99. As the state-by-state breakdown suggests, some states with a substantial number of proposed amendments included little of note. In some cases, proposals within a single state were inconsistent with one another, suggesting they may have been responses to diverse political pressures, rather than a reflection of educational best practices.

100. Fla. Const., art. IX, §§ 2 (changed appointive procedures for state board of education), 4 (specified nonpartisan election for local school boards), and 5 (made references to superintendent of schools gender neutral).

101. Fla. Const., art. IX, § 1 (1998).

102. *See,* for example, Daniel Gordon, "Failing the State Constitutional Education Grade: Constitutional Revision Weakening Children and Human Rights," 29 *Stetson L. Rev.* 271 (1999).

103. Fla. Const., art. IX, § 1(a) (setting maximum class size for prekindergarten through grade 3 at 18 students, for grades 4 through 8 at 22 students, and for grades 9 through 12 at 25 students, "[t]o assure that children attending public schools obtain a high quality education").

104. *See* Goodnough, "Florida Board Backs Retreat on Class Size," *New York Times,* Aug. 20, 2003. Interestingly, all the Board's members were appointed by Gov. Jeb Bush, who opposed the original constitutional amendment.

105. Fla. Const., art. IX, § 1(b) ("Every four-year old child in Florida shall be provided by the State a high quality pre-kindergarten learning opportunity in the form of an early childhood development and education program.").

106. The word *model* is placed in parentheses advisedly because the thrust of this chapter, indeed of the entire volume of which it is a part, is not really to produce a "model," in the usual sense of the word. Webster's dictionary defines a "model" as a "pattern, or standard of excellence." *Webster's New World Dictionary* 913 (2d ed., 1978). The Oxford dictionary defines it as a "thing regarded as excellent of his/its kind and worth imitating" or as "one that has been specially designed to be very efficient." *Oxford Advanced Learner's Dictionary* 797 (4th ed., 1989). These definitions suggest that drafting a "model" state constitutional education provision to serve as a "standard of excellence" and efficiency, to be "worth imitating," would be laudable. Yet, as a practical matter, seeking to produce a single model that could be adopted in each of the fifty states is impossible. To be a meaningful model, such a provision would have to consider and account for an extraordinarily complex and variable set of circumstances in each state derived, among others, from history, custom, politics, intergovernmental relations, state judicial traditions and state constitutional interpretation. The risk is that a "model," seeking to be sensitive to such complexity and variability, would wind up being either too detailed and unwieldy, or too general and unresponsive. Therefore, this chapter's focus is on the range of issues that must be considered in evaluating the effectiveness of state constitutional education provisions to respond to current needs, and the range of alternative approaches.

107. For some interesting musings on this subject, *see,* for example, National Municipal League, *Model State Constitution,* vii–viii (sixth ed., 1963; rev'd 1968).

108. An additional threshold question might be whether or not there should even be an education clause, but given the importance ascribed to education and the pervasiveness of education provisions in existing state constitutions, that question hardly seems to merit more than this brief note.

109. "The oldest constitutions are generally the shortest and the least amended. All those now effective that date from before 1850 are substantially shorter than the average length of all state documents. The most recently written state constitutions are usually far shorter than the average. All state documents formulated and adopted within the last two decades [of 1969] have fewer than 20,000 words, and most of them contain less than 15,000." Albert L. Sturm, *Thirty Years of State Constitution-Making: 1938–1968* 15 (1970). So, as of 1969, Alabama's constitution, adopted in 1901, had a total of 284 amendments, with an estimated length of 95,000 words. Ibid. at 7. Similarly, the notorious Louisiana constitution, adopted in 1921, had 530 amendments and an estimated word length of 253,800 by 1969. Ibid. at 8. In 1974, following a constitutional convention, Louisiana adopted its present constitution, with an estimated length of 51,448 words. Janice C. May, "State Constitutions and Constitutional Revision 1992–93," in *The Book of the States 1994–95* 19 (1995). On the other hand, Alaska's constitution, adopted in 1956, had two amendments as of 1969, and an estimated length of 12,000 words. Ibid. at 7. Connecticut is another example. Its constitution, adopted in 1965, by 1969 not surprisingly had zero amendments and an estimated length of 7,960 words. Ibid.

110. *See* California, Secretary of State, "A History of California Initiatives" (Dec. 2002), available at http://www.ss.ca.gov/elections/init_history.pdf_, for an explanation of California's initiative process, which began in 1911, and a partial list of proposals relating to education. Since 1960, "initiative measures have appeared on primary, general, and special election ballots." Ibid. at 2. Voters have approved a constitutional amendment regarding the school system (1920), funds for elementary schools (1944), public school funds (1952), property tax limitation (1978), prohibition of affirmative action programs by public entities (1996), English language instruction (1998), school facilities (2000). In the context of school finance measures, California voters have approved constitutional amendments in 1978, 1979, 1988, and 1990, engaging in a dance with the legislature and *court*. "School Finance Overview," available at http://nov2002.san mateo.org/background.htm (Sept. 2002) (summarizing briefly, and chronologically, actions taken by the California legislature, court and voters since 1972, changing that state's school finance system). In 1978, voters passed Proposition 13, limiting property tax rates; in 1979, Proposition 4, limiting government spending at every level, including school districts; in 1988, Proposition 98, "guarantee[ing] a minimum funding level from state and property taxes for K–14 public schools in a complex formula based on state tax revenues"; and in 1990, Proposition 111, which effectively raised the limit established by Proposition 4. Ibid. There has been substantial criticism of California's initiative and referendum system, precisely because of the ease with which it allows constitutional amendments. *See*, for example, Kevin M. Mulcahy, Comment, "Modeling the Garden: How New Jersey Built the Most Progressive State Supreme Court and What California Can Learn," 40 *Santa Clara L. Rev.* 863 (2000).

111. Fla. Const., art. XI, § 2.

112. Little, supra note lxviii, at 485.

113. Ibid.

114. *See,* for example, Paul G. Kauper, Citizens Research Council of Michigan, *The State Constitution: Its Nature and Purpose* 10 (1961); A. E. Dick Howard, "The Indeterminacy of Constitutions," 31 *Wake Forest L. Rev.* 383, 393 (1996) (averring that "American state constitutions offer vivid examples of the vices of excessive length and detail" and that "[r]ather than produce a constitution that looks like the state's code, drafters may prefer general propositions, even if that means a heightened need for interpretation."); Lawrence Schlam, "State Constitutional Amending, Independent Interpretation, and Political Culture: A Case Study in Constitutional Stagnation," 43 *DePaul L. Rev.* 269, 277–81, 278 n 18 (1994) (noting that the ease with which state constitutions can be amended has resulted in lengthy and detailed state constitutions, such that "almost all state constitutions contain extraordinary amounts of detail which seem absurd or superfluous" and that such detail inhibits effective state governance"). But *see* Christopher W. Hammons, "State Constitutional Reform: Is It Necessary?," 64 *Alb. L. Rev.* 1327, 1341 (2001) (suggesting that "the greater length and detail of modern state constitutions allow states to tailor constitutions to meet their specific needs."); G. Alan Tarr, "Understanding State Constitutions," 65 *Temple L. Rev.* 1169, 1182–83 (1992) (explaining that while "virtually all state constitutions contain numerous provisions that, in their detail and specificity, can only be called 'statutory,'" this phenomenon partly

"reflects the efforts of political majorities to write their policies into the fundamental law in order to shield those policies, insofar as possible, from change by future majorities," and that rather than look down on the so-called statutory provisions, perhaps "the dual character of state constitutions would seem to require a dual approach to their interpretation.") Interestingly, the New York Court of Appeals pointed to the detailed nature of the state constitution as reason for minimizing the import of its education clause, explaining that "the document concededly contains references to matters which could as well have been left to statutory articulation." *Board of Education v. Nyquist*, 439 N.E.2d 359, 366 n.5 (N.Y., 1982.) *See also* Robert A. Schapiro, "Identity and Interpretation in State Constitutional Law," 84 *Va. L. Rev.* 389 (1998).

115. *See*, for example, *Cal. Const.*, art. 1, § 31 ((a) "The State shall not discriminate against, or grant preferential treatment to, any individual or group on the basis of race, sex, color, ethnicity, or national origin in the operation of public employment, public education, or public contracting . . . (h) This section shall be self-executing."); and N. Car. Const., art. I, § 15 ("The people have a right to the privilege of education, and it is the duty of the State to guard and maintain that right.").

116. *Compare*, for example, *Helena Elementary Sch. Dist. No. 1 v. State*, 769 P.2d 684, 690 (Mont., 1989) ("specifically conclud[ing] that the guarantee of equality of educational opportunity applies to each person of the State of Montana, and is binding upon all branches of government whether at the state, local, or school district level.") *with City of Pawtucket v. Sundlun*, 662 A.2d 40, 47–48 (R.I., 1995) (rejecting the lower court's finding "'that there is a fundamental and constitutional right for each child to an opportunity to receive an education,'" and instead declaring that "[t]he education clause confers no such right, nor does it guarantee an 'equal, adequate, and meaningful education.'"). *See supra* note lxxiv, regarding the stance taken by the New Jersey Supreme Court and the Rhode Island high court's colorful criticism of it.

117. For example, in *Bennett v. City School District of New Rochelle*, 114 A.D.2d 58, 61–62 (N.Y.A.D., 1985), a New York appellate court considered whether the state could be compelled to admit petitioner into the state's full-time program for gifted elementary students, after she was found eligible but then failed to gain a spot after the lottery was drawn. The court upheld the lottery system and found that the "sound basic education" that the Court of Appeals had connoted "education" in the state constitution to mean "was never intended to impose a duty flowing directly from a local school district to individual pupils to ensure that each pupil receives a minimum level of education, the breach of which duty would entitle a pupil to compensatory damages." Ibid. at 67. Similarly, in *Agostine v. School District of Philadelphia*, 527 A.2d 193, 195 (Pa. Commonw. Ct., 1987), the court found that petitioner failed to state a cause of action when she "alleged that the District negligently diagnosed her," and sought damages. The court found that the education provision of the state constitution "does not confer an individual right upon each student to a particular level or quality of education but, instead, imposes a duty upon the *legislature* to provide for the maintenance of a thorough and efficient system of public school throughout the Commonwealth." Ibid. at 195. In *Pierce v. Board of Education of City of Chicago*, 370 N.E.2d 535, 536 (Ill., 1977), the plaintiff sued for damages after "he suffered severe and permanent emotional injury requiring hospitalization and medical treatment"

when the board "refused to place the plaintiff in a special education class," despite diagnosis of a learning disability. In declining to find a cause of action, the court held that the education clause is not self-executing and "does not impose a duty on boards of education to place students in special education classes." Ibid. In *Simmons v. Sowela Technical Institute*, 470 So.2d 913, 916 (La. Ct. App., 1985), the court rejected plaintiff's suit challenging her dismissal from a practical nursing program based on unethical conduct. In doing so, the court found that "the constitutional mandate to educate the people of the State . . . is a moral or imperfect obligation; rather than a natural obligation." Ibid. at 920. In contrast, courts have generally found their education provisions to be self-executing and enforceable when faced with challenges to school finance, requiring systemic reform.

118. *See*, for example, *Alabama Coalition for Equity, Inc. v. Hunt*, 624 So.2d 107 (Ala., 1993) (affirming "that Alabama schoolchildren have an enforceable constitutional right to an education," and requiring the legislature to follow the trial court's order for remedial action); *Tennessee Small School Systems v. McWherter*, 851 S.W.2d 139 (Tenn., 1993) (finding that the education clause of the state constitution "is an enforceable standard for assessing the educational opportunities provided in the several districts throughout the state."); *Abbeville County School District v. State*, 515 S.E.2d 535 (S.C., 1999) (holding that the education provision, which employs the term "shall," is mandatory and "requires the General Assembly to provide the opportunity for each child to receive a minimally adequate education."); *Spackman v. Board of Education of Box Elder County School District*, 16 P.3d 533 (Utah, 2000) (holding that "the Open Education Clause [which] requires that the public education system 'shall be open to all children of the state' . . . is self-executing" and allowing for damage awards in certain circumstances). But *see Lewis E. v. Spagnolo*, 710 N.E.2d 798 (Ill., 1999) (rejecting plaintiffs' argument that the education clause "grants them the right to a 'minimally adequate education,'" and barring them from "su[ing] state and local officials directly under this article for deprivation of that right").

119. This is, of course, a positively stated version of the prohibition against segregation or other discrimination, which appears subsequently.

120. Rights or interests characterized as "fundamental" are accorded the greatest protection under both the federal constitution and many state constitutions. In devising its 1998 education clause proposal, Florida's Charter Revision Panel used the word "fundamental," but imbedded it in the phrase "fundamental value" rather than "fundamental right." Tony Doris, "Little-Noted Lawsuit Says State Fails to Meet Constitutional Duty to Provide High-Quality Education," 48 *Miami Daily Bus. Rev.* No. 243 (May 24, 2002). This reportedly was done out of concern that using the "fundamental right" formulation could impose "too severe of a burden on school districts and the state, [because it] might ultimately make their actions subject to strict judicial scrutiny with regard to litigation by individuals." Ibid. By contrast, "fundamental value" was thought to focus more generally, and less actionably, on the education system and its adequacy. Mills and McLendon, supra note lxvii, at 365 (quoting *Abbott v. Burke*, 575 A.2d 359, 369 [N.J., 1990]).

121. *See*, for example, Wash. Const., art. IX, § 1 ("paramount duty"); Fla. Const., art. IX, § 1 ("fundamental value"); Ga. Const., art. VIII, § 1 ("primary obligation").

122. *See*, for example, La. Const., art. VIII, preamble ("The goal of the public educational system is to provide learning environments and experiences, at all stages of human development, that are humane, just, and designed to promote excellence in order that every individual may be afforded an equal opportunity to develop to his full potential"); Fla. Const., art. IX, § 1 ("The education of children is a fundamental value . . . It is, therefore, a paramount duty of the state to make adequate provision for the education of all children residing within its borders."); Geo. Const., art. VIII, § I, par. I ("The provision of an adequate public education for the citizens shall be a primary obligation of the State"); Ill. Const., art. X, § 1 ("A fundamental goal of the People of the State is the educational development of all persons to the limits of their capacities."); Kan. Const., art. 6, § 1 ("The legislature shall provide for intellectual, educational, vocational and scientific improvement"); Md. Const., art. VIII, § 1 ("The General Assembly . . . shall by Law establish throughout the State a thorough and efficient System of Free Public Schools"); Minn. Const., art. XIII, § 1 ("it is the duty of the legislature to establish a general and uniform system of public schools. The legislature shall make such provisions by taxation or otherwise as will secure a thorough and efficient system of public schools throughout the state."); Mont. Const., art. X, § 1 ("It is the goal of the people to establish a system of education which will develop the full educational potential of each person."); N.J. Const., art. VIII, § IV, par. 1 ("The Legislature shall provide for the maintenance and support of a thorough and efficient system of free public schools."); Pa. Const., art. III, § 14 ("The General Assembly shall provide for the maintenance and support of a thorough and efficient system of public education.").

123. For example, in New Jersey, a concurrent resolution was introduced seeking to amend the constitution to prohibit the State from regionalizing school districts to meet the goals of the education clause. "Education for All—Facing the Challenges of New Jersey's Public School System," at http://www.princeton.edu/~lawjourn/Fall97/II1morley.html (last visited Apr. 14, 2003). For a brief survey of discussed and proposed constitutional amendments relating to education and the school finance system in New Jersey, see Tractenberg, supra note lxxiv, at 938–40.

124. *See*, for example, Ala. Const., art. XIV, § 256 (ages 7 to 21); Ariz. Const., art. XI, § 6 (ages 6 to 21); Ark. Const., art. XIV, § 1 (ages 6 to 21, with authorization for legislature to expand); Colo. Const., art. IX, § 2 (ages 6 to 21); Idaho Const., art. IX, § 9 (ages 6 to 18); Neb. Const., art. VII, § 1 (ages 5 to 21); N.J. Const., art. VIII, § IV, par. 1 (ages 5 to 18); N.M. Const., art. XII, § 1 ("all the children of school age"); Va. Const., art. VIII, § 1 ("all children of school age"); Wis. Const., art. X, § 3 (ages 4 to 20); Wyo. Const., art. VII, § 9 (ages 6 to 21, also includes specified educational range in Wyo. Const., art. VII, § 1).

125. *See* Ga. Const., art. VIII, § 1, par. 1 ("Public education for the citizens prior to college . . . shall be free."); Ill. Const., art. X, § 1 ("Education in public schools through the secondary level shall be free. There may be such other free education as the General Assembly provides by law"); Mich. Const., art. VIII, § 2 ("free public elementary and secondary schools as defined by law"); Mont. Const., art. X, § 1 (elementary and secondary); N.D. Const., art. VIII, § 2 (providing for free public schools "beginning with the primary and extending through all grades up to and including schools of higher education," but authorizing tuition and other charges for higher education); Wyo. Const., art. VII, § 1 ("free elementary schools of every needed kind and grade").

126. Some states provide that the university system should be as close to free as possible. *See*, for example, Ariz. Const., art. XI, § 6 (ensuring that, in state educational institutions, "instruction furnished shall be as nearly free as possible"); N.C. Const., art. IX, § 9 (benefits of public institutions of higher education shall be extended to state residents "free of expense" to the extent practicable); Wyo. Const., art. VII, § 16. Other states authorize the legislature to determine whether higher education should be free. *See* N.D. Const., art. VIII, § 2 (providing for free public schools "beginning with the primary and extending through all grades up to and including schools of higher education," but authorizing tuition and other charges for higher education); Wyo. Const., art. VII, § 1 (providing for "establishment and maintenance" of "a university with such technical and professional departments as the public good may require and the means of the state allow"). Still other states provide for loan guarantees. *See*, for example, Ohio Const., art. VI, § 5 (state may "guarantee the repayment of loans made to residents . . . to assist them in meeting the expenses of attending an institution of higher education" to "increase opportunities to the residents of this state for higher education.").

127. Currently, most states address early childhood education by statute or regulation. *See*, for example, N.J.S.A. 18A:7F-16 (creating early childhood program for low-income areas); N.H. R.S.A. 186:6-a (limiting state board of education's authority to kindergarten through twelfth grade but authorizing board to "accept, distribute and supervise funds for pre-kindergarten programs"); N.Y. C.L.S. Educ. § 3602-e (universal prekindergarten); N.C. Gen. Stat. § 143B-168.10 (parents have primary duty to educate preschoolers, but state may help); O.R.C. Ann. 3313.646 (allowing districts to establish a preschool program if there is a demonstrated need). A few states already have constitutional provisions that might authorize early childhood education, however. *See* Mo. Const., art. IX, § 1(a) ("general assembly shall establish and maintain free public schools for the gratuitous instruction of all persons in this state within ages not in excess of twenty-one years as prescribed by law"); Wis. Const., art. X, § 3 (education provided beginning at age four).

128. *Abbott v. Burke*, 153 N.J. 480, 508 (1998) (Abbott V). The New Jersey Supreme Court reiterated its mandate in *Abbott v. Burke*, 163 N.J. 95 (2000) (Abbott VI). There, the court found "that the manner in which the Department of Education . . . has carried out the preschool mandate of Abbott IV [was] not consistent with the Commissioner's representations to the remand court in that case." Ibid. at 101. The New Jersey Supreme Court issued its early childhood mandates even though the state education clause guarantees a free public education to students "between the ages of five and eighteen years." *See* N.J. Const., art. VIII, § 4, par. 1. Its reasoning was twofold: that some students could not receive the constitutionally guaranteed education starting at age five unless they had been provided access to effective early childhood education; and, in any event, the legislature had adopted a policy in favor of such education, especially for disadvantaged students. *Abbott V,* at 507.

129. *See*, for example, Okla. Const., art. XIII, § 4 (all children between 8 and 16, "who are sound in mind and body," compelled to attend school, unless otherwise educated, for at least 3 months per year); N.C. Const., art. IX, § 3 ("every child of appropriate age . . . shall attend the public schools, unless educated by other means"); Okla. Const., art. XIII, § 4 (all children ages 8 to 16 must attend school for at least 3 months per year); Va. Const., art. VIII, § 3 (compulsory attendance for "every child of appropriate age").

130. *See*, for example, Colo. Const., art. IX, § 11 (general assembly may require that children ages 6 to 18 attend public school, but provides in § 2 for free education for children ages 6 to 21); Del. Const., art. X, § 1 ("The General Assembly . . . may require by law that every child, not physically or mentally disabled, shall attend the public school, unless educated by other means."); Idaho Const., art. IX, § 9 (legislature may require children ages 6 to 18 to attend school); Nv. Const., art. XI, § 2 ("legislature may pass such laws as will tend to secure a general attendance of the children").

131. *See* William E. Thro, "The Role of Language of the State Education Clauses in School Finance Litigation," 79 *Ed. Law Rep.* 19 (1993). Thro's categorization actually was derived from two much earlier articles, and especially the one by Gershon Ratner. *See* Norton Grubb, "Breaking the Language Barrier: The Right to Bilingual Education," 9 *Harv.C.R.-C.L.L. Rev.* 52, 66–70 (1974; Gershon Ratner, "A New Legal Duty for Urban Public Schools: Effective Education in Basic Skills," 63 *Tex. L. Rev.* 777, 814–16, n. 143–46 (1985).

132. Ibid. at 23. Thro cites Tennessee as a typical Category I clause: "The General Assembly shall provide for the maintenance, support and eligibility standards of a system of free public schools." Tenn. Const., art. 11, § 12. Other examples include Ariz. Const., art. 11, § 1 ("The legislature shall enact such laws as shall provide for the establishment and maintenance of a general and uniform public school system"); Neb. Const., art. VII, § 1 ("The Legislature shall provide for the free instruction in the common schools of this state of all persons between the ages of five and twenty-one years."); N.Y. Const., art. 11, § 1 ("The legislature shall provide for the maintenance and support of a system of free common schools, wherein all the children of this state may be educated.").

133. Thro, supra note cxxxiv, at 23–24. Pennsylvania's provision is typical: "The General Assembly shall provide for the maintenance and support of a thorough and efficient system of public education to serve the needs of the Commonwealth." Pa. Const., art. III, § 14. *See also* Colo. Const., art. 9, § 2 ("The general assembly shall, as soon as practicable, provide for the establishment and maintenance of a thorough and uniform system of free public schools throughout the state."); Ky. Const. § 183 ("The General Assembly shall, by appropriate legislation, provide for an efficient system of common schools throughout the State."); W. Va. Const., art. 12, § 1 ("The legislature shall provide, by general law, for a thorough and efficient system of free schools.").

134. Thro, supra note cxxxiv, at 24. Examples include Cal. Const., art. IX, § 1 ("A general diffusion of knowledge and intelligence being essential to the preservation of the rights and liberties of the people, the Legislature shall encourage by all suitable means the promotion of intellectual, scientific, moral, and agricultural improvement."); R.I. Const., art. XII, § 1 ("The diffusion of knowledge, as well as of virtue among the people, being essential to the preservation of their rights and liberties, it shall be the duty of the general assembly to promote public schools . . . , and to adopt all means which it may deem necessary and proper to secure to the people the advantages and opportunities of education.").

135. Thro, supra note cxxxiv, at 25. Examples include Wash. Const., art. IX, § 1 ("It is the paramount duty of the state to make ample provision for the education of all children residing within its borders, without distinction or preference on account of race, color, caste, or sex."); Ga. Const., art. VIII, § 1 ("The provision of an adequate public education for the citizens shall be a primary obligation of the State of Georgia.").

136. *See* Enrich, supra note lxxviii (discussing the relationship between local control and equality in public school funding).

137. Thro's treatment of the relationship among plain meaning, legislative history and judicial tradition is confusing. Although he gives lip service to the latter two elements, indeed suggests contrary to classic construction techniques that they should be consulted first, he seems to wind up giving exclusive weight to plain meaning in his categorization of the education clauses. Other commentators consider the role of legislative history and judicial tradition to be of crucial importance in the interpretation of state education clauses because some courts that have struck down school finance systems as unconstitutional and mandated sweeping reforms "have risen to the challenge of articulating a substantive content for the sparse language of the constitutional clauses." Enrich, supra note lxxvii, at 175. Such bold, or activist, judicial behavior "to define the contours of educational adequacy" also is partly a function of the political or social climate in a particular state. Ibid. Under such circumstances, disembodied parsing of constitutional terminology may be of limited or no value.

138. *See* Thro, supra note cxxxiv, at 22–23.

139. William J. Brennan, "State Constitutions and the Protection of Individual Rights," 90 *Harv. L. Rev.* 489, 491 (1977).

140. *See* Mills and McLendon, supra note lxvii, at app. II, at 402–09.

141. Molly McUsic, "The Use of Education Clauses in School Finance Reform Litigation," 28 *Harv. J. on Legis.* 307 (1991).

142. Ibid. at 315.

143. *See* Banks, supra note lxx, at 153–54 (finding a lack of any discernible relationship between the strength of constitutional commitment to education and the success of school finance challenges).

144. *See* William E. Thro, "Judicial Analysis During the Third Wave of School Finance Litigation: The Massachusetts Decision as a Model," 35 *B.C. L. Rev.* 597 (1994).

145. 487 P.2d 1241 (Cal. 1971).

146. William F. Dietz, "Manageable Adequacy Standards in Education Reform Litigation," 72 *Wash. U. L.Q.* 1193, 1195 (1996).

147. Ibid. at 1197 (discussing *San Antonio Independent School District v. Rodriguez,* 411 U.S. 1 [1973]).

148. McUsic, supra note cxliv, at 308.

149. Dietz, supra note cxlix, at 1198.

150. 303 A.2d 273 (N.J., 1973).

151. Thro, supra note cxxxiv, at 19.

152. *See,* for example, *Lujan v. Colorado State Board of Education,* 649 P.2d 1005 (Colo., 1982) (reversing trial court decision that disparities in wealth among districts

were a violation of state equal protection); *McDaniel v. Thomas*, 285 S.E.2d 421 (Ga., 1981) (rejecting claim that funding system violated equal protection clause); *Board of Education of the City School District of Cincinnati v. Walter*, 390 N.E.2d 813 (Ohio), *cert. denied*, 444 U.S. 1015 (1979).

153. Dietz, supra note cxlix, at 1200.

154. Ibid.

155. Thro, supra note cxlvii, at 603.

156. Dietz, supra note cxlix, at 1201.

157. See *Abbott v. Burke II*, 575 A.2d 359 (N.J. 1990).

158. *Abbott v. Burke II*, 119 N.J. 287, 575 A.2d 359 (1990); *Abbott v. Burke III*, 136 N.J. 444, 643 A.2d 575 (1994), *Abbott v. Burke IV*, 149 N.J. 145, 693 A.2d 417 (1997); *Abbott v. Burke V*, 153 N.J. 480, 710 A.2d 450 (1998); *Abbott v. Burke VI*, 163 N.J. 95, 748 A.2d 82 (2000); *Abbott v. Burke VII*, 164 N.J. 84, 751 A.2d 1032 (2000); *Abbott v. Burke VIII*, 170 N.J. 537, 790 A.2d 842 (2002); *Abbott v. Burke IX*, 172 N.J. 294, 798 A.2d 602 (2002).

159. "About *Abbott v. Burke*," Education Law Center, at http://www.edlaw center.org/ELCPublic/AbbottvBurke/AboutAbbott.htm (citing various *Abbott* decisions).

160. See *Abbott v. Burke I*, 495 A.2d 376, 382 (1985) (quoting *Robinson v. Cahill*, 62 N.J. 473, 515 [1973]).

161. *See*, for example, Md. Const., art. VIII, § 1; Minn. Const., art. XIII, § 1; N.J. Const., art. VIII, § 4, para. 1; Ohio Const., art. VI, § 2; Pa. Const., art. III, § 14; W.Va. Const., art. XII, § 1.

162. See *Pauley v. Kelly*, 255 S.E.2d 859 (W.Va., 1979).

163. In *DeRolph IV*, the Ohio Supreme Court held that the state school finance system was unconstitutional, and directed the state legislature to enact a thorough and efficient school financing system, as the court had set forth in its prior opinions. *DeRolph v. State*, 97 Ohio St.3d 434, 780 N.E.2d 529 (2002). See *DeRolph v. State*, 78 Ohio St.3d 193, 677 N.E.2d 733 (1997) ("DeRolph I"), *DeRolph v. State*, 89 Ohio St.3d 1, 728 N.E.2d 993 (2000) ("DeRolph II"). Plaintiffs then moved for a compliance conference "'to ensure that the State initiates, without further delay, the process of formulating a school funding system that satisfies the mandates of the [state] Supreme Court.'" *State ex rel. State v. Lewis*, 99 Ohio St.3d 97, 2003-Ohio-2476 (May 16, 2003). The State responded by filing for a writ of prohibition to prevent the common pleas court and the trial judge from exercising further jurisdiction in *DeRolph*. The Ohio Supreme Court granted the writ, holding that "the exercise of further jurisdiction in this litigation would violate [its] *DeRolph IV* mandate." The court specifically ended any further litigation in *DeRolph*, emphasizing that "[t]he duty now lies with the General Assembly to remedy an educational system that has been found . . . to still be unconstitutional."

164. Over half of state constitutional education clauses have quality standards, most of them of Thro's Category II, or relatively weak, variety. *See* Robert M. Jensen, *Advancing Education Through Education Clauses of State Constitutions*, 1997 B.Y.U. Educ.

and L.J. 1, 4–5. These include: "general and efficient"—*see,* for example, *Del. Const.,* art. X, § 1; "general and uniform"—*see,* for example, Ariz. Const., art. XI, § 1; Ind. Const., art. VIII, § 1; Minn. Const., art. XIII, § 1; N.C. Const., art. IX, § 2; Ore. Const., art. VIII, § 3; S.D. Const., art. VIII, § 1; Wash. Const., art. IX, 2; "thorough and uniform"— *see,* for example, Colo. Const., art. IX, § 2; "general, uniform, and thorough"—*see,* for example, Idaho Const., art. IX, § 1; "complete and uniform"—*see,* for example, Wyo. Const., art. VII, § 1; "liberal"—*see,* for example, Ala. Const., art. XIV, § 256; "basic"— *see,* for example, Mont. Const., art. X, § 1; "competent"—*see,* for example, Vt. Const. ch. 2, § 68; and "suitable"—*see,* for example, Me. Const., art. VIII, 1.

165. *See Rose v. Council for Better Education,* 790 S.W.2d 186 (Ky., 1989).

166. Building on this framework, Kentucky has devised a new educational system that, in many ways, is a national model. "Kentucky is best known for blazing a new frontier in the movement to set standards and hold schools accountable for results." "Quality Counts 2002: Kentucky," *Education Week, at* http://edweek.org/sreports/qc02/ templates/state.cfm?slug=17ky.h21 (last visited Mar. 6, 2003). *See* Kentucky Education Reform Act of 1990, 1990 *Ky. Rev. Stat. & R. Serv.* 476 (codified as amended in scattered sections of *Ky. Rev. Stat. Ann.* [Baldwin 2002]) [Reform Act]. *Ky. Rev. Stat. Ann.* § 157.310 (2002) declares: "It is the intention of the General Assembly to assure substantially equal public school educational opportunities for those in attendance in the public schools of the Commonwealth, but not to limit nor to prevent any school district from providing educational services and facilities beyond those assured by the state supported program. The program shall provide for an efficient system of public schools throughout the Commonwealth, as prescribed by Section 183 of the Constitution of Kentucky, and for the manner of distribution of the public school fund among the districts and its use for public school purposes, as prescribed by Section 186 of the Constitution." The standards established by the Kentucky court have been adopted and followed by other state courts. *See,* for example, *Leandro v. State,* 488 S.E.2d 249 (N.C., 1997). One commentator explained, "[I]n short, the Reform Act embraces a substantial number of provisions intended to enhance quality of schooling" and "presents an extraordinarily thorough reform plan" that resulted from successful school finance litigation. Benson, supra note lxxiv, at 420–21. "For a useful discussion of the provisions and implementation of [the Reform Act]," *see* Jacob E. Adams, Jr., *School Finance Policy and Students' Opportunities to Learn: Kentucky's Experience, The Future of Children,* Winter 1997, cited in James E. Ryan, "The Influence of Race in School Finance Reform," 98 *Mich. L. Rev.* 432, 466 n. 177 (1999).

167. *Campaign for Fiscal Equity, Inc. v. State of New York,* 801 N.E.2d 326 (N.Y., 2003). A lower court in Kansas, another Thro Category I state, even more recently struck down that state's school funding system. See *Montoy v. State of Kansas,* 62 P.3d 228 (Dist. Ct. Shawnee Co., Kan., 2003).

168. *See* http://www.accessednetwork.org (last visited Jan. 13, 2004).

169. *See,* for example, Va. Const., art. VIII, § 1 ("high quality"); Ill. Const., art. X, § 1 ("efficient system of high quality"). In *Scott v. Commonwealth,* 443 S.E.2d 138, 142 (Va., 1994), the Virginia Supreme Court held that while education is a fundamental right under the state constitution, "nowhere does the Constitution require equal, or

substantially equal, funding or programs among and within the Commonwealth's school divisions." The court found that the language in the education clause ("shall seek to ensure that an educational program of high quality is established and continually maintained") is "merely aspirational," and not mandatory. Ibid. In *Committee for Educ. Rights v. Edgar*, 672 N.E.2d 1178, 1189, 1193 (1996), the Illinois Supreme Court found, first, "that disparities in educational funding resulting from differences in local property wealth do not offend section 1's efficiency requirement," and second, "that the question of whether the educational institutions and services in Illinois are 'high quality' is outside the sphere of the judicial function." Thus, the court dismissed plaintiffs' complaint challenging the state's school funding system. Ibid. at 1197. The Illinois Supreme Court affirmed this holding in *Lewis E. v. Spagnolo*, 710 N.E.2d 798 (1999).

170. Thro is not alone, incidentally, in believing that strong educational quality language should lead to strong judicial action. *See*, for example, Jensen, supra note clxvii, at 4–5 ("The most effective language of state constitutions found in the efforts advancing and protecting the educational offering will inevitably be that which prescribes a high level of educational quality."). However, a relatively clear consensus has emerged, even including Thro himself, that the litigation experience of the past ten years has undermined any argument that education clause language alone has significant predictive value.

171. *See* Mills and McLendon, supra note lx, at 368–77.

172. *See* Thro, supra note cxlvii; Dietz, supra note cxlix; Michael Heise, "State Constitutions, School Finance Litigation, and the 'Third Wave': From Equity to Adequacy," 68 *Temple L. Rev.* 1151 (1995).

173. *See*, for example, *Serrano v. Priest*, 557 P.2d 929 (Cal., 1976); *Van Dusartz v. Hatfield*, 334 F.Supp. 870 (Minn., 1971); *Milliken v. Green*, 203 N.W.2d 457 (Mich., 1972), *vacated and overruled by* 212 N.W.2d 711 (Mich., 1973). For a discussion of the arguable advantages of education adequacy litigation, *see* Heise, supra note clxxiv. Mills and McLendon, supra note lxvii, at 368–77.

174. 63 N.J. 196, 306 A.2d 65 (1973).

175. *See*, for example, Ore. Const., art. VII, § 8 ("The Legislative Assembly shall appropriate in each biennium a sum of money sufficient to ensure that the state's system of public education meets quality goals established by law, and publish a report that either demonstrates the appropriation is sufficient, or identifies the reasons for the insufficiency, its extent, and its impact on the ability of the state's system of public education to meet those goals. Consistent with such legal obligation as it may have to maintain substantial equity in state funding, the Legislative Assembly shall establish a system of Equalization Grants to eligible districts for each year in which the voters of such districts approve local option taxes."); Mo. Const., art. IX, § 3(b) ("In the event the public school fund provided and set apart by law for the support of free public schools, shall be insufficient to sustain free schools at least eight months in every year in each school district of the state, the general assembly may provide for such deficiency; but in no case shall there be set apart less than 25 percent of the state revenue, exclusive of interest and sinking fund, to be applied annually to the support of the free public schools."); and N.M. Const., art. XII, § 7 ("The annual distributions from the fund shall be one hundred two percent of the

amount distributed in the immediately preceding fiscal year until the annual distributions equal four and seven-tenths percent of the average of the year-end market values of the fund for the immediately preceding five calendar years. Thereafter, the amount of the annual distributions shall be four and seven-tenths percent of the average of the year-end market values of the fund for the immediately preceding five calendar years.").

176. *See,* for example, Fla. Const., art. IX, § 1 ("It is . . . a paramount duty of the state to make adequate provision for the education of all children residing within its borders. Adequate provision shall be made by law for a uniform, efficient, safe, secure, and high quality system of free public schools that allows students to obtain a high quality education and for the establishment, maintenance, and operation of institutions of higher learning and other public education programs that the needs of the people may require."); Ill. Const., art. X, § 1 ("A fundamental goal of the People of the State is the educational development of all persons to the limits of their capacities. The State shall provide for an efficient system of high quality public educational institutions and services."); R.I. Const., art. XII, § 1 ("It shall be the duty of the general assembly . . . to adopt all means which it may deem necessary and proper to secure to the people the advantages and opportunities of education."); Ark. Const., art. 14, § 1 ("The State shall ever maintain a general, suitable and efficient system of free public schools and shall adopt all suitable means to secure to the people the advantages and opportunities of education."); and Mont. Const., art. X, § 1 ("It is the goal of the people to establish a system of education which will develop the full educational potential of each person. Equality of educational opportunity is guaranteed to each person of the State.").

177. *See,* for example, *Serrano v. Priest,* 557 P.2d 929 (Cal., 1976); *Campbell County School District v. State,* 907 P.2d 1238 (Wyo., 1995) (discussing its prior decision in *Washakie County School District No. One v. Herschler,* 606 P.2d 310 (Wyo., 1980), where the court "struck down the then-existing school finance system," acknowledging "the post-*Washakie* reform [input] measures," and emphasizing that "lack of financial resources will not be an acceptable reason for failure to provide the best educational system); *Brigham v. State,* 692 A.2d 384 (Vt., 1997) (determining "that the current system for funding public education in Vermont, with its substantial dependence on local property taxes and resultant wide disparities in revenues available to local school districts, deprives children of an equal educational opportunity in violation of the Vermont Constitution," and that while "[e]qual opportunity does not necessarily require precisely equal per-capita expenditures . . . it does not allow a system in which educational opportunity is necessarily a function of district wealth. However, in *Leandro v. State,* 488 S.E.2d 249, 260 (N.C., 1997), the North Carolina court, while acknowledging that "the level of the state's general educational expenditures and per-pupil expenditures" is a factor when evaluating whether the state is meeting its constitutional duty to provide a sound basic education, it alone is not dispositive. Other factors such as "the level of performance of the children . . . on standard achievement tests," as well as legislative "[e]ducational goals and standards," are also to be considered. Ibid. at 259–60.

178. *See,* for example, *Rose v. Council for Better Education,* 790 S.W.2d 186 (1989); *Claremont School District v. Governor,* 794 A.2d 744 (N.H., 2002). For a current constitutional provision that specifies an educational opportunity measure, see Mont.

Const., art. X, § 1(1) ("It is the goal of the people to establish a system of education which will develop the full educational potential of each person. Equality of educational opportunity is guaranteed to each person of the State.").

179. *See Robinson v. Cahill*, 62 N.J. 473, 515 (1973). In *Abbott v. Burke II*, 575 A.2d 359, 397 (1990), the New Jersey Supreme Court explained "thorough and efficient" as "mean[ing] the ability to participate fully in society, in the life of one's community, the ability to appreciate music, art, and literature, and the ability to share all of that with friends." The court aptly stated, "If absolute equality were the constitutional mandate, and "basic skills" sufficient to achieve that mandate, there would be little short of a revolution in the suburban districts when parents learned that basic skills is what their children were entitled to, limited to, and no more." Ibid. at 397–98. In *Abbott v. Burke IV*, 693 A.2d 417, 427–28 (1997), the New Jersey Supreme Court once again emphasized that "[a]t its core, a constitutionally adequate education has been defined as an education that will prepare public school children for a meaningful role in society, one that will enable them to compete effectively in the economy and to contribute and to participate as citizens and members of their communities." In a subsequent opinion and in furtherance of providing a constitutionally adequate education, the court mandated specific remedial relief, including whole-school reform and early childhood education for three- and four-year-olds. *Abbott v. Burke V*, 710 A.2d 450, 473–74 (1998). *See generally* Julie Zwibelman, Note, "Broadening the Scope of School Finance and Resource Comparability Litigation," 36 *Harv. C.R.-C.L. L. Rev.* 527 (2001), for a discussion of state cases that have reached beyond input measures and demonstrate a more complete approach to remedying educational inequality.

180. *See* N.C. Const., art. IX, § 2(1) ("The General Assembly shall provide . . . for a general and uniform system of free public schools . . . wherein equal opportunities shall be provided for all students."); Mont. Const., art. X, § 1(1): "Equality of educational opportunity is guaranteed to each person of the State."

181. *See*, for example, N.J. Const., art. I, par. 5 ("No person shall . . . be segregated . . . in the public schools, because of religious principles, race, color, ancestry or national origin."); Conn. Const., art. I, § 20 ("No person shall be denied the equal protection of the law nor be subjected to segregation or discrimination in the exercise or enjoyment of his civil or political rights because of religion, race, color, ancestry or national origin.").

182. *See*, for example, Ind. Const., art. VIII, § 1 ("[I]t shall be the duty of the General Assembly . . . to provide, by law, for a general and uniform system of Common Schools, wherein tuition shall be without charge, and equally open to all"); *see also* La. Const., art. VIII, pmbl.; N.D. Const., art. VIII, § 1 ("open to all children"); S.D. Const., art. VIII, § 1 ("equally open to all").

183. *See* Ariz. Const., art. XI, § 6 (ensuring that state educational institutions will be open to both sexes); Ky. Const. § 187 (race or color not to affect distribution of school fund); Mich. Const., art. VIII, § 2 ("without discrimination as to religion, creed, race, color or national origin"); Mont. Const., art. X, § 7 (prohibiting refusal of admission based on "sex, race, creed, religion, political beliefs or national origin"); Wash. Const., art. IX, § 1 preamble ("without distinction or preference on account of race,

color, caste, or sex"); and Wyo. Const., art. VII, § 10 (no discrimination between pupils "on account of sex, race or color").

184. *See* Mo. Const., art. IX, § 3(c) (requires state to withhold funding for schools discriminating against teachers); Mont. Const., art. X § 7 (prohibits "religious or partisan test[s] or qualification[s]" of teachers or students); Neb. Const., art. VII, § 11 (prohibits religious testing or qualifications of students or teachers).

185. *See*, for example, N.J. Const., art. VIII, § IV, par. 1.

186. *See* Minn. Const., art. XIII, § 1 ("The legislature shall make such provisions by taxation or otherwise as will secure a thorough and efficient system of public education throughout the state."); Ohio Const., art. VI, § 2 ("The general assembly shall make such provisions . . . as . . . will secure a thorough and efficient system of common schools throughout the state . . ."); N.J. Const., art. VIII, § IV, par. 1 (The legislature shall provide for the maintenance and support of a thorough and efficient system of free public schools. . . ."); Wyo. Const., art. VII, § 9 ("The legislature shall make such further provision by taxation or otherwise, as with the income arising from the general school fund will create and maintain a thorough and efficient system of public schools."). For a different formulation, using the phrase "by all suitable means." see Ind. Const., art. VIII, § 1; Iowa Const., art. IX, § 3; Nev. Const., art. XI, § 1; S.D. Const., art. VIII, § 1. *See also* R.I. Const., art. XII, § 1 ("all means which [the legislature] may deem necessary").

187. *See* Colo. Const., art. IX, § 17 (for the fiscal years 2001–02 through 2010–11, state funding for "all categorical programs shall grow annually at least by the rate of inflation plus an additional one percentage point." From 2011–12 on, the funding shall be increased at least at the rate of inflation); *see also* Okla. Const., art. XIII, § 1(a) (regarding appropriation and allocation of funds for support of common schools, $42.00 per capita shall be raised and appropriated by the legislature for schools, to be distributed by an agency "designated by the Legislature"); Ore. Const., art. VIII, § 8(1) (legislature appropriates "in each biennium a sum of money sufficient to ensure that the state's system of public education meets quality goals established by law, and publish[es] a report that either demonstrates the appropriation is sufficient, or identifies the reasons for the insufficiency").

188. *See* Mont. Const., art. X, § 1(3) (The legislature "shall fund and distribute in an equitable manner to the school districts . . ."); Ore. Const., art. VIII, § 8 ("Consistent with such legal obligation as it may have to maintain substantial equity in state funding, the Legislative Assembly shall establish a system of Equalization Grants to eligible districts for each year in which the voters of such districts approve local option taxes.").

189. *See* La. Const., art. VIII, § 13(B) (assures legislative appropriation of funding to assure a minimum foundation program of education in all public schools through a formula developed and adopted by the state board of education).

190. *See* Ore. Const., art. VIII, § 4 (income from the school fund shall be distributed among the counties proportionally to the number of children ages 4 to 24); S.D. Const., art. VIII, § 3 (fund income apportioned among schools in proportion to number of school-age children; revenue from fines for state law violations are distributed to public schools within the county in which the fine was imposed).

191. While historically, public schools have been funded mostly by local property taxes, the "general trend [now] has been toward a larger portion of state funding and control." *School Finance Overview, EdSource Online,* at http://www.edsource.org/edu_fin.cfm (Sept. 2002). In 1919–20, local funds comprised 83.2 percent of total revenue nationwide for public elementary and secondary schools, while the state provided 16.5 percent of total funds. Table 157, Revenues for public elementary and secondary schools, by source of funds: 1919–20 to 1998–99, National Center for Education Statistics, *Digest of Education Statistics,* 2001, available at http://nces.ed.gov//pubs2002/digest2001/tables/dt157.asp. However, by 1965–66, local funds made up 53 percent of the total revenue, state funds 39.1 percent, and the contribution of federal funds increased to 7.9 percent (from 0.3% in 1919–20). Ibid. In 1998–99, the percentages were: 44.2 percent local funds, 48.7 percent state funds, and 7.1 percent federal funds. Ibid. These statistics are nationwide. On an individual state basis, "proportions and funding structures vary." "School Finance Overview," *EdSource Online,* at http://www.edsource.org/edu_fin.cfm (Sept. 2002). States such as "California and Michigan . . . have state-controlled school finance systems," while other states such as Illinois and New Jersey depend on some state funds, "but still rely most heavily on local property taxes." Ibid. Federal funding provides for less than 10 percent of public school education throughout the nation. Ibid. Therefore, in California, state funds provided for about 60 percent of the total public school budget in 2001–02, and local funds for about 30 percent. "Proportions of Funding Structures," *EdSource Online,* at http://www.edsource.org/sch_revsrc.cfm (Aug. 2002). Federal funds made up the remaining 10 percent. Ibid. In Michigan, state funds accounted for over 70 percent of total revenue, local funds for a little over 20 percent, and federal funds made up the rest. Ibid. However, in Illinois, state funds provided only about 30 percent of the total budget, with local funds providing over 60 percent, and federal funds making up the difference. Ibid. In New Jersey, local funds made up 60 percent of total revenue and state funds about 35 percent. Ibid. To illustrate the divergence and variability of funding, in 1997–98, the state share of revenue in Vermont was less than 30 percent. George A. Clowes, "Just the Facts: Sources and Uses of Public Education Dollars," The Heartland Institute, available at http://www.heartland.org/Article.cfm?artId=10763 (Dec. 1, 2002). In 1999–2000, that number jumped to 73.6 percent. Ibid. For state data tables providing total revenues for public schools, grades K–12, from state and local governments, per state, for 2001–02 and 2000–01, *see* Rankings & Estimates Update, available at http://www.nea.org/edstats/reupdate02.html#TABLE (Fall 2002).

192. *See* S.D. Const., art. VIII, § 15 ("The Legislature shall make such provision by general taxation and by authorizing the school corporations to levy such additional taxes as with the income from the permanent school fund shall secure a thorough and efficient system of common schools throughout the state . . . Taxes shall be uniform on all property in the same class.")

193. *See,* for example, N.C. Const., art. IX, § 2(1) ("The General Assembly shall provide by taxation and otherwise for a general and uniform system of free public schools.").

194. *See,* for example, N.J. Const., art. VIII, § IV, par. 2 (school fund shall be perpetual and "securely invested;" income shall be appropriated for public school support

"for the equal benefit of all the people of the State;" legislature may not use fund for any other purpose; and fund may invest in bonds of any school district); S.D. Const., art. VIII, § 11 (permanent school fund to be invested by "state investment council . . . as provided by law"), § 2 (principal of perpetual trust fund for maintenance of public schools inviolate; trust fund cannot be used for any other purpose).

195. *See*, for example, Colo. Const., art. IX, § 5 (inviolable school fund consists of proceeds from land granted to state for educational purposes, all estates that escheat to state, and grants to state for education); Mont. Const., art. X, § 2 (detailed list of sources of funding, including escheats, grants and unclaimed shares and dividends of corporations), § 5 (revenue from school fund to be apportioned with 95% going to public schools and 5% being reinvested); *see also* Neb. Const., art. VII, § 5 (money from fines, penalties and license money goes to support of public schools in the areas they accrue, except fines for overloading vehicles; proceeds from sale of "conveyances" seized in drug busts goes exclusively to support of public schools); N.C. Const., art. IX, § 6 (detailed list of sources of funds, including sales of state-owned swamp land); S.D. Const., art. VIII, § 2 (sources of school fund, including "proceeds of the sale of public lands that have heretofore been or may hereafter be given by the United States for the use of public schools in the state" and escheated property); Utah Const., art. X, § 5 (established permanent public school fund and lists sources of revenue, including "all revenues derived from the use of school trust lands" and 5 percent of net proceeds from sales of U.S. public lands in Utah; unused balance at end of each year becomes part of permanent school fund).

196. *See*, for example, Ky. Const. § 184 (protecting school fund and requiring that raising funds for public schools be submitted to voters); R.I. Const., art. XII, § 2 (perpetual school fund "shall be securely invested and remain a perpetual fund" for the support of public schools; S.D. Const., art. VIII, § 3 (principal shall be increased by at least the rate of inflation before interest and income is apportioned).

197. *See*, for example, Ind. Const., art. VIII, § 3 (fund may be increased but never diminished and cannot be used for any purpose but support of public schools); Fla. Const., art. IX, § 6 (income from state school fund may be appropriated only for "support and maintenance of free public schools"); Wash. Const., art. IX, § 2 ("the entire revenue derived from the common school fund and the state tax for common schools shall be exclusively applied to the support of the common schools").

198. *See* S.D. Const., art. VIII, § 13 (any loss occurring through an unconstitutional act shall be remedied through a special appropriation); Wash. Const., art. IX, § 5 (any losses from the permanent fund become state debt).

199. *See Robinson v. Cahill*, 118 N.J. Super. 223 (Law Div. 1972), *overruled in relevant part by* 62 N.J. 473 (1973).

200. *See*, for example, *Buse v. Smith*, 247 N.W.2d 141 (Wis., 1976) (concluding that Wisconsin's power equalization legislation, under which certain school districts would not receive any state aid but rather would "be required to pay a portion of their property tax revenues into the general state fund to ultimately be redistributed to other school districts in the state," violated the uniform taxation clause in the Wisconsin

Constitution); *cf. Richland County v. Campbell*, 346 S.E.2d 470 (S.C., 1988) (upholding state funding plan that "provides for shared funding of a minimum program of public education by the state and local school districts," by which "school districts which lack a sufficient tax base receive proportionally more state funds and are required to pay proportionately less local revenue for public school operation" and concluding that the plan "is a rational and constitutional means by which to equalize the educational standards of the public school system and the educational opportunities of all students").

201. *See*, for example, N.C. Const., art. IX, § 10 (proceeds from escheats go to aid "worthy and needy students" who are state residents enrolled in state institutions of higher learning).

202. *See*, for example, Ala. Const., art. XIV, § 263 ("No money raised for the support of the public schools shall be appropriated to or used for the support of any sectarian or denominational school."); Alaska Const., art. VII, § 1 (no money shall go to the "direct benefit" of private or religious institutions); Idaho Const., art. IX, § 5 (sectarian appropriations prohibited—no appropriation may ever be made nor any public funds distributed to aid any "church or sectarian or religious society, or for any sectarian or religious purpose"); Minn. Const., art. XIII, § 2 (prohibition against aiding sectarian school); N.D. Const., art. VIII, § 1 ("free from sectarian control"); Utah Const., art. X, § 1 ("free from sectarian control"); Wis. Const., art. X, § 3 ("no sectarian instruction," but students may be allowed to leave during school hours for religious reasons).

203. *Zelman v. Simmons-Harris*, 536 U.S. 639 (2002).

204. *See*, for example, Gary J. Simson, "School Vouchers and the Constitution—Permissible, Impermissible, or Required?" 11 *Cornell J.L. & Pub. Pol'y* 553 (2002); Jason S. Marks, "What Wall? School Vouchers and Church-State Separation after *Zelman v. Simmons-Harris*," 58 *J. Mo. B.* 354 (2002). For an examination of "the more restrictive stance taken by many state courts interpreting state establishment clauses," *see* Linda S. Wendtland, "Beyond the Establishment Clause: Enforcing Separation of Church and State Through State Constitutional Provisions," 71 *Va. L. Rev.* 625 (1985). A few state courts already have weighed in with decisions about voucher and tax credit programs. *Compare Colorado Congress of Parents v. Owens*, No. 03-3734 (Colo. Dist. Ct., Dec. 3, 2003) (invalidating pilot private school voucher program on basis of state constitution's local control in education provision) *with Kotterman v. Killian*, 972 P.2d 606 (Ariz., 1999) (upholding constitutionality of tax credit for contributions to "school tuition organizations"). The Colorado decision has been appealed to the state supreme court and oral argument is expected to be held in March 2004.

205. *See* Cal. Const., art. IX, § 7.5 (authorizing free textbooks for grades one through eight); S.D. Const., art. VIII, § 20 (authorizing free textbooks).

206. *Compare* Okla. Const., art. XIII, § 6 (official textbook list created by committee of experts from which districts select textbooks) *with* Colo. Const., art. IX, § 16 ("Neither the general assembly nor the state board of education shall have power to prescribe textbooks to be used in the public schools."); Wyo. Const., art. VII (legislature and superintendent may not prescribe textbooks to be used).

207. *See,* for example, Fla. Const., art. IX, § 1 ("It is . . . a paramount duty of the state to make adequate provision for the education of all children residing within its borders."). *See also* Ark. Const., art. XIV, § 1; Ga. Const., art. VIII, § 1; Haw. Const., art. X, § 1; Ill. Const., art. X, § 1; N.M. Const., art. XII, § 3.

208. *See,* for example, Ala. Const., art. XIV, § 256 ("The legislature shall establish, organize, and maintain a liberal system of public schools throughout the state. . . ."). *See also* Alaska Const., art. VII, § 1; Ariz. Const., art. XI, § 1; Cal. Const., art. IX, § 1; Colo. Const., art. IX, § 1; Conn. Const., art. VIII, § 1; Del. Const., art. X, § 1; Idaho Const., art. IX, § 1; Ind. Const., art. VIII, § 1; Iowa Const., art. IX, § 3; Kan. Const., art. VI, § 1; Ky. Const., § 183; La. Const., art. VIII, § 1; Me. Const., art. VIII, pt. 1, § 1; Md. Const., art. VIII, § 1; Mass. Const., pt. 2, C.V., § II; Mich. Const., art. VIII, § 2; Minn. Const., art. XIII, § 1; Miss. Const., art. VIII, § 201; Mo. Const., art. IX, § 1(a); Mont. Const., art. X, § 1(3); Neb. Const., art. VII, § 1; Nev. Const., art. XI, §§ 1–2; N.H. Const., pt. 2, art. 83; N.J. Const., art. VIII, § IV, par. 1; N.Y. Const., art. XI, § 1; N.C. Const., art. IX, § 2(1); N.D. Const., art. VIII, § 1; Ohio Const., art. VI, § 2; Okla. Const., art. XIII, § 1; Ore. Const., art. VIII, § 1; Pa. Const., art. III, § 14; R.I. Const., art. XII, § 1; S.C. Const., art. XI, § 1; S.D. Const., art. VIII, § 1; Tenn. Const., art. XI, § 12; Tex. Const., art. VII, § 1; Utah Const., art. X, § 1; Vt. Const., § 68; Va. Const., art. VIII, § 1; Wash. Const., art. IX, § 1; W. Va. Const., art. XII, § 1; Wis. Const., art. X, § 3; Wyo. Const., art. VII, § 1.

209. *See,* for example, Ill. Const., art. X, § 2 (creating state board of education to be "elected or selected on a regional basis" and establishing board's duties, while providing that these may be limited by law); Mo. Const., art. IX, § 2(a) (providing for state board of education; number, appointment, term and political affiliation of its members; and their reimbursement for expenses and per diem compensation); Neb. Const., art. VII, § 3 (eight members, elected from eight districts of roughly equal population; four-year terms; no compensation but reimbursement for expenses; nonpartisan ballot; members cannot be "actively engaged in the educational profession"). *See also* Okla. Const., art. XIII, §§ 5, 8 to XIII-B, § 4 (establishing and explaining in detail structure of state board of education and of system of higher education and board of regents). But *see* Idaho Const., art. IX, § 2 (very general, indicating only that board's powers and duties will be prescribed by law).

210. *See,* for example, Kan. Const., art. VI, §§ 2–5 (creating state board of education to oversee educational interests of the state and board of regents to oversee higher education).

211. *See,* for example, Miss. Const., art. VIII, § 202 (state superintendent is elected in same time and manner as governor for four-year term).

212. *See,* for example, Cal. Const., art. IX, § 3.3 (permitting county charters to provide for the election, qualifications and terms of members of county board of education); N.C. Const., art. IX, § 2 (2) (allowing general assembly to assign responsibility for support of public schools to local governing entities "as it may deem appropriate").

213. *See,* for example, Ga. Const., art. VIII, § 5 ("Each school system shall be under the management and control of a board of education"); Kan. Const., art. VI, § 5 ("Local public schools . . . shall be maintained, developed and operated by locally

elected boards."); Ohio Const., art. VI, § 3 ("[E]ach school district embraced wholly or in part within any city shall have the power by referendum vote to determine for itself the number of members and the organization of the district board of education"); Va. Const., art. VIII, § 7 ("The supervision of schools in each school division shall be vested in a school board, to be composed of members selected in the manner, for the term, possessing the qualifications, and to the number provided by law.").

214. *See*, for example, Fla. Const., art. IX, § 4 (establishes non-partisan election process for county school boards and gives them power to "operate, control and supervise all free public schools within the school district and determine the rate of school district taxes").

215. *See* Fla. Const., art. IX, § 5 (establishes the office and election process of superintendent of schools for individual school districts, who will be employed by the school board); La. Const., art. VIII, § 9(A) (parish school board "shall fix the qualifications and prescribe the duties of the parish superintendent").

216. *See* Colorado, Amendment 17 (2002), available at http://www.state.co.us/gov_dir/leg_dir/96bp/amd17.html (this unsuccessful proposal to guarantee parents' authority to control their children's upbringing, education, values, and discipline was the first such proposal to be placed on a ballot).

217. *See*, for example, *Pierce v. Society of Sisters*, 268 U.S. 10, 534–35 (1925) (finding that an Oregon statute making attendance of all children between eight and sixteen at public schools compulsory, upon threat of prosecution, unreasonably interferes with the liberty of parents and guardians to direct the upbringing and education of children under their control," in the context of private schools.); *Wisconsin v. Yoder*, 406 U.S. 205, 215, 234–35 (1972) (recognizing that "however strong the State's interest in universal compulsory education, it is by no means absolute to the exclusion or subordination of all other interests" and holding that "the First and Fourteenth Amendments prevent the State from compelling respondents to cause their children to attend formal high school to age 16," where compelling attendance would violate respondents Amish religious beliefs).

218. *See* Zelman, supra note ccvi. In that case, the Court rejected an Establishment Clause challenge to Ohio's "pilot program designed to provide educational choices to families with children who reside in the Cleveland City School District." Ibid. at 611. One aspect of the program gave "tuition aid for students in kindergarten through third grade, expanding each year through eighth grade, to attend a participating public or private school of their parent's choosing." Ibid. at 612. The Court found that the challenged program "is a program of true private choice . . . [and] neutral in all respects toward religion. It is part of a general and multifaceted undertaking by the State of Ohio to provide educational opportunities to the children of a failed school district." Ibid. at 617. For an interesting discussion about parental rights versus children's interests, and that the constitutionalization of the former has trumped the latter and "perpetuated a view of the child as parental property," *see* Barbara Bennett Woodhouse, *Speaking Truth to Power: Challenging "The Power of Parents to Control the Education of Their Own,"* 11 *Cornell J. L. & Pub. Pol'y* 481 (2002).

219. *See* No Child Left Behind, 20 U.S.C.S., § 7201 et seq. (2003) (Title V entitled "Promoting Informed Parental Choice and Innovative Programs").

220. *See Abbott v. Burke V,* 153 N.J. 480, 489, 710 A.2d 450, 454 (1998) (explaining "the remedial measures that must be implemented in order to ensure that public school children from the poorest urban communities receive the educational entitlements that the Constitution guarantees them"). The court intervened again just two years later "to assure that the implementation of preschool in the Abbott districts is faithful to the programs proposed by the Commissioner and accepted by this Court." *Abbott v. Burke VI,* 163 N.J. 95, 101, 748 A.2d 82, 85 (2000).

221. For example, in 1978, California voters responded to *Serrano v. Priest,* 487 P.2d 1241 (Cal., 1971), "on the eve of the implementation of the legislature's response to *Serrano II* [557 P.2d 929 (1976)]" by passing Proposition 13, which limited property tax rates. *See* William A. Fischel, *How Serrano Caused Proposition* 13, 12 *J.L. & Politics* 607, 612 (1996). "Its intended and actual effect was a more than fifty percent reduction in local property tax collections across the state." Ibid. Subsequently, the legislature did meet *Serrano II*'s "equalized spending goal . . . but . . . at a greatly reduced level of spending," effectively leaving the state's "school finance in shambles." Ibid. at 613. In 1996, California voters also passed the controversial Proposition 209, prohibiting affirmative action in public education. Another example is provided by Colorado's "busing clause." *See* Colo. Const., art. IX, § 8 ("nor shall any pupil be assigned or transported to any public educational institution for the purpose of achieving racial balance"). This amendment was passed in 1974, the year busing began after a federal district court ordered the Denver public schools to desegregate. *See Keyes v. School Dist. No. 1,* 303 F. Supp. 279 (D. Colo., 1969).

222. Newsroom: Illinois Statewide Management Alliance, at wysiwyg://217/ http://www.iasbo.org/ newsroom/alliancecont.htm (updated Apr. 10, 2003). *See* Joseph L. Bast, Herbert J. Walberg, and Robert J. Genetski, "The Heartland Report on School Finance Reform Illinois" (May 1996), at http://www.heartland.org/pdf/21245j.pdf, for the text of the proposed amendment.

223. Newsroom: Illinois Statewide Management Alliance, at wysiwyg://217/http:// www.iasbo.org/newsroom/alliance_cont.htm (updated Apr. 10, 2003).

224. As indicated supra, predictive efforts by some commentators, *see,* for example, Thro, supra note cxxxiv, heavily based on the language of state education clauses, have been largely unsuccessful. Studies by others suggest that "courts interpreting a state constitution with a 'strong' education clause are [not] more likely to strike down school finance schemes than courts interpreting a 'weak' education clause." *See* Karen Swenson, "School Finance Reform Litigation: Why Are Some State Supreme Courts Activist and Others Restrained," 63 *Alb. L. Rev.* 1147, 1155, 1174–75. (2000). Rather, the best indicator of whether or not a court will invalidate a financing scheme under the education clause is whether the legislature is unable or unwilling to fix the problem. *See* Banks, supra note lxx. What the political affiliation of the court is and whether judges are appointed or elected are other relevant factors. Ibid.

Chapter Ten

The Environment and Natural Resources

Barton H. Thompson Jr.

INTRODUCTION

A majority of state constitutions seek to protect the public's interest in natural resources and the environment.[1] The constitutional provisions, however, vary substantially among states both in what they protect and in the nature and extent of the protections. Some provisions set out broad public rights to clean air and healthy environments; others guarantee very specific public rights, such as the right to use navigable waters or to fish; several merely authorize the legislature to pass environmental laws. A number of constitutional provisions establish new institutions or procedures for the management, allocation, and preservation of fish and wildlife, water, or other natural resources. Yet other provisions create and protect various categories of state public lands.

The environmental focus of state constitutions has evolved over time as public concerns have changed. Navigable waterways were of greatest concern to citizens in the nineteenth century because of the immense commercial importance of waterways. As a result, the earliest constitutional provisions established rights of navigation and of access to navigable waters.

As Americans immigrated to the western United States in the late nineteenth century, citizens of the new western states confronted the need both to protect and to allocate scarce water resources. Many of the new western states therefore adopted constitutional provisions asserting "public ownership" over water resources, while authorizing private appropriation of water resources on a first-in-time, first-in-right basis. Some western constitutions also banned nonbeneficial or wasteful uses of water.

The conservation movement of the early twentieth century generated interest in protecting fish, wildlife, and other natural resources from overexploitation. A number of state constitutions responded by creating new governmental institutions such as fish and game commissions, insulated from direct political influence, to manage such resources. Other constitutional provisions set out general guidelines for the management and conservation of natural resources.

Increasing public interest in the environment since the 1950s has generated the latest and largest body of constitutional provisions addressing the environment. Approximately a third of all state constitutions, including all constitutions written since 1959, contain provisions either directing the legislature to protect the environment or guaranteeing public rights to a clean and healthy environment. A handful of states also have created state land reserves, designed to protect undeveloped land for aesthetic, recreational, ecological, or historic purposes.

Yet questions remain about both the rationale for and effectiveness of broad environmental provisions in state constitutions. Although the public widely supports environmental protection, how to balance environmental protection with economic growth generates heated debate. At the same time, environmental advocates have been disappointed with the impact of many modern environmental provisions on actual policy. Most state courts have shied away from actively using the provisions and instead deferred to legislative judgments as to the appropriate level and types of environmental protection. Nor is there evidence that the recent growth in environmental provisions has had a significant impact on legislative and executive decision-making in the environmental field.

The drafters of twenty-first-century constitutions thus face several critical questions: Although environmental protection is an important subject of state policy, is there justification for addressing the environment in state constitutions? If there is sufficient justification, what provisions should be included? And finally, can environmental provisions be drafted in a fashion that makes them more effective than in the past?

UNDERSTANDING THE CONTESTED TERRAIN OF ENVIRONMENTAL POLICY

Environmental provisions are doomed to failure unless they build on a clear understanding of environmental problems and the constraints and trade-offs involved in solving them. Environmental policy encompasses a diverse array of issues, usefully divisible into three broad subject areas—control and cleanup of pollution and toxic products (health issues), conservation and allocation of natural resources (resource issues), and public access to and preservation of resources of recreational or other importance to the general population (public access issues). Each set of issues raises unique public policy questions that cannot be addressed effectively through a single universal provision. Many environmental issues, moreover, involve trade-offs. Environmental protection often comes at economic or other cost. Constitutional provisions that fail to address the trade-offs are avoiding the tough policy questions that the government must address.

Health Issues

The last third of the twentieth century generated scores of new federal and state statutes regulating pollution and toxic substances. While state governments once took the lead in pollution regulation, national laws from the Clean Air Act to the Safe Drinking Water Act now play the principal role.

The principal question in controlling pollution is how great of a health risk society should tolerate. Many forms of pollution do not have a safe threshold of exposure below which everyone is safe from injury. The cost of reducing pollution, moreover, generally increases as the government imposes stricter regulations. In deciding how much ambient lead to permit in the air or how much arsenic to permit in drinking water, the government thus inevitably is engaging in a trade-off between the health benefits of reduced pollution and the economic costs of increased regulation. People, moreover, differ strongly over how to resolve the trade-off between health risks and economic costs. Constitutional provisions that simply promise a "healthful" environment ignore these central issues. Additional pollution reductions can reduce the health risks but seldom to zero and, in most cases, only at a cost.

Scientific uncertainty further complicates pollution regulation. Scientists often do not know whether a particular pollutant presents a health risk or how large the risk is. The government must decide whether to err on the side of public safety, and restrict the pollutant as if it were hazardous (exercising what has come be called the "precautionary principle"), or err on the side of the economy and permit the pollution absent further evidence of risk. References in constitutions to general and vague terms such as "clean air" and "healthful environment" again provide little guidance on how to address uncertainty.

Resource Issues

1. Resource Extraction

States still play the principal role in regulating the extraction and use of natural resources. In managing each natural resource, states must decide the maximum extraction, if any, to allow in any time period and how to allocate that amount among competing users.

How much extraction to allow depends on whether the resource is "renewable" or "depletable." Nature continually replenishes renewable resources such as fish, wildlife, timber, and groundwater. So long as the rate of human consumption does not exceed the rate of natural replenishment, future generations can continue using the resource; consumption rates that exceed natural replenishment, by contrast, can risk destroying the resource. By contrast, depletable resources such as petroleum, coal, and hard minerals are finite, requiring government to apportion use across generations. Higher consumption today means less of the resource available in the future. Today's extraction decisions thus can affect the welfare of future generations. Although most people agree that renewable resources should be managed in a sustainable fashion for their optimum yield, there is little consensus on how to apportion depletable resources across generations.

2. Ecosystem Preservation

In recent years, society increasingly has recognized the importance of protecting wildlife habitat, instream waterflows, and other ecosystems. Although the federal government has taken the lead through laws such as the Endangered Species Act, a number of states have adopted their own laws providing greater or broader protections of various ecosystems.

There is no clear public consensus on either the goals to be achieved in protecting ecosystems or on how much protection to provide. To some people, the goal should be to avoid species extinction; to others, the goal should be to maximize the overall biodiversity in a region; yet others seek to protect and enhance ecosystems in order to maximize the "natural services," such as clean drinking water or flood control, that healthy ecosystems can provide. More important, people again differ on whether the appropriate degree of protection is an issue of ethics or of maximizing human utility. Many environmentalists argue that species, as well as individual animals and plants, have a right to protection even if the animals and plants are of no practical importance to humans. But other Americans believe that we should protect species, and thus their habitats, only to the degree that they provide value to humans.

The absence of "safe thresholds" again frustrates those looking for simple answers. Habitat destruction is the principal cause of species endangerment. By the time a species is listed as endangered, most of its historic habitat typically already has been destroyed or degraded. There is therefore no "safe" amount of development. Each additional acre of lost habitat generally will reduce the species' chances of survival and recovery, posing a difficult trade-off for policy makers.

Who should bear the burden of ecosystem protection is another contentious issue. In the view of many environmentalists, property owners should not have the right to develop or destroy environmentally sensitive lands and waters. Property owners, by contrast, often argue that, if society wishes to preserve such resources, society should pay for the protection. Arguments can be mustered for both views.

Public Access Issues

A final set of environmental issues focuses on public access to recreational and other resources of importance to the general population. Many state constitutions include a public right to use navigable rivers and waterways. The public also has long enjoyed a right in most states to use navigable waterways and tidal areas under what is known as the "public trust doctrine." To further meet public demands for recreation and open space, the fifty states have acquired and set aside over ten million acres of land as state parks and other public areas.

As public demand for recreational and aesthetic access has continued to increase in recent years, public advocacy groups have called on legislatures, courts, and voters to act. Most states have responded by acquiring and dedicating additional lands, often as part of comprehensive open-space programs or ballot initiatives. Courts in several states also have invoked the public trust doctrine or other common law doctrines to open access across or to privately owned beaches or waterways.[2] Finally, a number of states and local jurisdictions have begun to condition the development of beachfront or other properties by requiring the property owner to provide public rights of access.

Drafting Environmental Provisions

Basic Drafting Choices

1. *Issue Focus*
As cataloged in the previous section, environmental issues comprise a wide and diverse range of issues, having as their only overarching theme the relationship of humans to their natural environment. Only a handful of constitutions attempt to address the environment comprehensively, and those typically do so through broad policy announcements or prescriptions. The Virginia Constitution, for example, states that "it shall be the Commonwealth's policy to protect its atmosphere, lands, and water from pollution, impairment, or destruction,"[3] while the Michigan Constitution directs the legislature to "provide for the protection of the air, water, and other natural resources of the state from pollution, impairment, and destruction."[4]

Most state constitutions deal with only a subset of environmental issues, but in greater detail. California's constitution, for example, addresses fishing, wildlife conservation, water use, and tidelands, but says nothing about pollution, biodiversity, forestry, or energy.[5] Some constitutions address only a very limited class of environmental issues. The North Carolina Constitution provides for water conservation and forestry preservation, but is otherwise silent on the environment.[6] Idaho's and New Mexico's constitutions address only water allocation.[7] The particular issues singled out for constitutional attention, moreover, vary tremendously from state to state.

Whatever choices the drafters of a constitution make, environmental provisions should be as clear as possible as to scope. Where environmental provisions have been ambiguous as to scope, state courts often have interpreted them narrowly to avoid intervening in policy disputes not clearly within the language of the provisions. Like a number of states, for example, the Illinois Constitution provides that the "public policy of the State and the duty of each person is to provide and maintain a healthful environment for the benefit of this and future generations."[8] The Illinois Supreme Court has held that this language addresses only those actions such as pollution that might directly harm human health and does not require the state and its citizens to ensure the survival of endangered or threatened species (despite evidence that habitat preservation can promote a cleaner environment).[9]

2. Types of Environmental Provisions

A second question is what type of provisions to use in addressing the selected environmental issues. Environmental provisions array themselves along several overlapping dimensions. One dimension is the degree to which the provision constrains the ability of the legislature and executive branches to decide on the environmental policy of the state. A second distinction is whether the provision seeks to affect environmental policy by modifying traditional governmental *processes* (e.g., by requiring supermajorities in the legislature) or by dictating particular *substantive* results. A final difference among provisions is the degree to which the provision directly proscribes *private* actions that harm the environment.

Authorization Provisions. Some provisions merely empower the legislature or executive branch to address particular environmental issues. The Georgia Constitution, for example, provides that the "General Assembly shall have the power to provide by law for . . . [r]estrictions upon land use in order to protect and preserve the natural resources, environmental, and vital areas of this state."[10]

In most cases, such Authorization Provisions are constitutionally unnecessary. Given the inherent police power of state governments, legislatures generally enjoy the power to enact environmental legislation even absent explicit constitutional authorization.[11] In some cases, however, the framers of an environmental provision might want to clarify that environmental legislation does not violate other constitutional provisions. The Rhode Island Constitution, for example, specifies that environmental regulations "shall not be deemed to be a public use of private property" and thus not subject to challenge as an unconstitutional taking of property for private purposes.[12]

Value Declarations. A few state constitutions set out environmental policy goals for the state. The Virginia Constitution, for example, specifies that it is the "policy of the Commonwealth to conserve, develop, and utilize its natural resources" and "to protect its atmosphere, lands, and waters from pollution."[13] Courts have uniformly held that such Value Declarations do not require anyone, including the government, to take any particular actions. In constitutional terminology, Value Declarations are not "self-executing," but instead rely on legislative or administrative implementation. Government officials and others, however, often invoke Value Declarations in advocating for or defending particular actions,[14] and such Value Declarations may influence legislative and administrative decisions.

Institutional Specifications. Without directly dictating particular environmental actions, state constitutions also can influence environmental policy either by changing the rules by which governmental branches make environmental decisions or by creating new governmental organizations to manage specific environmental issues. In the first category, the constitution can modify legislative voting requirements or administrative procedures. In order to protect state lands of particular environmental importance, for example, several state constitutions require that the legislature approve any sale of protected tracts of land in multiple legislative sessions or by supermajority votes.[15] Constitutions also can modify the rules by which the courts review and enforce environmental laws. Rhode Island's constitution, for example, mandates that environmental regulations "be liberally construed."[16]

Constitutions also can take environmental issues away from the traditional branches of government and award the issues to new governmental organizations that are specially designed to ensure special expertise, to favor one or another interest group, or to provide a balanced perspective. For example, the California Constitution creates a Fish and Game Commission to manage fish and wildlife in the state.[17] In order to ensure a degree of independence from political influence, that constitution also requires that the five members of the commission be selected by the governor but confirmed by the Senate and serve six-year terms.[18]

Policy Directives. Constitutions also can protect the environment either by directing the government to adopt and implement particular policies or by restricting the actions that the government can take. These Policy Directives can bind all or selected branches of government and can set out the mandated policy in general or detailed terms. The Michigan Constitution, for example, provides broadly that the "legislature shall provide for the protection of the air, water, and other natural resources of the state from pollution, impairment, and destruction."[19] At a more detailed level, California's constitution requires the state, whenever it sells or transfers public lands, to reserve "in the people the absolute right to fish thereupon."[20]

Courts often have held that broad Policy Directives, such as the Michigan directive, do not give citizens the right to sue the state for failing to take particular actions either because the provisions are not "self-executing"[21] or because the constitution does not give private citizens a cause of action or standing to sue.[22] Although such Policy Directives might still play important political roles, directives that are not judicially enforced are effectively the same as Value Declarations.

Environmental Rights and Duties. Finally, some constitutions include Environmental Rights that assure citizens of particular protections. Again, the Environmental Rights can be either quite broad or relatively narrow and detailed. At the latter end of the spectrum, the Wisconsin Constitution provides that "the river Mississippi and the navigable waters leading into the Mississippi and St. Lawrence, and the carrying places between the same, shall be common highways and forever free, as well to the inhabitants of the state as to the citizens of the United States, without any tax, impost or duty therefor."[23] Colorado's constitution specifies that the "right to divert the unappropriated waters of any natural stream to beneficial uses shall never be denied."[24] At a much broader level, the Massachusetts Constitution sets out a public right to "clean air and water."[25] Constitutions can and often do couple such broad Environmental Rights with Policy Directives to the government.

Environmental Duties are the flip side of Environmental Rights. Any constitutional right implies a corresponding duty. If a constitution guarantees its citizens a right to clean air, there must be a duty in at least some individuals or entities not to pollute the air. Although constitutions can leave duties an implicit corollary to the listing of Environmental Rights, spelling out specific Environmental Duties makes clear who exactly is under a duty not to interfere with the right. The Illinois Constitution therefore states that "the duty of each person is to provide and maintain a healthful environment for the benefit of this and future generations."[26]

3. Enforcement

Policy Directives, Environmental Rights, and Environmental Duties raise the questions of who can enforce the provisions, in what courts, and in what circumstances. One option, which most constitutions have adopted, is to say nothing, leaving these questions to judicial resolution under the courts' standard rules of constitutional enforcement. There are risks, however, to this approach. Environmental litigation is relatively unique. In traditional constitutional litigation, plaintiffs seek to block governmental action that directly threatens to injure them. In environmental litigation, by contrast, plaintiffs who have not suffered a personal injury but are trying to vindicate a general environmental interest often seek to force the government to act. A nonprofit organization, for example, may try to use environmental provisions to force the government to protect an endangered species. Many states have not developed clear rules for dealing with such cases, and courts often have proven reticent to recognize private causes of action in such settings.

Policy Directives, Environmental Rights, and Environmental Duties therefore may wish to incorporate explicit provisions regarding judicial enforcement. The constitutions of Hawaii and Illinois explicitly authorize citizens to enforce their Environmental Rights in court against both governmental and private defendants, subject to "reasonable limitations and regulation as provided by law."[27] And the New York Constitution provides that a violation of its Policy Directives "may be restrained at the suit of the people or, with the consent of the supreme court in appellate division, on notice to the attorney-general at the suit of any citizen."[28]

Such enforcement provisions can address a number of important issues, without getting bogged down in unnecessary detail. First, who can bring a lawsuit seeking to enforce the environmental provision? Potential plaintiffs include various governmental attorneys (e.g., state attorneys general and local city or county attorneys), other governmental officials holding special responsibilities for representing the public interest (e.g., state public advocates), and private organizations and individuals. Second, should courts employ any special standing rules? In particular, should courts insist on a showing of actual injury or damage to the plaintiff? Finally, should the constitution affirmatively encourage such lawsuits by authorizing courts to award attorneys' fees to prevailing plaintiffs? "Citizen suit provisions" in national environmental statutes, such as the Clean Air Act, have helped promote enforcement of these laws by providing for fee awards, and similar constitutional authority is likely to lead to more active litigation under environmental provisions.[29]

4. Degree of Specificity

A final drafting question is the degree of specificity with which an environmental provision should be written. Both extremes present dangers. However, hyperlegislation, in which a constitution specifies environmental policy at a level of detail more traditionally associated with statutes, presents far greater problems. Hyperlegislation makes it difficult to adjust environmental policies to changing conditions and needs and to make midcourse adjustments to policies in light of experience. Hyperlegislation also clutters up a constitution and dilutes the importance of more fundamental constitutional provisions. To the degree that a constitution grows to resemble a statutory code, fewer citizens will be aware of the constitution's provisions, and the symbolic and educational value of the constitution will fade.

An example of counterproductive hyperlegislation is the appropriately named Marine Resources Protection Act, which constitutes Article X-B of the California Constitution. Approved by California voters in 1990 as a constitutional amendment, Article X-B bans the use of gill and trammel nets, which can entangle and thereby injure or kill sea-lions, porpoises, and other noncommercial marine life. Like statutes, the article sets out in exacting detail how the ban should be implemented, specifies enforcement procedures (including the exact penalties and fines to be imposed for violations), and even requires an annual report to the legislature. Any changes in the details of the article require a constitutional amendment, effectively freezing in place the current provisions.

Overly general provisions, by contrast, can be ineffective. Few people would disagree that states should protect their environments and carefully manage their natural resources. Constitutional provisions that merely mandate "healthy environments" and resource "conservation" thus contribute little to public policy. To be more than window dressing, constitutions must provide guidance on key policy questions regarding environmental trade-offs and uncertainty. The goal should be to provide useful guidance but at a broad level that governmental agencies and courts can apply in an evolving, flexible manner to each situation that arises.

Key Drafting Issues

1. Why Should State Constitutions Address Environmental and Natural Resource Issues?

A number of questions are relevant in choosing and drafting environmental provisions. The first and most important question is why a state constitution should include environmental provisions at all. One can readily imagine a constitution that does not include any environmental provisions whatsoever. The federal Constitution, as well as a handful of state constitutions, focus largely on shaping the process by which the government makes decisions and then trust that process to determine appropriate substantive policy. These constitutions generally authorize broad categories of governmental action, but include virtually no substantive directives. Even constitutions that include substantive mandates typically do not include provisions dealing with transportation policy, insurance, professional regulation, employment policy, and a host of other issues with which state governments regularly are engaged. Why then should a state constitution include environmental provisions?

Community Values. The state polity may wish to include environmental provisions in its constitution in order to recognize and stress the special importance of the environment to the polity. One of the original purposes of state constitutions was to define, highlight, and foster the identity and values of the state. Under such a "community values" rationale, environmental provisions serve an important constitutional function both by proclaiming the significance of environmental protection to the citizenry and by signaling to the government the importance of promoting the environment through legislation and administrative action. The environmental provisions constitute a dialogue, both among the state's citizens and between the citizens and their governmental officials, concerning the physical and symbolic value of environmental protection.

A community values rationale can justify Value Declarations that announce broadly supported environmental values and that leave the state government

with discretion in how to implement the values. But a community values rationale by itself cannot justify Policy Directives, Institutional Specifications, Environmental Rights, and Environmental Duties that modify, bypass, or constrain
the legislative and administrative processes by which the state typically makes
regulatory or social policy. To justify these politically more intrusive provisions,
the framers of a constitution must find a rationale for changing or restricting the
normal governmental decision-making process.

Process Imperfections. At least two rationales might justify such provisions. First,
despite constitutional efforts to create effective governmental processes, the legislative or administrative processes may suffer from unavoidable imperfections
that prevent the government from dealing efficaciously with some environmental issues. For example, legislators may underrepresent future generations, who
do not vote and cannot help legislators get reelected.

Framers of a state constitution, however, must be cautious before constraining or bypassing governmental decision-making on process grounds.
Legislative and administrative processes are inherently flawed to some degree,
but we tolerate the relatively minor flaws because of our commitment to and
valuation of democracy and pluralism. In deciding whether to "constitutionalize" a particular environmental issue, the question is whether there is something
unique about the issue that makes the risks of the standard governmental
processes greater than the benefits.

Fundamental Principles. A second rationale for more intrusive constitutional
provisions is that the subject matter of the provisions is ethically too fundamental or principle driven to leave to democratic discretion, no matter how well
governmental institutions reflect current majoritarian views. This rationale, of
course, is a primary justification for including civil rights provisions in state
constitutions: no matter what the views of the current electorate, the state
should not be permitted to discriminate against individuals or groups based on
immutable personal characteristics. The difficult constitutional question is
what, if any, other policies fall into this category. The framers of a constitution
must distinguish between strongly and widely held policy preferences that
nonetheless should be open to political debate, on the one hand, and fundamental principles that should be enshrined in the constitution, on the other.
Virtually everyone, for example, believes that drinking water should be safe
from injurious pollutants, but is safe drinking water of the same fundamental
character as freedom from invidious discrimination?

At least two questions seem central to determining whether a particular
policy is sufficiently "fundamental" to justify enshrinement in a constitution.
First, does support for the policy go beyond mere self-interest? Would citizens
agree with the policy even if it did not personally benefit them? Second, is the

principle sufficiently important to a well-functioning, industrious, and equitable society to justify inclusion in the state constitution?

2. Will Courts Implement and Enforce Environmental Provisions?

Because the purpose of Value Declarations is merely to proclaim and stimulate discussion of common values, rather than to impose particular policies, they do not need active judicial enforcement to be effective. Rights Declarations, by contrast, anticipate that the public can call on courts to vindicate their rights. Both Policy Directives and Institutional Specifications also can require active judicial intervention to be effective. If the legislature fails to comply with a Policy Directive or the legislative or executive branches of government intrude into the jurisdiction of commissions or other special entities created by Institutional Specifications, courts may need to step in if the constitutional goals are to be achieved.

In choosing and framing environmental provisions, another key question is thus whether courts are adequately equipped and willing to enforce the provisions. Although courts may feel uncomfortable enforcing all types of environmental provision, Policy Directives and Rights Declarations can raise special concerns for courts. Most courts have declined to use general environmental policy provisions to force legislatures to protect the environment or to constrict the actions of private or governmental entities that threaten the environment. Although the courts have relied on various legal grounds to avoid involvement, the courts' reticence to act appears motivated by more fundamental concerns, only some of which can be avoided by constitutional drafters.

First, many Policy Directives and Rights Declarations provide only the broadest and vaguest of guidance. The Hawaii Constitution guarantees everyone a "right to a clean and healthful environment,"[30] while the Michigan Constitution provides that the "legislature shall provide for the protection of the air, water, and other natural resources of the state from pollution, impairment, and destruction."[31] Presented with only the most general of charges, courts have found it difficult to apply such provisions to the difficult and complex trade-offs involved in real cases.

Courts, of course, frequently engage in hard trade-offs in other fields, such as free speech and procedural due process, with little guidance from the constitutional language. A far greater consensus, however, exists on the framework to apply in addressing these other constitutional issues. The societal split on how to resolve environmental disputes, by contrast, is both wide and deep. In the case of long-standing constitutional provisions, courts can turn to decades of jurisprudence to help frame and resolve new cases. By contrast, modern environmental provisions ask courts to develop and apply a totally new framework in a complex field. Absent both precedent and an existing or emerging societal norm, courts often feel rudderless trying to decide how much of society's resources to devote to increasing the chances that an endangered species will recover or to decreasing the chances that the most pollution-sensitive members of the population will suffer from asthmatic attacks.

Courts also must worry about the procedural complexity of applying and enforcing Policy Directives, Environmental Rights, and Environmental Duties in the environmental arena. Environmental law is a particularly technical field that often requires significant fact collection and scientific evaluation, as well as an active regulatory apparatus to monitor and pursue violations. Courts, however, generally do not have the expertise or comprehensive fact-finding ability of legislatures. Unlike legislatures, moreover, courts cannot create and fund expert administrative agencies to implement and enforce their policies.

The procedural problems that courts can encounter in trying to implement Policy Directives, Environmental Rights, and Environmental Duties should not be overstated. State and federal courts have dealt effectively with similar procedural problems in both a wide array of institutional litigation (involving school desegregation, prison reform, mental health care, and educational policy) and in multiplaintiff conflicts involving exposure to toxic substances. In drafting environmental provisions, nonetheless, framers of state constitutions must bear in mind the comparative limitations of courts in designing, implementing, and enforcing environmental policy.

THE LESSONS OF EXISTING ENVIRONMENTAL AND NATURAL RESOURCE PROVISIONS

The myriad environmental and natural resource provisions contained in existing state constitutions provides one set of potential models for new constitutional provisions. Drafters of future constitutions also might find valuable models in the provisions of several international agreements, including the Stockholm Declaration of the United Nations Conference on the Human Environment (signed by the United States and scores of other countries in 1972 at the first major United Nations conferences on the environment),[32] the World Charter for Nature (adopted by the United Nations General Assembly in 1982 over the sole dissent of the United States),[33] and the Rio Declaration on Environment and Development (which the United States and dozens of other nations signed during the 1992 "Earth Summit" in Rio de Janeiro).[34]

General Environmental Policy Provisions

1. Current Provisions

The most common environmental provisions in state constitutions seek in broad terms to promote general environmental protection. While over a third of all state constitutions now contain such provisions,[35] the provisions vary tremendously in their language and purpose. Georgia's Constitution, for example, contains merely an Authorization Provision, empowering the legislature to address environmental issues.[36] Four states go a step further and include Value Declarations announcing the importance of environmental protection.[37] Most of the state constitutions go further and at least purport to require environmental protection either through Policy Directives[38] or Environmental Rights and Duties.[39]

Most of these constitutional provisions refer broadly and vaguely to the need for or right to a "clean" or "healthful" environment or "scenic beauty."[40] A minority of the provisions refer to somewhat more specific environmental goals or mandates, such as clean air and water or noise abatement.[41] As discussed later, many of the provisions also provide for protection or conservation of wildlife and natural resources. None of the provisions, however, provide any guidance on what they mean by terms such as "clean" or "healthful."

Only a few constitutional provisions explicitly recognize and address the potential trade-offs between environmental protection and other societal goals. The New Mexico Constitution, for example, provides that the "legislature shall provide for control of pollution and control of despoilment of the air, water, and other natural resources of the state, consistent with the use and development of these resources for the maximum benefit of the people."[42] Louisiana's constitution mandates a "healthful" environment but only "insofar as possible and consistent with the health, safety, and welfare of the people."[43] In including this proviso, the delegates to Louisiana's 1974 Constitutional Convention intended "to strike a balance, or find a happy medium between the environmentalist on one side, and the agri-industrial interest on the other side" and hoped that they had found a policy statement that "strikes a balance, that is not extreme one way or the other."[44] Although the proviso is exceptionally vague on how this balance is to be struck, Louisiana courts have concluded that the proviso embodies a "rule of reasonableness" that "requires a balancing process in which environmental costs and benefits must be given full and careful consideration along with economic, social and other factors."[45]

Most environmental provisions are silent regarding how courts should deal with such trade-offs. A few constitutions recognize other public policy goals, implicitly suggesting that there should be a trade-off without informing either the state or its courts of how to perform the trade-offs.[46] But most environmental provisions ignore the trade-offs entirely, leaving state decision makers with no guidance whatsoever.

As discussed, virtually all the constitutional provisions are similarly silent regarding enforcement options, presumably deferring questions of standing and causes of action to the judiciary. Of those constitutions that contain Policy Directives, only New York's constitution addresses enforcement, authorizing private citizens and nonprofit organizations to sue if the state supreme court consents and the state attorney general has been notified.[47] Of the constitutions that create Environmental Rights, only Hawaii's and Illinois' constitutions explicitly authorize private citizens to enforce their rights in court, subject to "reasonable limitations" imposed by law.[48] The remaining constitutions are silent on whether and when private citizens can enforce their constitutionally vested environmental rights.

2. Judicial Reactions

Not surprisingly, state courts have held that Authorization Provisions and Value Declarations do not require either the state or private parties to take any particular action.[49] However, most state courts also have found ways to avoid taking any actions under Policy Directives, Environmental Rights, and Environmental Duties.

The legal grounds that courts have given for avoiding private enforcement efforts are legion. Where state constitutions are silent on enforcement, courts sometimes have concluded that there is no private or public cause of action.[50] Even when an environmental provision explicitly authorizes citizen enforcement, courts have dismissed lawsuits based on lack of standing or ripeness.[51]

One of the most common grounds for dismissing lawsuits has been that the provisions are not "self-executing."[52] If constitutional provisions are not self-executing, courts must wait for the legislature to pass implementing statutes. In deciding whether a constitutional provision is self-executing, courts not only look at the language and purpose of a provision but also ask whether the provision sets out a sufficient rule by which to decide cases without legislative guidance.[53] For the reasons discussed earlier, most courts have found that the general and vague language of environmental provisions provide inadequate guidance on how to resolve concrete disputes.

Even where courts have agreed to hear private enforcement actions and concluded that the constitutional provisions are self-executing, the courts typically have been very deferential to the legislature and executive branches. Although the Michigan Supreme Court has held that the state's constitution requires the legislature to provide environmental protection, the court also has concluded that the legislature "is not . . . under a duty to make specific inclusion of environmental protection provisions in every piece of relevant legislation."[54] So long as the legislature has paid some attention to the environment, Michigan courts do not appear eager to determine the exact level and type of protection constitutionally required. Despite entertaining multiple enforcement actions, the New York and Pennsylvania courts also have never used their states' environmental provisions to constrain state or private actions alleged to be harmful to the environment.[55]

The courts' historic reticence to actively wield the broad environmental provisions found in many state constitutions is understandable. As discussed, the environmental provisions typically fail to provide the courts with even the most fundamental policy guidance—for example, how the adequacy of environmental protection should be judged, how policy trade-offs should be addressed, and how scientific uncertainties should be resolved. Given that environmental law is still very much in its infancy, courts are inclined to defer to legislative and administrative judgments. Although courts have mechanisms for evaluating complex scientific issues and creating new administrative structures, courts also are reluctant to become the ultimate arbiter of environmental policy. Courts might be willing to undertake the risk and burden of "constitutionalizing" the environment if current levels of environmental protection were clearly deficient, but the existence of multiple national and state statutes and the varied regulatory activities of national and state environmental agencies normally undercut any sense of urgency.

These concerns have not stopped all courts from using the constitutional provisions to achieve greater environmental protection. Louisiana courts have taken a more active stance while avoiding the concerns just discussed by focusing on the process by which the state makes environmental decisions rather than on the substance of those decisions. The Louisiana courts in essence have converted the state's Policy Directive into a process requirement. In a lawsuit challenging the approval of a proposed hazardous waste facility by the Louisiana Environmental Control Commission, for example, the Louisiana Supreme Court held that the Commission must "make basic findings supported by evidence and ultimate findings . . . and it must articulate a rational connection between the facts found and the order issued."[56]

The Montana Supreme Court treats Environmental Rights and Environmental Duties in the Montana Constitution much like other, more traditional constitutional rights.[57] For the first quarter century after voter approval of the 1972 Montana Constitution, the Montana courts, like courts in most other states, found legal reasons to avoid employing the environmental provisions. In 1999, however, the Montana Supreme Court held that state legislation exempting specified mining operations from state laws prohibiting degradation in water quality was unconstitutional.[58] Finding that a "clean and healthful environment" is a "fundamental" right under the Montana Constitution,[59] the court concluded that "any statute or rule which implicates that right must be strictly scrutinized and can only survive scrutiny if the State establishes a compelling state interest and that its action is closely tailored to effectuate that interest and is the least onerous path that can be taken to achieve the State's objective."[60] Two years later, the court held that the constitution's environmental "guarantees" also directly constrain private actions that threaten a clean and healthful environment. In a contract dispute between two private parties, the court concluded that it would be unlawful to drill a well on private property "in the face of substantial evidence that doing so may cause significant degradation of uncontaminated aquifers and pose serious public health risks."[61]

The Montana Supreme Court's decisions, unfortunately, may open the door to an array of other, more troubling cases. Future cases, for example, may challenge the constitutionality of existing environmental quality standards, forcing the courts to determine the appropriate standard for pollutants with no safety threshold. Other cases may challenge the state's failure to address some environmental issues at all, presenting the courts with the daunting task of designing and implementing a regulatory system from scratch. In one recent lawsuit, a number of asbestos victims sought damages from the state for failing to regulate asbestos.[62] With some basis in existing constitutional case law, plaintiffs claimed that, by not ensuring them a "clean and healthful environment," the state committed a constitutional tort entitling them to damages for their asbestos injuries.

3. Future Directions

Given the importance of environmental protection to the citizens of most states, Value Declarations that articulate the public's interest in a healthful environment are easily justified. The justification for including Policy Directives, Environmental Rights, or Environmental Duties in state constitutions, however, is open to more question. Some proponents have argued that, absent such provisions, legislatures are likely to slight the public's interest in environmental protection in the face of strong business opposition. Empirical studies of environmental policy-making in the United States, however, provide no basis for concluding that biases in the legislative process are significant enough to justify having courts rather than the legislature make general environmental policy. Rather than being "captured" by industry, most legislatures appear to be responsive to both the need for environmental protection and public calls for environmental regulation.[63]

Proponents of stronger environmental provisions also have argued that a "healthful environment" is a fundamental right that should not be open to democratic derogation. No consensus currently exists, however, on how to address the trade-offs and scientific uncertainty involved in environmental policy-making. Given that trade-offs between the environment and other important policy goals will continue to evade any simple solution, legislatures rather than courts may be the better institutions to grapple with the issues at the current moment.

No matter what form general environmental provisions take, the provisions should furnish greater guidance on the principal issues underlying environmental disputes—trade-offs and scientific uncertainty. References to "clean" and "healthful" environments sound good; they provide effective sound bites. But they do not supply any of the branches of government with useful information for addressing concrete policy matters. As a result, all legislators and regulators can claim that they are acting in compliance with the constitution, and courts feel rudderless undertaking meaningful judicial review.

In drafting more useful environmental provisions, future state constitutions might find guidance in emerging international principles of environmental protection. These principles are still quite general, but they do a better job than existing state constitutions of addressing the key questions. For example, the Rio Declaration explicitly urges a "precautionary approach" to scientific uncertainty: "Where there are threats of serious or irreversible damage, lack of full scientific certainty shall not be used as a reason for postponing cost-effective measures to prevent environmental degradation."[64] Even though this provision leaves open many questions (e.g., how should uncertainty be weighed in making decisions?), it supplies two significant policy guidelines: uncertainty should not be used as a justification for postponing decisions, and protective efforts need not be taken if they are not cost-effective.

International environmental agreements set out a number of important principles of relevance to environmental policy. Many are of potential constitutional significance.

- *The Precautionary Principle:* International agreements vary in their framing of the Precautionary Principle. The Rio Declaration includes one of the weaker versions. At the stronger end of the spectrum, the World Charter for Nature provides that "where potential adverse effects are not fully understood, [activities that present a significant risk] should not proceed."[65] All versions of the Precautionary Principle address the problem of uncertainty and emphasize that uncertainty should not be used as an excuse for failing to take any action.
- *The Principle of Prevention:* This principle, which is closely related to the Precautionary Principle, states that governments should prevent pollution or other environmentally harmful activities *before* they cause harm.[66]
- *Balance:* Most international environmental agreements recognize that environmental protection often involves trade-offs with economic development and other interests. Like state constitutions, however, few provide useful guidance on how the trade-offs should be resolved.
- *The Polluter Pays Principle:* Several international environmental agreements emphasize the importance of ensuring that polluters bear the cost of any harm that they cause. The Rio Declaration, for example, states that governments "should endeavor to promote the internalization of environmental costs and the use of economic instruments, taking into account the approach that the polluter should, in principle, bear the cost of pollution."[67]

  The Florida Constitution has adopted the Polluter Pays Principle in one narrow context. In 1996, Florida voters approved a constitutional amendment to protect the Florida Everglades from water pollution.

The amendment specifically provides that anyone who causes water pollution in the area "shall be primarily responsible for paying the costs of the abatement of that pollution."[68]

- *Environmental Assessment:* International environmental documents also call on states to undertake "environmental impact assessments" for any activity that is "likely to have a significant adverse impact on the environment."[69] In the United States, about a third of the states have environmental quality acts that require such assessments for governmental actions.[70]

- *Information Dissemination and Public Participation:* Another emerging principle of international environmental law is that all citizens should have ready access to "information concerning the environment" in their community, "including information on hazardous materials and activities in their communities," and an "opportunity to participate in decision-making processes."[71]

- *Duty Not to Discriminate Regarding Environmental Harms:* International environmental instruments also emphasize that states should "discourage or prevent the relocation and transfer" of harmful substances or activities from one jurisdiction to another.[72] The environmental justice movement in the United States has similarly objected to environmental protection efforts that simply relocate risks from wealthier to poorer communities.[73]

Resource Management

Approximately a third of the current state constitutions address natural resource policy. Most of these provisions address specific resources, with water (11 constitutions), forestry (6), and fish and wildlife (6) most commonly covered.

1. General Provisions
Although few constitutions address natural resources as a class, a strong case again can be made for Value Declarations that emphasize the importance of conserving and not wasting a state's natural resources. Several state constitutions include Value Declarations emphasizing the importance of conservation (although sometimes balanced with development). Michigan's constitution, for example, declares that "conservation and development of the natural resources of the state" are of "paramount public concern."[74]

Given the importance of resource supplies to future generations, a strong case also can be made for Policy Directives, Environmental Rights, and Environmental Duties promoting resource conservation. Few people would disagree that each generation owes an ethical obligation to conserve resources for future generations, but people generally act in a more self-interested fashion than philosophers would argue is ethical, and political institutions reinforce this bias. Because politicians have only limited terms in office and future generations cannot vote, the political process tends to favor demands for current consumption over conflicting interests of future generations.

The difficult issue is how to express this obligation in constitutional terms. Most natural resource provisions tend to be quite vague in their directives. The Ohio Constitution thus calls expansively for the "conservation of the natural resources of the state,"[75] without providing any guidance on what is meant by conservation. Several other state constitutions implicitly call for a balancing of "conservation" and economic development without explaining how the two goals should be balanced.[76] The Montana Constitution proscribes the "unreasonable depletion and degradation of natural resources."[77]

Several constitutions go a step further and explicitly call for natural resource management to take into account the interests of future generations. The Hawaii Constitution thus requires the state to "conserve and protect" Hawaii's natural resources "for the benefit of present and future generations."[78] Although still quite general, these provisions at least emphasize the key ethical precept making natural resource policy of constitutional importance—the need to preserve resources for future generations. International environmental agreements make the same point. The Rio Declaration thus requires governments to safeguard natural resources "for the benefit of present and future generations."[79]

Only Alaska's constitution tries to provide more specific guidance for the management of natural resources. Under the terms of the Alaska Constitution, "Fish, forests, wildlife, grasslands, and all other replenishable resources belonging to the State shall be utilized, developed, and maintained on a sustained yield principle, subject to preferences among beneficial uses."[80] Even this standard leaves open numerous questions. Resources, for example, can be "sustained" at various stock levels. The Alaska standard, however, does not specify whether the yield of a resource should be sustained at the maximum level or some lower amount.[81] By contrast, the World Charter for Nature provides that resources should be "managed to achieve and maintain optimum sustainable productivity."[82]

No current state constitution provides specific guidance on the management of nonrenewable resources (other than general directives for the "conservation" or "reasonable depletion" of all resources). Several international environmental agreements, however, have tried to formulate standards. The Stockholm Declaration dictates that the "non-renewable resources of the earth must be employed in such a way as to guard against the danger of their future exhaustion."[83] The World Charter for Nature provides, in more expansive terms, "Non-renewable resources which are consumed as they are used shall be exploited with restraint, taking into account their abundance, the rational possibilities of converting them for consumption, and the compatibility of their exploitation with the functioning of natural systems."[84]

Taking a slightly different approach toward the conservation of natural resources, several state constitutions provide for the creation, funding, and use of "natural resources trust funds."[85] These provisions are designed to bypass the standard appropriations processes in the state and guarantee funding for natural resources conservation.[86] Michigan's constitution also creates a board to manage the trust fund.[87] These provisions suffer from several problems. First, the funds only help resource problems that can be solved through money; they do not help avoid the overuse of a resource. Second, the amount guaranteed is not calibrated to relative fiscal needs and thus is likely to be either not enough or too much. Finally, these and similar funding provisions can lead to the balkanization of the state's budget and an inability to weigh alternative funding needs in a rational fashion.

2. Water

Although the most common resource provisions in today's state constitutions address water resources, there is at best a weak case for including water-specific provisions in future state constitutions. The existing provisions are largely historical. Most date back to efforts in the late nineteenth century to ensure use of the "prior appropriation" doctrine, rather than the "riparian" doctrine, in the western United States.[88] A number of western state constitutions thus guarantee the right to appropriate water.[89]

The goal of firmly implanting the prior appropriation doctrine also explains why several western constitutions provide that water belongs to the state or is reserved for the public.[90] As the Colorado Supreme Court has explained, these "public ownership" provisions originally were meant to reject any claims that real property owners enjoyed riparian rights as part of their private land rights.[91] Today, however, these provisions have taken on new meaning and importance in many states. The Montana Supreme Court, for example, has used the public ownership provision in its constitution to meet the public's growing demand for recreational use of Montana's rivers and streams. In 1984, the court held that the public ownership provision authorizes public access and use of all state waterways even over the objection of private property owners.[92]

A number of western state constitutions also encourage water conservation. These constitutions typically permit appropriations only for "beneficial uses."[93] The California Constitution explicitly bans "waste" and permits people to extract only "such water as shall be reasonably required for the beneficial use to be served."[94] Although these provisions can be extremely valuable in ensuring efficient water use,[95] there is little reason to single out water for special constitutional protection rather than barring waste of all natural resources.

3. Fish and Wildlife

Only a few state constitutions include provisions designed to protect fish and wildlife. These constitutions, moreover, eschew directives and instead create independent expert commissions, insulated to some degree from direct political influence, to oversee fish and game policy.[96] As public concern for wildlife has increased, voters also have amended some constitutions to include hyper-legislation such as California's ban on gill-netting and Colorado's ban on various forms of traps and poisons.[97] Again, there seems little justification for addressing fish and wildlife separately from other important resources.

4. Forestry

Although there also seems little reason to address forestry separately from other renewable resources, half a dozen state constitutions do. Several constitutions provide for the management of forests on "forestry principles"[98] (implying that the state should use scientific tools and principles for managing their forests) or for the prevention or suppression of fires.[99] Several constitutions also establish state foresters or forestry commissions, seeking to affect forestry practices through institutional means.[100]

5. Other Specific Provisions

A smattering of other resource provisions can be found in state constitutions. All seem too specific for constitutional inclusion. Montana thus requires the reclamation of all lands "disturbed by the taking of natural resources."[101] Louisiana requires the conservation of wetlands and the reclamation of oilfield sites.[102]

Protection and Access to Navigation

The earliest "environmental" provisions in state constitutions dealt with public access to tidelands and navigable state waterways. Virtually all of these provisions remain in the state constitutions today. Half a dozen state constitutions, for example, declare that submerged and tidal lands are state public domain.[103] Although these provisions do not explicitly provide for public access, the provisions often emphasize that the lands are held by the state in "trust" for the public, implicitly indicating that the public should have access.[104] Under the public trust doctrine, courts long have held that the public has a right of access to such lands for fishing, boating, or recreational uses.[105]

Approximately the same number of constitutions go a step further and explicitly provide for a public right of navigation, free public access to navigable waterways, or both. The earliest of these provisions, found in several Midwestern and Southern states, guarantee that some or all of the state's navigable waters shall be "public" or "common highways," free to citizens of both the state and the nation without any tax, duty, or toll.[106] California and Alaska prohibit anyone from excluding access to navigable waters.[107]

The original constitutional justification for these provisions—the importance of waterways to commerce—is much weaker today. A new argument, however, can be made that public access to common property, such as waterways and beaches, is critical to both our democratic system and private property. An effective and healthy democracy arguably depends to a degree on the existence of commons where all citizenry can mingle and interact both with each other and with their shared physical environment.[108] Commons provide an opportunity for people to understand each other and learn how to socialize and live together. Commons also contribute to shared values. In addition, commons can help reduce the tensions that otherwise grow out of a highly uneven distribution of private property. The nonlanded majority of today's America may accept the nation's private property system in part because they have free access to roads, parks, beaches, and other public "commons."

Public Land Preservation

These "commons" justifications for public access suggest that the traditional navigation provisions are too narrow in their focus on navigation and in their application only to navigable waterways and foreshore. The "commons" arguments suggest that the public should have access to navigable waterways and foreshore, not just for navigation, but for a broader set of purposes including recreation, aesthetics, and quiet contemplation. "Commons" rationales also argue for extending public access and use to a broader set of lands. Although navigable waterways and foreshore remain important commons, public parks, forests, undeveloped foothills, and other open spaces provide equally important commons today.

A number of state constitutions have responded to the public demand for broader "commons." Historically, one of the most important forms of public recreation was fishing. Not surprisingly, therefore, half a dozen constitutions provide for some common public right to fish, often linked with a public right of access to rivers or other fishery resources.[109] California's constitution, for example, guarantees a public right to "fish upon and from the public lands of the State and in the waters thereof," although the legislature is authorized to regulate fishing seasons and conditions.[110]

In response to increasing public demands for recreation and open space, moreover, a growing number of state constitutions establish and preserve various forms of state land reserves that go beyond the historic preoccupation with tidelands and navigable waterways. In the earliest of these provisions, New York constitutionally created the Adirondack forest preserve in 1895.[111] Within the last two decades, environmental advocates have borrowed and expanded on this idea to constitutionally create the "Alabama Forever Wild Land Trust,"[112] the "Great Outdoors Colorado Program,"[113] and the North Carolina "State Nature and Historic Preserve."[114] Amendments to several other state constitutions also have dedicated funds or otherwise authorized the state to acquire and preserve land of particular aesthetic, recreational, or historic value.[115]

The purposes of these provisions include not only public access to shared "commons" but also preservation of environmentally or historically important lands. Here again, an argument can be made that society has an obligation to future generations to preserve those lands that are important to preserving a healthy functioning environment or to the historical heritage of the region. The Alabama Constitution explicitly notes that an underlying goal of the Alabama Forever Wild Land Trust is to protect lands of "unique ecological, biological and geological importance" in trust for "succeeding generations."[116]

Provisions creating "commons trusts" must address several issues. First, what lands should be included in the trust? Given the difficulties of specifying which lands now or in the future will be of recreational, ecological, or historical importance to the public, state constitutions should generally leave specification of some lands to legislative discretion. State constitutions might explicitly include all lands covered by the traditional public trust doctrine—that is, tidelands and navigable foreshore—because of their historic and continuing importance as public "commons." For other lands, however, state constitutions should be wary of the time boundedness of current presumptions regarding what lands to include. Rather than specifying particular "commons," constitutions more effectively could specify the criteria by which legislatures should determine what lands to acquire and include: for example, the value of the land for common recreational, social, or aesthetic use by a broad segment of the general public, the land's ecological importance, or the land's historic significance to the state and its citizens.

Second, what types of rights should the public enjoy in the protected lands? Existing constitutional trusts focus solely on acquiring and preserving lands and are silent on the public's rights to use the lands (although public access might be implied). The value of common use of the lands, however, is one of the bases for creating new constitutional trusts. Under a "commons" rationale, state constitutions therefore should provide for open public use of the land, except to the degree that the legislature determines that use must be regulated either to protect the ecological or historical value of the land or to maximize common benefits by restricting overcrowding or inconsistent uses.

Finally, under what, if any, circumstances should lands be removable from a constitutional trust and its protections? The California Constitution's current restrictions on tideland sales illustrate the dangers of placing inflexible limits on particular lands. Fearful of legislative misadventures, and responsive to the nineteenth century interest in protecting navigation, the 1879 California Constitution strictly prohibited sales of tidelands within two miles of any incorporated area and bordering on "any harbor, estuary, bay, or inlet used for the purposes of navigation." The rigidity of this prohibition has forced courts over the last century to develop a number of exceptions to the restriction to account for the need to alienate specific tidelands.[117] As the public interest has evolved to focus on other nonnavigable uses of tidelands, moreover, the constitutional protection, with its narrow focus on premium navigation sites, has grown increasingly misaligned with the public's actual interests.

Rather than imposing flat restrictions on alienation, process safeguards often may be more sensible. Requirements that land removals be approved by two separate legislative sessions, as the New York Constitution requires,[118] can help ensure full and deliberate consideration of the potential ramifications. Supermajoritarian requirements, as imposed by Maine and North Carolina,[119] can help protect against legislative tendencies to discount diffuse public values. Both procedural approaches permit land decisions to evolve with changing conditions, information, and needs, while still protecting against unwarranted privatization or development.

CONCLUSION

State constitutions today contain a varied mishmash of environmental provisions ranging from broad policy directives to hyperlegislation on subjects such as gill netting, mining reclamation, and animal trapping. Because the constitutions seldom provide guidance on the more difficult issues underlying environmental policy, state courts often have ducked enforcement of the existing provisions, and most provisions appear to have had little impact on actual policy decisions.

Future constitutions should return to first principles and address environmental issues at a broader and more fundamental level. Framers of the constitutions should focus on at least three categories of provisions. First, state constitutions for the twenty-first century should include environmental Value Declarations. Whether the constitutions should go further and include specific directives, rights, or duties that constrain the state government's discretion on environmental issues is a more difficult question. Whether or not the environmental provisions constrain governmental discretion, however, the provisions should give greater guidance than current provisions do on such underlying issues as scientific uncertainty and the potential trade-offs between environmental protection and economic development. In developing this guidance, the drafters of future constitutional provisions may find useful models in international environmental agreements.

Second, future constitutions should provide for the conservation of natural resources. The emphasis should be on society's trust responsibility to future generations. Here again, provisions should provide greater guidance on the appropriate management of both renewable and depletable resources and may be able to use international environmental agreements as models.

Finally, state constitutions for the twenty-first century should provide for "commons trusts." State constitutions' traditional focus on access to tidelands and navigable water for commerce and fishing is outdated. Commons trusts should encompass not only these traditional trust lands, but all lands of significant recreational, aesthetic, ecological, or historical value to the general public. The purposes of the trusts also should be expanded to include recreation, historical preservation, and environmental protection. The legislature should retain discretion to determine which lands should be placed in and removed from the trust, but constitutions should include process safeguards to ensure that land is removed only after careful thought.

NOTES

1. Articles providing general overviews or analyses of these provisions include Bret Adams et al., "Environmental and Natural Resources Provisions in State Constitutions," 22 *J. Land Resources & Envtl. L.* 73 (2002); Barton H. Thompson, Jr., "Environmental Policy and State Constitutions: The Potential Role of Substantive Guidance," 27 *Rutgers L.J.* 863 (1996).

2. *See*, for example, *Concerned Citizens v. Brunswick County Taxpayers Ass'n v. Rhodes*, 404 S.E.2d 677 (N.C., 1991) (using prescriptive easement doctrine to provide beach access); *Matthews v. Bay Head Improvement Ass'n*, 471 A.2d 355 (N.J., 1984) (using public trust doctrine to provide beach access); *Gion v. City of Santa Cruz*, 465 P.2d 50 (Cal., 1970) (using dedication doctrine to provide beach access); *State ex rel. Thornton v. Hay*, 462 P.2d 671 (Ore., 1969) (using doctrine of custom to provide beach access).

3. Va. Const., art. XI, § 1.

4. Mich. Const., art. IV, § 52.

5. For a detailed analysis of California's environmental provisions, see Barton H. Thompson, Jr., *Environmental Policy and the State Constitution: The Role for Substantive Policy Guidance, in Constitutional Reform in California 473* (Bruce E. Cain and Roger G. Noll, eds. 1995).

6. N.C. Const., art. XIV, § 5.

7. Idaho Const., art. XV; N.M. Const., art. XVI, § 2.

8. Ill. Const., art. XI, § 1.

9. *Glisson v. City of Marion*, 720 N.E.2d 1034, 1041–45 (Ill., 1999). In *Glisson*, the construction of a water supply dam by the city of Marion, Illinois, allegedly threatened to destroy the habitat of two species listed by the State of Illinois as endangered or threatened—the least brook lamprey and the Indiana crayfish.

10. Ga. Const., art. III, § VI, par. II(a)(1).

11. *See,* for example, *Hayes v. Howell,* 308 S.E.2d 170, 176 (Ga., 1983) (concluding that environmental legislation would be a legitimate exercise of state police power even absent the Georgia Authorization provision).

12. R.I. Const., art. I, § 16.

13. Va. Const., art. XI, § 1.

14. For an example involving the Montana legislature, see Barton H. Thompson, Jr., "Constitutionalizing the Environment: The History and Future of Montana's Environmental Provisions," 64 *Mont. L. Rev.* 157, 182 (2003).

15. *See,* for example, Maine Const., art. IX, § 23 (supermajority); N.Y. Const., art. XIV, § 4 (separate legislative sessions).

16. R.I. Const., art. I, § 16.

17. Cal. Const., art. IV, § 20.

18. Ibid. Many of the fish and game commissions created in state constitutions are modeled after a "Model Fish and Game Commission" developed by the International Association of Game, Fish, and Conservation Commissioners in 1934 to give fish and game decisions to expert entities, partially shielded from direct interest group pressures. See Arguments in Favor of Assembly Constitutional Amendment No. 45, in *Proposed Amendments to Constitution, Propositions, and Proposed Laws* 19 (Cal. Sec. of State, 1940).

19. Mich. Const., art. IV, § 52.

20. Cal. Const., art. I, § 25.

21. *See,* for example, Advisory Op. to the Gov'r, 706 So. 2d 278, 281 (Fla., 1997); Petition of Highway US-24, 220 N.W.2d 416 (Mich., 1974); *Commonwealth v. National Gettysburg Battlefield Tower,* 311 A.2d 588 (Pa., 1973).

22. *See,* for example, *Stop H-3 Ass'n v. Lewis,* 538 F. Supp. 149 (D. Haw., 1982), modified on other grounds, 740 F.2d 1442 (9th Cir., 1984), cert. denied, 471 U.S. 1108 (1985); *Enos v. Sec'y Envt'l Affairs,* 731 N.E.2d 525, 532, n. 7 (Mass., 2000); *City of Elgin v. County of Cook,* 660 N.E.2d 875, 891 (Ill., 1995); *State v. General Dev. Corp.,* 448 So. 2d 1074 (Fla. Dist. Ct. app., 1984), aff'd, 469 So. 2d 1381 (Fla., 1985).

23. Wisc. Const., art. IX, § 1.

24. Colo. Const., art. XVI, § 6.

25. Mass. Const., amend. XLIX.

26. Ill. Const., art. XI, § 1.

27. Haw. Const., art. XI, § 9; Ill. Const., art. XI, § 2.

28. N.Y. Const., art. XIV, § 5.

29. For a general discussion of citizen suit provisions in national environmental laws, see Barton H. Thompson, Jr., "The Continuing Innovation of Citizen Enforcement," 2000 *U. Ill. L. Rev.* 185.

30. Haw. Const., art. XI, § 9.

31. Mich. Const., art. IV, § 52.

32. Stockholm Declaration of the United Nations Conference on the Human Environment, 11 I.L.M. 1416 (1972).

33. World Charter for Nature, U.N.G.A. RES 37/7, 22 I.L.M. 455 (1983).

34. Rio Declaration on Environment and Development, 31 L.L.M. 874 (1992).

35. *See* Thompson, supra note 14, at 160.

36. Ga. Const., art. III, § VI, par. II(a)(1) (the "General Assembly shall have the power to provide by law for . . . [r]estrictions upon land use in order to protect and preserve the natural resources, environment, and vital areas of this state").

37. As noted earlier, for example, the Virginia Constitution declares that it is the "policy of the Commonwealth to conserve, develop, and utilize its natural resources" and to "protect its atmosphere, lands, and waters from pollution." Va. Const., art. XI, § 1.

38. New York's constitution, for example, provides that the legislature "shall include adequate provision for the abatement of air and water pollution and of excessive and unnecessary noise, the protection of agricultural lands, wetlands and shorelines, and the development and regulation of water resources." N.Y. Const., art. XIV, § 4. *See also* Fla. Const., art. II, § 78; La. Const., art. IX, § 1; Mich. Const., art. IV, § 52; S.C. Const., art. XII, § 1.

39. Typical is the Hawaii Constitution, which declares that "Each person has the right to a clean and healthful environment." Haw. Const., art. XI, § 9. *See also* Ill. Const., art. XI, §§ 1–2; Mont. Const., art. II, § 3; Pa. Const., art. I, § 27.

40. *See,* for example, Ill. Const., art. XI, §§ 1–2 ("healthful environment").

41. *See,* for example, N.Y. Const., art. XIV, § 4 ("abatement of air and water pollution and of excessive and unnecessary noise").

42. N.M. Const., art. XX, § 21.

43. La. Const., art. IX, § 1.

44. Charles S. McCowan, Jr., "Evolution of Environmental Law in Louisiana," 52 *La. L. Rev.* 907, 912 (1992) (quoting Records of the Louisiana Constitutional Convention of 1973, Convention Transcripts, 103rd Day's Proceedings, Dec. 18, 1973, vol. IX, pp. 2911–12).

45. *Save Ourselves, Inc. v. Louisiana Envtl. Control Comm'n,* 452 So. 2d 1152, 1157 (La., 1984).

46. Hawaii's constitution, for example, instructs the state not only to protect the environment but also to "promote the development and utilization" of the state's resources "in a manner consistent with their conservation and in furtherance of the self-sufficiency of the State."

47. N.Y. Const., art. XIV, § 5.

48. Haw. Const., art. XI, § 9; Ill. Const art. XI, § 2.

49. *See*, for example, *Robb v. Shockoe Slip Found.*, 324 S.E.2d 674, 676 (Va., 1985).

50. *See*, for example, *State v. Gen. Dev. Corp.*, 448 So. 2d 1074, 1080 (Fla. Dist. Ct. App., 1984), aff'd 469 So. 2d 1381 (Fla., 1985) (individual state attorney did not have authority under constitutional provision to challenge creation and modification of artificial waterways).

51. *See*, for example, *Enos v. Sec'y Envt'l Affairs*, 731 N.E.2d 525, 532, n. 7 (Mass., 2000) (constitutional provision does not provide separate standing); *Lockman v. Secretary of State*, 684 A.2d 415, 417, 420 (Me., 1996) (dispute not yet ripe for judicial review); *City of Elgin v. County of Cook*, 660 N.E.2d 875, 891 (Ill., 1995) (standing lacking to bring suit under environmental provision); *Parsons v. Walker*, 328 N.E.2d 920, 924–25 (Ill. App. Ct., 1975) (lawsuit dismissed as premature).

52. *See*, for example, Advisory Op. to the Gov'r, 706 So. 2d 278, 281 (Fla., 1997) (environmental amendment to Florida constitution is not self-executing); *County of Delta v. Michigan Dept. of Nat. Resources*, 325 N.W.2d 455 (Mich. Ct. App., 1982); Petition of Highway US-24, 220 N.W.2d 416 (Mich., 1974).

53. *See*, for example, Advisory Op. to the Gov'r, 706 So. 2d 278, 281 (Fla., 1997), citing *Gray v. Bryant*, 125 So. 2d 846 (Fla., 1960).

54. *State Highway Comm'n v. Vanderkloot*, 220 N.W.2d 416, 426 (Mich., 1974).

55. *See* Adams et al., supra note, at 182–83 (discussing the New York case law and concluding that the "New York courts have been reluctant to apply article XIV, section 4 in a manner that would limit State action"). The Pennsylvania courts were the first to hold an environmental provision to be self-executing, but have established a standard for invalidating state actions that is exceptionally hard to meet. Unless the plaintiff can show that the state failed to make a "reasonable effort to reduce the environmental incursion to a minimum" or that the environmental harm "clearly outweighs" the benefits of the challenged action, the state wins. *See Commonwealth v. National Gettysburg Battlefield Tower*, 302 A.2d 886 (Pa. Commw. Ct., 1973), aff'd, 311 A.2d 588 (Pa., 1973); *Payne v. Kassab*, 312 A.2d 86 (Pa. Commw. Ct., 1973).

56. *Save Ourselves, Inc. v. Louisiana Envtl. Control Comm'n*, 452 So. 2d 1152, 1159 (La., 1984). *See also* Matter of American Waste & Pollution Control Co., 642 So. 2d 1258 (La., 1994) (rejecting a decision by the Louisiana Department of Environmental Quality since the Secretary of the DEQ "did not list his basic findings or his ultimate findings, nor did he articulate a rational connection between the factual findings and his order"); Matter of Rubicon, Inc., 670 So. 2d 475 (La., 1996) (failure to provide sufficient analysis).

57. For a lengthier overview and discussion of the Montana Supreme Court's treatment of its state's environmental provisions, *see* Thompson, supra note 14.

58. *Montana Envtl. Info. Ctr. v. Department of Envtl. Quality*, 988 P.2d 1236 (Mt., 1999).

59. The "right to a clean and healthful environment" leads the list of "inalienable rights" set out in the Montana Constitution's "Declaration of Rights." Mont. Const., art. II, § 3.

60. Montana Envtl. Info. Ctr., 988 P.2d at 1246.

61. *Cape-France Enterprises v. Estate of Peed,* 29 P.3d 1011, 1017 (Mont., 2001). In confirming that any violation of the constitutional guarantee would require a compelling state interest, the court emphasized that a compelling state interest is "at a minimum, some interest 'of the highest order and . . . not otherwise served'" and that generally the defendant must show that a violation of the guarantee is justified by "the gravest abuse, endangering a paramount government interest." Ibid. at 1016–17 (quoting *Armstrong v. State,* 989 P.2d 364, 375, n. 6 (Mt., 1999)).

62. *Orr v. State of Montana,* No. BDV-201-423. In August 2002, the trial court dismissed plaintiffs' claims as not stating a cause of action, but the case is currently on appeal.

63. For a discussion of the empirical evidence, *see* Thompson, supra note 1, at 892–93; Evan J. Ringquist, Environmental Protection at the State Level: Politics and Progress in Controlling Pollution (1993). Ringquist, however, did find that "mining strength," as measured by the value of mining output as a percentage of gross state product, was correlated with weaker water quality regulation. Ibid. at 161–65.

64. Rio Declaration, supra note 34, principle 15.

65. World Charter, supra note 33, principle 11.

66. *See,* for example, Stockholm Declaration, supra note 32, principle 6.

67. Rio Declaration, supra note 34, principle 16.

68. Fla. Const., art. II, § 7(b).

69. Rio Declaration, supra note 34, principle 17.

70. *See* Daniel Mandelker, NEPA Law and Litigation, ch. 12 (2d ed., 1994).

71. Rio Declaration, supra note 34, principle 10.

72. Ibid., principle 14.

73. For an expansive review of environmental justice issues, *see* Clifford Rechschaffen and Eileen Gauna, *Environmental Justice: Law, Policy, and Regulation* (2002).

74. Mich. Const., art. IV, § 52. *See also* R.I. Const., art. I, § 17 (legislature must provide for the "conservation" of natural resources and for "adequate resource planning for the control and regulation of the use of natural resources of the state").

75. Ohio Const., art. II, § 36. *See also* Fla. Const., art. II, § 7 (instructing the legislature to make "adequate provisions" for the "conservation and protection of natural resources"); N.C. Const., art. XIV, § 5 (policy of state is to "conserve and protect its land and waters").

76. Thus the Texas Constitution requires the "conservation and development" of the state's natural resources. Tex. Const., art. XVI, § 59. *See also* La. Const., art. IX, § 1 (requiring the legislature of the state to enact laws protecting, conserving, and replenishing natural resources "insofar as possible and consistent with the health, safety, and welfare of the people"); Va. Const., art. XI, §§ 1–2 (state policy is "to conserve, develop, and utilize its natural resources," and legislature can enact laws in support).

77. Mont. Const., art. IX, § 1(3).

78. Haw. Const., art. XI, § 1. The Pennsylvania Constitution similarly declares that the state's "public natural resources are the common property of all the people, including generations yet to come" and requires the state, as "trustee of these resources," to "conserve and maintain them for the benefits of all the people." Pa. Const., art. I, § 27.

79. Rio Declaration, supra note 34, principle 2. *See also* Stockholm Declaration, supra note 32, principle 2 ("natural resources of the earth . . . must be safeguarded for the benefit of present and future generations through careful planning or management, as appropriate").

80. Alaska Const., art. VIII, § 4.

81. The Alaska legislature has statutorily defined "sustained yield" as "the achievement and maintenance in perpetuity of a high level annual or regular periodic output of the various renewable resources of the state land consistent with multiple use." Alaska Code § 38-04-910(12).

82. World Charter for Nature, supra note 33, principle 4 ("Ecosystems and organisms, as well as the land, marine and atmospheric resources that are utilized by man, shall be managed to achieve and maintain optimum sustainable productivity, but not in such a way as to endanger the integrity of those other ecosystems or species with which they coexist."). The World Charter for Nature also provides that "[l]iving resources shall not be utilized in excess of their natural capacity of regeneration." Ibid., principle 10(a).

The Stockholm Declaration can be read also to mandate a sustained yield. Principle 3, in particular, provides that the "capacity of the earth to produce vital renewable resources must be maintained and, wherever practicable, restored or improved." Stockholm Declaration, supra note 32, principle 3.

83. Stockholm Declaration, supra note 32, principle 5. The same provision also mandates that the benefits from non-renewable resources should be "shared by all mankind." Ibid.

84. World Charter for Nature, supra note 33, principle 10(d).

85. Mich. Const., art. IX, § 35; Minn. Const., art. XI, § 14; Ore. Const., art. XV, § 4.

86. Under Michigan's constitution, the funding comes from any revenues collected by the state for the "extraction of nonrenewable resources from state owned lands." Mich. Const., art. IX, § 35. The Minnesota Constitution provides that "not less than 40 percent of the new proceeds from any state-operated lottery" must be deposited in the fund. Minn. Const., art. XI, § 14. Oregon's constitution dedicates 15 percent of lottery proceeds. Ore. Const., art. XV, § 4.

87. Mich. Const., art. IX, § 35.

88. The historic water-law doctrine in the eastern United States had been the riparian doctrine, which permitted riparian property owners, but no one else, to make limited use of water from streams and rivers; diversions to distant uses were prohibited. Many western settlers believed that the riparian doctrine would stunt growth in the West where water was more limited, and they lobbied for the prior appropriation doctrine, under

which water was assigned on a first-come, first-served basis and could be diverted and moved tens or hundreds of miles to water-starved uses.

89. *See*, for example, Colo. Const., art. XVI, § 6; Idaho Const., art. XV, §§ 1–4; Neb. Const., art. 15, § 6; N.M. Const., art. XVI, § 2. Not all the appropriation provisions, however, are a century old. When Alaska adopted its constitution in 1959, it also provided that all waters, except mineral and medicinal waters reserved to the people for common use, "are subject to appropriation." Alaska Const., art. VIII, § 13. And when Montana rewrote its constitution in 1972, it continued the original guarantee of appropriation. Mont. Const., art. IX, § 3.

90. *See*, for example, Mont. Const., art. IX, § 3 (continuing earlier provision); N.M. Const., art. XVI, § 2; Wyo. Const., art. 8, § 1.

91. *People v. Emmert*, 597 P.2d 1025, 1028 (Colo., 1979).

92. *Montana Coalition for Stream Access, Inc. v. Curran*, 682 P.2d 163, 170 (Mont., 1984).

93. *See*, for example, Alaska Const., art. VIII, § 13; Colo. Const., art. XVI, § 6; Idaho Const., art. XV, § 3; Mont. Const., art. IX, § 3; Neb. Const., art. 15, § 6; N.M. Const., art. XVI, § 2. Although courts seldom invoke these provisions to limit water use, they on occasion have used them to bar waste. *See*, for example, *Wilkins v. State*, 313 N.W.2d 271 (Neb., 1981).

94. Cal. Const., art. X, § 2. The Hawaii Constitution also directs the legislature to provide for a water resources agency that will "set overall water conservation, quality and use policies." Haw. Const., art. XI, § 7.

95. California courts have actively used the state's constitutional provision to restrict water usage deemed excessive or unjustified. *See*, for example, *Imperial Irrigation Dist. v. State Water Resources Control Bd.*, 231 Cal. Rptr. 283 (Cal. Ct. App., 1986); *Joslin v. Marin Mun. Water Dist.*, 429 P.2d 889 (Cal., 1967).

96. *See*, for example, Ark. Const., amend. 35; La. Const., art. IX, § 7; Mo. Const., art. IX, § 40(a).

97. Colo. Const., art. XVIII, § 12b.

98. *See* La. Const., art. IX, § 8; Minn. Const., art. XI, § 11; Mo. Const., art. IV, § 36.

99. *See* Mo. Const., art. IV, § 36; N.M. Const., art. V, § 2.

100. *See*, for example, La. Const., art. IX, § 8.

101. Mont. Const., art. IX, § 2.

102. La. Const., art. VII, §§ 10.2, 10.6.

103. *See*, for example, Alaska Const., art. VIII, § 6 (applying to all lands "possessed or acquired by the State, and not used or intended exclusively for governmental purposes"); Fla. Const., art. X, § 11; Haw. Const., art. XII, § 4 (applying to all lands "granted to the State of Hawaii" on statehood); La. Const., art. IX, § 3; Wash. Const., art. XVII, § 1.

104. *See* Fla. Const., art. X, § 11 (land held "in trust for all the people"); Haw. Const., art. XIII, § 4 (land held "as a public trust for native Hawaiians and the general public").

105. *See* Joseph L. Sax, "The Public Trust Doctrine in Natural Resource Law: Effective Judicial Intervention," 68 *Mich. L. Rev.* 471 (1970).

106. *See* Ala. Const., art. I, § 24; Minn. Const., art. II, § 2; S.C. Const., art. 14, §§ 1, 4; Wisc. Const., art. IX, § 1.

107. Courts have cited these provisions to establish a public right to use the waterways themselves and to strike down ordinances limiting use of the waters. *See*, for example, *People ex rel. Younger v. County of El Dorado*, 157 Cal. Rptr. 815 (Cal. App., 1979) (invalidating county ordinance banning public navigation of South Fork of American River for safety and antilittering reasons); *Wernberg v. State*, 516 P.2d 1191 (Alaska, 1973) (constitution designed to ensure broadest possible use of state waters).

108. For a wonderful elaboration of this theme, *see* Carol Rose, "The Comedy of the Commons: Custom, Commerce and Inherently Public Property," 53 *U. Chi. L. Rev.* 711 (1986).

109. *See* Alaska Const., art. VIII, § 3, 15 (reserving both fish and wildlife for "common use" of the public); Cal. Const., art. I, § 25; Haw. Const., art. XI, § 6 (covering "fisheries in the sea waters of the State not included in any fish pond"); R.I. Const., art. 1, § 17 (protecting both fishery rights and "the privileges of the shore"); Va. Const., art. XI, § 3; Vt. Const., § 67.

110. Cal. Const., art. I, § 25.

111. N.Y. Const., art. XIV, § 1. Sometimes known as the "forever wild" provision, it provides that the "lands of the state, now owned or hereafter acquired, constituting the forest preserve as now fixed by law, shall be forever kept as wild forest lands." Ibid.

112. Ala. Const., amend. 543. According to the constitution, these lands are to be protected and used "for conservational, educational, recreational, or aesthetic purposes." Ibid. § 3(a).

113. Colo. Const., art. XXVII, § 1.

114. N.C. Const., art. XIV, § 5.

115. *See*, for example, Mass. Const., amend. art. 49; Mich. Const., art. IX, § 35 and art. X, § 5.

116. Ala. Const., amend. 543, § 1.

117. *See*, for example, *City of Long Beach v. Mansell*, 3 91 Cal. Rptr. 23, 38–39 (Cal., 1970); *Forestier v. Johnson*, 127 P. 156, 159 (Cal., 1912).

118. N.Y. Const., art. XIV, § 4.

119. Maine Const., art. IX, § 23; N.C. Const., art. XIV, § 5.

Bibliography

Those interested in pursuing the subject of state constitutional reform in greater depth are urged to consult *State Constitutions for the Twenty-first Century: The Politics of Constitutional Reform* and *State Constitutions for the Twenty-first Century: Drafting State Constitutions, Revisions, and Amendments*.

The following works provide more detailed analysis of topics treated in this volume.

GENERAL WORKS ON STATE CONSTITUTIONS

Abrahamson, Shirley. "Divided We Stand: State Constitutions in a More Perfect Union." 18 *Hastings Const. Law Q.* 723 (1991).

Book of the States (annual publication).

Dishman, Robert B. *State Constitutions: The Shape of the Document* (rev. ed., 1968).

Elazar, Daniel J. *American Federalism: A View from the States* (3d ed., 1984).

Elazar, Daniel J. "The Principles and Traditions Underlying American State Constitutions." 12 *Publius* 11 (1982).

Grad, Frank P. "The State Constitution: Its Function and Form for Our Time." 54 *Va. L. Rev.* 928 (1968).

Kincaid, John. "State Constitutions in the Federal System." 496 *Annals Am. Acad. Pol. & Soc. Sci.* 12 (1988).

Lutz, Donald. "The Purposes of American State Constitutions." 12 *Publius* 25 (1982).

Model State Constitution (6th rev. ed., 1968).

State Constitutional Law Issue, *Rutgers Law Journal* (annual publication).

Sturm, Albert L. "The Development of American State Constitutions." 12 *Publius* 57 (1982).

Tarr, G. Alan. *Understanding State Constitutions* (1998).

Williams, Robert F. *State Constitutional Law* (3rd ed., 1999).

CONSTITUTIONAL REFORM

Allen, Tip H., Jr., and Coleman B. Ransome Jr. *Constitutional Revision in Theory and Practice* (1962).

Benjamin, Gerald, and Henrietta N. Dullea, eds. *Decision 1997: Constitutional Change in New York* (1997).

Cain, Bruce E., and Roger G. Noll, eds. *Constitutional Reform in California: Making State Government More Effective and Responsive* (1995).

Connors, Richard J. *The Process of Constitutional Revision in New Jersey: 1940–1947* (1970).

Cornwell, Elmer E., Jr., Jay S. Goodman, and Wayne R. Swanson. *State Constitutional Conventions: The Politics of Revision in Seven States* (1975).

Dishman, Robert B. *The Revision and Amendment of State Constitutions* (1970).

Graves, W. Brooke, ed. *Major Problems in State Constitutional Revision* (1960).

Hammons, Christopher W. "State Constitutional Reform: Is It Necessary?" 64 *Alb. L. Rev.* 1327 (2001).

Sturm, Albert L. *Thirty Years of State Constitution-Making: 1938–1968* (1970).

Tarr, G. Alan. ed. *Constitutional Politics in the States* (1996).

Teaford, Jon C. *The Rise of the States* (2002).

Wheeler, John P., Jr. *Salient Issues of Constitutional Reform* (1961).

Williams, Robert F. "Is Constitutional Revision Success Worth the Popular Sovereignty Price?" 52 *Fla. L. Rev.* 249 (2000).

RIGHTS AND STATE CONSTITUTIONS

Collins, Ronald K. L. "Bills and Declarations of Rights Digest." *The American Bench* (3d ed., 1985).

"Developments in the Law—the Interpretation of State Constitutional Rights." 95 *Harv. L. Rev.* 1324 (1982).

Dowlut, Robert, and Janet A. Knoop. "State Constitutions and the Right to Keep and Bear Arms." 7 *Ok. City U. L. Rev.* 177 (1982).

Feldman, Jonathan. "Separation of Powers and Judicial Review of Positive Rights Claims: The Role of State Courts in an Era of Positive Government." 24 *Rutgers L.J.* 1057 (1993).

Friedelbaum, Stanley, ed. *Human Rights in the States* (1988).

Friesen, Jennifer. *State Constitutional Law: Litigating Individual Rights, Claims, and Defenses* (2d ed., 1996).

Latzer, Barry. *State Constitutions and Criminal Justice* (1991).

Neuborne, Burt. "State Constitutions and the Evolution of Positive Rights." 20 *Rutgers L.J.* 881 (1989).

Sachs, Barbara Faith, ed. *Fundamental Liberties and Rights: A Fifty State Index* (1980).

Tarr, G. Alan. "Church and State in the States." 64 *Wash. L. Rev.* 73 (1989).

Tarr, G. Alan. "The New Judicial Federalism in Perspective." 72 *Notre Dame L. Rev.* 1097 (1997).

Tarr, G. Alan, and Mary Cornelia Porter, eds. "Special Issue: New Directions in State Constitutional Law." 17 *Publius* 1 (1987).

Williams, Robert F. "Equality Guarantees in State Constitutional Law." 63 *Tex. L. Rev.* 1195 (1985).

VOTING, ELECTIONS, AND CONSTITUTIONAL CHANGE

Constitutional Change

Colatuono, Michael G. "The Revision of American State Constitutions: Legislative Power, Popular Sovereignty, and Constitutional Change." 75 *Calif. L. Rev.* 1473 (1987).

Cronin, Thomas E. *Direct Democracy: The Politics of Initiative, Referendum, and Recall* (1989).

Dinan, John J. "'The Earth Belongs Always to the Living Generation': The Development of State Constitutional Amendment and Revision Procedures." 62 *Rev. of Pol.* 645 (2000).

Ellis, Richard J. *Democratic Delusions: The Initiative Process in America* (2002).

Gais, Thomas, and Gerald Benjamin. "Public Discontent and the Decline of Deliberation: A Dilemma in State Constitutional Reform." 68 *Temple L. Rev.* 1291 (1985).

Gerber, Elisabeth R. *The Populist Paradox: Interest Group Influence and the Promise of Direct Legislation* (1999).

Gerber, Elisabeth R. *Stealing the Initiative: How State Government Responds to Direct Democracy* (2001).

Lutz, Donald. "Toward a Theory of Constitutional Amendment." 88 *Am. Pol. Sci. Rev.* 355 (1994).

Magelby, David. "Let the Voters Decide? An Assessment of the Initiative and Referendum Process." 66 *U. Colo. L. Rev.* 13 (1995).

May, Janice C. "Constitutional Amendment and Revision Revisited." 17 *Publius* 153 (1987).

Reed, Douglas S. "Popular Constitutionalism: Toward a Theory of State Constitutional Meanings." 30 *Rutgers L.J.* 871 (1999).

Williams, Robert F. "Are State Constitutional Conventions Things of the Past? The Increasing Role of the Constitutional Commission in State Constitutional Change." 1 *Hofstra J. Pub. Pol.* 1 (1996).

Witte, Harry L. "Rights, Revolution, and the Paradox of Constitutionalism: The Processes of Constitutional Change in Pennsylvania." 3 *Widener J. Pub. L.* 383 (1993).

Voting and Elections

Carey, John M., Richard G. Niemi, and Lynda W. Powell. *Term Limits in the State Legislature* (2000).

Jones, Matthew C. "Fraud and the Franchise: The Pennsylvania Constitution's 'Free and Equal Election' Clause as an Independent Basis for State and Local Election Challenges." 68 *Temple L. Rev.* 1473 (1995).

Keyssar, Alexander. *The Right to Vote: The Contested History of Democracy in the United States* (2000).

State and Local
Governmental Institutions

General

Advisory Commission on Intergovernmental Relations. *The Question of State Governmental Capability* (1985).

March, James G., and Johan P. Olsen. *Rediscovering Institutions* (1989).

Rossi, Jim. "Institutional Design and the Lingering Legacy of Antifederalist Separation of Powers Ideals in the States." 52 *Vand. L. Rev.* 1167 (1999).

Smentkowski, Bret. "Legal Reasoning and the Separation of Powers: A State Level Analysis of Disputes Involving Federal Funds Appropriations." 16 *Law and Policy* 395 (1994).

Legislative Branch

Catalano, Michael W. "The Single Subject Rule: A Check on Anti-majoritarian Logrolling." 3 *Emerging Issues in State Con. Law* 77 (1990).

Citizens Conference on State Legislatures, *The Sometimes Governments: A Critical Study of the Fifty American State Legislatures* (1971).

Devlin, John. "Toward a State Constitutional Analysis of Allocation of Powers: Legislators and Legislative Appointees Performing Administrative Functions." 66 *Temple L. Rev.* 1205 (1993).

Dragich, Martha J. "State Constitutional Restrictions on Legislative Procedure: Rethinking the Analysis of Original Purpose, Single Subject and Clear Title Requirement." 38 *Harv. J. on Legis.* 103 (2001).

Huefner, Steven F. "The Neglected Value of the Legislative Privilege in State Legislatures." 45 *W. & M. L. Rev.* 221 (2003).

Linde, Hans J. "Due Process of Law Making." 55 *Neb. L. Rev.* 197 (1976).

Marritz, Donald. "Making Equality Matter (again): The Prohibition Against Special Laws in the Pennsylvania Constitution." 3 *Widener J. Pub. L.* 161 (1993).

Rosenthal, Alan, Burdett A. Loomis, John R. Hibbing, and Karl T. Kurtz. *Republic on Trial* (2003).

Sibley, Joel H., ed. *Encyclopedia of the American Legislative Process* (3 vols., 1994).

Williams, Robert F. "State Constitutional Limits on Legislative Procedure: Legislative Compliance and Judicial Enforcement." 48 *U. Pitt. L. Rev.* 797 (1987).

Executive Branch

Beyle, Thad L. "The Governors," in *Politics in the American States* (ed. Virginia Gray and Russell Hanson, 8th ed., 2003).

Chi, Keon S. "State Executive Branch Reorganization: Options for the Future." 1 *State Trends Forecasts* 1 (1992).

Garnett, James L. *Reorganizing State Government: The Executive Branch* (1980).

Sabato, Larry. *Goodbye to Good-Time Charlie: The American Governorship Transformed* (2nd ed., 1983).

Judicial Branch

American Bar Association, Commission on Standards of Judicial Administration. *Standards Relating to Court Organization* (1974).

American Bar Association. "Report of the Commission on the Twenty-first Century Judiciary," *Justice in Jeopardy* (2003).

Baar, Carl, and Thomas Henderson. "Alternative Models for the Organization of State-Court Systems," in *The Analysis of Judicial Reform* (ed. Philip Dubois, 1982).

Berkson, Larry Charles, and Susan B. Carbon. *Court Unification: History, Politics, and Implementation* (1978).

Douglas, James W., and Roger E. Hartley. "The Politics of Court Budgeting in the States: Is Judicial Independence Threatened by the Budgetary Process?" 63 *Public Admin. Rev.* 441 (2003).

Dubois, Philip L. *From Ballot to Bench: Judicial Elections and the Quest for Accountability* (1980).

Flango, Victor Eugene, and Nora F. Blair. "Creating an Intermediate Appellate Court: Does It Reduce the Caseload of a State's Highest Court?" *Judicature* 64–*Judicature* 74 (1980).

Goldschmidt, Joan. "Merit Selection: Current Status, Procedures, and Issues." 49 *U. Miami L. Rev.* 1 (1994).

Maute, Judith L. "Selecting Justice in State Courts: The Ballot Box or the Backroom." 41 *S. Tex. L. Rev.* 1197 (2000).

Note, "The State Advisory Opinion in Perspective." 44 *Fordham L. Rev.* 81 (1975).

Porter, Mary Cornelia, and G. Alan Tarr, eds. *State Supreme Courts: Policy-Makers in the Federal System* (1982).

Tarr, G. Alan. "Rethinking the Selection of State Supreme Court Justices." 39 *Willamette L. Rev.* 1445 (2003).

Tarr, G. Alan, and Mary Cornelia Porter. *State Supreme Courts in State and Nation* (1988).

Tobin, Robert W. *Creating the Judicial Branch: The Unfinished Revolution* (1999).

Tobin, Robert W. *Funding the State Courts: Issues and Approaches* (1996).

Yackle, Larry W. "Choosing Judges the Democratic Way." 69 *B.U. L. Rev.* 273 (1994).

Local Government

Barron, David J., Gerald F. Frug, and Rick T. Su. *Dispelling the Myth of Home Rule* (2004).

Briffault, Richard. "Our Localism." 90 *Col. L. Rev.* 1, 346 (1990).

Clark, Gordon L. *Judges and the Cities* (1988).

Frug, Gerald E. "The City as a Legal Concept." 93 *Harv. L. Rev.* 1059 (1980).

Krane, Dale, Platon N. Rigos, and Melvin B. Hill, Jr. *Home Rule in America: A Fifty State Handbook* (2000).

Libonati, Michael E. "Home Rule: An Essay on Pluralism." 64 *Wash. L. Rev.* 51 (1989).

Maass, Arthur, ed. *Area and Power* (1959).

Nicolaidis, Kalypso, and Robert Howse, eds., *The Federal Vision* (2001).

Ostrom, Vincent, Robert Bish, and Elinor Ostrom. *Local Government in the United States* (1988).

United States Advisory Commission on Intergovernmental Relations. *Local Government Autonomy* (1993).

United States Advisory Commission on Intergovernmental Relations. *Measuring Local Discretionary Authority* (1981).

United States Advisory Commission on Intergovernmental Relations. *State Laws Governing Local Government Structure and Administration* (1993).

United States Advisory Commission on Intergovernmental Relations. *The Organization Of Local Public Economies* (1987).

United States Census Bureau. *Census of Federal, State and Local Governments* (2002).

PUBLIC POLICY PROVISIONS

Taxing, Borrowing, and Spending

Briffault, Richard. *Balancing Acts: The Reality Behind State Balanced Budget Amendments* (1996).

Gelfand, M., David Gelfand, Joel A. Mintz, and Peter A. Salsich, Jr. *State and Local Taxation & Finance* (2d ed., 2000).

Hellerstein, J. R., and W. Hellerstein. *State and Local Taxation: Cases and Materials* (6th ed., 1997).

Rubin, Dale F. "Constitutional Aid Limitation Provisions and the Public Purpose Doctrine." 12 *St. Louis U. Pub. L. Rev.* 143 (1993).

Sexton, Terri A., Steven M. Sheffrin, and Arthur O'Sullivan. "Proposition 13: Unintended Effects and Feasible Reforms." 52 *Nat'l. Tax J.* 99 (1999).

Valente, W., D. McCarthy, Richard Briffault, et al. *State and Local Government Law* 536 (5th ed., 2001).

Environment

Adams, Bret, et al., "Environmental and Natural Resources Provisions in State Constitutions." 22 *J. Land Resources & Envtl. L.* 73 (2002).

Thompson, Barton H., Jr. "Constitutionalizing the Environment: The History and Future of Montana's Environmental Provisions." 64 *Mont. L. Rev.* 157 (2003).

Thompson, Barton H., Jr. "Environmental Policy and the State Constitution: The Role for Substantive Policy Guidance." 27 *Rutgers L. J.* 863 (1996).

Education

Alexander, Kern. "The Common School Ideal and the Limits of Legislative Authority: The Kentucky Case." 28 *Harv. J. on Legis.* 341 (1991).

Banks, Jonathan. "State Constitutional Analyses of Public School Finance Reform Cases: Myth or Methodology?" 45 *Vand. L. Rev.* 129 (1992).

Benson, Charles S. "Definitions of Equity in School Finance in Texas, New Jersey, and Kentucky." 28 *Harv. J. on Legis.* 401 (1991).

Bosworth, Matthew H. *Courts as Catalysts: State Supreme Courts and Public School Finance Equity* (2001).

Cochran , Kelly Thompson. "Beyond School Financing: Defining the Constitutional Right to an Adequate Education." 78 *N.C.L. Rev.* 399 (2000).

Dayton, John. "Examining the Efficacy of Judicial Involvement in Public School Finance Reform." 22 *J. Educ. Fin.* 1 (1996).

Dietz, William F. "Manageable Adequacy Standards in Education Reform Litigation." 72 *Wash. U. L.Q.* 1193, 1195 (1996).

Eastman, John C. "When Did Education Become a Civil Right? An Assessment of State Constitutional Provisions for Education 1776–1900." 42 *Am. J. Legal Hist.* 1, 3 (1998).

Enrich, Peter. "Leaving Equality Behind: New Directions in School Finance Reform." 48 *Vand. L. Rev.* 101, 185–191 (1995).

Fischel, William A. "How Serrano Caused Proposition 13." 12 *J.L. & Politics* 607 (1996).

Gordon, Daniel. "Failing the State Constitutional Education Grade: Constitutional Revision Weakening Children and Human Rights." 29 *Stetson L. Rev.* 271 (1999).

Grubb, Norton. "Breaking the Language Barrier: The Right to Bilingual Education." 9 *Harv. C.R.-C.L.L. Rev.* 52 (1974).

Heise, Michael. "State Constitutions, School Finance Litigation, and the 'Third Wave': From Equity to Adequacy." 68 *Temple. L. Rev.* 1151 (1995).

Heise, Michael. "The Effect of Constitutional Litigation on Education Finance: More Preliminary Analyses and Modeling." 21 *J. Educ. Fin.* 195 (1995).

Matzen, John Mathiason. *State Constitutional Provisions for Education* (1931).

McUsic, Molly. "The Use of Education Clauses in School Finance Reform Litigation." 28 *Harv. J. on Legis.* 307 (1991).

Mills, John, and Timothy McLendon. "Setting a New Standard for Public Education: Revision Increases the Duty of the State to Make 'Adequate Provision' for Florida Schools." 52 *Fla. L. Rev.* 329 (2000).

Mulcahy, Kevin M., Comment, "Modeling the Garden: How New Jersey Built the Most Progressive State Supreme Court and What California Can Learn." 40 *Santa Clara L. Rev.* 863 (2000).

Murray, Sheila E., William N. Evans, and Robert Schwab. "Education Finance Reform and the Distribution of Education Resources." 88 *Am. Econ. Rev.* 789 (1998).

Ratner, Gershon. "A New Legal Duty for Urban Public Schools: Effective Education in Basic Skills." 63 *Tex. L. Rev.* 777 (1985).

Ryan, James E. "The Influence of Race in School Finance Reform." 98 *Mich. L. Rev.* 432 (1999).

Swenson, Karen. "School Finance Reform Litigation: Why Are Some State Supreme Courts Activist and Others Restrained?" 63 *Alb. L. Rev.* 1147 (2000).

Thro, William E. "Judicial Analysis During the Third Wave of School Finance Litigation: The Massachusetts Decision as a Model." 35 *B.C. L. Rev.* 597 (1994).

Thro, William E. "The Role of Language of the State Education Clauses in School Finance Litigation." 79 *Ed. Law Rep.* 19 (1993).

Tractenberg, Paul L. "The Evolution and Implementation of Educational Rights Under the New Jersey Constitution of 1947." 29 *Rutgers L.J.* 827 (1998).

Tyack, David, Thomas James, and Aaron Benavot. *Law and the Shaping of Public Education, 1785–1954* (1987).

White, Frank S. *Constitutional Provisions for Differentiated Education* (1950).

Zwibelman, Julie. Note, "Broadening the Scope of School Finance and Resource Comparability Litigation." 36 *Harv. C.R.-C.L.L. Rev.* 527 (2001).

STUDIES OF SPECIFIC STATES AND THEIR CONSTITUTIONS

Alabama

Stewart, William H. *The Alabama State Constitution: A Reference Guide* (1994).

Thomson, Bailey, ed. *A Century of Controversy: Constitutional Reform in Alabama* (2002).

Alaska

McBeath, Gerald. *The Alaska State Constitution: A Reference Guide* (1997).

Arizona

Leshy, John D. *The Arizona State Constitution: A Reference Guide* (1993).

Arkansas

Goss, Kay Collett. *The Arkansas State Constitution: A Reference Guide* (1993).

California

Cain, Bruce E., and Roger G. Noll, eds. *Constitutional Reform in California: Making State Government More Effective and Responsive* (1995).

Grodin, Joseph R., Calvin R. Massey, and Richard B. Cunningham. *The California State Constitution: A Reference Guide* (1993).

Colorado

Oesterle, Dale A., and Richard B. Collins. *The Colorado State Constitution: A Reference Guide* (2002).

Delaware

Holland, Randy J. *The Delaware State Constitution: A Reference Guide* (2002).

Florida

D'Alemberte, Talbot. *The Florida State Constitution: A Reference Guide* (1991).

Georgia

Hill, Melvin B., Jr. *The Georgia State Constitution: A Reference Guide* (1994).

Hawaii

Lee, Anne Feder. *The Hawaii State Constitution: A Reference Guide* (1993).

Meller, Norman. *With an Understanding Heart: Constitution-Making in Hawaii* (1971).

Idaho

Crowley, Donald, and Florence Heffron. *The Idaho State Constitution: A Reference Guide* (1994).

Indiana

McLauchlan, William P. *The Indiana State Constitution: A Reference Guide* (1996).

Iowa

Stark, Jack. *The Iowa State Constitution: A Reference Guide* (1998).

Kansas

Heller, Francis H. *The Kansas State Constitution: A Reference Guide* (1992).

Kentucky

Ireland, Robert M. *The Kentucky State Constitution: A Reference Guide* (1999).

Louisiana

Hargrave, Lee. *The Louisiana State Constitution: A Reference Guide* (1991).

Maine

Tinkle, Marshall J. *The Maine State Constitution: A Reference Guide* (1992).

Maryland

Wheeler, John P., Jr. *Magnificent Failure: The Maryland Constitutional Convention of 1967–1968* (1972).

Michigan

Fino, Susan P. *The Michigan State Constitution: A Reference Guide* (1996).

Minnesota

Morrison, Mary Jane. *The Minnesota State Constitution: A Reference Guide* (2002).

Mississippi

Winkle, John W., III. *The Mississippi State Constitution: A Reference Guide* (1993).

Montana

Elison, Larry M., and Fritz Snyder. *The Montana State Constitution: A Reference Guide* (2001).

Nebraska

Miewald, Robert D., and Peter J. Longo. *The Nebraska State Constitution: A Reference Guide* (1993).

Nevada

Bowers, Michael W. *The Nevada State Constitution: A Reference Guide* (1993).

New Jersey

Connors, Richard J. *The Process of Constitutional Revision in New Jersey: 1940–1947* (1970).

Williams, Robert F. *The New Jersey State Constitution: A Reference Guide* (rev. ed., 1997).

New Mexico

Smith, Chuck. *The New Mexico State Constitution: A Reference Guide* (1996).

New York

Benjamin, Gerald, and Henrietta N. Dullea, eds. *Decision 1997: Constitutional Change in New York* (1997).

Galie, Peter J. *The New York State Constitution: A Reference Guide* (1991).

North Carolina

Orth, John. *The North Carolina State Constitution: A Reference Guide* (1993).

North Dakota

Leahy, James E. *The North Dakota State Constitution: A Reference Guide* (2003).

Ohio

Steinglass, Steven H., and Gino J. Scarselli. *The Ohio State Constitution: A Reference Guide* (2004).

Oklahoma

Adkison, Danny M., and Lisa McNair Palmer. *The Oklahoma State Constitution: A Reference Guide* (2001).

Pennsylvania

Gormley, Ken, ed. *The Pennsylvania Constitution: A Treatise on Rights and Liberties* (2004).

Tennessee

Laska, Lewis L. *The Tennessee State Constitution: A Reference Guide* (1990).

Texas

May, Janice. *The Texas State Constitution: A Reference Guide* (1996).

Utah

White, Jean Bickmore. *The Utah State Constitution: A Reference Guide* (1998).

Vermont

Hill, William C. *The Vermont State Constitution: A Reference Guide* (1992).

Virginia

Howard, A. E. Dick. *Commentaries On The Constitution Of Virginia* (1974).

Washington

Utter, Robert F., and Hugh D. Spitzer. *The Washington State Constitution: A Reference Guide* (2002).

West Virginia

Bastress, Robert M. *The West Virginia State Constitution: A Reference Guide* (1995).

Wisconsin

Stark, Jack. *The Wisconsin State Constitution: A Reference Guide* (1997).

Wyoming

Keiter, Robert B., and Tim Newcomb. *The Wyoming State Constitution: A Reference Guide* (1992).

Contributors

GERALD BENJAMIN is Dean of the College of Liberal Arts and Sciences and SUNY Distinguished Professor of Political Science at the State University of New York at New Paltz. He has published extensively on state and local government, with a particular focus on New York. His most recent book (with Richard Nathan) is *Regionalism and Realism: A Study of Governments in the New York Metropolitan Area* (2002).

THAD L. BEYLE is Thomas J. Pearsall Professor of Political Science at the University of North Carolina (Chapel Hill). He served as an assistant to North Carolina Governor Terry Sanford and as the Director of the Center for Policy Research and Analysis of the National Governors Conference. His publications include *Governors and Hard Times* (1992), *Gubernatorial Reelections* (1986), and *The American Governor in Behavioral Perspective* (1972).

RICHARD BRIFFAULT is Vice Dean and Joseph P. Chamberlin Professor of Legislation at Columbia Law School. He has served as a consultant to the New York City Charter Revision Commission and to the New York State Commission on Constitutional Revision. His publications on state and local government law and election law have appeared in leading law reviews, including *Columbia Law Review, University of Chicago Law Review,* and *Stanford Law Review.* He is the author of *Balanced Budgets: The Reality Behind State Balanced Budget Requirements* (1996).

JAMES A. GARDNER is Professor of Law at the University at Buffalo Law School. He is the author of *Interpreting State Constitutions: A Jurisprudence of Function in a Federal System* (2005), as well as of articles on state constitutional law and on electoral systems in leading law reviews, including *William & Mary Law Review*, *Georgetown Law Journal*, and *Texas Law Review*.

MICHAEL E. LIBONATI is Laura H. Carnell Professor of Law at Temple Law School. He is the coauthor of *Legislative Law and Statutory Interpretation* (3rd ed., 2001) and of *State and Local Government Law* (2000). His publications on state and local government law have appeared in leading law reviews, and he has served as a consultant to national, state, and local governments.

G. ALAN TARR is Director of the Center for State Constitutional Studies and Distinguished Professor of Political Science at Rutgers University–Camden. He is the author or editor of several books dealing with state constitutionalism, including *Understanding State Constitutions* (1998), *Constitutional Politics in the States* (1996), and *State Supreme Courts in State and Nation* (1988). His research focuses on American state constitutions, subnational constitutions in other federal systems, and American constitutional law.

PAUL L. TRACTENBERG is Board of Governors Distinguished Service Professor and Alfred C. Clapp Service Professor of Law at Rutgers Law School (Newark), where he directs the Institute on Education Law and Policy. He is the author of numerous books, articles, and other publications on education law and has served as a consultant to national, regional, and state agencies on educational policy. He has also participated in several landmark cases involving education.

BARTON H. THOMPSON JR. is Robert E. Paradise Professor of Natural Resources Law at Stanford Law School and Director, Stanford Institute for the Environment. He is coauthor of *Enviromental Law and Policy: Concepts and Insights* (2004) and of *Legal Control of Water Resources* (3rd ed., 2000). He has published widely on environmental law in leading law reviews.

ROBERT F. WILLIAMS is Associate Director of the Center for State Constitutional Studies and Distinguished Professor of Law at Rutgers University–Camden. Professor Williams is the author of *State Constitutional Law: Cases and Materials* (3rd ed., 1999) and *The New Jersey State Constitution: A Reference Guide* (rev. ed., 1997). He also has more than thirty articles on state constitutional law and legislation in the *Rutgers Law Journal*, the *William & Mary Law Review*, and in other law journals. He has been active as counsel in many public interest cases.

Index

Abbot v. Burke, 263, 291*n128*, 298*n179*

Abortion: parental consent for, 26

Adams, John, 67

Agnew, Spiro, 75

Alabama constitution: administrative authority in court system and, 94; amendments and revisions, 183, 185, 200, 206*n19*, 206*n31*; borrowing and debt limitations in, 216; election procedures and, 156; environmental provisions in, 329, 330; funding for court system and, 96; judicial rule making authority and, 95; jurisdiction of state courts and, 106*n16*; local immunity from state legislative interference, 114; positive rights in, 25; provision for care of old and needy, 25; provisions for education in, 275*n37*, 275*n39*, 283*n89*, 289*n118*, 290*n124*; school segregation in, 275*n39*; selection of judges and, 94; special laws provision, 32*n68*; special/private law rules in, 58; structural autonomy of local government and, 114; suffrage in, 1

Alaska constitution: administrative authority in court system and, 93, 94; amendments and revisions, 183, 193, 194, 195, 199, 205*n14*, 206*n19*;

attorney general appointment/election, 76; best practices in education in, 252; budgetary/appropriation powers in, 41; court jurisdiction and, 90, 91; electoral victory standards in, 158; eminent domain and, 24; environmental provisions in, 326, 328, 337*n81*; home rule issues, 116; legislative immunity and, 49; privacy rights, 26; property rights and, 24; selection of judges and, 93, 94, 105n3; special laws provision, 32*n68*; spending limits and, 43; structural autonomy of local government and, 116; unenumerated rights and, 27; voting apportionment rules, 161, 165

Amendments and revisions, 9; basic principles, 177–200; constitutional, 177–204; constitutional commission and, 191–192; constitutional initiative and, 186; court challenges to, 184; in criminal procedure area, 12; defining, 178; difficulty of, 180; election timing and, 183; error correction in, 187; guidelines for process, 200–204; home rule and, 184–185; limits of, 183–184; methods, 178; as modification rather than

357

Amendments and revisions (*continued*), radical change, 12; number offered, 183; popular ratification of, 180–181, 200–201; procedural and substantive limitations, 189–191; process administration, 182, 187; proposal and adoption through legislature, 181–182; ratification, 185; responsibility for process of, 183; resubmission limits, 184; revision by convention, 192–200; separate vote for, 184; signature gatherers and, 187–188; signature requirements and, 188–189; single purpose, 183; special elections and, 187; special majorities and, 185; substantive limits on, 185; through initiative, 192; timing of, 187; without legislative participation, 185

American Bar Association, 85; Commission on the Twenty-First Century Judiciary, 101; on judicial selection, 99; Model Judicial Article, 104

American Judicature Society, 85, 99

Apportionment, electoral, 160–166, 175*n70*; authority for, 163–164; bases of, 162; district qualities and, 164–166; requirements for, 160–162; timing, 162–163

Arizona constitution: amendments and revisions, 189, 190, 193, 195, 206*n19*; campaign finance provisions, 171; civil litigation rights and, 18; functional autonomy of local government and, 118; judicial qualifications and, 98; legislative compensation, 48; primary elections and, 171; provisions for education in, 281*n86*, 290*n124*, 291*n126*, 298*n183*; spending limits and, 43; voter approval of taxation and, 224; voter eligibility and, 151

Arkansas constitution: amendments and revisions, 183, 190, 206*n19*, 208*n54*; best practices in education in, 253; judicial qualifications and, 98; provi-

sions for education in, 245, 276*n41*, 278*n61*, 283*n91*, 285*n98*, 290*n124*, 297*n176*; school funding, 253

Assembly rights, 15

Baker, Lynn, 13

Benjamin, Gerald, 4

Beyle, Thad, 4, 67–82

Bill of Rights, 8, 13; selective incorporation of, 8

Bipartisan Campaign Reform Act, 171, 172

Blaine Amendment, 16

Bonds: nonguaranteed, 217; revenue, 217–218; self-liquidating project finance, 217

Briffault, Richard, 4

Brown v. Board of Education, 247, 278*n56*

Bush, George W., 75

California constitution: administrative authority in court system and, 93; affirmative action programs, 253; amendments and revisions, 182, 185, 189, 194, 195, 197, 206n19; antidiscrimination in education provision, 247; best practices in education in, 253; constitutional limitations on taxation, 223; death penalty and, 17; debt approval process and, 237n35; election procedures and, 159; environmental provisions in, 311, 313, 315, 327, 328, 329, 330; fiscal autonomy of local government in, 119, 133; forced linkage approach, 9; functional autonomy of local government and, 117, 118; home rule issues, 115, 124, 125; intergovernmental relations in, 118; interpretations going beyond federal requirements in, 9; judicial rule making authority and, 95; judicial selection and, 99; limitations on taxation/expenditures and, 224, 225; lockstep amendment approach, 9; personnel autonomy in local government and, 121; primary elections and, 170; privacy amendment, 11; privacy rights, 26; provisions for education in, 274*n29, 275n30, 276n45, 277n47, 277n48, 279n63, 281n86, 283n91, 285n97, 287n110, 288n115, 297n177*; recall policy in, 51; school busing and, 9; school funding, 248; selection of judges and, 93; spending limits and, 43; state auditor appointments, 77; subject-to-appropriation debt and, 220; use of City Republic version of home rule, 125; voter approval of taxation and, 224; voting apportionment rules, 161

Capital punishment, 28*n3*

Cellucci, Paul, 75

Citizens Conference on State Legislatures, 52, 53, 54, 83*n12*

Citizens for Independent Courts, 99

Civil service: goals of, 68

Clean Air Act, 309

Colorado constitution: amendments and revisions, 183, 187, 188, 189, 195, 197, 200, 205*n15, 206n19*; antidiscrimination in provisions for education in, 275*n39*; appropriation powers in, 61*n28*; best practices in education in, 253; campaign finance provisions, 171; compulsory education in, 275*n44*; environmental provisions in, 314, 327, 328; fiscal autonomy of local government in, 119; home rule issues, 115, 125; initiative/immunity powers of local government and, 110; jurisdiction of state courts and, 106*n16*; positive rights in, 25; provisions for education in, 275*n39, 276n44, 277n47, 281n86, 283n91, 284n92, 284n94, 290n124, 292n130, 299n187*; recall policy in, 51; school funding, 248, 253, 275*n38*; structural autonomy of local government and, 116; voter approval of taxation and, 224; voter el-

igibility and, 150; voting apportionment rules, 162, 163, 164, 165

Common Cause v. Maine, 214

Compact for Education, 83*n12*

Connecticut constitution: amendments and revisions, 182, 183, 195, 206*n19*; court structure and, 89; delegation of authority in, 40; educational funding provisions, 273*n18*; election crimes in, 147; electoral victory standards in, 158; equality provision in education, 244; initiative/immunity powers of local government and, 111; judicial tenure and, 107*n44*; legislative veto and, 40; provisions for education in, 273*n18, 298n181*; structural autonomy of local government and, 116; voting apportionment rules, 163

Constitution, federal: Antifederalist criticism of, 13; Equal Opportunity Clause, 263; Equal Protection Clause, 20, 32*n57*, 146, 153, 162; Fourteenth Amendment, 20, 263; Fourth Amendment to, 28*n4*; indifference to public finance, 211; Sixteenth Amendment, 211; Twenty-fifth Amendment, 75, 84*n23*; Twenty-sixth Amendment to, 150

Constitution, state. *See also* Constitution, state; executive branch; judicial branch; legislative branch: ages of, 3; amendments to, 9, 177–204; autonomy of local government, 110–113; best practices in education clauses in, 250–255; borrowing and debt limitations in, 215–221, 231–232, 236*n32*; boundaries between public and private sector and, 40; changeability of, 7; City Republic version of home rule in, 125; civil liberties and, 15, 16; civil litigation rights and, 18, 19; common benefits clauses in, 21; common features of, 1; comprehensiveness in educational

Constitution, state (*continued*), provisions, 256–257; conflicts of interest and, 49, 50; curbs on special/exclusive privileges, 21–24; devolution-of-powers version of home rule in, 128–129, 131–132; discretionary authority of local government, 113–121; distribution of franchise by, 145; as documents of limitation rather than empowerment, 5*n1*; due process of law and, 25; electoral practices, 148–166; enforceability of educational provisions, 257–258, 271; environment and natural resources in, 307–332; equality provisions, 20–24; establishment of agencies outside executive branch, 68; establishment of electoral rules and practices by, 145; establishment of institutions of state government by, 1; establishment of political ground rules by, 145; evasion of debt limits in, 217–221; executive branch, 67–82; fiscal autonomy of local governments and, 119–120; functional autonomy of local government, 117–118; function of, 145; as fundamental law of the state, 1; governmental institutions and, 4; home rule issues, 123–133; impact on national politics, 2; inclusion of elements not in federal constitution, 2; insertion of new rights into, 8; as instruments of limitation, 37; interbranch conflicts, 38, 39, 42; inverse condemnation and, 24, 25; lease financing in, 218; legislative branch issues, 37–59; legitimacy of rulings different federal standards, 19; local Bill of Rights version of home rule in, 125–127; local government and, 109–138; methods of changing, 177; "model" provisions for education, 255–271; modification of existing clauses in, 8; personnel autonomy in

local government, 120–121; piecemeal amendments in, 3; political rights in, 154; positive rights and, 25, 26; privacy rights in, 26; privatization decisions and, 40; property rights in, 24, 25; protection of rights under, 4; provisions for education in of, 241–272; reform agenda for state/local finance, 228–235; reform of, 1; restrictions on state supremacy and, 122–133; revenue bonds and, 217–218; revisions, 177–204; rights and, 7–27; rights of accused and, 16, 17; rules on interlocal collaboration, 130–131; school financing, 249–250; specificity in educational provisions, 256–257; state/local finance and, 211–235; status of rights in, 15–27; structural autonomy of local governments and, 113–117; structural provisions of, 13; subject-to-appropriation debt and, 218–221; taxation and expenditure limitations in, 221–228, 232–235; unenumerated rights and, 26, 27; victims' rights and, 20; voter approval of taxation, 224, 234, 235; voter eligibility and, 149–154; voting and, 4; voting apportionment rules, 160–166; voting protections, 155–156; as works in progress, 3
Constitution, state; executive branch, 67–82; attorney general and, 76, 77; current state of, 69–72; gubernatorial ambition ladder and, 79; gubernatorial budget and veto power, 81, 82; gubernatorial elections, 73, 74; gubernatorial reorganization authority, 80, 81; gubernatorial tenure and, 72, 73; history of, 67–69; lieutenant governor in, 74–75; power sharing and, 68; powers of appointment, 44, 45; process officials in, 72–78; restrictions on governorships in, 67, 68; role in budgetary process, 41;

secretary of state positions in, 78; separately elected officials in, 74–79; state auditor position in, 77; treasurer appointments, 77, 78; veto powers of, 41

Constitution, state; judicial branch, 85–104; accountability and, 86; administrative authority in, 93, 94; administrative issues, 92–95; commission approach to compensation, 102; compensation and, 102–103; constitutionalization of court structure, 89, 90; court jurisdictions and, 90–92; discipline and, 102, 104; federal model of compensation, 102; funding/budgeting for court system, 96, 97; institutional autonomy and, 86; judicial independence and, 86, *106n23*; judicial tenure, 100–101; mechanisms for enforcement of accountability and, 87; models for court systems, 89; prohibitions on judges in, 97, 98; qualifications of judges in, 97, 98; recall of judges, 102, 104; reeligibility in, 100–101; removal of judges in, 102, 104; rule making and, 94, 95; sanctions and, 102, 104; selection of judges and, 85, 98–102; service delivery in, 86; shared-burden model of compensation, 102; state/local financing, 96, 97; structure of court system, 87–90; trial-court consolidation and, 87, 88; unification of courts and, 90

Constitution, state; legislative branch: accountability, 37; adjournment/dissolution rules, 54, 55; appropriation powers, 41–43; bans on dual office-holding and, 47; barriers to authority to delegate powers of, 39; budgetary powers, 41–43; compensation in, 48; confirmation powers of, 44, 45; control over federal funding by, 42; criteria for office beyond reach of majority rule politics, 46, 47; distribution of policy-making authority and, 38; efficiency of, 37; expulsion, exclusion, and recall devices, 50–52; full-time professional v. part-time citizen, 47, 48; impeachment issues, 45, 46; imposition of spending limits and, 42; informational powers, 43, 44; institutional autonomy, 37; investigative powers, 43, 44; leadership rules, 48; legislative ethics and, 49, 50; legislative immunity in, 48, 49; legislative procedure in, 55–57; legislative veto and, 40; managerial constitutionalism and, 39, 40; membership in, 46–52; nondelegation doctrine and, 39, 40; powers of, 37–46; processes of, 55–59; qualifications/disqualifications for membership, 46, 47; representativeness, 37; role with respect to federal grants, 42; separation of powers and, 37–39; sessions rules, 53, 54; shared power with Executive, 38; shared power with Judiciary, 38; single-district representation/district residency requirements and, 47; size of, 53; strengthening of executive powers over adminstrative agencies and, 40; structure of, 52–55; terms of office in, 47; transparency, 37

Constitutional conventions: amendments and revisions by, 192–200; automatic convention calls, 193; districting for delegates, 197; frequency of, 197; operation of, 194–197; popular vote requirements, 193; preparation for voting in, 193; proposed by legislature, 192; proposed through initiative, 192; referendum election timing and, 193; size of, 197; specific logistics of, 197–200; staffing and convening, 194–197

Courts. *See* Constitution, state; judicial branch
Court systems: administration of, 92–95; constitutionalization of, 89, 90; federal model, 89; full-articulation model, 89, 90; jurisdictional issues, 90–92; modified federal model, 89; multiple-court model, 90; multiple-level model, 90; overruling of judicial interpretations and, 9; single-court model, 90; structure of, 87–90; trial-court consolidation, 87–88; unification in, 90
Criminal procedure rights, 16, 17

Declaration of Independence, 54; on judicial independence, 105*n4*; language of equality in, 21
Delaware constitution: amendments and revisions, 181, 185, 195, 197, 199, 206*n19*, 209*n69*; election procedures and, 158; electoral crimes and, 154; judicial qualifications and, 98; jurisdiction of state courts and, 106*n16*; provisions for education in, 292*n130*; voter eligibility and, 149, 154; voting apportionment rules, 165
Democracy: deliberative, 56; direct, 3, 169; popular, 12
Development: economic, 3; historical, 4; policy, 3
DiFrancesco, Donald, 74
Dillon, John, 121
Dillon's Rule, 121, 122, 127, 129, 130, 132

Education: adequacy of current provisions, 249–250; *Brown v. Board of Education*, 247; centralization of, 246; comprehensiveness of provisions for, 256–257; constitutional issues, 241–272; enforceability of provisions for, 257–258, 259, 271; equality standards in, 258, 267–268; evolution of provisions for, 242–249; extent of commitment to, 242; foundational stage of history of, 242, 244–247; funding, 248, 259, 268–269; funding for sectarian schools, 246; governmental responsibility for, 259; hortatory clauses in constitutions, 243; identification of best practices in, 250–255; introductory stage of history of, 242, 243, 244; obligatory clauses in constitutions, 243; prohibitions/limits in, 259, 269; public school systems, 247; quality standards specifications, 258, 261–267; responses to legal and advocacy efforts in, 243, 247–249; responsibility for, 241, 270; role of parents/family in, 259; scope of provision coverage, 260–261; segregation and, 246; specificity in provisions for, 256–257; specific services in, 259; state commitment to, 260; structure of state systems, 242
Education Commission of the States, 83*n12*; State Constitutions and Public Education Governance, 251
Eisenhower, Dwight, 69
Elections, 145–172. *See also* Voting; administrative authority for, 157–158; blanket primary, 170; campaign finance and, 171–172; "coattail" effect, 74; congressional, 145; constitutionalization of process, 147, 148; constitutional practices of, 148–166; crimes in, 147; gubernatorial, 73, 74; judicial, 98–102; lieutenant governor, 74, 75; media coverage of, 76; open primary, 170; primary, 170–171; procedures, 156–160; recall, 145; reform agenda for, 166–172; special, 187; tie-breaking procedures, 159; timing, 73; victory standard, 158; voter falloff in, 76; voting eligibility in, 146
Eminent domain, 24

Endangered Species Act, 310

Environment and natural resources: access to navigation, 328–329; authorization provisions for, 312; Clean Air Act, 309; community values and, 316, 317; conservation movement and, 307, 308; constitutional provisions for, 307–332; contested terrain of policy for, 308–311; costs of regulation in, 309; diversity of issues in, 308; drafting constitutional provisions for, 311–319; ecosystem preservation, 310; effectiveness of constitutional provisions for, 308; Endangered Species Act, 310; enforcement provisions, 314, 315; evolution of focus of, 307; existing provisions, 319–331; fish and wildlife, 327–328; forestry, 328; health issues, 308, 309; information dissemination and, 325; institutional specifications for, 313; judicial reactions to provisions for, 321–323; policy directives for, 313; polluter pays principle and, 324, 325; pollution reduction, 309; precautionary principle in, 309, 324; principle of prevention and, 324; process imperfections in provisions, 317; public access issues, 308, 310, 311; public interest in, 308; public land preservation, 329–331; public participation and, 325; public right of access and, 311; public trust doctrine and, 311; recreational issues, 310, 311; resource extraction and, 309, 310; resource issues, 308, 309, 310; resource management and, 324–328; rights and duties, 314; Rio Declaration on Environment and Development, 319; Safe Drinking Water Act, 309; scientific uncertainty and, 309; specificity of provisions, 315, 316; Stockholm Declaration of the United Nations Conference on the Human Environment, 319; trade-offs in protecting, 308; value declarations for, 312, 313; water management, 327; World Charter for Nature, 319, 324

Equality guarantees, 20–24

Equal Opportunity Clause, 263

Equal Protection Clause, 146, 153, 162

Equal Rights Amendment, 23

Ethics: biomedical, 27; legislative, 49, 50

Executive, state. See also Constitution, state; executive branch: current status of, 69–72; election of officials in, 74–79; gubernatorial budget and veto power, 81, 82; gubernatorial reorganization authority, 80–81; gubernatorial tenure and election, 72–74; history of, 67–69

Federalism: horizontal, 1, 6n3; judicial, 8, 19, 44; majoritarianism and, 12; vertical, 2, 6n3

Finance, state and local, 211–235; bills for raising revenue, 211; borrowing and debt limitations, 215–221, 231–232, 236n32; constitutional provisions, 212; educational, 246, 248, 249–250; evasion of debt limits and, 217–221; fees and assessments, 225–227; lease financing, 218; lending of credit and, 214, 215, 230, 236n26; nontax revenue sources, 225–227; public purpose limits, 212–215, 229–230, 235n12, 236n21; reduced role of property taxes, 225; reduction in local revenue growth, 227–228; restrictions on borrowing and taxation, 211; revenue bonds and, 217–218; subject-to-appropriation debt and, 218–221; taxation and expenditure limitations in, 221–228, 232–235; voter approval of taxes, 224, 234, 235

Florida constitution: abortion rights, 26; amendments and revisions, 9,

Florida constitution (*continued*), 179, 185, 187, 188, 190, 191, 192, 200, 206n19; best practices in education in, 252, 253, 254, 255; campaign finance provisions, 171, 172; conflicts of interest and, 50; court structure and, 89; educational funding provisions, 273n18; educational quality issues, 253; election procedures and, 159; forced linkage approach, 9; functional autonomy of local government and, 117, 118; home rule issues, 115, 130; intergovernmental relations in, 118; interpretations going beyond federal requirements in, 9; judicial prohibitions and, 98; judicial rule making authority and, 95; judicial selection and, 101; jurisdiction of state courts and, 106n16; legislative ethics and, 50; legislative investigation powers in, 43, 44; lockstep amendment approach, 9; personnel autonomy in local government and, 120; primary elections and, 171; privacy rights, 26; provisions for education in, 273n18, 274n28, 274n29, 279n69, 283n89, 283n90, 285n103, 286n105, 289n120, 297n176; public employee pensions/benefits and, 120; right to provisions for education in, 274n27; school funding, 248, 249; search and seizure clause, 9, 17; voter approval of taxation and, 224; voter eligibility and, 151; voting apportionment rules, 163, 164, 166

Ford, Gerald, 75

Fordham-Model State Constitution, 111

Gardner, James, 4, 46, 52, 53

Georgia constitution: administrative authority in court system and, 94; alternative voting means, 169; amendments and revisions, 179, 184, 197, 199, 200, 206n19; best practices in education in, 253; court structure and, 89; debt limitations and, 237n33, 237n36; environmental provisions in, 312, 320, 333n11, 334n36; home rule issues, 115; legislative structure in, 52; obligatory approach to provision of education, 243; provisions for education in, 274n29, 290n125; rights of prisoners and, 19; school funding, 248, 253; selection of judges and, 94; structural autonomy of local government and, 116; trial court system and, 88; voter eligibility and, 151

Gerrymandering, 162

Government, local, 109–138; citizen choice and, 134; constitutional drafting considerations, 135–138; discretionary authority of, 113–121; eligibility for local autonomy and, 134–135; fiscal autonomy of, 119–120; functional autonomy of, 117–118; guidelines for alterations to, 109, 110; home rule issues, 112, 113; immunity powers of, 110–113; initiative powers of, 110–113; intergovernmental cooperation and, 112, 135; personnel autonomy in, 120–121; privatization and, 112; relations with state governments, 109, 121, 122; restrictions on state supremacy and, 122–133; role of judiciary in, 135; structural autonomy and, 113–117

Governorships: ambition ladder and, 79; appointment powers of, 71, 72; budget power, 81; elections and, 73, 74; indices of power of, 70, 70tab, 71; institutional powers of, 70, 70tab, 71; reorganization authority, 80–81; restrictions on, 67, 68, 69, 70, 71, 72; selection process, 68; tenure issues, 72, 73

Great Society Programs, 69

Hamilton Fish Institute: Review of State Constitutions: Education Clauses, 25

Hancock Amendment, 225

Hansen v. Owens (1980), 17

Hawaii constitution: amendments and revisions, 185, 190, 193, 195, 198, 199, 200, 206*n19*; attorney general appointment/election, 76; best practices in education in, 253; campaign finance provisions, 171, 172; debt limitations and, 237*n33*, 240*n93*; election procedures and, 159; environmental provisions in, 314, 321, 326, 334*n39*, 334*n46*, 337*n78*; fiscal autonomy of local government in, 120; legislative immunity and, 49; provisions for education in, 281*n86*, 283*n89*, 285*n98*; school funding, 253; voting apportionment rules, 165

Hayes v. State Property & Buildings Commission, 214

Headlee Amendment, 224

Help America Vote Act, 170

Hershkoff, Helen, 26

Hickel, Walter, 158

Hoover Commissions, 69

Idaho constitution: amendments and revisions, 179, 184, 189, 195, 197, 206*n19*; environmental provisions in, 311; expulsion standards in, 51; provisions for education in, 290*n124*, 292*n130*; recall policy in, 51; voting apportionment rules, 161

Illinois constitution: amendments and revisions, 182, 183, 185, 186, 190, 193, 195, 197, 198, 199, *206n19*; civil litigation rights and, 18; curbs on special/exclusive privileges in, 22; election procedures and, 158, 159; environmental provisions in, 312, 314, 321; equal protection clause, 33n69; functional autonomy of local

government and, 118; Granger Constitution of 1870, 3; home rule issues, 112, 115, 124; intergovernmental relations in, 118; judicial selection and, 99; legislative structure and, 53; personnel autonomy in local government and, 121; provision of local services and, 118; provisions for education in, 297*n176*; public employee financial disclosure and, 121; special laws provision, 32*n68*; term limits, 61*n46*; tort reform and, 18; trial court system and, 88; use of devolution-of-powers approach in, 131–132; voting apportionment rules, 163

Impeachment, 45, 46; depoliticization of, 46

"Index of Formal Powers of the Governorship" (Schlesinger), 69, 70

Indiana constitution: amendments and revisions, 195, 206*n19*, 208*n54*; civil litigation rights and, 18; curbs on special/exclusive privileges in, 22; debt limitations and, 237*n34*; local immunity from state legislative interference, 114; prisoners' rights and, 31n47; provisions for education in, 274*n29*, 276*n45*, 298*n182*; state role in provision of education, 244; structural autonomy of local government and, 114; tort reform and, 18; voting protections and, 155

Institute for Court Management, 96

International Association of Game, Fish, and Conservation Commissioners, 333*n18*

Inverse condemnation, 24, 25

Iowa constitution: amendments and revisions, 195, 206*n19*, 209*n69*; election of state judges and, 1; fiscal autonomy of local government in, 119; home rule issues, 115; voting apportionment rules, 163

Jefferson, Thomas, 3, 177

Johnson, Lyndon, 69

Judiciary, state, 85–104; accountability in, 86; administration of court systems, 92–95; compensation in, 102–103; constitutionalization of court structure, 89, 90; court jurisdictions, 90–92; discipline and, 102, 104; effective delivery of services in, 86; funding/budgeting for court system, 96, 97; institutional autonomy and, 86; judicial independence and, 86; judicial independence in, 106n23; models for court systems, 89; prohibitions on judges in, 97, 98; qualifications of judges in, 97, 98; recall of judges, 102, 104; reeligibility, 100–101; removal of judges and, 102, 104; rule making, 94–95; sanctions in, 102, 104; selection of judges and, 85, 98–102; structure of court system, 87–90; tenure issues, 100–101; unification of courts and, 90

Kansas constitution: administrative authority in court system and, 93, 94; amendments and revisions, 183, 195, 198, 206n19; home rule issues, 115; judicial discipline and, 104; selection of judges, 93, 94, 105n3; special laws provision, 32n68; voting apportionment rules, 162

Kentucky constitution: amendments and revisions, 179, 183, 193, 195, 197, 206n19; best practices in education in, 253; civil litigation rights and, 18; debt limitations and, 237n34; educational entitlement and, 263; efficiency of education provision, 265; election procedures and, 159; provisions for education in, 280n73, 295n166, 298n183; public purpose limitations in, 214; school segregation issues, 253; voter eligibility and, 154; voting apportionment rules,

175n70; voting protections and, 155

King, Angus, 158

Laws: civil rights, 146; due process of, 25; freedom of information, 44; local, 22, 57–59; motor voter, 146, 167; nondelegation doctrine and, 40; private, 57–59; special, 22, 32n68, 57–59; sunshine, 44

Legislature, state. See also Constitution, state; legislative branch: accountability and, 37; bicameral, 52; constitutional issues, 37–59; efficiency of, 37; election of, 2; institutional autonomy of, 37; membership in, 46–52; powers of, 37–46; processes of, 55–59; representativeness, 37; single member/multimember districts and, 52, 53; structure of, 52–55; transparency and, 37; unicameral, 52

Libonati, Michael, 4, 37–59, 109–138

Linde, Hans, 19, 22

Litigation rights, 17, 18

"Little Hoover Commissions," 69

Louisiana constitution: administrative authority in court system and, 94; amendments and revisions, 27, 183, 184, 192, 206n19; best practices in education in, 253; civil service system and, 121; court jurisdiction and, 91; environmental provisions in, 320, 322, 328; equality provision, 27; home rule issues, 115; judicial rule making authority and, 95; personnel autonomy in local government and, 121; provisions for education in, 281n86, 283n91, 299n189; rules on interlocal collaboration, 131; school funding, 253; selection of judges and, 94; structural autonomy of local government and, 116; voting apportionment rules, 163

Lowden, Frank, 68

Madison, James, 38

Maine constitution: amendments and revisions, 192, 195, 206*n19*; attorney general appointment/election, 76; court structure and, 89; electoral victory standards in, 158; environmental provisions in, 331; home rule issues, 115; jurisdiction of state courts and, 106n16; voting apportionment rules, 160, 161, 162, 163, 165

Marriage, same-sex, 21

Maryland constitution: amendments and revisions, 184, 195, 197, 206*n19*, 209*n69*; election procedures and, 156, 159; electoral crimes and, 154; legislative compensation, 48; provisions for education in, 276*n41*; structural autonomy of local government and, 116; voter eligibility and, 154

Massachusetts constitution: amendments and revisions, 181, 186, 189, 190, 194, 195, 206*n19, 208n54*; capital punishment and, 28*n3*; constitutional limitations on taxation, 223, 224; election procedures and, 159; environmental provisions in, 314; fiscal autonomy of local government in, 119; hortatory approach to provision of education, 243; on judicial independence, 105*n4*; judicial tenure and, 107*n44*; jurisdiction of state courts and, 106*n16*; legislative immunity and, 49; positive rights in, 26; separation of powers in, 38; structural autonomy of local government and, 116

May, Janice, 12

Michigan constitution: administrative authority in court system and, 94; amendments and revisions, 187, 190, 193, 195, 200, 206n19; antidiscrimination in education provision, 247; best practices in education in, 253; court structure and, 89, 90; debt approval process and, 237*n35*; debt limitations and, 237*n34*; envi-

ronmental provisions in, 311, 313, 321, 325, 327, 336*n74*, 337*n86*; expulsion standards in, 51; fiscal autonomy of local government in, 119; functional autonomy of local government and, 117; home rule issues, 115; judicial prohibitions and, 98; judicial rule making authority and, 95; limitations on taxation/expenditures and, 224, 225; provision for intersession legislative powers, 60n15; provisions for education in, 274*n28*, 274*n29*, 278*n53*, 278*n55*, 278*n57*, 283*n91*, 290*n125*, 298*n183*; search and seizure clause, 17; selection of judges and, 94; special laws provision, 32*n68*; structural autonomy of local government and, 116; voter approval of taxation and, 224; voter eligibility and, 151; voting apportionment rules, 164, 165

Minnesota constitution: amendments and revisions, 185, 195, 206*n19*; campaign finance provisions, 171; election procedures and, 157; electoral victory standards in, 158; home rule issues, 116; judicial qualifications and, 98; provisions for education in, 274*n27*, 276*n41*, 299*n186*; recall policy in, 51; right to provisions for education in, 274*n27*; special laws provision, 32*n68*; voting apportionment rules, 165

Mississippi constitution: amendments and revisions, 186, 189, 190, 191, 205*n15*, 206*n19*, 208*n54*; conflicts of interest and, 50; educational funding provisions, 273n18; election procedures and, 159; legislative ethics and, 50; provisions for education in, 245, 273*n18*, 275*n30*, 275*n37*, 277*n46*, 278*n55*; public purpose limitations in, 214; unenumerated rights and, 27; voting apportionment rules, 163, 166

Missouri constitution: amendments and revisions, 178, 184, 190, 193, 195, 198, 199, 200, 206n19; best practices in education in, 253; electoral victory standards in, 158; fiscal autonomy of local government in, 119; functional autonomy of local government and, 118; home rule issues, 124; intergovernmental relations in, 118; judicial selection and, 99, 101; limitations on taxation/expenditures and, 225; provisions for education in, 291n127; rules on interlocal collaboration, 131; school funding, 253; selection of judges, 105n3; structural autonomy of local government and, 116; use of devolution-of-powers version of home rule in, 128, 129; voter approval of taxation and, 224; voting apportionment rules, 163, 165

Model Fish and Game Commission, 333n18

Model State Constitution, 4, 6n10, 68, 75, 84n22, 128, 250

Montana constitution: amendments and revisions, 179, 187, 189, 194, 195, 206n19, 208n43; best practices in education in, 252; educational entitlement and, 263; environmental constitution of 1972, 3; environmental provisions in, 322, 323, 326, 327, 328, 335n59; expulsion standards in, 51; local electoral approval of legislative power, 115; privacy rights, 26; provisions for education in, 278n57, 284n92, 288n116, 290n125, 297n176, 298n180, 298n183, 299n188; structural autonomy of local government and, 115, 116; voter approval of taxation and, 224; voting apportionment rules, 175n70

National Center for State Courts, 85
National Governor's Association, 73
National Municipal League, 6n10, 68, 84n22, 99, 128, 250

National Summit on Improving Judicial Selection, 99

National Voter Registration Act, 167

Nebraska constitution: amendments and revisions, 185, 187, 189, 190, 191, 193, 195, 206n19; educational funding provisions, 273n18; election procedures and, 159; impeachment model in, 46; provisions for education in, 275n34, 275n37, 275n38, 283n91, 284n92, 285n98, 290n124; school funding, 275n38; structural autonomy of local government and, 116; tenure of governors, 73; voting apportionment rules, 160, 161, 162, 165, 175n70

Nevada constitution: amendments and revisions, 187, 188, 189, 195, 206n19; campaign finance provisions, 171; debt limitations and, 237n33, 237n34; election procedures and, 158; provisions for education in, 274n28, 274n29, 276n44, 277n48, 283n91, 292n130; special laws provision, 32n68; structural autonomy of local government and, 116

New Hampshire constitution: amendments and revisions, 183, 185, 193, 195, 200, 206n19; attorney general appointment/election, 76; fiscal autonomy of local government in, 119; gubernatorial elections and, 73; judicial tenure and, 107n44; jurisdiction of state courts and, 106n16; provisions for education in, 275n38; rights of prisoners and, 19; school funding, 275n38; structural autonomy of local government and, 116; tenure of governors, 72; voting protections and, 155

New Jersey constitution: administrative authority in court system and, 94; amendments and revisions, 182, 184, 195, 206n19, 208n54; antisegregation in education provision, 247; attorney general appointment/election, 76; civil liberties and, 15; educational entitlement and, 263; equality guarantees in, 24; equal protection clause, 32*n60*; freedom of assembly and, 15; home rule issues, 124, 129–130; initiative/immunity powers of local government and, 112; judicial selection and, 99; legislative confirmatory powers in, 44; lieutenant governorship issues, 74, 75; local immunity from state legislative interference, 114; personnel autonomy in local government and, 120; provisions for education in, 263, 276*n41*, 277*n49*, 278*n57*, 280*n73*, 290*n124*, 291*n127*, 291*n128*, 298*n181*; public employee pensions/benefits and, 120; selection of judges and, 94; structural autonomy of local government and, 114; subject-to-appropriation debt and, 220; term limits, 61*n46*; use of devolution-of-powers version of home rule in, 129–130; voting apportionment rules, 164

New Judicial Federalism, 8, 19

New Mexico constitution: amendments and revisions, 184, 185, 192, 195, 206*n19*; confidentiality privilege in, 44; environmental provisions in, 311, 320; legislative investigation powers in, 44; provisions for education in, 290*n124*; structural autonomy of local government and, 116; voter eligibility and, 151; voting apportionment rules, 164, 166

New York constitution: amendments and revisions, 179, 181, 183, 195, 196, 199, 205*n18*, 206*n19*; budgetary/appropriation powers in, 41; civil service system and, 121; debt limitations and, 237*n34*; educational entitlement, 265, 266; election of state judges and, 1; election procedures and, 158; electoral crimes and, 154; environmental provisions in, 315, 320, 321, 329, 331,

334*n38*; equal protection clause, 33*n70*; executive role in budgetary process in, 41; finance issues, 212; functional autonomy of local government and, 117, 118; funding for court system and, 97; home rule issues, 124, 125–127; intergovernmental relations in, 118; local immunity from state legislative interference, 114; personnel autonomy in local government and, 121; positive rights in, 25; provision for care of old and needy, 25; provisions for education in, 288*n117*, 291*n127*; public purpose limitations in, 212, 213; structural autonomy of local government and, 114, 116; trial court system and, 88; use of local Bill of Rights version of home rule, 125–127; voter eligibility and, 154; voting apportionment rules, 162, 165, 166

Nixon, Richard, 75

No Child Left Behind Act, 270

North Carolina constitution: amendments and revisions, 179, 194, 206n19; environmental provisions in, 311, 330, 331; positive rights in, 26; provisions for education in, 263, 288*n115*, 291*n126*, 291*n127*, 291*n129*, 297*n177*, 298*n180*; public purpose limitations in, 214; structural autonomy of local government and, 116; veto power of governors and, 71; voter eligibility and, 152; voting apportionment rules, 161

North Dakota constitution: amendments and revisions, 187, 189, 195, 206*n19*, 208*n54*; election procedures and, 159; local electoral approval of legislative power, 114; primary elections and, 171; provisions for education in, 284*n92*, 290*n125*, 291*n126*; size of legislature in, 53; structural autonomy of local government and, 114, 116; voter eligibility and, 151; voting apportionment rules, 164

Ohio constitution: alternative voting means, 168; amendments and revisions, 184, 187, 195, 198, 206n19; citizen initiation of local legislation, 115; civil litigation rights and, 18; civil service system and, 121; educational equality provisions, 273n17; election procedures and, 159; environmental provisions in, 326, 336n75; equality provision in education, 244; equal protection clause, 32n59; fiscal autonomy of local government in, 119; functional autonomy of local government and, 117, 118; home rule issues, 115, 125, 127; hortatory approach to provision of education, 243; intergovernmental relations in, 118; personnel autonomy in local government and, 121; provisions for education in, 273n17, 275n38, 276n41, 277n49, 277n50, 279n62, 291n126, 294n163; religion guarantees, 15, 16; rights of conscience and, 16; school funding, 248, 275n38; state and local borrowing in, 123; structural autonomy of local government and, 115; tort reform and, 18; unenumerated rights and, 26; voting apportionment rules, 162, 164, 165, 166, 175n70

Oklahoma constitution: amendments and revisions, 188, 189, 193, 195, 206n19; best practices in education in, 253; campaign finance provisions, 171; citizen initiation of local legislation, 115; election procedures and, 158; functional autonomy of local government and, 118; provisions for education in, 263, 281n86, 283n89, 283n91, 284n95, 291n129; school funding, 253; structural autonomy of local government and, 115, 116; voting apportionment rules, 161, 163

Oregon constitution: alternative voting means, 168; amendments and revisions, 179, 184, 189, 193, 195, 206n19, 208n43; best practices in education in, 253; campaign finance provisions, 171; citizen initiation of local legislation, 115; civil litigation rights and, 18; curbs on special/exclusive privileges in, 2, 21; fiscal autonomy of local government in, 119; home rule issues, 115, 125; prisoners' rights and, 31n47, 31n48, 31n49, 31n50; provisions for education in, 278n61, 281n86, 283n91, 284n92, 285n96, 296n175, 299n190; rights of prisoners and, 19; school funding, 248, 253; structural autonomy of local government and, 115, 116; tort reform and, 18; voter approval of taxation and, 224; voter eligibility and, 152; voting apportionment rules, 164

Panic of 1837, 213, 216
Patronage: excesses of, 68
Pennsylvania constitution: amendments and revisions, 184, 194, 195, 206n19, 208n54; appropriation powers in, 61n28; budgetary/appropriation powers in, 41; conflicts of interest and, 50; electoral crimes and, 154; environmental provisions in, 321, 337n78; equal protection clause, 33n70; functional autonomy of local government and, 118; funding for court system and, 96; home rule provisions, 112; initiative/immunity powers of local government and, 111; intergovernmental relations in, 118; judicial selection and, 99; legislative ethics and, 50; legislative investigation powers in, 44; legislative procedures and, 55, 56; legislative structure in, 52; obligatory approach to provision of education, 243; privacy interests of witnesses and, 44; prohibitions on discrimination in exercise of civil

rights, 23; provisions for education in, 276*n45*, 288*n117*; ripper clause in, 123; structural autonomy of local government and, 116; use of devolution-of-powers version of home rule in, 128, 129; voter eligibility and, 149, 154

People v. Anderson (1972), 17

Policy: choices, 1; development, 3; direct democracy and, 3; making, 3; public, 1, 4

Pound, Roscoe, 85

Power: appropriations, 41–43; confirmatory, 44, 45; contested, 38; of legislative branch, 37–39; plenary legislative, 27; separation of, 43, 67; shared, 38; veto, 41, 81, 82

Prisoners: rights of, 19, 20, 31*n47*

Privacy: rights, 26, 27

Progressivism, 145, 167, 168

Property: eminent domain, 24; inverse condemnation, 24, 25; rights, 24, 25

Recall devices, 50–52

Reform, constitutional: administrative organization and, 68, 69; campaign finance, 145; of court systems, 85; educational, 241–272; electoral, 146, 147, 148, 166–172; executive branch reorganization, 69; gubernatorial, 72, 73; impetus for, 2, 3; to increase responsiveness of state institutions, 3; judicial, 85–104; redistricting state legislatures, 69; regulation of political parties and, 145; state and local finance arrangements, 228–235; term limits, 61*n46*, 145, 169–170, 172*n1*, 207*n35*; voting, 166–172

Reform, penal, 19

Reform, tort, 18, 95

Religious rights, 15, 16

Rhode Island constitution: amendments and revisions, 193, 195, 206*n19*; campaign finance provisions, 171, 172; conflicts of interest and, 50;

election procedures and, 159; environmental provisions in, 312; fiscal autonomy of local government in, 119; home rule issues, 115; jurisdiction of state courts and, 106*n16*; legislative ethics and, 50; local immunity from state legislative interference, 114; provisions for education in, 288*n116*, 297*n176*; selection of judges, 105n3; structural autonomy of local government and, 114, 116; victims rights and, 20

Ridge, Tom, 75

Rights, 7–27; of accused, 16, 17; amendments by electorate and, 11; to bear arms, 7, 14; civil, 20, 22, 23, 28*n1*, 146; civil liberties, 15, 16; civil litigation, 18, 19; collective bargaining, 13, 28*n1*; of conscience, 16; criminal procedure, 16, 17; current state of, 15–27; of disabled, 12, 14; educational, 247, 274*n27*; enforceable, 14; environmental, 12; equality guarantees of, 20–24; evolution of guarantees, 13–14; fishing, 14; franchise, 146; to freedom of assembly, 15; to free speech, 15; guarantees of, 7; imposition of obligations by, 11; inclusion of restrictions on private actions, 11; individual, 7; judicial enforcement of, 11; judicial interpretation of, 8; lack of protection for some, 12; litigation and enforcement of, 8; location in constitution, 10; loss of, 7; majoritarianism and, 12; may differ from federal Bill of Rights, 9–10, 14; of minorities, 12, 13; modification of existing clauses of, 8; overrule of, 8; political, 154; popular supervision over guarantees, 12; positive/negative, 10, 25, 26; principles to guide changes in declarations of, 9–13; of prisoners, 19, 20, 31*n47*; privacy, 12, 26; property, 7, 24, 25; protection of, 4; relationship of state and federal, 14;

Rights (*continued*), as reflections of fundamental values of state, 9; similar to federal constitutional guarantees, 7; to strike, 7; unemumerated, 26, 27; victims, 14, 20; victims', 7; voting, 155–156; water, 14; of witnesses, 44; women's, 7, 13, 28n1
Rio Declaration on Environment and Development, 319
Robinson v. Cahill, 263, 266, 298*n179*
Rockefeller, Nelson, 75
Roosevelt, Franklin, 68

Sabato, Larry, 69
Safe Drinking Water Act, 309
San Antonio Independent School District v. Rodriguez, 263
Sanford, Terry, 67, 69, 83*n12*
Sato, Sho, 112
Schlesinger, Joseph, 69, 70
Search and seizure clauses, 9, 17, 28*n4*
Serrano v. Priest, 263
Sharpless v. Mayor of Philadelphia, 213
Smith, Alfred, 68
South Carolina constitution: alternative voting means, 169; amendments and revisions, 182, 206*n19*; best practices in education in, 253; debt approval process and, 237*n35*; functional autonomy of local government and, 118; judicial selection and, 99; provision of local services and, 118; provisions for education in, 281*n86*, 289*n118*; school funding, 253; structural autonomy of local government and, 116; voter eligibility and, 149; voting apportionment rules, 175n70
South Dakota constitution: amendments and revisions, 192, 195, 199, 206*n19*; best practices in education in, 253; judicial selection and, 101; jurisdiction of state courts and, 106*n16*; provision for intersession legislative powers, 60*n15*; provisions for education in, 281*n86*, 283*n91*,

284*n93*; school funding, 253; structural autonomy of local government and, 116; voting apportionment rules, 163, 175n70
Speech rights, 15
State Justice Institute, 85
States: assumption of responsibility for policy development, 3; budget issues in, 3; constraints over power of, 146; educational responsibilities and processes, 241–272; possession of plenary legislative powers by, 5*n1*; proliferation of administrative agencies in, 39; provision of services by, 23; revenues originating with federal government, 42; traditional responsibilities of, 3; use of power devolved from federal government, 3
Stockholm Declaration of the United Nations Conference on the Human Environment, 319
Suffrage, 1

Tarr, G. Alan, 4, 55, 56, 85–104, 207*n35*
Taxes: commercial, 222; income, 222; limits on, 221–228; property, 221, 222, 225; sales, 222; school, 245, 246; state and local, 221–228; substantive limitations on levels of, 222, 223, 224, 232–235; uniformity requirements of, 222, 223, 232–233, 239*n58*, 239*n59*; voter approval of, 224, 234–235
Technology: law enforcement and, 27; privacy rights and, 27; reproductive, 27; voting, 170
Tennessee constitution: amendments and revisions, 181, 185, 194, 197, 206n19; fiscal autonomy of local government in, 119, 120; provisions for education in, 274*n28*, 276*n45*, 289*n118*; right to provisions for education in, 274*n27*; structural autonomy of local government and, 116; voting apportionment rules, 164

Tenure: gubernatorial, 72, 73; judicial, 100–101

Term limits, 47, *61n46*, *172n1*, *207n35*

Texas constitution: amendments and revisions, 206*n19*, 208*n54*; educational entitlement and, 263; environmental provisions in, 336*n76*; functional autonomy of local government and, 118; home rule issues, 116; intergovernmental relations in, 118; legislative compensation, 48; legislative confirmatory powers in, 44; legislative immunity and, 49; provisions for education in, 274*n29*, 276*n45*, 280*n73*; spending limits and, 43; structural autonomy of local government and, 116; trial court system and, 88; voting apportionment rules, 162, 163, 164

Thompson, Barton Jr., 4

Thompson, Tommy, 75

Thoughts on Government (Adams), 67

Thro, William, 262, 263, 264, 265, *292n131*, *292n132*, *292n133*, *292n134*, *292n135*, *293n137*, *296n170*

Tocqueville, Alexis de, 55

Tractenberg, Paul, 4

Tribe, Lawrence, 23

Truman, Harry, 69

United States Supreme Court: application of Bill of Rights to state/local actions by, 8, 13

United States v. Nixon, 44

Unruh, Jess, 69

U.S. Advisory Commission on Intergovernmental Relations (ACIR), 113, 120, 130

Utah constitution: administrative authority in court system and, 93; amendments and revisions, 192, 195, 206*n19*; election procedures and, 159; electoral crimes and, 154; initiative/immunity powers of local government and, 111; provisions for education in, 274*n29*, 276*n45*; selection of judges and, 93; self-incrimination and, 17; structural autonomy of local government and, 116; tenure of governors, 73; voter eligibility and, 154

Van Alstyne, Arvo, 112

Ventura, Jesse, 158

Vermont constitution: amendments and revisions, 181, 183, 195, 206*n19*, 208*n54*; budgetary/appropriation powers in, 41; Common Benefits Clause in, 21; dissolution rules, 54; electoral crimes and, 154; expulsion standards in, 51; gubernatorial elections and, 73; legislative structure in, 52; obligatory approach to provision of education, 243; provisions for education in, 297*n177*; tenure of governors, 72; voter eligibility and, 154; voting apportionment rules, 163

Veto: gubernatorial power of, 69, 70, 71, 81, 82; item, 41

Virginia constitution: alternative voting means, 169; amendments and revisions, 206*n19*; best practices in education in, 253; compulsory education in, 275*n44*; election procedures and, 158; environmental provisions in, 311, 312, 334*n37*, 336*n76*; impeachment model in, 45, 46; initiative/immunity powers of local government and, 111; judicial selection and, 99; legislative confirmatory powers in, 44; provisions for education in, 263, 278*n53*, 290*n124*, 291*n129*, 295*n169*; regulatory jurisdictions and, 40; school funding, 253; size of legislature in, 53; tenure of governors, 73; trial court system and, 88; voting apportionment rules, 166

Virginia Declaration of Rights, 21

Voting, 145–172. *See also* Elections; age requirements, 150; alternative systems of, 167–168; apportionment

Voting (*continued*), rules, 160–166; ban on discriminatory practices in, 146; citizenship status and, 149–150; convenience issues, 167; cumulative, 53; dilution of, 146; disabled access to, 167; disqualifications, 152, 153; eligibility provisions, 149–154; felony convictions and, 152, 153; instant runoff, 168; property qualifications and, 151–152; proportional representation method, 168; protections, 155–156; reform agenda for, 166–172; registration, 146, 151; residency and, 150–151; technology, 170; turnout, 167

Voting Rights Act, 53, 146, 158, 161

Washington constitution: amendments and revisions, 189, 195, 206*n19*; antidiscrimination in provisions for education in, 275n39; debt limitations and, 237*n33*, 237*n36*; home rule issues, 127; provisions for education in, 246, 275*n39*, 276*n45*, 298*n183*; structural autonomy of local government and, 116; tenure of governors, 73; voter approval of taxation and, 224; voting apportionment rules, 162, 164, 165

Weicker, Lowell, 158

West Virginia constitution: alternative voting means, 168; amendments and revisions, 183, 195, 206*n19*; election procedures and, 159; electoral crimes and, 154; home rule issues, 115; legislative compensation, 48; provisions for education in, 279*n69*; voter eligibility and, 149, 154; voting apportionment rules, 161

Whitman, Christie, 74, 75

Williams, Robert, 4, 7–27

Wisconsin constitution: amendments and revisions, 185, 194, 195, 196, 206*n19*; environmental provisions in, 314; home rule issues, 115; provisions for education in, 290*n124*, 291*n127*; voting apportionment rules, 165, 175*n70*; voting protections and, 155

Witte, Harry, 12

World Charter for Nature, 319, 324

Wyoming constitution: amendments and revisions, 185, 190, 195, 206*n19*; attorney general appointment/ election, 76; home rule issues, 115; provisions for education in, 290*n125*, 290*n124*, 291*n126*, 297*n177*, 298*n183*; rights of prisoners and, 19